Character Development:

Encouraging Self-Esteem & Self-Discipline in Infants, Toddlers, & Two-Year-Olds

Polly Greenberg

A 1990–91 NAEYC Comprehensive Membership benefit

National Association for the Education of Young Children
Washington, DC

We gratefully acknowledge the authors and publishers listed below for permission to reprint excerpts as follows:

p. 2 from *The Policing of Families* (p. 10–11) by Jacques Donzelot, 1979. New York: Random House. Originally published in French as *La Police de Familles* by Editions de Minuit, copyright © 1977. English edition copyright © 1979 by Random House with Preface copyright © by Jacques Donzelot. Reprinted by permission.

p. 3 from *Early Childhood Education: The Year In Review. A Look At 1987* (p. 19) by James L. Hymes, Jr., 1987. Carmel, CA: Hacienda Press. Copyright © 1988 by James L. Hymes, Jr. Reprinted by permission.

pp. 12–13 from *A Children's Defense Budget, FY 1989: An analysis of Our Nation's Investment in Children.* Copyright © 1988 by Children's Defense Fund, Washington, DC. Reprinted by permission.

p. 22 from "Poverty's Legacy—Fragile Families, Vulnerable Babies" by M. Gardner, December 18, 1989, (p. 10). Reprinted by permission from *The Christian Science Monitor,* Copyright © 1989 by The Christian Science Publishing Society, Boston, MA. All rights reserved.

pp. 42, 43–44, 119 from the "Cementing Family Relationships" by T. Berry Brazelton, copyright © 1984 by T. Berry Brazelton in *The Infants We Care For—Revised Edition* (pp. 9–20) by Laura L. Dittman (Ed.). Washington, DC: NAEYC. Copyright © 1984 by NAEYC. Reprinted by permission.

p. 53–54 from "Infants in Day Care: Reflections on Experiences, Expectations, and Relationships" by Jeree Pawl, 1990, *Zero-to-Three, 10* (3), p. 6. Copyright © 1990 by the National Center For Clinical Infant Programs, Arlington, VA. Reprinted by permission.

p. 54 from *Quality in Child Care: What Does Research Tell Us?* (pp. 122–123), NAEYC Research Monograph, Vol. 1., by Deborah A. Phillips (Ed.). Washington, DC: National Association for the Education of Young Children. Copyright © 1987 by Deborah A. Phillips. Reprinted by permission.

p. 54 from "The Effects of Infant Day Care Reconsidered" by Jay Belsky, 1988, *Early Childhood Research Quarterly, 3* (3), pp. 265–266. Copyright © 1988 by Jay Belsky. Ablex Publishing Corp.: Norwood, NJ. Reprinted by permission.

p. 89 from *You Are Your Child's First Teacher* (p. 101) by Rahima Baldwin. Copyright © 1989 by Rahima Baldwin. Reprinted by permission of Celestial Arts, Berkeley, CA.

p. 90 from *The Psychoanalytic Study of the Child* (p. 131) by Helen Buchsbaum and Robert Emde, 1990. New Haven, CT: Yale University Press. Copyright © 1990 by Yale University Press. Reprinted by permission.

p. 96 from "Susanne and Her Two Mothers" by Jan Hare and Leslie A. Koepke, 1990, *Day Care and Early Education, 18* (2), pp. 20–21. Copyright © 1990 by Human Sciences Press. Reprinted by permission.

pp. 108–109, 110–116, and 159–160 reprinted with permission of Charles Scribner's Sons, an imprint of Macmillan Publishing Company, from *The Magic Years* (pp. 51–54 and 124–126) by Selma H. Fraiberg. Copyright © 1959 by Selma H. Fraiberg; copyright renewed.

p. 120 from "Seeing Children as Individuals" by Judith Leipzig, 1988, *Day Care and Early Education 16* (2), p. 41. Copyright © 1988 by Human Sciences Press. Reprinted by permission.

p. 133 reprinted with permission from *Infant/Toddler Caregiving: An Annotated Guide to Media Training Materials* (p. v) by Alice S. Honig and Donna Wittmer. Copyright © 1988 by California Department of Education, P.O. Box 271, Sacramento, CA 95802-0271.

table on p. 134 from *A Great Place To Work: Improving Conditions for Staff in Young Children's Programs* (p. 4) by Paula Jorde–Bloom, 1988. Washington, DC: NAEYC. Copyright © 1988 by Paula Jorde–Bloom. Reprinted by permission.

p. 154 from *Two To Four From Nine To Five* by Jean Roemer and Barbara Austin. Copyright © 1989 by Jean Roemer and Barbara Austin. Reprinted by permission of HarperCollins Publishers.

pp. 158–159 from *First Feelings* (pp. 83–84) by Stanley Greenspan and Nancy Thorndike Greenspan. Copyright © 1985 by Stanley Greenspan and Nancy Thorndike Greenspan. Reprinted by permission of Viking Penguin, a division of Penguin Books USA Inc.

p. 166 from "Assessing the Communication Of Infants and Toddlers: Integrating A Socioemotional Perspective" by Barry M. Prizant and Amy M Wetherby, 1990, *Zero to Three, 11* (1), p. 2. Copyright © 1990 by National Center for Infant Clinical Programs, Arlington, VA. Reprinted by permission.

p. 166 from *Language Thought and Personality in Infancy and Childhood* (p. 13) by M.M. Lewis, 1963. New York: Basic Books. Copyright © 1963 by M.M. Lewis. Reprinted by permission.

National Association for the Education of Young Children
1834 Connecticut Avenue, N.W.
Washington, DC 20009-5786

The National Association for the Education of Young Children attempts through its publications program to provide a forum for discussion of major issues and ideas in our field. We hope to provoke thought and promote professional growth. The views expressed or implied are not necessarily those of the Association.

Library of Congress Catalog Card Number: 91-060826
ISBN Catalog Number: 0-935989-43-9
Series ISBN Catalog Number: 0-935989-46-3
NAEYC #175
Cover design: Polly Greenberg and Jack Zibulsky. Book production: Jack Zibulsky
Printed in the United States of America

CONTENTS

CHAPTER 4. What Is Curriculum for Infants and Toddlers in Family Day Care (or Elsewhere)? What Is the Goal? . . . 67

CHAPTER 5. How Does Good Character Develop? Self? Self-Esteem? Self-Discipline? Do We Have Anything To Do With It? 75

CHAPTER 6. For Infants, Toddlers, and Twos, Keep It Like Home (But Not Like a Boring Home): The Job of an Optimal Home Is Building "Good Character" 101

Contents   v

OVERVIEW

If early childhood experts are to be taken at their *literal* (not rhetorical) word, then in our profession—child developing—our aim should be to create and maintain *optimal* settings in order to help each child develop *optimally*—to his or her "fullest potential." Our aim should *not* be to operate services that will do little or no harm, with the goal of ensuring that each child develop "normally." Most of the 12 lively essays in this book, each of which starts with a question or viewpoint that commonly comes up in onsite staff development discussions, delve into realistic ways in which we can move from where we are (much American day care is rated by the experts as merely "adequate" or actually *in*adequate) to where many of us *want* to be—providing *high-quality* center-based or family child care.

If strong character development, positive self-esteem, and sensible self-discipline are the important foundations of mental health and good citizenship that many ordinary people and experts believe them to be, and if the early years are the impressionable, formative period that many ordinary people and experts believe them to be, then it matters how we treat our youngest children on a daily basis, whether they're at home or elsewhere and regardless of who is caring for them.

All families need support and services in addition to what they can offer their children. For some, these assists come from kin and friends and/or fee-paid help and include, for example, the doctor, the orthodontist, school, perhaps camp, maybe some lessons, certainly a good deal of child care (do you know any parents who *really* stay home with the children full-time?), elder care (it could be a nursing home), and very likely—if the family is middle-class—some household help so parents have more free time for their children and for themselves.

People who don't have available kin or friends or money to purchase these services need assistance too. For the long-term good of the community, shouldn't we make sure such services exist and are plentiful enough and of good enough quality "to do good?" When it comes to child care services, who, if not we, will champion this cause?

The purposes of these pages are to encourage those who regularly spend many, many hours a week giving care to infants, toddlers, and two-year-olds to appreciate more fully the incredibly important character development work they're doing and to encourage them to deepen both their understanding of child development and their child caring skills.

CHAPTER 1

. . . addresses the concern heard from many Americans—including many early childhood educators and child development specialists—that this "modern," "feminist" phenomenon of women "working" when they have children younger than three years old may be somewhat harmful to the children.

The thrust of the chapter is that most women throughout the world, throughout history, have not been wealthy and have worked *more* than what we currently call "full-time" (a 40-hour week) in field, factory, and household. Mothers' pre-dawn to post-dusk drudgery, with no help from large or small household appliances and little or no help from most husbands, left them little time for providing what is known these days as "quality child care." But very few people other than radical social reformers worried about the quality of care these families' babies and toddlers were getting.

Wealthy women weren't tending their tots full-time either—for better or worse, servants were.

The differences between "then" and "now" are

1. We now know too much about what kinds of childrearing conditions usually create good physical health, mental health, and character; high self-esteem; sensible self-discipline; etc.; and about the high price society pays if—through its negligence—it fails to budget as needed to support families in raising *the community's children, the nation's future citizens*—if it looks the other way and lets children grow up *without* these basics.

2. As any country develops, standards and expectations rise (about technology, medical care, everything, including child care), and what was quite acceptable yesteryear (the privy, the horse and buggy) is no longer tolerable; in our cultures "custodial care," which much of day care still is, is no longer considered tolerable; and

3. Large numbers of well-educated, upper-middle-class women, who can articulate the details of what "quality care" is and how critical it is to the well-being of each child, are now employed away from home, and so have become concerned about the availability and affordability of "quality" child care arrangements—this is why we're hearing so much about the need for good day care.

Chapter 1 concludes that, whether or not we "approve," half of all American mothers of babies younger than a year and more than half of the mothers of one- and two-year-olds are employed at least part-time—most of them full-time—outside the home. Thus, it's the obligation of our child-caring profession to struggle against all the odds and biases hampering us in an effort to create family day care homes and child care centers that are good for infants, toddlers, and two-year-olds. For people now directing child care programs, this means hiring individuals who are "good with children" and enhancing their effectiveness as child developers through staff development and supervision. The highlights of good child care are touched upon.

CHAPTER 2

... points out that although positive self-esteem, a buzz-phrase in the child care community these days, is fundamental to mental health, children need some things that are even *more* basic, such as prenatal care, food, pure water, shelter, and immunizations. These are basics we overburdened, overwhelmed caregivers may be too inundated to think much about.

This chapter documents worldwide child neglect and speculates on the cause of the fact that in almost all countries, children are not a budget priority. These speculative queries and considerations may seem controversial to some. They *are*. Readers are asked if they'd like to question "the way it is"; to use their higher level critical thinking skills to imagine how it *might* be.

The probability—or even the possibility—that children will be able to do well in school when they are hungry, unhealthy, and homeless is questioned. The assumption that there's nothing significant *we* can do about child poverty is challenged. Caring people of all kinds and categories can become advocates for children of low-income families and for children without constructively functioning families. It's hard for either group to effectively advocate for itself because both are politically disenfranchised.

Studies show that many Americans feel disenchanted with the political picture—feel manipulated by big money, political public relations pros, and the media—yet wistfully say they'd like to make a difference. Well, here's a way! We can get involved in children's issues in our localities.

CHAPTER 3

... and the various people quoted in it who frankly tell us what they think, urges parents, practitioners, teacher educators, and decision makers to avoid deciding where babies should be solely according to the doctrine of the day ("mothers should stay home full-time," "full-time child care programs are perfectly OK for babies") and to consider many other concerns:

1. What are the parents' goals for themselves and their children? Socioeconomic status, ethnic and religious background, educational level, and, above all, individual differences influence what parents want for themselves and their children. What are the parents' preferences? If there are two parents, do both want to work full-time? Is work refreshing and enriching or stressful and draining? Does each parent feel good about his or her life or ambivalent and guilty? To a large extent, what's least stressful and feels happily best for the whole family—all things considered—is best for the baby, too. In this segment, many parents share their strong opinions and varied experience with readers.

2. What's the baby's home situation? Is this an "optimal" home, to use the researchers' word? Or is it disastrous, dysfunctional, or detrimental? How about babies from average homes—not especially child-oriented, but OK situations to grow up "OK" in? We say that full-time out-of-home child care of less than high quality is not good for babies, and we know that most specific child care settings for infants, toddlers, and two-year-olds are *not* high quality, yet we don't oppose full-time day care for this age group. How do we reconcile these clashing realities? What are the implications for policy makers, teacher educators, employers, and directors of babies' need for ample and leisurely parenting from one or two parents or guardians, whether they're in or out of home care? In this segment, we "overhear" a lively debate—researchers, parents, teachers, all tell it like *they* think it is. In the next segment, we meet real people, too—this time *children*—who challenge our thinking.

3. What's best for the individual child? Because of a young child's temperament, personality, family circumstances, special health needs, or whatever the situation, family day care, center-based care, care by kin, in-home care by a caregiver who comes to the home, a male caregiver, a grandmotherly caregiver, a mother substitute caregiver, or three-quarter or half-time care by those other than mothers or fathers may be most desirable. What setting is most desirable for *this individual baby*? What about the child with poor coping skills who lacks flexibility? The wild child? The abandoned child? There are many exceptional family child care providers and center caregivers who are insightful in their relationships and offerings with individual children. But most child care situations are pretty much one-size-fits-all, and that is *never* high quality.

What's best for the whole family? There may be other children to consider. Each of them has individual needs. Each adult has needs, too. How essential is the parent's (or two parents') full-time salary during this period of months or two or three years? The cost of high-quality infant child care in some parts of the country is $6,000 a year; one of four children live in single-parent households, most of which are supported by women earning between $15,000 and $26,000 a year. How does this add up? Do *all* parents have equal opportunity in deciding what they'll do about family and work in the first year? Does society permit and assist each family to do what seems wisest with a full array of affordable support services, such as paid parent assurance leave, high-quality out-of-home infant care, part-time jobs, and job-sharing options? Is it ethical to exclude most parents and babies from what we say is best for babies (and from what many socioeconomically privileged people arrange for their families)? Is it best for America to condemn most families to choicelessness? In this chapter, we are asked the tough questions, and challenged to face them head first.

This chapter suggests that the child caring community may want to discuss and work toward ways of ensuring all families equal choices, including high-quality infant/toddler care programs, which we know are costly, and ways of participating in regular and leisurely ways in their babies' daily lives, whether or not they're in child care.

CHAPTER 4

. . . returns from global, national, and philosophical issues affecting a child's care to what should be two down-to-earth, everyday questions: (1) What is curriculum for infants and toddlers in family day care (or elsewhere)? and (2) What is the goal?

Caregivers are encouraged to

1. notice individual needs and respond promptly to them;

2. *prevent* discipline problems by observing what's going on and responding *in time*!;

3. notice and appreciate each child's natural, spontaneous growth in all dimensions; and

4. remember that lots of positive relationship and lots of positive communication between the caregiving adult and the individual tyke are the core of character development and are the "core curriculum" for infants, toddlers, and two-year-olds.

CHAPTER 5

. . . investigates, in-depth, the psychology of personality development, character development, and the development of mental health in the first three years. Probably because this has been one of the author's favorite areas of study (book study and child study) for many decades, a number of pre-publication reviewers found this chapter quite unique and fascinating. Where does one's physical self-image come from? I know I'm myself, but what is "self?" How does a person develop low self-esteem? What can we do to *increase* a child's self-esteem? What are the three major parts of personality? Which one should we encourage in a very young child? What is conscience and where does it come from? Why are we advised not to shame children? How do race, disabilities, culture, etc., relate to high or low self-esteem, and how can we encourage the former? How do trusting and respecting a toddler help develop good character?

Of course, little children bustle through this chapter giving us glimpses of "applied theory" as they go about their business — growing into grownups, hopefully good ones.

*   *   *

The second half of *Character Development: Encouraging Self-Esteem & Self-Discipline In Infants, Toddlers, & Two-Year-Olds* offers an unusual mixture — within each chapter — of detailed psychological, social, intellectual, and physical child development — entwined, as they are in real children — *and details the intricacies of what to do to enhance all of it in actual, non-ideal child care settings, while guiding each child toward good character, self-esteem, and self-discipline.*

CHAPTER 6

. . . informally offers a practical, what-to-do-about-it, age-by-stage "course" in understanding and enhancing the development of younger-than-one-year-olds — in all dimensions. Emphasis is on noticing and encouraging the details that add up to general development in a way that also encourages an embryonic version of positive self-esteem and self-regulation (which precede self-discipline). Babies with special needs and their parents are mainstreamed into the chapter, as is recommended that they be in family day care and center-based programs. Both should be a natural part of the warp and woof of a child care setting.

Good ideas for providing

● sensible routines,

● stimulating variety,

● care for the unique needs of each baby,

● help with mother/child and child/mother discomfort during separations, and

● standards of "good behavior" for babies

are discussed. The incomparable experts Selma Fraiberg and T. Berry Brazelton are quoted extensively. Dr. Fraiberg describes the dawn of autonomy, and Dr. Brazelton urges us to consider strengthening the family as the major priority of any program for children under two. This means extensive parent inclusion.

CHAPTER 7

. . . responds to a director's dilemma — unfortunately, a dilemma that's all too common in the child care world. The director says she can't pay enough to get well-trained people, and wants to know

● how she can work toward a better toddler program with the far-from-perfect staff she has, and

● what she should look for as she hires new staff, considering that credentialed caregivers may not be a possibility.

The following suggestions are made and discussed:

1. Hire people who have a way with little children, and then establish an ongoing, on-the-job staff development program.

2. Acquire enough adult participation — by regularly using parents and volunteers — to be able to give toddlers family-style group sizes and informality.

3. Move toward a developmentally appropriate program to maximize development and learning and minimize discipline problems.

Tips on timing, transitions, potty training, grouping children, and other preventive discipline practices, as well as a number of useful tricks of our trade, are discussed. Practitioners' wisdom is shared. Solutions for problems are sought. The tone is collegial.

CHAPTER 8

. . . explores the amazing *mental* development that takes place during the second year of each child's life (12–24 months). The entrancingly realistic examples and helpfully insightful comments reveal some toddler oddities and some reasons that toddlers' not surprisingly incomplete expertise about how the world around them works occasionally causes them to appear to be fairly peculiar little people. Thoughts are offered on how to handle everyday happenings during our hours with toddlers in a way that promotes the emotional organization of "self," positive self-esteem, and sensible self-discipline.

CHAPTER 9

. . . a short chapter, notes admiringly that language is developing (through maturation and interaction) almost miraculously rapidly in infants, toddlers, and two-year-olds. We are reminded that the promoting of relationship—connecting—communicating—is the central function of language. Every caregiver, whatever her language, is invited to chat casually, frequently, and appreciatively with each child each day, extending what the child is doing, wanting, or feeling into words and comments. If we do this, we're encouraging language development, self-esteem, self-awareness, and self-discipline.

CHAPTER 10

... even shorter than chapter 9, continues to emphasize the importance of using informal language throughout the day with "pre-preschool" children, but focuses on using *playful* language and making baby-level jokes as a form of child guidance (toward good behavior, good character, self-discipline, and self-esteem—why would we want to guide our tiny charges toward anything else?). Fun-filled friendship is central to what we are trying to achieve with young children.

CHAPTER 11

... is an exceedingly practical chapter about the specifics of disciplining two-year-olds and other young children firmly and fairly while avoiding adversarial interactions in which somebody "wins" and somebody else feels crushed, angry, and retaliative. A person's intuitive feeling of self-worth (or

worthlessness) is formed at a very young age from a collection of perceptions about his body, race, intelligence, similarity to others in the peer group, socioeconomic status, and other "self-images." Probably the most major among them is the child's perception of parents' and significant others' continuing evaluation of him. Nothing is more consistently and intimately linked to a wide variety of emotional and behavioral disturbances than is a low opinion of oneself. This chapter offers suggestions about guiding children unequivocally but encouragingly toward good behavior and good character.

CHAPTER 12

... sums it all up. If "instructing" infants, toddlers, and two-year-olds isn't advised, then what, beyond wiping bottoms and noses, have we accomplished in the three years—thousands of hours—we've been living busily and patiently with these little children? **If we have been giving culturally appropriate guidance along with our care** (in all senses of the word *care*), **we have helped build the foundations of good character in each child.** Dozens of specifics are listed here. What more could anyone ask of us? What career could be more important?

* * *

Volume II of this series of child development books by Polly Greenberg —*Character Development: Encouraging Self-Esteem & Self-Discipline*—(to be published in 1992) takes it from here. It discusses these same subjects, in equal depth and detail, as they relate to three-, four-, and five-year-olds. Volume III, (to be published in 1993) addresses the same topics in the same manner, continuing with five-year-olds and then focusing on six- and seven-year-olds as they develop and learn in classroom settings.

* * *

A Word of Thanks

As I developed this book, nineteen reviewers helped me better express what I was trying to say, showed me holes in my thinking, or amended some sentences to render them more accurate.

Several reviewers helped with all chapters; all reviewers helped with several chapters. Everyone didn't agree with me all the way, but most people did seem to agree that the book boldly confronts urgently important sticky issues usually skirted by early childhood education writers.

I especially want to thank Jack Zibulsky, my partner in journal- and book-making at NAEYC, for his technical expertise, good ideas and patience as together we constructed these pages.

The purposes of these pages are to encourage those of you who regularly spend many, many hours a week giving care to infants, toddlers, and two-year-olds to appreciate more fully the incredibly important character development work you're doing, and to encourage you to deepen both your understanding of child development and your child caring skills.

The book can be used in various ways. People who aren't big readers can benefit and enjoy by looking up something that concerns them in the Index and reading about it (biting, fears), or by browsing through the chapters, hitting the headings and highlights, catching the captions, and warming to the dozens of adorable photos—scanning, skimming, and reading paragraphs or segments that appeal to them. Directors, other on-site staff development people, and teacher educators may want to use one chapter per session or class as the centerpiece of a discussion. Perhaps staff or students who like to read this sort of thing—as well as the group leader—can read the chapter and present its key points; everyone can participate in discussion. Then too, there are many caregivers—parents and others—who *are* readers, and are tremendously interested in child developing, who just might choose to read the whole book.

CHAPTER

1

Infants and Toddlers Away From Their Mothers?
Is It Good for Their Mental Health?
Is It Good for Their Self-Esteem?

QUESTION: I am considering adding an infant/toddler component to my child care center. There is so much demand in my town. The ethics of it keep me feeling uneasy, though. For the first time in history, all these babies not being taken care of tenderly by their mothers? Is it good for such young children to be cared for by people other than their mothers?

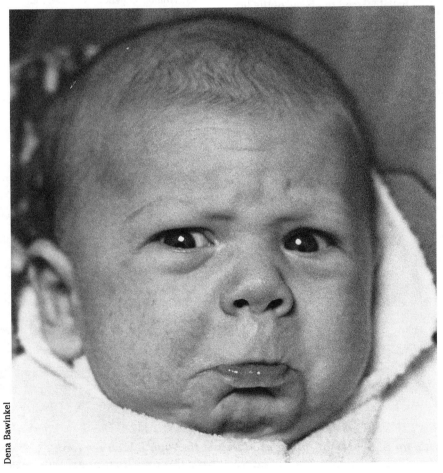

Who will best take care of me?

Most of us have a hazy and highly inaccurate view of family history because until recent years, as a result of what has been called "gender-warped historical writing," the white male scholars who wrote our history books did not know much about young children firsthand, and did not research the lives of women and children. (They preferred, as we know, to focus on the military exploits and political events most of us studied in school.) However, we now know more about the history of childhood, and one thing we know is that babies were *not* all tended by their mothers. We must not discuss out-of-home child care as if it's happening "for the first time in history," as you put it.

Dena Bawinkel

Infants and Toddlers Away From Their Mothers?

1

Historically, few babies have had the luxury of quality care

The poor women of the world, and of our country, that is, the *majority* of women, were in the fields growing food, in the homes of the rich serving them, in factories toiling, and so forth. Who took care of their young children? Perhaps other adults, who may have been caring and who may have been care*less*. Perhaps older children. Perhaps the littlest ones were pretty much on their own, seven-year-olds tending infants and toddlers. In fact, millions of young children *themselves* labored and sweated in field and factory, even in the United States. Farm and slave children were valued as a source of free labor. Babies barely able to walk were assigned chores. Our child labor laws were not passed until 1916 and 1938! Luckily, as psychobiological specialists (e.g., Kagan, 1984) believe, much mental development in young human beings is programmed into the species; this belief formed the basis of the life work of Arnold Gesell and his followers at the Gesell Institute. While most mothers do the best they can, under these difficult life conditions it seems

MYTH #1: Babies of the world always received wonderful care before 20th century women "went to work." (Women didn't work before this century?)

safe to guess that infants were not benefiting from the excellent care they could get in a first-rate infant/toddler child care program. No one was worrying about the quality of their mental health and the level of their self-esteem!

All the babies of the world were being taken care of tenderly by their mothers? Many were, of course, but not all, not even most, not even all the children of the wealthy, really. For example, read this about the situation in 18th Century France:

Reliance on nurses from the country was the prevailing custom in the population of the cities. Women depended on them, either because they were too taken up with their own work (as wives of merchants and artisans) or because they were rich enough to be able to avoid the thankless task of breastfeeding. The villages in the immediate environment of the cities supplied nurses to the rich, and the poor had to search for theirs much farther away. The distance involved and the absence of contact between nurses and parents . . . meant that the placing of

children with nurses was often a means of disguising desertion. . . . [T]he death rate of children entrusted to nurses was huge: around two-thirds for nurses living at a distance and one-fourth for those nearby.

The wealthy could buy themselves the exclusive services of a nurse but rarely her good will, and doctors suddenly discovered in the behavior of nurses the explanation for many of the defects that afflicted the children of rich parents. (Donzelot, 1979, pp. 10–11)

This problem was not unique to Europe.

A more direct form of abandoning babies was to leave them on doorsteps, in churchyards, or at foundling hospitals. In France in the year 1833, for example, St. Vincent de Paul sheltered 131,000 children. An enormous number of them died.

Even in much more recent times and in the United States, growing up for many children was laced with beatings and whippings, for to spare the rod was to spoil the child. Look around today. While many families in all walks of

Arthur Jones

National Archives

It's an indicator of the classist lenses through which we look at issues in our society that child care for working mothers became of interest to researchers, to the early childhood education "establishment," and to the nation only when the women working away from home were middle-class mothers.

life are reliably kind and sensibly involved, many are not. Many of us have relatives and neighbors who shame and ridicule their children as a way of life, even though they do not physically abuse them. Most of us have friends who routinely ignore their little children's eagerness, usually neglect to provide appropriate challenges, and so on. Let's face it, not every young child in out-of-home care has been expelled from the Garden of Eden!

Not every young child being cared for at home has been encouraged to become and to feel *competent,* to feel good about herself, to develop high self-esteem. There is more to the matter of helping a child feel confident and lovable than whether she is at home or in out-of-home care.

Most parents provide the best care they can, but what about when they're off at work?

On the other hand, most parents do the very best they can, and really do a great job. Many marvelous parents, married or single, need or want very much to be employed—to have paid work, and seek care as good as they would give if they were home—as good as they *do* give all the hours and days, weeks, months, and years that even parents who work away from home *are* home with their children. Parents are the primary people in children's lives, no matter how many hours the children spend in care.

You're worried about the ethics of having infants and toddlers in child care programs. **But nearly half of all mothers of babies younger than a year work away from home.** If we developmentalists don't take care of these little ones, who will? Wonderful grammas and nannies and other fine caregivers in some cases, and in other cases, not-so-hot "sitters"—whose role, it would seem, is to *sit,* often with eyes glued to the one-eyed electronic babysitter of the babysitter (TV). Regardless of our cherished beliefs, we must acknowledge reality. The reality is that many mothers work away from home.

Many startling statistics appear each year throwing light on aspects of American family life. From the Census Bureau in June: Forty-eight percent of all mothers of infants under one year of age work outside the home. And of the 1.4 million mothers who gave birth for the first time between June 1984 and June 1985, 57% returned to work. Some experts predicted that by the year 2000 four out of every five infants would have a mother in the labor force. Such figures lent strong weight to the recommendation of the Yale Bush Center Advisory Committee on Infant Care Leave that employees be allowed a minimum of six months leave, with 75% replacement of salary for three months, to recover from pregnancy and to care for their newborn or newly adopted infants. They also led to the publication of "The Crisis in Infant and Toddler Care," a statement by 11 organizations ranging from the American Academy of Pediatrics to the National Board of the YWCA, . . . suggesting a variety of approaches employers, communities and the government could follow to meet the infant care problem (Hymes, 1987, p. 19).

long way toward gradually building the little person's positive self-esteem.

We know too much now about the development of young children's mental health and well-being to run emotionally negligent programs

Now that so much is known that wasn't known until this century was well under way about what babies need to be healthy and happy, many well-known child development specialists think that out-of-home care is unethical if the program is inferior, and ethical if the program is excellent. What *is* an excellent program? What do babies and toddlers need?

MYTH #2: Anyone can provide good enough care to infants and toddlers. (To create strong "character," good self-discipline, and high self-esteem?)

Even if and when our country establishes reasonable parental leave policies, and even if and when employers, communities, and the government get more helpfully involved in infant/toddler care issues, we will need expert caregivers—especially for abused and neglected babies. Anything you, as a director, can do to help develop these expert caregivers will be a plus. The core of good caregiving is ensuring that each child experiences good feelings almost every time he is needy—feels his needs are being respected and responded to—and almost every time he engages with an adult. Factors other than the primary caregiver's opinion influence a child's opinion of himself. Moreover there are many dimensions of what adds up to be high or low self-esteem. But in infancy and toddlerhood, respecting and warmly responding to each individual goes a

To live, to thrive, **to develop their fullest potential,** babies need relaxed, responsive grown-ups who promptly tend to the many kinds of discomforts that babies communicate through fussing and fretting.

This means that each baby must have one or two primary caregivers who can really get to know him and whom he can really learn to trust as a sensitive, responsive, caring person. This means that no caregiver should be responsible for too many children, work too many hours, be alone with the babies too much, or lack reasonable job security, reasonable wages, and reasonable benefits. To regulate these factors is beyond the control of the caregiver. Good working conditions must be created by the people planning and running the program (see Godwin & Schrag, 1988; Jorde-Bloom, 1988), "and insisted upon by concerned, conscientious citizens," Alice Honig reminds us. Alice Sterling Honig, Ph.D., is Professor of Child Development at Syracuse University, New York. For the past 13 years, she has been program supervisor of the Syracuse Children's Center, the longest federally funded infant/toddler child care center in the United States.

If these dangers leading to burnout and turnover are not considered and guarded against—if these necessities are not built in during the construction of the program—most staff will probably not be able to meet children's needs **immediately, generously,** and **kindly,** nor feel safe, secure, respected, and in the sort of good mood that's contagious to babies. Staff members may become sour and are likely to leave for jobs offering more "sweeteners."

It all depends on the caregiver, so select "the right stuff"

Careful selection of staff at hiring time is vitally important. Because infants and toddlers need adults' emotional focus, warmth, and steady, good-natured calmness, people who appear self-centered or distracted by problems in their own lives, essentially angry, cold, rigid, humorless, or unusually anxious, are not good bets if optimal development in all dimensions is the goal. To put it bluntly, there are "basics" about people that cannot be changed simply through training, if at all.

One basic that can't always be

Subjects & Predicates

At home or elsewhere, quality care is essential if optimal development is desired. If adequate development rather than optimal development is deemed sufficient, our nation still has a long way to go; nationwide, we have a great deal of inadequate day care.

changed—one that can probably **never** be changed without the active willingness of the person in question is this: **Parents and caregivers (some inadvertently and some intentionally) reproduce the social strategies** **for daily living that make sense for them in the world as they see it from their socioeconomic position.** This fact greatly affects how people relate to children: rigid and authoritarian, or flexible and egalitarian; gruffly barking orders, or giving melodiously toned reasons; removing a child to stand in the corner while harshly reprimanding him, or redirecting the child to another activity by enticingly inviting her; ignoring needs individual children signal and conversations they start, or responding promptly to child-initiated ideas, behaviors, and conversations; "instructing" children and believing that activities *they* select are trivial, or developing curriculum *from* activities children are deeply involved in—believing that "instruction" and imposed curriculum are inappropriate; strictly teaching gender stereotyping,

---

MYTH #3: There are plenty of potential caregivers with "the right stuff" who are willing to work for low wages. In a short time we will have excellent infant/toddler care programs for all parents who work away from home. (Raise your hand if you believe this myth. If you don't believe it, we childcarers have a lot of work to do!)

---

or strongly encouraging androgynous living; restricting language primarily to brief imperative commands, or considering conversations with children of utmost importance and expanding them as much as possible. **Views on the desirability of developing high self-esteem and strong self-discipline in young children differ markedly in various socioeconomic groups.** (See Chapter 3 for more issues of social class reproduction in childrearing/child care settings.) You can teach people to conform to certain schedules, perform specific acts, use assorted tips and techniques—but you cannot develop an entirely different character, personality, and self-esteem level in a staff person.

There is evidence, also, that the more schooling, specialized infant/toddler training, and prior teaching experience with a similar age group an applicant has had—providing he or she has had "the right stuff" to start with—the more likely it is that the individual will be a success in your program.

Children seem to benefit from having close contact with some staff of the same racial, ethnic, or socioeconomic group. Certainly parents do! A few men in a program for even the youngest children seem to be a good influence. It's important to start with "the right stuff!"

Giving a great deal of thought before hiring to what very young children need, and what grown-ups must do to meet these needs optimally, guarantees that you will have fewer misfits on your staff, thus fewer headaches. Effective parents and caregivers typically:

● provide the body-nourishing, cuddling, carrying, and holding that babies need to become secure and feel calm and safe

● enjoy playing and chatting with children of this age
  ○ in small groups, and
  ○ individually (frequently);
● are interested in
  ○ how babies' and toddlers' minds work,
  ○ what little ones are trying to communicate,
  ○ helping babies and toddlers help themselves (become competent and confident in many dimensions,

knowing that the younger the child, the more learning occurs through the senses, not through instruction),
  ○ assisting the very inexperienced youngest children in getting along with one another (neither yielding too easily, nor bullying),
  ○ planning simple activities, such as water play, singing, or looking at books,
  ○ being involved in, but not directing, a collage of activities at once, like a carefully supervised home scene, and do not feel that children should all be doing the same thing at the same time;

● are able to
  ○ adjust the schedule to meet the ever-changing needs of small groups and individuals,
  ○ offer almost constant positive encouragement,
  ○ gently guide children toward desired behaviors,

  ○ work warmly as a team with babies' family members; and
● have good judgment, which results from a mix of the way *they* were brought up, common sense, training, and reading.

Speaking of families—well, families *are* one of the most important points pertaining to infants and toddlers to speak of! In a nutshell, the better the program, the more parent participation there will be:

● indirectly (preparing snacks, typing newsletters),
● in the classroom (in a wide variety of roles),
● in collaborative conferencing and planning for their child,
● in parenting education projects, and
● in meaningful decision making.

All this is only a start. But if you decide to add an infant/toddler component to your child care center, these are some important first steps to think about.

Nancy P. Alexander

We can get easy solace by stubbornly planting our heads in the sand and insisting that all mothers should be home with their young children. Well, they aren't.

Bettye Caldwell, Donaghey Distinguished Professor of Education at the University of Arkansas at Little Rock, is the person who established what is generally considered to be the nation's first research-oriented infant day care center in Syracuse, New York, in 1964. She has written:

I think we will have infant care of reasonable quality for all children needing it and all parents wanting it by the beginning of the 21st Century — if not by the midpoint of the nineties. My prediction is based on the fact that the young adults moving into position as the movers and shakers in this country have, with minimal fanfare but maximum conviction, assimilated the concept that parenting should be a shared project, not one carried out exclusively by the mother.

The concept is based on the philosophy that children need fathers as well as mothers and that society needs the talents and contributions of women as well as men. And with the philosophy comes the recognition that society at large, with the responsibility of ensuring its own collective future, must also participate in the process through the provision and support of high-quality services. Although, demographically speaking, this is a small segment of the population needing and wanting infant services, it represents the power elite, whose support has been lacking in the past. These future movers and shakers, in 1990, are no longer asking whether it is OK for babies younger than a year to be in full-time weekly family or center-based day care. Instead, they are in effect saying to those who design and operate the programs: "This is the way we say it is going to be; now you find out how to do it and do it right." (Caldwell, 1990)

The bottom line is that if the mental health and general well-being of children younger than three *is in our hands,* it is our obligation to do everything we can to build each little child's good feeling about herself. Feeling good about oneself is self-esteem. Self-esteem is the prerequisite of good mental health. Good mental health is a necessity if a good life is to follow.

MYTH #4: Taking time to build a little child's self-esteem dozens of times a day is a frill. (Well, the evidence doesn't seem to substantiate this. Really, self-esteem is a basic. Low self-esteem is found in most dysfunctional people.)

References

Caldwell, B. (1990). Personal communication to author, response to queries.

Donzelot, J. (1979). *The policing of families.* New York: Pantheon.

Godwin, A., & Schrag, L. (1988). *Setting up for infant care: Guidelines for centers and family day care homes.* Washington, DC: NAEYC.

Honig, A. J. (1990). Personal communication to author, response to queries.

Hymes, J. L., Jr. (1987). *Early childhood education: The year in review. A look at 1986.* Hacienda Press, Box 222415, Carmel, CA 93922.

Jorde-Bloom, P. (1988). *A great place to work: Improving conditions for staff in young children's programs.* Washington, DC: NAEYC.

Kagan, J. (1984). *The nature of the child.* New York: Basic.

CHAPTER

What Do Babies Need To Develop Optimal Self-Esteem?

2

QUESTION: For a long time, many of us who care about little children have expressed concern that the world does not do enough for its youngest citizens. We all know that babies grow up to be future leaders and followers in each nation; why do we fail to focus on meeting their needs? Even their survival needs! Babies need a lot of basics before they can develop high self-regard. How can we talk about self-esteem when babies are starving and lack life-saving immunizations? Why do we neglect to notice the basics that come *before* the development of self-esteem? What *do* babies need?

Many early childhood educators, both practitioners and academics, tend to think very narrowly when talking about infant and toddler care. This is probably partly because there is so much to do and to learn that we don't have time to look much farther away than our nurseries or specialized work. Another reason for our strong tendency to think small is that there are too many issues in the world, and the amount of information is overwhelmingly massive. In order to feel competent instead of confused, all people learn young to put blinders on, and to confine our search for knowledge, information, and expertise to one or another narrow area. This is a major fac-

tor behind the arbitrary and otherwise absolutely counterproductive splitting of knowledge into academic and professional disciplines and fields. Making knowledge more manageable by attempting to master only a small designated portion of it prevents us from losing our minds, but it also severely interferes with our ability to keep our part of the job in an accurate context, and to form collections of "whole" (thus accurate) knowledge, or coalitions for effective political action.

When considering what babies need in order to develop high self-regard, let's not think about books full of "affirmations" that we will verbally distribute, or the exact right way to phrase our praise, until we first consider the big picture and the basics. **As Abraham Maslow explained to us more than two decades ago (Maslow, 1970), the human organism cannot concentrate on achieving higher level goals until it has met its physical and psychological survival needs.**

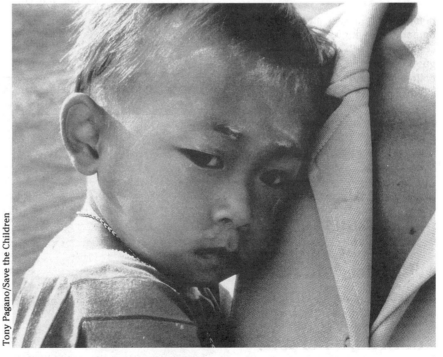

Tony Pagano/Save the Children

Worldwide, 40,000 children a day die of hunger-related causes. It's hard to tighten your belt when you're wearing diapers.

Under normal conditions, maturation just happens. However, what kind of a person each child turns out to be is more up to us than to nature.

First, the basics — nutrition, health care . . .

Babies need good prenatal care and safe deliveries; reliable, predictable shelter; a warm and comfortable temperature; protection from harm and fear; nutritious food suited to the infant's age; regular weighing and measuring to ensure that growth is going forward normally; immunizations; sensible sanitation and cleanliness; treatment of physical problems and illnesses; preventive dental care; and attachment to one primary person and care by that person and other consistent, continuous familiar people who provide a great deal of pleasant physical, social, and emotional contact, through which, and from which foundation, babies learn in all domains and dimensions. Babies need warmly loving care.

From this healthy and mentally healthy foundation grow trust, independence, initiative and motivation, empathy, lovingness, cooperation, **self-esteem, self-discipline**—all the good qualities that add up to what is colloquially called "character."

Whether they are being cared for by their mothers or by other caregivers, at home or somewhere else, this is what babies need.

But it's not what all of the world's babies get.

What kinds of people do you like? What are you doing to help each child become a lovable, admirable person?

As you well know, the governments of the world don't make "getting off to a happy, healthy start" a national priority. Every nation has a budget, and providing the best beginning for babies is rarely a big budget item. Even the most basic *basics* on the above list of necessities are not available to millions of the world's babies.

Babies in developing countries, not a budget priority

Right now at the end of the 20th century, right now while we read this sentence, millions of babies and young children in the developing countries are being denied—by world decision makers, including our own, **who could make different decisions**—not only quality care, but health, freedom from extraordinary handicaps, and life itself. Consider the numbers in Figure 1. They probably won't surprise *you*, but they may surprise some people who've never thought much about it.

Some of this misery is unavoidable. Much could be avoided. Some of these

---

When considering what babies need, let's not fret so much about refinements that we forget the basics.

Because they are not given such simple things as careful prenatal and delivery care, plenty of food, pure water, immunizations, preventive health care, and treatment of life-threatening but curable conditions, millions of infants die. Others are needlessly handicapped by illness or other serious disabilities.

are poor countries and/or newly organizing countries and don't have money enough to do everything rich countries do in the way of health and mental health systems, education systems, transportation systems, housing, economic development, job training, social services, and so on—all things

Figure 1. **Number of infant and child deaths in selected countries in 1987**

Country	Ages 0–1	Ages 1–5	Ages 0–5	Country's population (in millions)
India	2,537,440	1,409,690	3,947,130	800.3
Nigeria	533,590	386,220	919,810	108.6
China	659,830	247,430	907,260	1,062
Bangladesh	512,110	335,670	847,780	107.1
Pakistan	504,150	291,390	795,540	104.6
Indonesia	412,260	256,270	668,530	174.9
Ethiopia	314,380	255,300	569,680	46
Brazil	261,970	99,490	360,660	141.5
Iran	205,910	103,920	309,830	50.4
Afghanistan	160,960	146,090	306,970	14.2
Zaire	141,010	99,280	240,290	31.8

Sources: Population Reference Bureau, 1987; Ross, Rich, Molzan, & Pensak, 1988.

As Marian Edelman writes in her book Families in Peril: An Agenda for Social Change *(1987), "Poverty is the greatest child killer in the affluent United States of the mid-1980s. More American children die each year from poverty than from traffic fatalities and suicide combined. Over a five-year period, more American children die from poverty than the total number of American battle deaths during the Vietnam War" (p. 29). If the same people who are concerned about children's self-esteem and school success are not concerned enough about avoidable child death to act, who is?*

that all countries do, all things that affect families, thus children. Nonetheless many of the world's health, educational, and human services leaders wonder if good beginnings for babies are a world priority (Doxiadis, 1979; Greenberg, 1979). In this regard, there may be more than sparsely filled treasuries to consider.

For example, perhaps the high infant death rate (and adult death rate) is a practical part of these countries' passive, unspoken population control policy (Population Education Interchange, 1986).

Or perhaps the problem is that men run countries and **the majority** of those in key leadership positions, regardless of how good they may be *individually,* to their *own* children *individually,* have not yet come to consider young children *as a social class* of primary importance. (In some countries, for instance, when there's a shortage of food, custom dictates that the men in the family are fed first, then the women, and finally the children.) It should not be necessary to say that some of the world's greatest children's champions are men, but because of many people's sensitivity on the subject of male and female characteristics, roles in society, and so on, we may need to say it anyway.

We are *not* talking about infants in other countries, some readers may (irritably) say. We are *not* talking about needs greater than day care. We are *not* discussing good care before

---

The United States is more than *twice* as wealthy as the nearest runner-up, Japan, and almost *four times* as wealthy as the third in rank (the Soviet Union). Why does the United States have the highest child poverty rate of eight industrialized Western countries?

What Do Babies Need To Develop Optimal Self-Esteem?

birth, safe delivery, immunizations, nutrition, and drinking water free of killer germs, a reader may say. **We're talking about children in the United States of America, someone may say.**

Babies in contemporary America, not a budget priority

Though wealthy, the United States does not do so well in meeting the basic life-preserving needs of babies either. In the U.S. in 1987, 46,371 children younger than five died: 38,891 children younger than one year and 7,480 children aged one to five (Ross, Rich, Molzan, & Pensak, 1988). The United States' population that year was 243.8 million.

Even in the United States, the facts about children are sobering. For example, consider these, from the Children's Defense Fund (1989):

● *In 1986, the infant mortality rate was 10.4 deaths per 1,000 live births: 8.9 White babies died per 1,000 births; 18 Black babies died per 1,000 births.* Is the government ensuring that Black mothers in America are getting a fair share of prenatal care? Making sure it's *given* is one challenge facing us; making sure it's *gotten* is another. There are many reasons why health care apparently available is never actually delivered. There are also many known ways to alleviate this problem. What is our child caring community doing about this?

● *4,818,000 children younger than six (22.3%) live at or below the poverty level* (1987 figures). (The child poverty rate has increased two-thirds for Whites in recent years in contrast to one-sixth for Black children.) Do we believe that these almost five million little children are getting optimal developmentally appropriate physical, emotional, social, and intellectual care? That their self-esteem is being fostered? Many of these children are at far greater risk of

Public domain

There is no safety net for the millions of heartbroken refugees from the American Dream, scattered helplessly, homelessly, hopelessly in any U.S. city you can name. As award-winning educator and author of Death At An Early Age *and* Illiterate America *Jonathan Kozol discovered when working on his unforgettable newest book,* Rachel and Her Children *(1988), the basic problem is a criminal lack of affordable housing in the wealthiest country in the world. As city governments pay millions for dilapidated "temporary" housing, desperate men, women, and many, many children struggle hourly for survival. Desperate parents, starvation, fear, and cold aren't good for a child's school success or self-esteem.*

serious health and academic problems and teen-age problems (pregnancy, dropping out of school, substance abuse, delinquency) that will, in turn, affect *their* children than are children from more fortunate socioeconomic circumstances. Much is known about the prevention of all these problems. What is our child caring community doing about this? Is this the best we can do?

● *An estimated 100,000 children are homeless each night.* Read Jonathan Kozol's (1988) book about them and weep. Living in dilapidated rural shacks and rat-infested ghetto flats, all the while peering enviously in the windows of this conspicuously affluent so-

Since babies grow up to be the world's leaders and citizens, why aren't they a budget priority in any country?

The United States is one of the very few developed countries that does not give a children's allowance to each family in that country, regardless of socioeconomic level, at the birth of each of its children.

In our own small communities, what are we childcarers doing about prenatal care for all mothers, and health care for all children? This baby was born in a migrant labor camp where there is a nurse and clinic for prenatal care. In every community there are people who need us to ensure that they connect with health care.

ciety, is not good for children's self-esteem. But it's worse yet for them to exist in an unpredictable series of crowded rat- and crack-riddled "shelters." What is our rich country's government doing to guarantee that all children's families have a permanent roof over their heads? What are *we* doing to push decision makers? What is our child caring community doing about this?

● *The teen birth rate was 50.6 per 1,000 teen women aged 15 to 19 in 1986. Of the total number of babies born that year, 12.5% had mothers 19 and younger.* Can children be excellent mothers? Very seldom, especially if there's no money. We do have expertise in operating mother-empowering, multi-service parent-child programs. What is our child caring community doing to help teen-agers have babies later when their bodies and personalities are more mature, and their finances are in better shape? To help them and their babies if they have them? Is this the best we can do?

● *One in five children has a single parent.* Sometimes this works just fine. Sometimes it's excessively stressful to all involved, especially economically. The rising proportion of births to single Black mothers is explained (by people of such stature as Lisbeth Schorr and Marian Edelman) as a result of a lost generation of fathers—young Black males unable to marry and support a family, jobless from lack of appropriate education and job training. Actually, the birth rate for Black unmarried women is stabilizing, while that for unmarried White women is rising. What's going on in our communities that helps, economically or otherwise, the single parents who want help? Is this the best we can do?

● *In 1986, 30.1% of poor Black children and 33.7% of poor White children lived in families without health insurance. In low-income homes (family income less than twice the poverty level), 30.9% of Black children and 30.4% of White children had families without health insurance.* Are we all aware that the United States is the only developed country in the world that does not have some form of national health insurance that helps *everybody*? At all levels, legislators deal with public health and health

What Do Babies Need To Develop Optimal Self-Esteem?

insurance issues. They listen to their constituents. Do we ever tell them our views? Is this the best we can do?

• *A quarter of a million children live apart from their families in foster care, group homes, residential treatment centers, and other institutions.* Watchdog groups such as the Children's Defense Fund report that too many of these children are lost in the system, left in limbo, not properly arranged for, not well taken care of. Why is this not only allowed to happen, but even allowed to be a common occurrence? Few of us monitor our local agencies on this subject. If we child caring people don't, who will? Is what we do the best we can do?

• *In 1986, 675,000 children* (that we *know* of) *were abused.* We've all heard tell of child abuse cases being reported, sometimes repeatedly, yet the child not being rescued. Why do we allow the laws of our land and the reams of bureaucratic red tape to permit this? Why do we fund child protective services so inadequately that staff case loads don't allow immediate and complete attention to these situations? Is this the best we can do?

*   *   *

It's possible that the United States would do better by its babies if there were "enough" money. However, the money our country *does* have goes where most citizens *want* it to go; if we objected, as voters we would elect leaders, male or female, who would allocate the dollars differently. *This being a democracy, we're free to elect leaders who implement our values and strive to reach our goals.* Men and women have the power of the vote, but most, especially women, don't use it.

You ask why we fail to focus on meeting babies' needs, when we are aware that they grow up to be the future leaders and followers of the world; that was your question. For some of us, the answer is that we fail to see the connection between children's issues and elections; we don't vote. For others among us, the answer is that we vote by rote; we don't think. Figure 2 shows where America's money went in 1981 and in 1988.

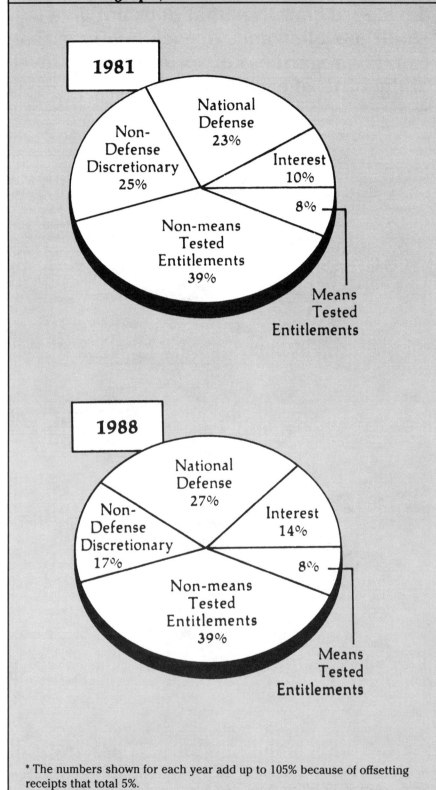

Figure 2. The Children's Defense Fund explains the division of the federal budget pie, FY1981 and FY1988*

* The numbers shown for each year add up to 105% because of offsetting receipts that total 5%.

Source: Congressional Budget office

A portrait of our nation's values, the federal budget reflects the relative priority we place on alternative and often competing interests and needs. The importance America places on children—their health and well-being, education and training, care and support—is determined by the decisions made in the development of the federal budget. . . .

The federal budgets of the 1980s placed little value on America's children and sacrificed their future and the nation's future, creating both budget deficits and human deficits of crisis proportions. . . .

The federal budgets of the 1980s were characterized by:

• An immense overall increase in military spending.
• A major shift in budget priorities with a dramatic increase in the proportion of the federal budget going to the military and **a dramatic decrease in the proportion for children, families, and the poor.**
• An insufficient amount of federal revenue; and
• Budget deficits of enormous and dangerous proportions.

These budgets mortgaged the future of all Americans, but none will bear so heavy a burden as our children. Ironically, our nation has left this legacy of deficit and debt to the same generation of children that has simultaneously been neglected by the shortsighted budget policies of the 1980s.

Budget "Winners" in the 1980s

Defense spending has skyrocketed under the Reagan Administration, significantly increasing the proportion of the federal budget devoted to military hardware and weapons systems. . . .

• Federal spending for early research alone for the unproven Star Wars (Strategic Defense Initiative) venture **is more than three times greater than our spending for the proven Head Start preschool program.**
• More federal spending supports military musical bands than grants **for the immunization of our children. . . .**

Budget Losers in the 1980s

Federal spending for means-tested entitlement programs directed to recipients with limited means or income below specified amounts, always a small portion of the federal budget, barely held even from

FY 1981 to FY 1988 despite a more than 10 percent growth in the number of persons living in poverty during that period. Both in 1981 and 1988 only 8 percent of federal spending was devoted to entitlement programs for the poor, including Medicaid, food stamps, child nutrition, and Aid to Families with Dependent Children (AFDC). Currently:

• **AFDC, the major welfare program, and child support enforcement efforts together consume only 1 percent of federal spending.**
• **Child nutrition and food stamps programs consume less than 2 percent of federal spending.**

The biggest loser in the 1980s was federal spending for all the remaining programs and services of the federal government, the budget category referred to as non-defense discretionary spending. Through these programs the nation invests in its future, funding efforts to educate and train our children and youths, to immunize infants, to prevent child abuse, to protect our environment, and to maintain and enhance our highways, bridges, air, and water. Yet funding for non-defense discretionary programs has been slashed from 25 percent of federal spending in FY 1981 to 17 percent in FY 1988.

Among discretionary programs, those serving children and the poor have been hardest hit by the budget policies of the 1980s. In 1981 and 1982 massive cuts, ranging up to 25 percent and more, were made in virtually all discretionary children's programs, including education and job training, child abuse, maternal and child health, child care, and nutrition. Many of these programs were the target of deficit reduction efforts in 1986 and 1987 as well. Overall, spending for discretionary programs for low-income Americans was cut by more than 50 percent between FY 1981 and FY 1987 after adjusting for inflation, according to the Center for Budget and Policy Priorities.

• **Federal spending for Chapter 1, the highly effective compensatory education program, was cut more than 10 percent (adjusted for inflation) during this period.**
• **Federal support for low-income housing was cut by nearly 80 percent after inflation.**

America's children and, ultimately, our economy and our future are the biggest loser from the budget policies of the 1980s. (Children's Defense Fund, 1988, pp. 1–4, **bold** emphasis added by P.G.)

As the Children's Defense Fund, the National Association for the Education of Young Children, and many other child-concerned organizations constantly point out, communication from constitutents — letters, visits, and phone calls — can have a powerful effect on shaping and reshaping the priorities reflected in our federal budget. What will we child carers do to help the low-income babies among us obtain the basics? Is it ethical for us to focus solely on important issues in day care, such as the ratio of staff per child, yet give no thought at all to ensuring a daily ration of food for each?

You ask why we fail to focus on meeting babies' needs, when we are aware that they grow up to be the future leaders of the world; that was your question.

Some of us keep wondering, does gender imbalance in the world's decision making, and in the world's history, have anything to do with young children's low status in most nations' budgets?

Glance, for example, at the percentage of female participation in the world's parliamentary assemblies. These statistics (United Nations, 1989) refer to both elected and appointed members of national legislative bodies — governing bodies corresponding to the U.S. House of Representatives (our lower chamber) and the U.S. Senate (our upper chamber). Only one third of countries with lower chambers have upper chambers, however.

● As of 1986, *no country in the world had, or ever had had,* more than 34.5% of the seats in its *lower* national legislative body occupied by women. **The average percent of women in the world's lower national legislative bodies is 9.6%.**

● As of 1986, no country in the world had or ever had had more than 31.1% of the seats in its *upper* national legislative body occupied by women. **The average percent of women in the world's upper national legislative bodies is 10.1%.**

© Jim Bradshaw

Why can't our communities give every young child the basics, including love, respect, and appreciation?

- In the United States in 1986, 5.3% of the House of Representatives was female; 2% of the Senate was female— and 1986 was a vintage year.
- In only five countries in the world could women vote even by 1915.
- In the United States, women could not vote before 1920.

If all these gender percentages were reversed, men would, most likely *literally*, be up in arms! And possibly, policies pertaining to children, particularly low-income children, would be quite different. Imagine, for instance, that 94.7% of the U.S. House of Representatives and 98% of the Senate were female. Do you think this country would have publicly funded, "subsidized" child care as we have publicly funded, "subsidized" public schools?

It should go without saying that *some* male leaders are strong advocates for services and programs (including minimum guaranteed income and/or job training programs, family leave after the arrival of a new child in the household, etc.) that benefit young children and their families. It should go without saying that a great many men are excellent participants in creating good lives for their own children. It should go without saying that many women are *not* politically or professionally active in behalf of children, and are *not* excellent parents. However, it's best to emphasize these points because commenting, even if calmly and with clear documentation, on the masculinist bias in our world is as taboo a thing to do as it is to comment on the white bias and on the middle class bias that, though usually invisible, dominate economic, political, social, and psychological systems all over the world. As with race and class bias, most of us feel very threatened when asked to face gender bias, probably because acknowledging the reality would make it uncomfortable for us to continue to acquiesce to it. Feeling that we are part of biased institutions clashes with

many people's self-image; we don't believe we *should* be biased—we don't want to see ourselves as essential supports of biased systems.

These days we hear a great deal about the importance of learning "thinking skills." Among the thinking skills that are important are the skills of stepping out of the comfortable, conventional assumptions and thoughts we're used to and questioning them.

more favorable to the world's babies and children if more women (women having traditionally been in closer touch with the nature and needs of young children) were in the countries' top decision-making roles. Figure 3 illustrates a possible problem in making young children a higher national budget priority in the United States.

Of course, even if an equitable number of women did co-lead our country,

---

Those of us who care for America's children must, in addition to working to help them achieve mental health and high self-esteem, get involved in the politics of child poverty. At least in our own communities!

Questioning "authority" and "conventional wisdom" can be quite illuminating. For instance, we're accustomed to assuming that governments do all they can for the citizenry, and for the children of their countries. Do they? Is this really true? We're used to saying, "Well, they'd do more if they could; there just isn't enough money." Would they? Is there truly not enough money? There *is* money for a great number of other things; why not for young children? We can't come to conclusions on this matter without examining a complex set of facts, but we can practice our thinking skills: We can think critically about these (literally) life-and-death issues. It is not necessarily true that there isn't enough know-how, money, and food on this Earth to keep a higher percentage of the world's young children alive and well. In fact, there is considerable evidence to the contrary (Doxiadis, 1979).

It is possible that the United States would do better by its babies if there were "enough" money. It's also possible that budget priorities would be

budget priorities might remain the same. This is an interesting question to think about. It's not known that if women had more political power, children's needs (including the health, care, educational, and special needs of *all* children regardless of their parents' income and socioeconomic status) would be better met. We do not know, as women have never had enough top-level decision-making power for us to make a comparison. The information given in this chapter proves this statement. In spite of the facts that a woman Supreme Court judge exists and that there are a few female heads of state somewhere in the world, we can see that beyond a doubt men— **and therefore men's priorities**—have determined national budgets. Since the national budget began, men have budgeted stunningly inadequately even for the basic basics for babies, such as food, sanitation, immunizations, shelter, and kindly care by a few constant people; we are talking about the United States of America, the richest country in the world,

---

Are we voting for local, state, and federal officials who are known for making significant efforts of one kind or another on behalf of low-income families?

Figure 3. Number of women and men in top official positions in the United States 1789–1989

Position	Women in position in 1989	Men in position in 1989	Women in position 1789–1989	Men in position 1789–1989
President	0	1	0	40
Vice-President	0	1	0	44
Presidential Cabinet Members	2	14	10	537
Senators	2	98	16	1,807
Representatives	26	409	113	9,875
Governors	3	47	9	2,124
Lieutenant Governers	4	39	17	*
State Legislators	1,261	6,200	*	*
Mayors (of 100 largest U.S. cities)	17	83	*	*
Supreme Court Judges	1	8	1	103
Federal Judges	68	694	*	*
Military Generals and Admirals				
Air Force	1	338	12	*
Army	4	403	14	*
Marine Corps	1	71	2	*
Navy	2	319	7	*

* Figures not available

Note. Compiled in part from fact sheets from the Center for the American Woman and Politics (CAWP), National Information Bank on Women in Public Office (NIB), Eagleton Institute of Politics, Rutgers University.

and one that talks nonstop about democracy.

To repeat: *We don't know if women would run the world any differently.* There is evidence that when women rise to executive levels they act like men, but this may not be a valid indication of what they would do if 50% of the world's decision-making power (or the 99+% that men have *now*) were in the hands of women. Women executives today have to fit into a context of nearly absolute male power. We don't know how they would behave if the show were theirs, to run for 100 years or so (a short trial period, compared to the number of years men have had). We *do* know, however, that all areas of work traditionally considered women's work—nursing, teaching the early grades, social work, being a homemaker, being a child care worker—always have been very low paid or unpaid altogether. This is an indicator of male-architectured society's lack of respect for these kinds of work.

Child development expert Bettye Caldwell laughingly says, "If men thought childrearing was important they wouldn't leave it to women" (Caldwell, 1990). Joking aside, it isn't a radical feminist stance to state what can be learned in any sociology, political science, history, or economics class. And it's neither illegal nor immoral for each of us to wonder if, were the gender of the voters or the elected different, children could be made a higher priority in our national life. We do know that after women won the vote in 1920 and became more politically active, wages and salaries as well as opportunities started improving, and the women's movement of the 1970s and '80s has fostered faster, perhaps lasting, improvement.

Well, at least we do better for babies than any other country, some readers may say—or do we?

An exceptionally well-done study done by the Urban Institute (Smeeding, Torrey, & Rein, 1988) examined poverty among children and the elderly in eight industrialized western countries. Countries beside the U.S.

covered in this study were Canada, Great Britain, Australia, Switzerland, West Germany, Norway, and Sweden.

Among the major findings of the study were the following:

● For children, the U.S. had the highest poverty rate—slightly above Australia, and well above all the other countries.

● For children in one-parent families, the U.S. had the second highest poverty rate—after Australia.

What are we doing to ease the situation for single parents in our programs?

Some have suggested that a major reason for the high U.S. child poverty rate is the high proportion of children in one-parent families. However, with slightly higher proportions of children in one-parent families than the U.S., Norway and Sweden had absolute poverty rates for all children of only 7.6% and 5.1%, respectively, compared to 17.1% for the U.S. Even if the demographic composition of the seven other countries is statistically adjusted to give them the same proportion of all children in one-parent families as the U.S. had for 1979, their overall (adjusted) absolute poverty rates for children would still be well below the U.S. rate in every country except Australia.

Some have suggested that a major reason for the high U.S. child poverty rate is the high proportion of minority-group children. However, even the U.S. poverty rate for White non-Hispanic children is higher than the overall poverty rate for children in every other country except Australia.

In our own small communities, what are childcarers doing to reduce teen pregnancy?

Hmmm, actually we do worse for babies than almost any other developed country!

The U.S. and Switzerland are the only two countries in the Urban Institute study without a children's allowance program. A children's allowance is given by many countries to each family in that country, regardless of socioeconomic level, at the birth of its children. The two countries that fill the smallest proportion of the poverty gap for their children (the U.S. and Australia) depend much more heavily on *means-tested* programs to aid families with children.

A *means-test* is proof a family must supply, usually in intricate and documented detail, that it is very, very poor. Many poor people, particularly borderline, "working poor" people, are proud and are not willing to "prove" how destitute they are. Others never learn about the programs that could help their children ("the establishment" does not promote these programs to the poor, to say the least!), are

unable to collect the documentation or fill out the forms (for example, psychiatrically ill, mentally retarded, or extremely disorganized parents), or are ineligible for a variety of technical reasons pertaining *not* to need, but to bureaucratic and regulatory absurdities.

Because of the many problems involved in *means-tested* programs for poor people and their children, a number of governments favor *social insurance programs*. This means that entitlement is established, in the words of the study, by "common citizenship in society." In other words, you are entitled to whatever the program is because you are part of that society and everyone in it is believed to "deserve" the benefits of the program. In Figure 4, the Urban Institute makes some interesting points on this subject.

In the five countries (excluding Australia, Switzerland, and the United States) with both children's allow-

ances and social insurance programs aiding **all** families with children, social insurance programs play an "overwhelmingly more important" role in reducing the poverty gap for families with children.

It's intriguing that the four English-speaking countries have the highest child poverty rates. This suggests the possibility that the English poor-law tradition may result in a higher proportion of children remaining in poverty than do continental European social policies. Perhaps the emphasis on property and individual rights in English common law is related to our reluctance to consider all babies our babies. Perhaps the fact that the English-speaking countries experienced (relatively) far less population loss in this century's wars encourages a heedlessness toward the country's babies as the country's future manpower, military, and so forth. Whatever the causes, the neglect is deplorable.

The Growth Program

Helping young children get dressed, learn their colors, and all the rest is certainly important. But isn't it important to be sure they have food, homes, and other such essentials too? Many of our child care programs include children who don't have these necessities.

What Do Babies Need To Develop Optimal Self-Esteem?

There's a place for ordinary people to go who care about curing the problem of pervasive, paralyzing child and family poverty in America. If you are an amateur advocate and want detailed advice about doing political work for children, see Goffin and Lombardi (1988).

The high U.S. child poverty rate probably reflects the fact that the U.S. has always been one of the most begrudging of all industrialized nations in terms of both adopting and funding social programs. (This is probably also a major factor in the longstanding poor U.S. showing in infant mortality; infant mortality rates have dropped sharply in the U.S. and other countries during this century, but the number of countries with lower infant mortality rates than the U.S. was at least eight in 1916 and 18—including Hong Kong, Singapore, and Spain—in 1985.)

We are not talking poverty

We are not talking about low-income and minority infants in America, a frustrated reader may say. We are not talking about families who live at half the government-defined poverty level. We are not talking about infant mortality, or the fact that **almost a fourth of all American children younger than six live in poverty,** or the fact that 100,000 children are homeless each night. We are not talking about all those children in foster care, group homes, residential treatment programs, and other institu-

tions. We are talking about what ordinary babies need.

Yes, we will talk in considerable detail throughout the next ten chapters about what "ordinary" babies need, but **we** of all people must not ignore the 25% whose basic needs are being ignored by a wealthy society.

You ask why we fail to focus on meeting babies' needs, when we are aware that they grow up to be the future leaders and followers of the world; that was your question. Why are we *not* talking about poverty? Is it because many of us are paralyzed by the *on-*

Almost one-fourth of all children younger than six in the wealthy United States of America live at or below the government-defined poverty level. And many child-caring teachers devote their professional lives to teaching four- and five-year-olds splinter skills and testing for mastery of them. Are our priorities sensible?

Figure 4. Notes from the Urban Institute Study

Despite their presumably more effective targeting, countries that rely on means test[ed programs] seem politically unable or unwilling to raise benefits high enough to be as effective in moving children out of poverty as universal and social insurance approaches. This situation is particularly glaring in the United States. (Smeeding, Torrey, & Rein, 1988, p. 116)

As noted in a hearing before the Select Committee on Children, Youth and Families (U.S. House of Representatives, 1988), U.S. means-tested benefits, although presumably better targeted [on the poor] than social insurance benefits [which *all* people receive, not exclusively *poor* people], were simply too low . . . to lift the average poor family with children out of poverty in 1979. U.S. social insurance benefits . . . did not provide a great deal of assistance to families with poor children.

When basic needs are not met, higher level human developments such as trust, autonomy, self-esteem, and self-discipline can rarely occur

True, it seems weirdly out of place to be touching upon these more *basic* needs of the world's infants and toddlers, and it even seems loony to be reciting the sad facts of death and homelessness affecting large numbers of American children. **We should realize, though, that as Abraham Maslow (1970) so clearly illustrated for us, until survival and critical health needs are taken care of, the human organism cannot focus on more advanced needs, such as the need for the high self-regard that permits achievement and personal fulfillment; or the need to discipline oneself so as to gain these glories. So if we're not talking about these basics we *should* be. We've come full circle,**

looker syndrome? We watch, we wait, we sigh, we tolerate. . . . Who do we imagine will right the great wrong being wrought against a fourth of America's little children? We care, but caring just isn't enough. Effective *action* is also essential to convert caring to curing. **There are ways to work away at the colossal problem of pervasive child and family poverty: It's important to send financial contributions, even if small, to any "cause" in which people are taking *action* on *any* issue, *any* aspect of the child poverty disgrace, or to pitch in with elbow grease at the local level. It's important to keep on making a good beginning for babies and all children real—transforming rhetoric into reality. The need for political advocacy and vigilance on the part of the child caring community will never end. There are no short cuts, there is no magical one-shot solution.**

At the leader level of our field, is our failure to focus on meeting the needs of *all* babies rooted in the ruthlessly competitive, "want-to-be-the-winner" mentality our culture encourages? Is that why we so seldom build coalitions, collaborate, and cooperate to give young children a powerful constituency? Do we fear that controversy will hurt our careers? A world class children's crusader discusses our lack of action in behalf of poor children in Figure 5.

Yes, some may say, this is all very well, but **what does it have to do with developing self-esteem, self-discipline, and good character in infants, toddlers, and two-year-olds?** But you, in your original question, stated the connection. You said, **"It seems that babies need a lot of basics in order to develop high self-regard."**

Figure 5. From the writings of Marian Wright Edelman

Democracy is not a spectator sport. I worry about people who opt out of political, bureaucratic, and community processes, even while I recognize that those processes are sometimes discouraging. I worry about men and women who refuse to take a position because of the complexity or controversy that often surrounds issues of life and death. I hold no brief for those who are content to kibitz intellectually about the life choices of millions of poor children without seeing the hunger and suffering behind the cold statistics, or for those who hide behind professional neutrality and shift responsibility for hard societal problems on to others — problems that must be shared if they are to be solved.

Feeding a hungry child or preventing needless infant deaths in a decent, rich society should not require detailed policy analysis or quantifiable outcome goals or endless commissions. They require compassionate action. By all means let us have more careful definition and justification for our policy goals and spending. Let us apply the same cost-benefit standards consistently to the military and to programs for the nonpoor. But let us be careful not to hide behind cost-benefit analyses when human survival is at issue.

Each of us must reflect hard within ourselves, our families, our churches, synagogues, universities, and home communities, about the national ideals we want America to hold. Each of us must then try, "by little and by little," as Dorothy Day recognized, to live them and be moved to act in the personal arena through greater service to those around us who are more needy, and in the political arena to ensure a more just society. One without the other is not enough to transform the United States. (Edelman, 1987, pp. 101–102)

Have leaders in your community looked at projects in model communities that are preventing families from becoming homeless?

back where we were at the beginning of this chapter. Children need:

- good prenatal care and safe deliveries
- reliable, predictable shelter
- a warm and comfortable temperature
- protection from harm and fear
- nutritious food suited to the infants' age
- regular weighing and measuring to ensure that growth is going forward normally
- immunizations
- sensible sanitation and cleanliness and treatment of physical problems and illnesses
- preventive dental care
- attachment to one primary person and care by that person and other consistent, continuous familiar people, who collaborate in the care and who provide ample amounts of physical, emotional, and social contact (not a series of foster mothers, however well-meaning, or a slew of day care workers of the sort who don't have much to give)
- a balance of active and quiet activities, and sleep, all based on observation of each individual infant's needs, natural rhythms, and what he himself indicates he needs

Are we advocating for the babies without basics in our communities?

Harvard's Jerome Kagan has specialized in worldwide research and writing emphasizing the close correspondence between maturation of the human organism's central nervous system from birth through age two and psychological development. He's not as big a believer in the importance of infinite planning and every mini-move caregivers make as we in early childhood education are—**as long as the *big* things (emotionally, environmentally, and *economically*) are OK:**

There is probably a broad range of early environments that have similar effects on infants. As long as caregivers provide food, protection from pain, and playful interaction with children on a regular schedule, it is likely that the small differences among two-year-olds raised on such regimens will have little predictive consequences for differences among them five or ten years hence. But there is no question that infants who frequently experience prolonged periods of distress, and do not enjoy playful interaction with adults, will be more fearful, irritable, and perhaps more aggressive and less cognitively proficient at age three than children treated in more benevolent fashion. (Kagan, 1984, p. 108)

Kagan doesn't think that all of an infant's characteristics (irritability, etc.) correlate with characteristics seen in the same individual later in life (though many of us *do*). **This is what distinguished researcher, scholar,** and thinker Jerome Kagan says really matters:

In contrast to the difficulty of using an infant's qualities to predict his or her future, a family's education, vocation, and income are excellent predictors of many aspects of a child's behavior at age ten. . . .

In general, about 10 percent to 20 percent of adolescents in a typical modern community fail to adjust to the demands of the school or to other local norms for socialized behavior. The best predictor of these apparent failures in adaptation is continued rearing in a family that is under economic stress and believes itself powerless to change its status. Children who grow up in such settings are less well prepared for school mastery and, as a result of identification with their social class, grow to doubt their potency. Hence, they lower their expectations and create defenses against middle-class standards. A child's social class constitutes a continuing set of influences on development. (Kagan, 1984, pp. 106–107)

In spite of cutbacks, a partial system of providing some basics exists

Although the bitter legacy of "trickle down" economics, joined with massive defense spending, has eroded the previous, partial commitments to babies, which had been laboriously established by the child caring community throughout the 20th Century, Congress and the states are making "a promising start," in CDF's (1989) phrase, toward improving our sadly lacking but still existent maternal and infant health system.

- Medicaid can be extended to more poor women and infants.
- Vaccinations, once nearly universal, then cut by stagnant federal funding, since 1989 are available for full immunization of infants, toddlers, and preschoolers.
- Migrant health centers are being expanded to serve more women and infants.

Do you suspect that a child you know is being abused? Or seriously neglected? What are you doing to help?

Much remains to be done, however.

- The Women and Infant Care program (WIC), which provides nutritional supplements to pregnant women and infants and has, in some communities, *eliminated* iron deficiency anemia with its potential legacy of lowered I.Q.; WIC, a proven saver of later health costs, *still reaches less than half of eligible, needy families!*

- AFDC, minimal as its payments are, in 1977 reached 84% of poor children and in 1987 reached only 60%. Increasing homelessness among the poor is a direct result.

It's foolish, unfair, and futile to expect young children without basics such as food and housing to "perform" and "achieve" on worksheets and tests. Perhaps we should toss the tests and house the children.

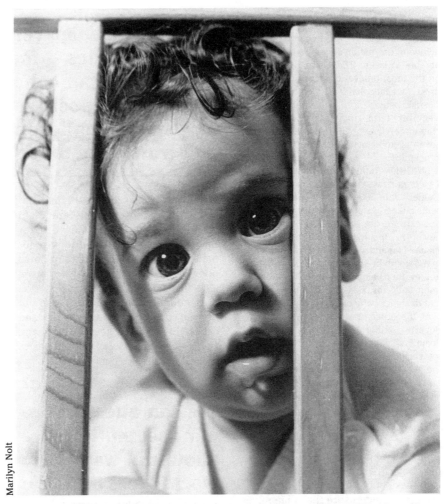

Marilyn Nolt

• Food stamp programs *miss serving one-third to one-half of those who are eligible!*

• School lunch programs improve children's nutrition, *but the program served fewer children after 1981.* And there have been cutbacks in quality. Do you remember the sly attempt to declare ketchup a "vegetable"? School breakfast programs in some states may be expanded through recent federal funding.

The existence of each of these important programs demonstrates a national consciousness: We know what needs to be done. The will to do it, for everyone's sake, must strengthen.

Many children arrive in kindergarten and the early grades with these needs unmet. **Therefore, it's foolish, unfair, and futile to expect them to have high confidence in and respect for themselves (positive self-esteem), or strong self-discipline,** which requires one to forgo instant gratification and work diligently for rewards in the future. (Astonishingly, some children with unmet basic needs *do* have high self-esteem and self-discipline.)

How well, for instance, will the babies described below, many of them born blind or suffering seizures, do in school?

In her book **Within Our Reach**, *Lisbeth Schorr writes: "The American Enterprise Institute's New Consensus on Family and Welfare says the crisis has reached the point of threatening to 'corrode a free society.' Sociologist James S. Coleman says that we are faced with a breakdown in American society of 'the process of making human beings human.' Senator Daniel Patrick Moynihan describes the combination of disintegrating families and rampant childhood poverty as 'life-threatening to the great cities of the land.'*

"But greater emphasis on the problem has not been accompanied by corresponding attention to promising solutions. . . . It will take more than economic measures alone. It will take more than the expansion of access to traditional services. Some of our helping systems may, in fact, be beyond repair and will require rebuilding. The 'inverse care law,' which holds that those who need the best services get the worst, must be repealed.

"This will not happen without a national commitment of consequence — specific in its objective, broad in its scope, and enduring in its staying power.

"Every American — as voter and taxpayer, as church, PTA, or hospital board member, as business, labor, political, or professional leader — has a role in translating such a commitment into action." (Schorr, 1988, p. 292)

What Do Babies Need To Develop Optimal Self-Esteem?

Day after day, in high-tech neonatal intensive care units across the country, heart-rending dramas . . . are being played out involving the nation's youngest, most vulnerable citizens. These are babies born on the most unlevel of playing fields. Call them "welfare babies," "crack babies," "at-risk babies," or "deficit babies"—by whatever term, they constitute a new "bio-underclass" of infants who are disadvantaged almost from the moment of conception.

Like the 16th-century England Mark Twain portrays in "The Prince and the Pauper," late-20th century America represents a land of stark contrast for babies. At one extreme are the babies of affluence—newborn "princes" and "princesses." Planned for and wanted, they are monitored in the womb by sophisticated medical technology, then pampered after birth with $800 imported cribs, $300 strollers, infant gyms, and designer baby clothes.

At the other extreme are the babies of poverty—under-cared for, often unwanted "paupers" who may be born too early and too small. So desperate is their plight that the '80s phrase, "the feminization of poverty," is now joined by another closely related term, the "infantization of poverty" (Gardner, 1989, p. 10).

Those of us who care for America's youngest children must, regardless of what else we do for them, advocate for the above "basics for babies."

Babies should be with families, and society should ensure that all families have the basics. All families need a variety of health, counseling, and child caring support services. Some families purchase these services privately, others are unable to, but all families need them. Some families should be offered an array of other helping services, too.

When no family whatsoever is available to a baby, as is the case for crack cocaine-addicted, and AIDS-afflicted, abandoned hospital-"boarding" babies (and many other deserted children), should we ensure that perma-

Why should a child without hope sacrifice instant gratification to maintain *self-discipline?*

nent group homes with as-permanent-as-possible houseparents are right there, right away? What will we do for these children beyond wringing our hands and lamenting that they do so poorly and/or are such behavior problems in school?

As child carers, we must reach out beyond the colors and shapes and catchy little songs, get involved, and advocate for the babies without basics at least in our own communities!

We can question our assumptions about the way the world "just is." (We made it this way, we can change it.)

For further reading

Keniston, K. (1977). *All our children: American family under pressure.* New York: Harcourt Brace Jovanovich.

O'Hare, W. P. (1989). *Poverty in America: Trends and new patterns.* Washington, DC: Population Reference Bureau.

References

Caldwell, Bettye. (1990). Personal communication.

Children's Defense Fund. (1988). *A children's defense budget, FY 1989: An analysis of our nation's investment in children.* Washington, DC: Author.

Children's Defense Fund. (1989). *A vision for America's future: An agenda for the 1990s—A children's defense budget.* Washington, DC: Author.

Doxiadis, S. (Ed.). (1979). *The child in the world of tomorrow.* Athens, Greece: Greek Ministry of Health and Social Services.

Edelman, M. W. (1987). *Families in peril: An agenda for social change.* Cambridge, MA: Harvard University Press.

Gardner, M. (1989, December 18). Poverty's legacy—fragile families, vulnerable babies. *The Christian Science Monitor* (pp. 10–11). [First article in a series of three. "Children of the Good Life" and "Quest for Infant Day Care Challenges Working Parents," also by Marilyn Gardner, appeared on December 19 and 20.]

Greenberg, P. (1979). *Changing the world through child caring.* Athens, Greece: Greek Ministry of Health and Social Services.

Goffin, S. G., & Lombardi, J. (1988). *Speaking out: Early childhood advocacy.* Washington, DC: NAEYC.

Kagan, J. (1984). *The nature of the child.* New York: Basic.

Kozol, J. (1988). *Rachel and her children.* New York: Fawcett/Ballantine.

Maslow, A. H. (1970). *Motivation and personality.* New York: Harper & Row.

Population Education Interchange. (1986). *Nature's checks on population growth.* Washington, DC: Population Reference Bureau.

Population Reference Bureau. (1987). *World population data sheet.* Washington, DC: Author.

Ross, J. A., Rich, M., Molzan, J. P., & Pensak, M. (1988). *Family planning and child survival: 100 developing countries.* New York: Columbia University, Center for Population and Family Health.

Schorr, L. B., & Schorr, D. (1988). *Within our reach: Breaking the cycle of disadvantage.* New York: Doubleday.

Smeeding, T., Torrey, B. B., & Rein, M. (1988). Patterns of income and poverty: The economic status of children and the elderly in eight countries. In J. L. Palmer, T. Smeeding, & B. B. Torrey (Eds.), *The vulnerable* (pp. 89–119). Washington, DC: The Urban Institute.

United Nations. (1989). *Compendium of statistics and indicators on the situation of women 1986.* Series K, No. 5. New York: United Nations, Department of International Economic and Social Affairs, Statistical Office.

U.S. House of Representatives. (1988, February 25). *Children and families in poverty: The struggle to survive. Hearing before the Select Committee on Children, Youth and Families.* Washington, DC: U.S. Government Printing Office.

While it's transparently true that children need the basics — food, shelter, health — before they can behave well, learn well, and develop positive self-esteem, most of us give "the children without" only fleeting and transitory thought.

CHAPTER

3

Where Should Babies Be To Develop Optimal Self-Esteem, Self-Discipline, and Good Character —In Other Words, To Develop "Optimally" All Around? Does Science Really Know?

QUESTION: As a recently graduated college student who majored in early childhood education, I have read zillions of studies, theories, and "expert" opinions about what infants and toddlers need in order to learn and develop normally, how language develops normally, and so on. I have also read innumerable books and articles about "quality child care programs." I still know zilch about what infants and toddlers need in order to develop *excellently* (*high* self-esteem, *high* everything, not merely "normal"). *How good* does a child care program have to be to be actually *beneficial* to a child (in other words, *a benefit* in addition to and beyond what a good home can give him)?

My husband and I are about to have our first baby. We are in fairly good financial shape. I like teaching. Should I work or not work? My friends say of course I should. My mother says of course I shouldn't. What does research really know for sure about all this? Where should babies be?

No wonder you're confused! "Experts" are always writing about what young children need, and whether day care is bad for babies, without ever discussing parents' *goals* for their children and for their own lives! Are we talking about what zero- to three-year-olds need in order to develop optimal mental health? Optimal motivation to learn? Optimal conversational skills? Optimal socioeconomic opportunity? Or is adequate— average—not dysfunctional our goal? Are we talking about day care enriching and providing soul-nourishing experiences that add up to a balanced week as part of a package for zero- to three-year-olds? Or are we talking about covering stretches of time while parents are away? Are we talking about parents whose main goal is to get childrearing safely over with, or parents whose main goal is to

Is it actually beneficial to a baby from "a good home" to be in out-of-home, nonfamilial care all day? How good does the care have to be to be an actual "plus" for a baby from a mentally healthy, loving home?

relish as much of the complex project as they can, during the brief span of years that childhood lasts?

It seems evident, but apparently is *not,* that one can't give directions without first knowing the destination. One can't assess the "appropriateness" or "quality" of a course of action or a program without knowing the intended and desired outcome. Even knowing the goals, the answers are not guaranteed to be correct, and the journey is not guaranteed to end where intended—at least surely not without a bunch of potholes, pitfalls, and detours. But in the end, if you put enough care into it, you're likely to at least approach your goal. In families where choice is possible, and it seems to be in *your* case, the parents' *goals* must **first** be examined. If there is any research on how mothers' choices regarding "to work or not to work"

are influenced by their life goals, it isn't widely known.

A **second** piece of information without which sound advice about where a baby should be cannot be given is: What's the baby's *home situation?*

Only very recently have significant numbers of infant researchers gotten around to examining this essential question, obvious to most people with common sense. Prior to the late 1980s, most researchers seemed either to assume that all mothers and home situations are excellent (so surely babies should be there!), or to assume that all homes are average (so adequate care could be readily replicated). Most researchers' writings—except for Burton White's views which we'll touch upon later—give no evidence that the authors know about marvelous mothers in all socioeconomic and cultural groups, and that it would be next to impossible to replicate the super care they give. Probably the reluctance of so many academics and professionals to acknowledge and credit expert mothers is part of the effort to professionalize the child care field. The thinking may be, "if they haven't had training, they can't be considered expert." The flaw in this idea is that the model we're training child care workers *toward* is that of the expert mother!

Another cluster of questions that spring like toadstools after a rain from this question about the baby's home situation are: How good does out-of-home child care have to be to be *beneficial* to a baby if she's from

- an extremely troubled home,
- a very unfortunate home, or
- an "average" home?

If it has been determined that the baby will be taken care of for significant amounts of time each week by someone other than mother, a **third** key consideration in making a judgment about where an **individual baby** should be is where the care should be given, and who the caregiver should be? *What's best for this particular baby?* This will depend, among other things, on special circumstances that may exist in an individual baby's life—having a "hyper" or easily overstimulated temperament, for instance, or an extremely shy introverted nature, or a serious disability.

And **fourth,** the needs and limitations of the **whole family** must be taken into account. To a large extent, except in unusual instances, what's least stressful and feels happily best for the overall family is best for baby too.

Whether center-based or family day care is being considered, the overall setup is important, especially in the area of health-ensuring practices, but equally important is the quality of the experience *this* baby will have. It must be carefully guesstimated; some caregivers in any center are much better than others—which specific person(s) will care for *this* baby? Except for overarching considerations such as health, hygiene, and

safety standards, and the quality and quantity of ongoing staff development and supervision, **the quality of "the child care program" means the quality and quantity of interactions between a few caregivers and each individual baby.** This implies that *enough* staff must be around, but a body count is not sufficient to guarantee good quality. *Who* will primarily take care of the baby? Caregiver X is excellent, Caregiver Y is OK but doesn't notice individual differences very much, and Caregiver Z shouldn't work with young children; apparently she can't stand them. We must look beyond "the program" at the pertinent *persons.*

How will the person(s) caring for "my" child younger than three help his self-esteem? Help him develop healthy self-discipline? Help him grow to be "of good character"? The more time a young child spends in care, the more important it is to ask, "What kind of a person are the caregiver and the care setting shaping my child toward being?"

Let's talk about each of these four major areas of consideration one at a time:

© Florence Sharp

© Cleo Freelance Photo

Where Should Babies Be To Develop Optimally

I. What are parents' goals for themselves and for their children?

II. What is baby's home situation?

III. What arrangement is best for the individual baby?

IV. What arrangement is best for the whole family, all things considered?

© Nancy P. Alexander

For the past six months, Tina has been at the center where Tim is.

My wife drops the kids off at 7 A.M. on her way to work. I get them at 6 P.M. on my way home. My wife *could* pick them up at five, but this way she has an hour at home to shower and start dinner before the hordes descend. Thank goodness they're bedded down by 7:30!

When this couple was queried as to whether or not they had considered deferring the purchase of a home for a few years so the children could be cared for by a parent while still infants, they answered that the cost of homes keeps going up, so they thought it best to buy as soon as possible. This meant that both of them had to work full-time.

Asked whether they thought that they or the children were missing anything, these parents agreed that they felt "no guilt" when the husband's mother was taking care of Tim, but "feel a little guilty" about having the babies "in a commercial center." (It's a fascinating fact that many couples prefer a relative they don't like and

I. *Where babies should be depends in part upon what the parents' goals are*

Even parents with a great deal of freedom to make choices don't all have the same goals. You and your husband may want to think about *your* goals.

Where does raising your children fit into the hierarchy of your values and lifelong priorities? What type of lifelong family life do you want?

Is it your priority to accrue whatever wealth and to achieve whatever career success you possibly can, as soon as feasible, tucking family life and children into the crevices as best you can fit them in? Many adults do this and the children grow up "normal." That's what *this* couple, **Karen and Ken,** want:

To us, the most important thing is to have a nice house in a nice neighborhood with a good public school nearby, and to be able to afford restaurants, vacations, and other amenities. It will take my wife and me both working to accomplish this. We believe that this will be best for our two children in the long run.

My wife returned to work when our first child was six weeks old. My mother took care of our son. When he was 18 months old,

Parents who are guilt-free and secure about their choices regarding whether or not to work full-time when their children are infants (probably most parents) usually don't at all mind discussing their values and goals.

we put him in a family day care home because my wife didn't like it that my mother spanked our son a lot — You know how this age is, they get into everything. My mother felt that he had to be trained. My wife said that wasn't the right way to teach him. When our son was two, the day care provider decided to stop taking children younger than school-age. For a while, he went to a Montessori school in the morning and a neighbor kept him in the afternoon. The neighbor took care of a lot of children, and didn't have much time for Tim. We put him in a day care center. We don't like it very much, but it's convenient and affordable.

When our daughter came along, we considered having my wife take more time off, but her employer wouldn't hold her job for more than six months, and if she changed jobs we would've lost out financially, so starting at three months, Tina was taken care of by the neighbor who watched Tim.

whose child care methods they don't approve of to a "commercial" child care program, which *might* be much better! This may be because of societal bias against leaving young children with "strangers," but it doesn't make a whole lot of sense. It's wiser to look at specifics than to base decisions on stereotypes or preconceptions.)

The couple agreed, also, that "we're probably missing a few milestones, but the kids will grow up OK, one way or another, and at least this way we'll be able to afford whatever they need, braces on their teeth and all that."

The viewpoints expressed by this couple, and shared by many other young modern middle-class American parents, provide food for thought, for professional caregivers as well as for parents:

26

1. Parents: Is your goal to get the kids grown and get on with your lives, or to enjoy a rich and fulfilling family life during the short period of years—approximately 18 years apiece—that children "live in" before they fly the nest? Families define the ties that bind in various ways.

Valerie hasn't seen her sister for seven years, since the sister moved from Arkansas to Utah, and Valerie moved to Montana. "We talk on holidays. We get along OK. We each go back to visit our parents about every other year." This is a normal family. Is this the type of thing you see in your family's future?

Carl wouldn't leave the community his kin are in "for any amount of money, as long as we can make ends meet." He says that his wife stayed home when the four children were young—"they need that special concern that parents have." Margie, the mother, says:

We did without a lot of material things for that 10 years, but we have a terrifically close-knit family, and that's what matters. I've been working ever since. If you're lucky, life is long. There's plenty of time to earn money and buy things later. The kids say that when I'm old and need it they'll take care of *me*. I'm sure they *will*; I take

What middle-class people mean by "have to" work varies. And whether or not they both work full-time away from home during their infant's first seven or eight months, how special parents with choice hope their relationships with their children will be, influences how much time they invest in their babies.

meals to my mom and Carl's mother every day, and do their cleaning, shopping, all that. What goes around comes around. It's the family life cycle. Take good care of the young ones, and later they take good care of the old folks. At both ends of the age spectrum, they're slow, they're needy, it takes time and patience.

This, too, is a normal family. Is this more the kind of life you and your husband envision?

To some, like comedian George Burns, happiness is having a large, loving, caring, close-knit family in a distant city. Others value more family connectedness, intimacy, and frequent

© Nancy P. Alexander

contact. No research studies on the subject come to mind, but one might suppose that—in most cases—the more quality time you give, the more you get; if a healthy form of lifelong togetherness is your goal, there are clues here as to which way to go. Similarly, one might guess—with no official research to back up the hunch, just personal observation—that the more you "make arrangements" for your very young children (that may be *good* arrangements but don't include much of yourself), the more likely it is that when you are very old, your adult children will "make arrangements" for you (that may be *good* arrangements but don't include much of themselves).

Traditionally in this country, child care and elder care have been provided within the extended family—which, in the African American community, for example, often includes the entire small community. In middle-class—especially Caucasian—America using child care programs, retirement communities, and nursing homes as needed is becoming culturally accepted. Whether this is "as good," "better than," "necessary," or "not right" is a personal opinion. However, though our influence isn't the *only* influence, we do teach our children many things that imprint deeply upon them, simply by the way we live our lives—by the example we set or *don't* set.

A stay-at-home-by-choice married mother whose family income is $23,000 a year says:

I'm not a scholar and I've done no research, but my experience is that loving, respecting

Parents with choice may want to consider their long-term goals regarding childrearing and family life.

people with time for each other generate *other* loving, respecting people with time for others. That's the kind of people I aim to create. There are certain characteristics we're trying to develop in our children. I'm taking great care of my little kids and I hope they'll be caring people who'll take time for me and others later. We *do* pay a dollar price for our way of life.

Marta tearfully tells that all her friends have moved somewhat away from her because she has chosen to take time out from her life in the away-from-home work force to be (temporarily) a stay-at-home mother. She still works part-time:

They say I'm old-fashioned. They say I'm just out of tune with the times. They say they want to stay home BUT. None of them are on the brink financially. Everybody could use more. Either I think they don't *really* want to stay home—they just say it to soothe what could be guilty consciences if they didn't tell themselves they want to stay home but can't—or I think they are pitifully disempowered women. If they have economic choice and choose to work, fine. But admit you want to work for any of dozens of reasons. Take responsibility for what you do, don't claim you have to if you're doing exactly what you want. And don't call stay-at-home mothers names. To each her own. Or if you honestly want to be home for a few

At this point, we're talking only about people who can more than make ends meet without working full-time when their children are younger than one year, or who want to work away from home and can make good child care arrangements. Many people truly do have to work; we'll talk about their needs later in this chapter (pages 45–63), where we urge that society offer them the same choices as more affluent parents.

years, do it, don't act so helpless and overwhelmed by the tune of the times. To me, feeling disempowered to think through alternatives and make choices is as big a problem for today's middle class mothers as the money squeeze is.

(We must add that stay-at-home mothers sometimes also disapprove of "working" mothers; unfortunately, there is tension between the two groups.)

In these reflections, prudence in prioritizing family financial allocations and wise consideration of personal and economic necessities are not being scoffed at, nor is the pressure they exert being ignored or trivialized. But smart people ponder values and goals as well as peer into their purses.

➡ **Professionals:** What is the teacher educator's role in helping early childhood education students think about goals in their own lives, and in their future positions as the parent counselors that all teachers are? What is the family child care provider's and child care center director's role in counseling parents who seem to have some choice but who emanate vibes of anxious ambivalence?

2. Parents: What are your priorities in life? A house, yes, but how expensive a house do you need to be happy? A car, yes, but how many cars, VCRs, etc.? How frequently do you need to go to restaurants to be happy, and will only The Palm satisfy, or will, for a while, McDonald's do? When you say "vacations," must it be summer trips to Europe and winter ones to the islands, or are camping and Motel 6

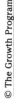
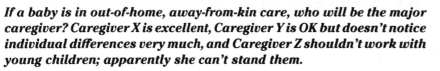

If a baby is in out-of-home, away-from-kin care, who will be the major caregiver? Caregiver X is excellent, Caregiver Y is OK but doesn't notice individual differences very much, and Caregiver Z shouldn't work with young children; apparently she can't stand them.

OK? How immediately do you have to have what you hope eventually to have? And ultimately, would you rather bequeath the kids a trust fund and family business or memories of cookies baking, family fun, and parental availability as needed?

Inheritances and trust funds may not be such a great thing to give a child (at least until late in her life) because they permit, thus often promote, childish dependency with a resulting assumption of inability to "make it on my own" (e.g., low self-esteem with regard to competence and personal power, important areas of overall self-esteem).

This is all extreme, but you see the point. There's no doubt that it costs money (money lost) to work part-time or not at all when children are babies, and there's no doubt that good quality in-home or out-of-home care is expensive. **People with choices may want to review their values and do what seems wisest,** *all things considered,* **which may be to work full-time.**

Some people may have been startled to realize in Chapter 2 how many families have no choice; they don't even have *food.* It may be equally surprising to realize how many people *do* have a choice — but don't even know it.

According to the Internal Revenue Service, 1.5 million American families have a net worth of more than $1 million. Not all of them have young children, or babies in full-time out-of-home care, but some of them do. Over 50,000 Americans have annual incomes over $500,000. They don't all have babies, and all the babies they *do* have aren't in full-time other-than-mother-or-dad care, but some are. Approximately 3.3 million of this nation's families have incomes over $75,000, an income usually allowing for a nice house in an affluent neighborhood, two late-model cars, private schools, and ample paid help. Many of these families have young children, and many of them are in full-time child care settings away from home.

Says **Sylvie,** a single mother by choice,

I love my career, and also I don't want to fall out of the bottom of the middle class. (I'm saying I'm just up from the top of the poor.) But I was willing to do without a lot of things — including any semblance of financial security beyond exorbitant self-paid health insurance — while my three children were each under two. I don't know or care what research says. (Researchers do the sorts of research and get the sorts of results that support what they value anyway, and people who rely on research to decide what they think read and believe only the research results that fit what they want to think anyway. Research is one important part of what we know about young children. Only *one.*) I'm simply convinced that it's good for babies to be with family, specifically with their mommies or daddies or grammas, a lot of each day. They feel more at ease.

It certainly was good for *me* not to feel too pressured and stressed out and exhausted. I didn't want my adorable, cherished, tremendously wanted babies to feel like an interruption and a nuisance — and that's what little kids *do* feel like when you're distracted in all directions or too damn tired. I don't, but most people have marriages to make work well, too. That *also* takes leisure time. I knew I didn't have supermom potential, and I didn't want to be one of the ones who says to a 14-month-old, "OK, so I'm not Supermom. Adjust."

Wouldn't it be wonderful if all parents had lots of choices?

It was only six years total 'til Hank was two. I worked half-time for a time, was a three-quarter-day consultant for a year; then I worked five mornings a week — It can be done if you're fortunate enough to be middle class. You can choose to be at the bottom of it or on a higher rung. I'm talking *temporary,* when the babies are young. Then I returned to full-time earning (and paid most of it to child care programs and providers).

➡ **Professionals: What values and priorities do we character development specialists transmit to children about the relative importance of money as status, materialism, how much work is too much work, consumerism, family life, good interpersonal relations, how important the individual child is to us, and other such basic attitudes? We do transmit values, even to children younger than three. Do we discuss these critical issues with parents?**

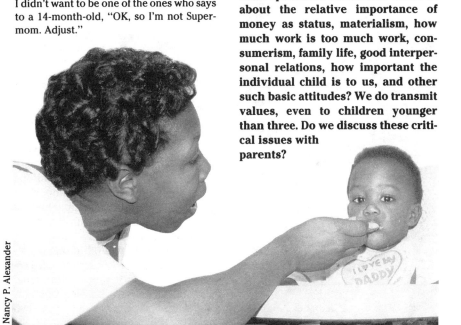

© Nancy P. Alexander

We train child care workers to be like expert mothers. Expert infant/ toddler caregivers are copies of excellent mothers.

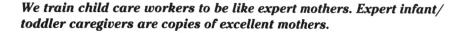

Another variable for parents with choice is how important they feel it is to invest in building their child's confidence and fine-tuning his character.

3. Parents: Which seems more important to you right now, securing the good neighborhood and public school (and money for orthodontia) that your child will need four or five (or more) years hence, or ensuring quality care one place or another during the most formative years for the child's relationship with her parents, self-esteem, self-discipline, and good character?

Few people, expert or not, will deny that as the twig is bent, so grows the tree; daily interaction patterns, experiences, and informal exposures (or lack of them) during the earliest years form the foundation for later feelings, behaviors, and attitudes toward self, parents, teachers, peers, and learning.

What would it do to your self-esteem if the people you loved best had little time for you and, even then, always seemed distracted and in a hurry to do something else?

© Anne Crabbe

Certainly *you*, as a person who has spent years studying the nuances of physical, emotional, social, and intellectual development, understand the crucial importance for later life of a good beginning for babies! What would it do for your opinion of yourself if the most important people in your life — including your husband, perhaps — had hardly any time for you, except to hustle you off to one or another unhappy or borderline OK "arrangement," and then, with relief ("thank goodness"), off, alone, to bed?

Do you think more money and the privileges it can buy would mean more to you than the knowledge that your best beloveds seek and appreciate time with you?

Infants, toddlers, and two-year-olds are very impressionable and have marvelous memories. They're *made* that way because they have so much to absorb, adjust to, and learn in order to ready themselves for the rest of their lives. They are trusting. They believe what they're told by *our actions as well as our words*. They accept as gospel whatever we communicate to them about how the world works and their place in it. Communicating through our hectic daily schedules to our very youngest children, who have few other sources of information on the subject of their self-worth, that no one regularly has time to leisure and pleasure with them, erects a barrier in the path of normally evolving positive self-esteem (e.g., mental health).

With this in mind, you may be interested in the box on the next page. It takes time and freedom from tension to live the kind of family life suggested in the first column, a luxury not available to many families. **Note:** Family characteristics usually are far more influential in determining the state of a "normal" child's mental health than are almost any other factors. Whether a baby from the type of family described in the first column is cared for at home or elsewhere during the day isn't likely to compare in significance to the family's influence on her — as long as the care is adequate.

* * *

Do child care professionals concerned about what's best for babies' emerging and developing self-esteem have an obligation to encourage undecided or ambivalent parents to consider all their alternatives? Many middle class parents have more choices than they think. Babies' self-esteem is enhanced when they feel cherished by their parents — which, of course, can be the case even though both parents work full-time.

Family Characteristics Often Mentioned by Mental Health Professionals As Being Associated With Child and Adolescent Mental Health; None of Them Relate in Any Way to Whether or Not Infants Were in Child Care Programs

Mental health is more likely in the children of these families*:

Responsive, supportive, affectionate parent-child relationship with one or two parents.

Firm, fair, authoritative approach to discipline on the part of one or two parents.

Child is expected to make a contribution to family well-being (chores, some child care, participate in care of older or infirm family member).

Positive relationships among family members, often including extended family. Family is involved in the community in some way — church, charitable work, the arts, the school; believes in God or Doing Good.

Family has reasonably high aspirations for child's age-appropriate successes, and is proud of her accomplishments.

Child feels good about his family.

Parents support most of society's values and rules, including the expectation that the child should work hard and do well in school; parents are not alienated from "the establishment," thus don't send the child double messages —"Do it although it's absurd."

---

*Mental health and serious behavior problems can occur even in the most healthy families.

Personality and behavior problems are more likely in the children of these families**:

One or more of the parents are emotionally unavailable to, and perhaps also actually negligent of, the child, perhaps due to mental illness, alcohol or drug abuse, or for other reasons; child feels rejected.

One or more of the parents are dominating, unfair, and employ harsh disciplinary methods; or neglect to establish and enforce sensible behavioral and interpersonal standards within and outside the family.

Family members feel lonely and angry, communication is very poor; the family may be isolated from others either in fact or by a strictly maintained facade of happy family life that hides the real situation, occasionally even child abuse.

Family has low expectations for the child, does not encourage him, may disparage his efforts or successes.

Child feels unhappy, sad, anxious, or angry with her parents, who may fight frequently and seriously.

Parents denigrate society's rules and standards, including the child's teachers and the worthiness of cooperating in school.

**Miraculously, some children survive the most unlikely families.

Where Should Babies Be To Develop Optimally

I Loved My Baby Daughter's Child Care Center

I love my work and chose to take off only eight weeks when Bridgette was born. We "bonded" just fine. My husband took off two weeks, and he and Bridgette bonded very well, too. With both of us working full-time as professionals, paying for our excellent center wasn't hard. Because there were two of us adults, Bridgette got plenty of parenting during all the before, after, weekend days, and holiday days. My husband and I split the household chores. With the two incomes, we were able to have some household help, too, and usually a Saturday night sitter.

There were the customary adjustments people have to becoming parents, but Bridgette's first year wasn't all that stressful for us. Briggie is a joy! Working was replenishing and refreshing, not a drain. The center the baby went to was a life-saver. There was none of the early morning frenzy many of my friends went through when their caregiver called in sick, or the family day care mother moved to Minnesota. I prefer the caregiver supervision you can count on in a center. In my opinion, having a group of nice grown-ups to be friends with helped our daughter develop flexibility and gregariousness, two traits I've always liked.

I'm pregnant now and plan to use the same center again. (Bridgette is two-and-a-half; she's still there and we think it's very good for her at her present age, too.)

All this doesn't answer your question: "Should I work or not work" (or work half-time), but the implication of this line of thinking is that as heavy an investment as is possible for *you* in your child's first years is a wise investment. This might mean that you

● drive that extra mile to the grandmother whose caregiving is heartfelt and high quality in your (child development trained) eyes, or

● pay a painstakingly selected, caring, careful in-home caregiver who is likely (based on references) to stay awhile, or

● pay more to the better family day care provider (she takes fewer children, so needs a higher fee from each client to cover the allotted slot she intentionally keeps empty), or

● pay more for the center that has fewer babies per staff person—

adequate salaries for plenty of staff is what zaps the cost of care up, or

● elect to work part-time, go to grad school (gradually), take a two-semester leave of absence from med school, or do 20 hours a week of work for a cause you care about, or

● decide to make baby the highlight of your work life for a sizable chunk of time.

Shortly, we *will* talk about what some of the leading child development/infant day care experts say *they* think, based on their years of experience and familiarity with research on the subject, but because you have a choice, think about this:

Researchers are not character developers, which parents and other regular full-day

© Shia Photo

Saying that most child development specialists believe that babies need lots of relaxed family time is not saying they shouldn't be in out-of-home, not-with-kin care. Both can co-exist.

caregivers are. Researchers can't tell you what characteristics you want most to encourage in your child, or whether you are aiming at optimal or adequate childrearing. They can't tell you if you can find a convenient and affordable caregiver or child care setting that's good enough, and sufficiently in sync with your values to help you raise the kind of child you want to raise. They can't tell you what makes you feel that you've made the best decision from among all imaginable routes open to you for the baby's first six months, first year, first two years, or first three years. They can't tell you whether creating and savoring family life—at least during the child's early years—is your first, second, or last priority. Researchers' values and the realities of their lives impact upon their conclusions just as much as yours will.

For life in which socioeconomic class are you preparing your child?

Beyond the shared belief that children need nutritious food, secure shelter, comprehensive health care, and people to look after them, there are dramatic differences in what people believe children need (and where they should *be* depends in part upon what we believe they *need*). It isn't primarily because people haven't received *training* in theory that causes the extreme differences in the way adults live and work with infants and toddlers. In large part, these differences result from the differing subgroups in society that the people possessing the childrearing beliefs belong to. **People prepare children, from infancy onward, for "the real world" as they see it (in other words, as they've experienced it and expect it will be for their grown children).** Any society that's economically, politically, and socially stratified, as ours is, reproduces, via subtle but systematic interactions during the processes of childrearing and education, the system of inequality.

Sociologists, anthropologists, and educational sociologists have produced quite a large pool of literature about this, although only in recent years have they investigated how it works with very *young* children. Most

Satellite Family Day Care Homes and Family Child Care Systems

Where should babies be? Many parents and child developmentalists prefer to see infants and toddlers in family day care *homes* —**family** and **homes** being the key words — *if* the child care provider is "good with babies." There is only one child care provider, who is always the same except on the rare occasions when she has a substitute, and during the fringes of the day when her husband, friends, older children, and the other child care children's parents are around for human variety. Assuming that she doesn't, for one reason or another, go out of business (which mothers sometimes say is a problem, one that causes abrupt caregiver changes for the baby or toddler), the arrangement tends to offer more continuity of care for the child than many centers can offer. As one mother who is devoted to the family day care concept says, "When it works, it's the best, really homelike, a home away from home."

A family child care home can be "softer" than a center, in all senses. And because it's smaller, there are fewer children and staff from whom to catch colds, coughs, flus, diarrhea, and other illnesses. Many (though not all) family day care homes offer the advantages of family-style mixed-age grouping. A center may be and do these things, but all three are less likely to happen there than in someone's home.

There are advantages in linking isolated family child care homes in a system of some sort. Because so many family day care providers work as lone adults in their separate homes, most of them lack and yearn for the support that being part of a network offers. Banding together under an umbrella organization appeals to many providers. They like being independent business people, but an over-all administration enables them to

- buy in bulk
- share their experiences (each one teach one)
- benefit from staff development
- share centrally hired and trained substitutes
- learn about resource and referral services.

If more children in a community require care, more family day care homes can open up. The network simply expands; experienced caregivers orient and help launch newcomers to the field. This kind of network is known as a **family day care system.**

Satellite family child care homes for infants and toddlers cluster around the center that children will probably feed into when they are three and four years old. New York City used a version of this approach as long ago as the 1960s. In New York, each week, the family day care mothers received some on-the-job training from a visiting staff developer, right in their own homes. Each week, the family child care provider and her flock (only two of whom, according to today's standards, can be younger than two) went to the satellite child care center. There, the children could have an exciting group experience, and the providers could too. They could share good ideas, put their heads together to pool and solve problems common among them, view and chew the fat about child development films and videos, hear speakers, attend workshops on subjects they selected, and so forth. Caregivers, who had not had formal training in child development, et al., could also assist center teachers, who were well-trained early childhood educators, thus expanding their horizons through occasional apprenticeship. This model seems to have enough merit to warrant modifying and reconsidering.

Talking about which socioeconomic class parents and caregivers are socializing a young child toward is uncouth, but what we do in this "domain" has as much impact upon his character and life as what we do in other "domains" — physical, emotional, social, and cognitive. Expectations about the importance of listening to and chatting with babies, gently offering intellectual challenges at the edges of what the baby can do or understand, encouraging self-esteem and self-discipline, appropriate behavior, and much else vary widely from one socioeconomic group to another.

early childhood teacher educators appear to be unaware of this expertise on the part of their colleagues in adjacent fields. Or for some other reason they don't bring it to their students' attention. As an early childhood major, you're unlikely to have been taught the intricacies of how families, caregivers, and teachers inculcate the culture (including the language or dialect) of their own social class into the children

for whom they're responsible. ("But I bet she's had to memorize gobs of useless theoretical and research detail about the learning process," laughs an expert infant/toddler practitioner. "The *main ideas,* the *principles,* that's what students need, but some of the teacher educators obfuscate them in such clouds of bejargoned detail that the students miss the entire idea! When they get to us, we have to teach them the point of it all, what it all adds up to, how to implement the theory, on-the-job.")

Perhaps the reason that the entire territory of how caste and class are transmitted to very young children is typically off limits to people studying to be teachers of young children is that

most of us early childhood educators are "good people" with "good intentions." We strongly believe we're preparing all children for citizenship in a **democracy;** therefore, we can't tolerate the cognitive dissonance we suffer if we consciously acknowledge that our democracy is structured so very few people have wealth, unlimited opportunity, and political or personal power, very *many* people must struggle to keep their heads above water, and a great number of people begin and are forced to end their lives below or hovering just above the poverty line. Or maybe so many leading early childhood teacher educators and other people in our field avoid the issue of class because besides not being pretty, it isn't politically palatable—in fact it's explosive. Nonetheless, **social class is unquestionably one of the most formative influences on the process of socialization** (Greenberg, 1969/1990; Bernstein, 1971).

Many studies have shown that in the areas of class and race, socioeconomic strata not only exist but reproduce themselves with only minimal crossing of barriers upwardly—or even downwardly—from generation to generation. The vehicles carrying this socioeconomic class maintenance from one generation to the next are childrearing, caregiving, and education. Parents usually pick child-caring arrangements in which the approach to childrearing is consistent with parents' socioeconomic class and education level—if such care is available.

Public schools have often been accused of teaching different characteristics, traits, and expectations that perpetuate differentiated class cultures. (For example, read the work of Apple, 1982; Bourdieu & Passeron, 1977; Bowles, 1971; Bowles & Gintis, 1971, 1976; Collins, 1971; Giroux, 1981; Kohn, 1969; and Willis, 1981; all of whom are called *reproduction theorists*.) Less frequently do we read that **families and child care programs also, albeit unwittingly, socialize children into their own distinct social classes.**

What babies are believed to need beyond the basics is significantly influenced by the eyes of the

beholder, and a powerful influence on our vision is the one our socioeconomic class has bestowed upon us (while we were growing up and not looking).

For example, the approach and standards agreed upon in the 1980s by early childhood authorities nationwide, and published by NAEYC as *Developmentally Appropriate Practice in Early Childhood Programs Serving Children From Birth Through Age 8,* repre-

Not all parents have the same childrearing goals. Respecting parents means discussing our different perspectives, not insisting that our goals are the only right goals.

Where Should Babies Be To Develop Optimally

sent primarily people from a social class consisting of well-educated, fairly affluent, professional, academic, and arts-oriented, leader-level people.

Like any other social class, this social class strives to reproduce—at home, in child care settings, and in school—citizens who will be able to function **as it functions** or desires to function—in this case with self-confidence (self-esteem), quite autonomously, assertively, and creatively, at a high verbal level, with excellent impulse control (self-discipline) and social skills. Children are encouraged to explore, to share, to care, to cooperate, negotiate, plan, choose, and decide. Infants and toddlers are to be respected and responded to because they're expected to grow up to be adults who are respected and listened to in their communities (both geographically and professionally speaking). *Developmentally Appropriate Practice* advocates that from infancy onward, every effort be made to enable children to encounter optimal options for developing the kind of character and characteristics that make maximum feasible opportunity as great a possibility as possible. *Developmentally Appropriate Practice* urges adults to allow children to take advantage of a great many advantages so they will have advantaged adult lives.

Because not all social groups *have* this goal (e.g., because this goal does not appear to some groups desirable, or to other groups, in any way realistic), not all want the characteristics listed above to be emphasized in child-rearing, childcaring, and education. At the opposite extreme of people with privilege are politically disenfranchised, educationally disadvantaged, low-income minority groups. The future many parents and caregivers in this situation foresee for their children is a place at the bottom of the socioeconomic system, a lowly role; they may not want children raised in such a way that, as the caregivers see it, the children will be headed for a fall or for trouble. (A very interesting book about this is *First Steps Toward Cultural Difference: Socialization in Infant/Toddler Day Care* by Darla Ferris Miller.) Professional child development people probably have an obligation to discuss with parents the parents' goals—and what to do to get their children there. (Greenberg 1969/1990). Most parents want their children raised in accordance with the family's cultural beliefs, or want to be in on any decision to do otherwise.

How do you and your husband want your child raised during weekday hours? It's much easier to find a child care setting in which we see practices such as those in Column 1, than those in Column 2, of the box below. This issue is much less relevant in infant than in toddler care.

With regard to child care centers, as with regard to so much else, Lady Luck is on the side of the adequate family. Research suggests

. . . that family background is the most salient determinant of development in children attending day care centers whose quality varies from adequate to good. The strength of family background as a predictor in and of itself ought not to come as a total surprise. These results are consistent with a major study of public school quality and children's cognitive development and educational attainment (Jencks, 1972). In that study family background explained half of the variance in children's educational attainment while school quality added little or nothing to predictions of cognitive development or educational attainment. (Kontos & Feine in Phillips, 1987, p. 75)

	Differences in childrearing emphases	
	Column 1	**Column 2**
Child Management Methods	authoritarian (expect obedience based on fear); impose ourselves; give monosyllabic orders; use corporal punishment; trivialize children's play, needs, comments, conversations; teach children their "place" (their inadequacies)	egalitarian (expect cooperation based on explanation); fit in with what children are doing; engage in explanation, conversation; empower them
Individualizing Children	treat children as a group	notice and meet *individual* needs, listen to each child, have private time with each child
Many Mini-Things We Do	try to get children to conform to the world as it is, even if it is destructive to the child or to others	encourage children to comprehend and creatively cope with the world, even to try to change elements in the environment
Language We Use and Pass On	is predictable and limited	elaborate and original
Goal	to attempt to control or restrict curious, creative, and assertive characteristics	to encourage curious, creative, and assertive characteristics

A Reader Inquires

Question: As I understand it, this chapter is not reporting research results about what infants need to develop normally; it offers the thoughts and speculations of some thinking people about what infants need to develop unusually strong (optimal) self-esteem, self-discipline, and good character. Is this the intent?

Response: Yes.

Question: On page 23, you mention "covering long periods of time while parents are away" as if it's a questionable thing to do. Do we know that to grow up OK, zero- to three-year-olds need "enriching" and "soul nourishing" experiences during the day every day? Do we know that parents who "relish" childrearing turn out better "products" than "parents whose main goal in childrearing is to get it safely over with" (e.g., no major psychological or other kinds of mishaps)?

Response: To both questions the answer is, no, research has not given us this information.

Question: On page 25, the assumption in the first column seems to be that "marvelous mothers" are much better for infants than is "adequate care." Isn't most infant development during the first six to twelve months maturational? As long as the child care is "good enough," does research show for sure that "marvelous" care matters much in the long run?

Response: You are correct. Much infant development during the first year is maturational. You're also correct that the assumption here is that if optimal development in all dimensions, self-esteem, etc., is the goal, not just "normal" development, then marvelous care is preferable — more "optimal." This is why infant caregiver training specialists work so hard to help caregivers provide "better" quality care. There's another assumption here, but it is research-based — that is, the quality of care in most infant child care settings is not "optimal." Probably an equal amount of in-home care by parents isn't "optimal" either. The paragraph you refer to does not state where babies should be; it discusses the recency of attention to researching what it is that expert mothers in all socioeconomic groups do.

Question: On page 26, you ask parents if their goal is "to get the kids grown and get on with their own lives, or to enjoy a rich and fulfilling life during the short period of years that children 'live in' before they fly the nest." Has research found that parents with the first-mentioned feeling are more likely to be employed full-time during their children's first six or nine months than are parents who want to "enjoy a rich and fulfilling family life?"

Response: No. In fact, scholars may not even have studied the subject. However, there are parents who feel each of these ways and say so openly. There are probably others who have never clarified their values on this subject. The purpose of the discussion on pages 23–33 is to highlight some important issues to consider in deciding what choice to make about an infant's care, and encourage a particular group of early childhood professionals and parents to reflect on their priorities. The group of people we are thinking of in most of these few pages at the front of this chapter feels guilty about working full-time during a child's early months, and could do otherwise, but has never brainstormed options; these are the people we all know who feel pressured by outside forces not to let up. In this small portion of the chapter, we're presenting alternatives for consideration, and encouraging adults to take initiative in solving a problem *they feel they have, not* reporting a research-based recommendation. Readers can think of this segment as a values clarification exercise, or as listening to friends talk about this topic, or can skip over it to the other three questions this chapter considers with regard to where an infant should be cared for:

- What is the baby's home situation?
- What arrangement is best for the individual baby?
- What arrangement is best for the whole family, all things considered?

Question: Does research show that if you are employed full-time during your baby's first six or seven months you can't enjoy a rich and fulfilling family life?

Response: No, research has never suggested this. Many stressed-out new parents complain about it, though.

II. *A second consideration: What is the baby's home situation?*

If at home a baby is experiencing a great amount of overt adult pathology (alcoholic or drug-addicted parents, psychotic parent who has attacks of crazed behavior, physically or sexually abusive parents, etc.); or if the responsible parent is not *able* to be reliably responsible (a 13-year-old mother, a mentally retarded mother); or if there *are* no operative parents (babies abandoned in a hospital or elsewhere); all authorities are understandably unanimous.

If a family is dysfunctional, all agree that baby is best off elsewhere during the day.

Even Harvard's **Burton White,** a well-known nonadvocate of full-time, out-of-home child care for infants and toddlers, says what most of us would very likely say if asked:

Clearly, if a family situation features alcoholism, drug dependence, or some other very serious deficiency or problem, substitute care even of average or slightly above average quality might be better for babies than their own home. (White & Meyerhoff, 1984, p. 27)

Many of us would add, as no doubt Burton White would if asked, that these children need topnotch care even more than ordinary children. We would not wish average care upon them, though surely it would be better than none. We would want the very *best* to make up, to whatever extent possible, for what they've missed, and to reduce the high risk of developing mental ill health that threatens them.

However, at present, the United States practices the law of "maximum feasible risk build-up"; the children most at risk are often also made victims of the lowest quality day care, thus increasing their risk of growing up in poor shape.

© 1991 Robert Maust

© Jean-Claude Lejeune

How minimal can a program be and it still remain ethical for us experts to say that day care for infants is OK? **Alice Honig** answers:

The baby is the yardstick of how minimal a program can be to be OK. If your baby sleeps a deep sleep, nurses rhythmically and leisurely, drapes sensuously and molds into the contours of your body, looks up with delicious, 3-chinned grins when you coo and use motherese and raised voice tones and stroke her or his body to express your sheer delight and pleasure and joy at this wonderful, round-bellied being—then the care is probably OK.

When babies can sink into somatic peacefulness upon their caregiver's body and when they work intensely hard at grasping a mobile toy overhead or over feet, if they cry full-bodied howls of righteous indignation when they are thirsty and hungry, then you know that the baby has good beginnings in

relationship with caregivers.

If you go to observe your infant's caregiver and s/he is body-cuddling, eyeshining, voice-caressing, and language turn-taking with every coo the baby gives —then this care is fine even though the caregiver may not be able to tell you what are the Eriksonian dialectic stages nor what the tasks and gains of Piaget's sensorimotor period are! (Honig, personal communication, 1990)

We know how to operate excellent therapeutic child care programs, but they're costly. Except for a rare program here and there, our communities apparently have other priorities. Again we may wonder as we did earlier: Of what use is knowledge if we ignore it? Have you read *Within Our Reach: Breaking the Cycle of Disadvantage* by Lisbeth Schorr?

But what about babies from inadequate yet less dramatically unhealthy homes? Where should they be?

We assume that *you,* as a concerned pre-parent and recent early childhood education major, and your caring husband, who both say you seek "optimal," will provide a good home life for your baby, whether in your baby's first year or two or three you do full-time mother work, or "mother work and other work," a distinction often made by infant specialist Dr. Honig. But as professionals and professors eager to profess opinions about where babies should be, we have to consider *all* kinds of home settings, not just the extremes—"untenable" and "optimal." Most families are not at either end of the spectrum.

On this subject, infant day care specialist **Bettye Caldwell** (introduced in Chapter 1, page 6), says

We need to recognize that there are some (probably all too many) babies who would be much better off in day care 50 hours a week than spending that time in a chaotic, unloving, unstimulating home. Believe it or not, there are homes like that in this country, and they are not all in the slums. (Caldwell, personal communication, 1990)

Even child development specialists who feel strongly that a baby should be with his parents as much as possible— with other caregivers supplementing around the edges—agree that there are parents in all walks of life who, while not neglecting the child's *physical* needs, neglect him *emotionally.* Perhaps both parents are attorneys, or executives gone from home from 8 A.M. to 8 P.M., and who, *in addition, do not enjoy their baby when they are home.* It's possible to be "on duty" with a baby but to be emotionally unavailable to him. Maybe these busy parents entertain a lot, go out socially many times a week, have homework or hobbies that don't include young ones. They *are* home, but as far as savoring their baby is concerned, they are out to lunch. As one such mother, **Diane,** dismissively says,

Babies are boring. He's in an OK day care center. I'm not a good mother; I don't pretend to be a good mother. We manage to get through the weekend with our group of babysitters and a few migraines. . . . He has

© Nancy P. Alexander

I. What are parents' goals for themselves and for their children? II. What is baby's home situation? III. What arrangement is best for the individual baby? IV. What arrangement is best for the whole family, all things considered? Some babies are best off in good child care settings and some do best at home.

And babies from homes that child development people would decry, but are not "certifiably" intolerable? Where should these babies be? Is adequate child care OK, or is the best necessary?

tons of toys and so much gear you can hardly get into the house. In about ten years, he'll be more interesting. Then we can teach him to play tennis like we do.

This mother may be surprised to find that by the time her son has been deprived of parental friendship for ten years, he no longer longs for it. He may, by then, have adjusted to the lack of lovingness that has been his lot, and have shut down emotionally. He may have become involved in other dimensions of self and life, or have found comfort elsewhere. He may have become addicted to *possessions,* because his parents showered him with *things* rather than with their affection. Or he may have a cavalier attitude toward possessions because they're easy to come by, easily replaced, and essentially meaningless anyway. An overabundance of them surrounds the child—he has never had to wait and work for one single truly wanted treasure. He may harbor resentment against his parents and retaliate by disappointing, disgracing, or dismaying them—flunking, drinking, drugging, etc. In any case, he may be permanently out of his parents' reach: His relationship to his parents may have come to seem as meaningless and low priority to *him* as they have led him to believe that it has always been to *them.*

There are young children who are growing up feeling very inadequate (who devalue themselves and are developing *low* self-esteem) because they see how low spending time with them is on their busy, fast-track parents' list of preferred things to do. As these children grow, so, in many cases, do their problems. Either their parents or they *themselves* expect them to achieve as much as their super-achiever adults. These parents often put excessive pressure on their children to achieve because "achievement" is one of their highest values.

Essential Points on Which Specialists Seem To Agree

In spite of great debates, storms of studies, and flurries of critical comments about colleagues' "findings" and viewpoints, it doesn't appear that infant/toddler researchers disagree significantly! They're interested in differing aspects of the picture and have different personal opinions, but apparently they agree with many expert parents and practitioners that:

1. Child care programs of reasonably good quality, whether in family day care homes or centers, are not harmful to most infants, toddlers, and two-year-olds. A definition of "reasonably good quality" has been established.

2. The quantity of out-of-home, not-by-kin care is equally as important as the quality of that care. Most authorities agree that if *optimal* development is a goal, not just *normal* development, babies are best off with their parents for the first six-to-twelve months; and after that, part-day care is preferable to full-day care—five four-or-five-hour days a week are less stressful to a baby than are several marathon days. Although some child development specialists are known for advocating that babies should be with good parents if they are fortunate enough to have them, none of them object to fifteen-to-twenty-five hours a week of high-quality non-parental care if that's what's best for the family. Conversely, other child development specialists are known for advocating that non-kin infant/toddler care is OK for babies, but few of them recommend more than twenty-five hours for babies younger than a year, if there is a choice. **Note: There is a group of specialists who believe 40 hours is also ok.**

3. All families should have more options. We all should advocate for paid parental leave, part-time jobs with job security and fair pay, job-sharing, flex-time, and a wide variety of *high*-quality, federally subsidized child care homes, centers, and other kinds of programs.

You may want to read an interesting book—*Children of Fast-Track Parents* by A. A. Brooks, a journalist knowledgeable on the subject—a subject neglected by most researchers and writers except for David Elkind, who is well-known for his writings about *The Hurried Child.*

We aren't speaking of parents who enjoy preschoolers or school-age children much more than babies. These parents just aren't baby people. We hear critics say, "Why do they have children if they aren't willing to spend any time with them?" If people are sure they want children, the fact that they aren't baby people is insufficient reason to "pass" on having them, as long as they "do their best," including making the very best child care arrangements they can, and meeting their baby's needs for positive attention and warmth as best they can, even if they consider it a sacrifice. (After all, some parents who enjoy *babies* very much aren't great with *older* children because they can't let go and grant their children increasing independence.)

But it would be hard to disagree with Dr. Caldwell in some instances. For example, **Alma** is a middle-class married mother of four who's home full-time. She bitterly resents the fact that she is, quote, "stagnating," while her husband is rapidly becoming famous in his field. She advertises the fact that she's "a terrible mother." She was the fifth child of a mother who didn't want any, and who grievously neglected and frequently punished her. Alma coped adequately with her first two, both girls, but when the third turned out to be twin boys, it was more than her fragile tolerance for parenting could bear. Emotionally, she gave up.

Each day, Alma filled and propped more milk bottles than the boys, kept in adjoining cribs, could need in a week, and every morning and evening she changed their soaked sheets and gave them each a fresh diaper. On and off throughout the day, if and when it was convenient, Alma boosted a baby or two into the air and coochy-cooed him a little bit, or tossed a few toys into the cribs, taking out several others. The babies could howl, whine, or be deathly still for hours

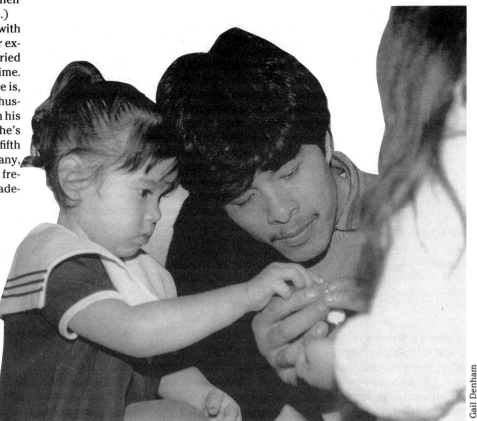

© Gail Denham

Parents should be an integral part of an infant/toddler program. We need to work especially closely and supportively with those among the parents we serve who seem not to be very involved with their young children, or who feel that they aren't good parents. We don't want them to believe that we're better "parents" than they; they might give up altogether. Some parents believe that their child is "always good" with the caregiver and "always bad" at home. We must combat this discouraged feeling.

When parents parent in a manner that's developing in their children low self-esteem, lack of self-discipline, and behavior patterns and emotions known to hinder successful functioning in the middle-class world of school, community, work, and future family, is it our responsibility to include the parents in our thinking and discussion of cause and effect so that, equipped with new information, they can decide if they want to try some new approaches? Some parents find counseling with a skillful mental health professional helpful if they are trying to attempt new parenting behaviors.

Where Should Babies Be To Develop Optimally

on end, but Alma went to them only when it suited her 'til 5 P.M. At that time, she bathed and dressed them "for Daddy," and they were up and about 'til 10 P.M. (being reprimanded right and left for "being wild," "getting into everything," "not listening," and being "holy terrors"); 10 P.M. is when they were returned to their cages for another 19-hour incarceration. This was life for the twins until they recently turned two-and-a-half and started half-day preschool.

In a situation such as this, most authorities would agree that the parents need intensive, extensive counseling, and the boys would be better off in a good child care setting, possibly "50 hours a week." But even when parents seem to child developmentalists utterly inadequate, solutions are by no means simple.

The less a parent is positively involved with her or his baby, the more urgent it is for caring people to strengthen the parent's confidence, parenting abilities, and willingness to engage with the parent-needing baby

T. Berry Brazelton, indisputably recognized as both a pro-child and pro-parent authority, says:

If we separate parents and their babies physically in a way that creates emotional separation between them, we say implicitly to parents that what *we* can do for babies is more valuable than what *they* can give. Then they experience one more fulfillment of the prophecy that nothing they do as adults really matters. We cannot afford to let emotional detachment become a part of early care outside the home, whether it is group or family care. It can happen unless each member of the caretaking team consciously works to cement parents to their children.

In a stressful environment, it is too easy for parents to abdicate the psychological care of their children, as well as their physical care, to a group which they consider to be more expert and better equipped than they. In the process of such abdication, one of two possible detrimental outcomes can result. The parents will feel competitive with the child care staff and will resent having given the child over to them. In this case they may unconsciously undermine the positive effects on the child, or more consciously resent the child's different behavior which results from the group care. While based on positive feelings, these competitive feelings can interfere with the environment at home and diminish any benefits which the child may otherwise accrue.

The second possible result might be a kind of compartmentalization of the child in the parents' minds — for example, the good part of the child belongs to the child care situation, the bad part to the family. With such an expectation on their part, the likelihood of the child's compartmentalizing her or his behavior is greatly increased (Brazelton, 1982).

With these possibilities in mind, it becomes even more important that we account for the negative potential of early separation of child from family. We must understand it better than we do. Very little work has been done to uncover the effects of multiple caretakers on the early development of the child (Freud and Dann, 1951). Much of what has been done has been biased in order to prove the thesis that early group care will not matter to the child, or to rely for proof on the model of multiple caregiving in the extended family. Citing the existence of many different caregivers in an extended family is obviously not a justification, as this is not a separation for either mother or child. Also, when caregivers are members of the same large family group, they do not represent significant differences from the mother. There are too many built-in similarities in their values and behavior to represent to the infant the kind of separation we are talking about.

Seashore et al. (1972) suggest that the self-confidence of the mother is impaired by early separation if the baby is her first, less so with the second and third babies. The literature on attachment behavior has sorely neglected fathers. We do not know what early separation of the infant may do to vulnerable father-infant attachment, but we can speculate that this relationship may be even more fragile and easily abdicated than with the mother. (Brazelton, 1984, pp. 12–13)

Evie is a young mother whose family disapproved of the guy she married right after high school. Her husband is young and spends many evenings out with "the boys." Evie works in a factory for four dollars an hour. When she picks two-year-old Zeke up after work, the family day care provider, who is quite nice with children, usually says things like, "Here, take this bad boy — I don't want to see any more of him today." (When asked why she says this, she says, "Oh, I'm just joshing. Anyway, by four o'clock I *am* tired of all these toddlers! Zekie comes in at 6 A.M.!") Evie's face falls. She says, "Oh no, was he bad today? I had a bad day, too!" Evie has no confidence in her maternal abilities anyway, and every little jesting slap cracks like a clap of thunder across her feelings. Like most young children, Zeke has trouble with transitions, so he cries and clings to the caregiver. This further convinces Evie that she isn't much of a mother — her own son, as she sees it, doesn't like her. The smiling caregiver is exhausted, hands over the squirming child, and turns away, leaving Evie and her screaming son to let themselves out. Evie would've like to talk, but . . . .

Evie and Zeke go home to drink one Coke after another and watch TV, Zeke whines and fusses at her feet, causing Evie to reach out fairly frequently to smack him and yell, "Shut up!"

In order to really help infants, toddlers, and two-year-olds from families in which parent-child bonds are frail and ailing, a center or child care home has to be exceptionally good. That is, the family child care provider or staffperson has to be un-

---

Too many toys, pieces of equipment, activities, and events, and not enough affectionate relationship, may shape a child's values toward materialism and away from humanism. What kind of character are we character developers trying to develop?

When parents have low interest in parenting, and/or a low estimation of their ability to be "good" parents, child development professionals — family child care providers, center staff, and others — must work sensitively and creatively to increase parents' interest and to raise their self-esteem regarding the parenting endeavor. The best way to help children is to help strengthen their parents' parenting motivation, confidence, and skills. Child care workers are in a good position to do this.

usually able to rise above the almost automatic temptation to feel and behave disapprovingly toward the parents, or to feel like a better parent to the child than the actual parent is. The caregiver has to work ceaselessly and sensitively to help parents develop a new style of parenting more adequately and feeling more adequate as parents. Dr. Brazelton writes about this:

In *Infants and Mothers* (Brazelton, 1969), I point to the importance of recognizing and supporting the marked individual differences in infants and their mothers' and fathers' reactions to them. If surrogate caregivers wish to enhance attachment rather than increase separation, they must give constant attention to the stage of development and the individual qualities of the infant and the parents. Through their surveillance and record keeping, they will need to assess and react to changes in each member of the mother-child dyad or the father-mother-child triad (Provence, Naylor, and Patterson, 1977). This is a demanding expectation. Many of parents' cues will be rather subtle. The mother's own unconscious feelings about abdicating care of

her baby may lead to a kind of acting out on her part. She may either withhold pertinent information about the child's behavior or stage of development, or manipulate the baby at home in such a way that she or he presents a difficult picture at the center. For similar unconscious reasons, she may also distort the picture of herself in such a way that she presents a negative, difficult image to the child's caretakers. For example, a mother may deliberately underfeed her baby at home, or keep the child up so late that she or he will be exhausted at the center. Another mother might instruct the caregiver in minute detail about how to take care of her baby—implicitly suggesting that the caretaker wouldn't know how—and setting up a negative response in the caregiver. Yet, on closer examination of these examples, it is easy to see that in the first, the mother might be setting it up for her baby to fail in another's care because she does not want to give the baby up to another. In the second, her own need and wish to be the one who does all the things for her child interfere with any recognition for the caregiver's competence. Her behaviors need to be dealt with, but helping her understand them will be therapeutic as well as helpful.

It is necessary for the child care staff to constantly emphasize the strengths in the mother-child relationship which produce such behaviors in order to continue to enhance them as strengths rather than to allow them to interfere with the child's best interest. Analysis of the competitive feelings in the mother can lead to her understanding them and using these feelings as strengths for the mother/child attachment.

Feelings of self-devaluation are all too easily reinforced in mothers and fathers. Pressures in the environment which result in giving up the child—such as mother needing extra income or an outlet for herself as a person, or in the father's case, his inability to be enough support for the family—simply synchronize with the model for abdication on the basis of inadequate feelings. Unless these perceived inadequacies can be seen by the staff as only one side of the parents' ambivalence, the family may be further devalued. Their effort has to be directed toward strengthening any positives in the situation—such as offering helpful advice to parents about structuring the child's playtime in the evening or the weekends so that their fatigue at the end of a long day does not interfere with the period of good interaction between them. Likewise, the staff should seek to preserve any cultural differences in children and to stress them as important to the families. In this way, their individuality and strengths, as well as the child's, are implicitly accepted and explicitly reinforced. As a negative ex-

ample, one child care center encourages Chinese infants to be messy by having them finger feed themselves at a time when chaos inevitably results, thereby ignoring the cultural importance of neatness and cleanliness in the Chinese. This kind of insensitivity is destructive to the parents' self-image and indirectly must affect the child. (Brazelton, 1984)

It would appear that the less good the home, the better the child care home or program must be, particularly in the area of parent support work, in hopes of offsetting to a degree some of the damage the child is experiencing. How often does it happen this way? Most researchers haven't seriously looked into the question, although **Carolee Howes** has. Judging by *her* work, our country is doing nothing to stop a scary game of double jeopardy. In a review of research on infant/toddler child care issues, Howes says that studies of middle-class families, equally able to pay child care costs, show that, in general, families who are unable to provide optimal parenting *also* select non-optimal child care programs.

Parents who are stressed (Howes & Stewart, 1987), who lead more complex lives (Howes & Olenick, 1986); who lack social supports (Howes & Stewart, 1987), and who are less developmentally appropriate in their childrearing practices and values (Howes & Olenick, 1986; Howes & Steward, 1987) are more likely to enroll their child in low-quality child care than in high-quality child care. Mothers whose infants were classified as insecurely attached

What about other-than-mother care for the infant from an optimal home?

to them enrolled their infants in family day care homes with more children per caregiver (Howes et al., 1988). We have no research comparing the infant child care choices of families with different financial resources but the cost of care suggests that low-income families have more difficulty than more affluent families in finding high-quality care. (Howes, 1989, p. 26)

To this, let's add that although *some* low-income families are well-educated middle-class college or graduate students, or are informed people who for one reason or another are temporarily living on low incomes, many are low socio-educational families. This may mean that experience or information about optimal childrearing and quality child care never have been available to

© The Growth Program

Parents may feel competitive with the child care staff and resent the relationship the baby has with the caregiver. In this case, parents may unwittingly undermine the care provider. Feeling unhappy about how well their baby appears to be doing in care, parents may influence her to "be bad" when with the caregiver. A lot of thought should go into building a healthy, real friendship with each parent, especially, to the extent possible, with the hard-to-reach parent.

CHAPTER 3

them. **Added to the difficulty of finding high-quality care may be lack of exposure to what high-quality care looks and feels like.**

At the happiest end of the continuum, what about babies from optimal homes? Where should these babies be?

If you and your husband are able to parent lovingly, generously, gently, and firmly, your young child will, in all likelihood, have the glow of good feeling that eventually differentiates into the various aspects of positive "self" feelings that add up to high self-esteem. If one, or better yet, *both* of you are able to parent positively and with pleasure, and with firmly enforced, reasonable behavioral expectations, your child will very likely have the emerging early attitudes, personality aptitudes, and evolving attributes that will later add up to good character. If the child is in excellent health and mental health, and in an excellent home (called in our trade an "optimal" home to avoid the judgmental sound of "excellent," but meaning, in fact, exactly the same thing), **there is no scientific data indicating that it would hurt her to be in adequate, full-time, out-of-home care of one kind or another.**

But unless it turns out that you have no choice (because you *have* to work—many of us mothers do!—or because it's very important to you to practice your profession, and no satisfactory child care arrangement can be found), *why*—if you're capable of recognizing and actualizing an *excellent* setting for your baby's growth and development and since you say that your baby's *optimal* development is your goal—*why* would you *choose* to put her in a merely *adequate* setting, full-time, and pay dearly for the privilege? (We're speaking, of course, about your baby's first year or two or three, not her entire early childhood.) Wouldn't you insist on an excellent child care setting? **Ruby** says,

For me, "adequate" is OK so I can work half-time—five four-hour mornings, plus an hour a day to get there and back. I *love* my work, as well as my child. This is my compromise to keep my life balanced. I have to think of *my* needs too. I'm "optimal" almost all the time I'm with him; probably partly because I'm *not* with him every minute.

Clarece says,

Adequate is OK with me, but only because it's part-time. My little boy is with a family child care provider who's very affectionate and low key, but not very stimulating—she doesn't talk to him or play with him, but she lugs him around a lot, and loves him—two days a week. I take classes and have a chance to get out. A friend has her baby with the same caregiver the other three days a week; she works part-time. When he's two and needs more activities and conversation, I'll make different arrangements.

Of course *you* could search and probably find a wonderful child care situation, way above "adequate," because you know what to look for. Would you be able to afford it? After your baby is born and you've interviewed trained nannies, and untrained but experienced in-home caregivers with good references, who appear likely to *stay* awhile, and after you've looked at available family child care homes and center settings, the best suggestion might be to do what your gut indicates feels most comfortable to you.

If parents have choices, where do the experts think their babies should be? What does research really know about where babies ought to be, you ask? It is not clear that research really *does* know, but here's what some of the most expert experts say:

Dr. Bettye Caldwell:

I think there is something unique and special about the mother-child relationship. I would like to see every mother remain home with her baby for at least six months, preferably nine or ten months. And I am a strong supporter of part-time work. Around that time, healthy and robust babies appear more than ready to move out and enlarge their worlds. They become excited when they see other babies and older children and adults. Their hands want to explore and hold the whole world of objects. A baby from even the most stimulating home environment probably gets extra development support from quality alternate care after that age. (Caldwell, personal communication, September 1990)

Dr. Alice Honig:

I personally am uncomfortable with babies under one year being in full-time day care. Clinically, babies wilt when they don't have access to the body and smell and feel and ministrations of the beloved special one (the parent) for more than four or five hours—and this, even when they are in the arms of a loving family day care provider.

It takes time to fall in love, for two bodies to become attuned, for deep intimacy of signaling and responses to grow.

Choosing optimal care is difficult. However, at present, nanny care is extremely expensive, and often the home-based caregiver has no or little specific training in the development of zero- to three-year-olds. Center care presents extra risks for hemophilus influenza, for gastrointestinal disease, for increased annual frequency of respiratory disease. When family day care providers are chosen particularly for their

---

Reminder: **"Optimal childrearing" as defined by child development specialists does not refer to socioeconomic status.**

Infant child care specialist Bettye Caldwell says that after nine or ten months, a baby from even the most stimulating home probably gets extra developmental support from quality alternate care.

body availability, their loving kindness and empathy with the miseries of baby life when hunger pangs, gas bubbles, lonesomeness, teething, or colic lead to despairs and inconsolability, then small family day care settings may be most appropriate. However, this will require adding to the caregiver's repertoire of songs, chants, stories, and rhythmic sing-songs. For language, I have observed, is *often* not rich and responsive even though the bodily snuggling does get done well in loving family care settings.

If the baby has been at home with a loving, tuned-in, responsive parent for the first nine months, then data suggest that half-time child care in a nurturing center (no walkers, good ratios, tender hands-on ministrations, with focused eye contact and talk while diapering, etc.) will not attenuate the positive attachment of infant and parent. As always, let the baby be our guide. If a baby becomes apathetic, dead-eyed, very quiet, or irritable, back-arching—then the child care setting is not OK for that baby. Each baby is a unique human being.

Care for 50 hours a week in the first year is not a good idea for a baby. Sure the baby will grow up, do his homework, etc. But will she or he be able to be warm, empathic, intimate, loyal in a marriage 25 years later? And will that baby grow up to parent in a nurturing manner ...? Why don't we value mother-work as much as other-work? Why can't we have a wave theory of life—with dignity given to the at-home time as well as the wave time spent in out-of-home-work. Let us cry dignity for baby-care work! And sacredness! And let us say amen to the distinguished child psychoanalyst Selma Fraiberg's call for every baby's "birthright" to be tended to by a special person who adores and cuddles the new little one. (Honig, personal communication, 1990)

Among the group of distinguished child development researchers who believe that more than part-time care outside the average home is probably detrimental are **Jay Belsky** and **Burton White**. Jay Belsky's views will be discussed shortly.

Burton White and his associates at Harvard University undertook a 13-year study of exactly *what* families who have successfully raised "wonderful" six-year-olds *do* to achieve these optimal results. During the 1960s and '70s, while many early childhood researchers were narrowly focused on cognitive skill learning, White concentrated on **how well-balanced, pleasurable children, who are also (but not only) intelligent and motivated are "made."** He studied families *who had already succeeded in raising outstanding children* as they parented subsequent children, infancy through three years of age. White discovered that raising a bright three-year-old is much easier than is raising "a pleasant, unspoiled three-year-old," and that *parents* (not "programs") are pivotal in achieving *optimal* (not "adequate") child development. **Burton White** believes:

Even though what reports we have show no obvious harm being done to the infants in superior programs, I still would not endorse such programs, except for families with special needs, or on a part-time basis after a child reaches six months. I am not concerned *only* with avoiding obvious harm, but with encouraging the best development as well, and none of the few evaluations performed so far has addressed the question of what situations are actually *good* for children.

In How Many Infant/Toddler Caregiving Settings Available to Average Families Do We See These Signs of Quality?

1. Caregivers develop enthusiastic, appreciative, respectful, responsive real relationships with each and every child, regardless of how unappealing or difficult they may find the child.

2. Caregivers (and the director in a center setting) form a collegial relationship, a partnership, with each parent. Information and ideas are shared respectfully, and by both parties. Educarers do everything they can to support or increase parents' self-esteem pertaining to parenting.

3. Director, family child care provider, and other staff support each mother's decision to work, find ways for mother and baby to enjoy each other in the child care setting, and suggest ways of working quiet private moments for baby and mother into busy lives at home.

4. Director and staff or family child care mother take active steps to help parents meet and get to know each other, especially parents who seem likely to benefit from the connections.

5. Educarers keep a daily record sheet for each baby's family, showing what the baby ate, drank, played, who she or he played with, length and times of naps, presence of diarrhea or signs of illness, bruises, mood, and any special information ("Juan's major caregiver is leaving next Monday"; "Juan is very much afraid of Miss Joanne's wheelchair"). A caregiver reviews the record sheet with the person who picks up the child.

6. Providers collect, read, view, and share with parents brochures, pamphlets, suitable books, and videos about infant/toddler development and care.

To put it bluntly, after more than 25 years of research on how children develop well, I would not think of putting a child of my *own* in any substitute-care program on a full-time basis during the first few years of life—especially a center-based program. (White, 1985, p. 270)

To the surprise of some, I am a strong advocate of substitute child care *on a part-time basis,* for all families who would like it, from the time a child is six months of age. (White, 1985, p. 271)

Excellent parenting can occur in average income and below-average income families, but *1)* getting by without both parents working full-time and *2)* finding excellent child care arrangements may well be impossible.

And "average" babies from average "non-optimal" homes? The majority of babies? What do they need? Where should they be?

Common sense suggests that what experts are recommending for the babies of people with choice, including families whose childrearing practices are consistent with what we know about developing excellent mental health—encouraging optimal development and therefore optimal future opportunities—would also be best for typical babies from typical homes. This includes families whose childrearing practices are *in*consistent with what we know about encouraging optimal development, therefore optimal future opportunities.

The average household income in the United States is $30,000. Your household income may be more than that, but this means a large number of families live on incomes *below* "average"; above poverty level ($11,611 for a family of four

What about families where choice is not possible — where the economic struggle to squeak by dominates all else? Don't their babies need what babies from the most fortunate families need, high-quality child care by parents or other caregivers? Don't all babies deserve equally good care? Isn't investing in healthy and emotionally healthy children a wise societal investment? Shouldn't democratic ideals be implemented beginning with babies?

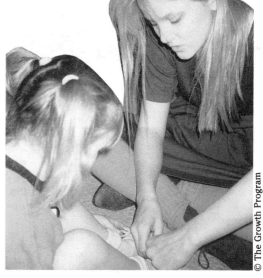

in 1987), but less than $30,000. To make ends meet, even minimally, both parents in many families with very young children must work full-time. "The dirty little secret of family income in this country is that it has risen — or kept even — because two people instead of one are now employed" (Cohen, 1990).

➡ **For many families in this income range, to permit one parent or the other to be the baby's caregiver during much of her first year generous, paid parent assurance leave is required.**

This is something the entire childcaring community — parents, grandparents, and paid educarers — can unite and fight for, just as the major organizations and associations that focus on the young child are doing. Of note is the fact that even *without* paid leave, many couples prefer working two different shifts (literally or figuratively) so their infants and toddlers can be taken care of by family. A number of parents with young children have this arrangement.

Quality care for infants and toddlers is labor intensive. Promptly meeting individuals' needs takes up 25 hours a day, and is only part of what's necessary: Time is required, also, for the child and the caregiver to stop and smell the flowers.

© Jean-Claude Lejeune

© The Growth Program

➡ **Many child development specialists encourage the mothers of children younger than three to work part-time,** but we need to be aware that the more than 25% of employed women who *do* work part-time *earn only 59% of the hourly wage of full-time workers.* Why is their hourly wage not the same? We need to be aware that part-time jobs typically provide few or no benefits, limited job security, and few opportunities for advancement. This is another area in which we must unite and fight for a situation in which we can do what's right for babies: More of the parents who must work might be able to cut back to part-time or take part-time jobs for the brief duration of their babies' infancies if benefits, job security, and opportunities for advancement were present.

➡ **We can also advocate job sharing:** two people do one job—the one who needs them takes the fringe benefits.

Because in the 1970s and 1980s they have been scrutinizing the situation, scholars have discovered what many families have long known: Some couples schedule themselves on different shifts so the children are always cared for at home by one parent or the other (Lein, 1974; Presser, 1988); increasing numbers of women have become at-home, self-employed entrepreneurs (Horvath, 1986); many mothers of very young children work part-time, chiefly to keep their feet in the door so as not to be closed out for "the duration"; and there are mothers who come up with other quite creative coping strategies (Elman & Gilbert, 1984). Among the

© The Growth Program

Are we fair? Do we care?

many interesting publications discussing all this are those by Abbott; Kamerman and Hayes; Diamond; Chow and Berheide; Cott; Kahn-Hut, Kaplan-Daniels, and Colvard; General Mills, Inc.; Gilligan; Kamerman; Kanter; Kessler-Harris; and Pleck and Lang.

➡ **Flex-time is urgently needed,** so that even parents who work full-time (hopefully not until their toddler is at least two and talking, unless wonderful alternative care is available, and the parents are free to spend lots of leisurely time with their toddler when home) can work hours that mesh well with their families' needs and schedules. We can all inform ourselves about, and support the work of, efforts such as those being made by Ellen Galinsky and Dana Friedman through their Families and Work Institute to encourage employers to adjust to their employees' family needs, especially the need to care for the very young and the very old. The Institute conducts research on business, government, and community efforts to help people balance their work and family lives.

Many mothers and fathers who **really** have to work also have to take whatever jobs they can get, wherever they are; therefore, many find themselves doing quite a bit of commuting. Many infants, toddlers, and twos are in out-of-home child care settings for 40 and 50 hours a week, nine or ten hours per day, so their mothers can earn $3.75 or $4.75 an hour toiling at the factory and getting no fringe benefits whatsoever. Does the early childhood education field's leadership have these ordinary people and extraordinary hours in mind when it states that "full-time" care is OK for infants and toddlers? Doubting that even the "mothers" of quality infant child care centers (Caldwell and Honig), both of whom are strong believers in the possibility and existence of such centers, advocate 50 hours of care a week for such young children, I *asked* them.

Paid parental leave and job security, more desirable part-time jobs, job sharing, and flex-time are needed so working people can have important leisure time with infants, toddlers, and two-year-olds. A country benefits when its citizenry is in good mental health — when there are fewer costly problem people. Ensuring happy childhoods is part of building mental health.

Bettye Caldwell:

I don't know how to answer your question about the 50-hour-a-week baby. Our research has simply not looked at that closely enough. I know this: It can't be all that good for the mothers, because many of them have another 50 hours of work at home, and that doesn't leave but 68 hours in a week for everything else, including sleep! Talk about burn-out! Many of us experience burn-out at an early age, and I don't mean boredom. We just get worn out. (Caldwell, personal communication, 1990)

Alice Honig:

Babies need time—at least 25 hours of a caregiver's day! They need leisurely feeds, leisurely croons, leisurely rocks, walks while leaning on the shoulder, long tummy caresses while being wiped and diapered, and long assurances that they are delicious and wonderful talkers as they coo and babble to us.

The hurried parent who rushes home at the end of the day is tired, resentful, armored with the righteous armor of the marketplace. Mothers need to come home and take off the armor—put on a housedress and cuddle, smooch, and feed faces together. How many parents can throw off their workplace armor and become the mama whose breast can be clutched, hair yanked, mouth poked with exploring baby fingers? Babies are delighted to sniff, taste, feel and get to know this wonder-of-wonders, the mother who he so loves and who loves him passionately and of a surety. Can the 50-hour-a-week mama find the energy, or the desire? Alas, I fear we expect superhuman energy from such a woman.

Only when we *value the work of baby-rearing,* the awesomeness of the task of rearing a human to become the kind of person we can value as a friend, be interested in as a person, only when we can value that *work*—only then will we value the quality of care that it takes to produce a small child after the infancy period, who, at three years, is a sturdy, sociable, serious, regulated, articulate, little being. The handiwork of high-quality infant caregiving is splendid. But until we become convinced of its importance to prevent misspent loves, and misspent lives (drug abuse, family violence, and the rest), we will continue to ignore the importance of the job—whether performed by a parent or an infant caregiver. (Honig, personal communication, 1990)

Why should the married mother have "50 hours" of work to do at home after she puts in her 50 hours *away* from home? Shouldn't her husband do half of it? According to studies, it doesn't work that way, especially in working class families; only 6% of the fathers in dual out-of-home job families of *any* socioeconomic level do 50% of the child care and housework when home.

What are the implications of infants' and toddlers' need for abundant parenting? For some time, many well-credentialed child development specialists have agreed (often off the record) that whether or not there is *yet* a wealth of definitive research to prove it, the *average* group child care arrangement, available to the *average family's infants and toddlers, is not beneficial and may be harmful to them because*

● too many caregivers and family child care providers don't really love and enjoy each baby, and lack both child development training and training in working collaboratively with parents,

● much too often, staff and provider turnover occurs, preventing infants and toddlers from being able to count on people, preventing them from being known and responded to appropriately as *individuals,* preventing them from forming genuine *friendships,*

The political climate in which researchers work and report their results, and their personal situation (socioeconomic status, optimal mother or not) must always be considered in evaluating their recommendations.

● too many babies are in the total group (more than nine), making home-like interactions, activities, conversations, and outings virtually impossible,

● too few adults per cluster of babies are ever present (fewer adults than one to be the primary caregiver for each three or four infants and six to eight toddlers), and

● there is too casual an approach to safety and sanitation.

With regard to this last point, Earline Kendall, a prominent early childhood educator and former operator of four day care centers, worries because diseases spread speedily among babies due to their low immunities. According to the Centers for Disease Control, while the situation isn't usually dangerous, there is increasing evidence that group care for babies probably is hazardous to their health: They are likely to get more colds, flu, strep throat, infectious hepatitis, and spinal meningitis, among other things.

Sick babies are sad little creatures. They are also often cranky and difficult, therefore even more needy of their caregivers' time than usual. They strain the patience of a saint. How many "average" mothers want to send a miserable, sick baby off to a caregiver? How many average mothers, working for average employers, can

---

Until very recently, most day care researchers have shown little interest in average families' child care arrangements, the quality of care available to them, and its effect on their babies. Just like the rest of us, many researchers have had strong opinions and little evidence.

---

manage to stay home from work (again!) to take care of the sick baby?

Half of the states don't even require immunizations and handwashing in day care. How can some of these regulations be enforced even in states that have adequate ones? Many infant/toddler providers and programs that are quite good in lots of ways, are negligent with regard to safety and sanitation.

So? I still don't know: Where should "average" babies from "average" families be?

Researchers who, politically, are "for" day care (e.g., for women's right to work away from home if they choose to, a category which most of the pro-infant day care researchers themselves are in) have either not examined typical infant/toddler day care in the U.S. (they've studied better-than-average settings, or day care in another country), or have not been sufficiently familiar with expert parenting and expert infant/toddler caregivers to realize what was missing (warm, real, focused *friendship* between baby and caregiver and so much more!), or have neglected to discuss *full*-time *average* day care for *infants,* while endorsing *high quality* 30–40-hour-a-week child care programs for *preschoolers*—an entirely different matter.

Few child development specialists have wanted to risk being trounced by a group of privileged, young, academic, professional and business women, who *love* their work, and *want* to work and have everything necessary to ensure *quality care* for their young children *while* they work; so until very recently those who harbor them haven't been writing much about their hesitations and reservations pertaining to

● *full-time* (45-or-more hours a week)

● *non-familial* care for

● *infants and toddlers*

● *in less-than-excellent* settings.

(Although sometimes the astute reader can read a lack of enthusiasm between the lines that child development people with serious reservations *do* write accepting the necessity of day care in our society.) Some of the educated, articulate, young women who the child development specialists have feared are *also* researchers of infant/toddler day care, and some have been its staunch defenders.

Because you've just graduated from the early childhood education department of a university where anything flying the flag of research gets more unquestioning respect than other writings or viewpoints, let's step back a moment to reflect upon research as a product of *people,*

and people as possessed of *perspectives biased* by their owners' socioeconomic and educational levels, sociopolitical opinions, and personal experience (or lack of it). None of us can escape seeing the world through eyes tinted by our social class, the times we live in, our personal persuasions, and our personal limitations.

Is Full-Time Average Care Away From the Clan O.K. for Babies?

● Whether it's possible to find or develop excellent day care providers and programs for infants, toddlers, and two-year-olds is not the issue. (It *is* possible.)

● Whether part-time care in a good setting is O.K. for babies is not the issue. (It *is* O.K.)

● Whether babies from dysfunctional, damaging, or nonexistent families are helped by being in adequate infant care settings on a full-day basis rather than being left at home or in a hospital is not the issue. (Probably so, but it's doubtful that a routine day care program would be enough to reduce the risks these babies face, whereas therapeutically excellent care might possibly be enough.)

● Whether full-time day care of only average quality is all right for preschoolers from O.K. homes is not the issue. (It may be, although early childhood educators are not likely to recommend it.)

● The issue we're looking at here is whether full-time average (minimally adequate) day care is beneficial to, or O.K. for, babies (not three- and four-year-olds) from average (not especially "optimal") families. This is a concern of many child development authorities, and they do not all agree.

Some of the developmentalists who defend full-time day care for babies have no children, which may, in the minds of many, create doubts about what arrangements *they* would make if they did have little babies. Would these mothers choose full-time care, 45-hour-a-week for their babies younger than a year, as the average parents who have to work often have to do? In a merely "average" setting outside the home and outside the extended family? Or would they select a good center or family child care provider, probably for about 25 hours a week? Or maybe a carefully selected caregiver to take care of the child younger than one, two, or three in the child's own home?

Some of the mother-researchers who have been ready to pounce on other researchers who question the OKness of the average infant/toddler day care available in average places to average people have older children. When their children were babies, this type of "average" care is not what the mothers subjected them to. Some of the mothers were at home a lot being graduate students during their children's earliest year or two or three, or being part-time consultants or writers, or being three-quarter-day employees with ample flex-time, or did volunteer work pertinent to careers they developed *later*. Their full-scale careers began later, or they scaled down during each of their children's infancy. This is not the life that average mothers living on average American incomes are privileged to lead.

Others shared care of the babies with devoted husbands, supplemented by grandmothers and/or good babysitters, or live-in help. All of this somewhat dilutes these developmentalists' advocacy of full-time infant/toddler care for the masses *now*. (Whether or not other countries

---

Why Do So Many Programs for Toddlers and Twos Pressure-Cook Them?

In this chapter, we've focused mostly on babies younger than a year. The truth is that, if we're talking **optimal,** toddlers and twos need lots of leisurely time with their own grown-ups, too. And during any hours they *are* in out-of-home care, they need to lead a normal toddler "lifestyle." They may be in school, but they're not yet school-age children. Why do so many of the less-than-best child care settings run inferior first grade programs for two-year-olds?

Speaking of the National Child Care Staffing Study (which was being presented at a congressional briefing by primary investigators Marcy Whitebook, Carollee Howes, and Deborah Phillips), NAEYC Governing Board member **Jerlean Daniel** said,

There was one finding of the staffing study that shocked me. I read this section a half dozen times, not wanting to believe what the words were saying. That finding was that 55% of the infant/toddler rooms . . . had only one teacher available for the bulk of the day. There is no way that even a trained teacher can provide meaningful, sensitive, growth-enhancing experiences for young children under such circumstances. With numbers like one adult to 10 toddlers, let alone 14, I am amazed that the overall quality of care provided scored even minimally adequate in the study. (Daniel, May 1990)

One reason that many programs for toddlers and two-year-olds gather them together and give them inappropriate group lessons to do (learn the ABCs, everybody color the ditto) is that meeting the individual needs of 10 to 14 babies of this age is impossible.

Many parents don't know a lot about the ages and stages of child development. They want the best for their children. This includes doing well in school. Parents know that schools judge children almost exclusively by their academic success. (How too bad!) In a misguided effort to help their children do well in school (years away from *this* year when the child is only one or two), they eagerly accept the child care providers' wish to feel that they are "teaching." **Parents and staff alike misunderstand what "educational excellence" at this age is. This is a second reason that we see so many toddler programs that look like first grades.** When caregivers themselves are convinced about what's developmentally appropriate, are good practitioners, and can clearly explain the value both of the approach and of the representative details that parents see, the understanding and approval of most parents grows.

A third reason why some parents and teachers pressure-cook little children is that, in their view, it makes them look good. It takes a skilled trainer to teach monkeys meaningless and difficult tricks. The more adequate an adult feels as a parent or teacher, the less necessary he or she feels it is to do this.

Fourth, there are some parents who feel guilty about working full-time when their children are so small. Their guilt causes them to want to ensure that their children aren't "missing anything." They erroneously fix on school skills. Their children—at this age—aren't lacking school skills, but they may well be "missing something"—enough relaxed time with their parents and other family members.

Probably the infant/toddler child-caring community will be able to better articulate to parents what high-quality toddler care is, as child-carers receive more training in this area.

have developed good nationwide child care and development systems for average families, and whether or not the U.S. *should* or *could* do so too, is a separate discussion. "Should" and "could" are different from how it is *now*. We mustn't misguide families who seek answers for their infants and toddlers *today*.

Some acceptors of full-time infant day care as all right if it meets minimal standards have never been the full-time caregiving person for one or more of their own babies and toddlers during the child's early years (maybe their wives did the job), or if they have, have not been gifted at it. Therefore, we have no particular reason to trust that they know what high-quality care for this age group really is, and the enormous investment of self and patience it requires. Quite likely, when they toss around the term "high-quality," they mean "adequate," "good enough." It's possible that adequate *is* good enough, but science is supposed to be precise, and prides itself on this precision. Parents who in many instances are not informed consumers, shouldn't be told by people called social "scientists" that K-Mart and Saks Fifth Avenue are one and the same, regardless of whether or not K-Mart is adequate and good enough. And probably the majority of these pro-"average" infant day care researchers have simply been, until very recently when they've begun to suggest caution, naive. They simply haven't been acquainted with the inferior care for babies that's all many average families living in average places can find (or even know to seek).

Although there are super excep-

tions, **much of the average child care in our country doesn't guarantee each baby and little child a loving, reliable person with whom to evolve a strong relationship. Jeree Pawl,** member of the board of directors, National Center for Clinical Infant Pro-

grams, emphasizes the essentialness of *relationship* for little children, regardless of where they are:

Perhaps a quotation from a short story of Tillie Olsen's will convey what the essence is of what I am trying to say about parents, infants, and day care.

"She was a beautiful baby. She blew shining bubbles of sound. She loved motion, loved light, loved color and music and textures. She would lie on the floor in her blue overalls patting the surface so hard in ecstasy her hands and feet would blur. She was a miracle to me, but when she was eight months old I had to leave her daytimes with the woman downstairs to whom she was no miracle at all.... Then she was two. Old enough for nursery school they said, and I did not know then what I know now—the fatigue of the long day, and the lacerations of group life in the kinds of nurseries that are only parking places for children."

Tillie Olsen describes what will *not* do. While we must know that not all babies are miracles to their parents, while we must

Concluding that high-quality child care in small amounts (15–25 hours a week) may be good for senior babies and toddlers has a flip side: Minimally adequate day care in large amounts (40–50 hours a week)—which is what a lot of little tykes get—is probably harmful to babies and toddlers; in fact, to a young child of any age.

know that no baby is perceived as a miracle all the time by parents, we must also steadfastly insist that each child in day care deserves the highest probability of being perceived as unique, of being appropriately and respectfully interacted with and of having predictable, trusting, mutually determined relationships. By the same token, each parent, and each caregiver, deserves respect, understanding, and support for his or her unique investment in the child. If we can also find ways to help ensure mutually respectful, trusting, and ongoing relationships *between* parents and caregivers then we will have the best kind of shared care for the child.

Day care must not be a "parking place for children" but a viable, rich place for safely learning more about the very complicated, but very worthwhile, things in the remarkable world of human relationships. (Pawl, 1990, p. 6)

One of the few and one of the first infant/toddler day care researchers who *did* during the 1980s dare to voice skepticism about the wisdom of placing infants in ordinary full-time child care progams (programs less than *excellent*) was Jay Belsky from the Pennsylvania State University; he was blasted right out of the water by some of his female colleagues, and was not protected by some of the progressive male researchers who didn't want to be seen by the females as reactionary. Of all of this, **Dr. Belsky** writes:

A decade ago a major question about day care was whether the absence of risks associated with high quality, university-based, research-oriented day care programs would also prove to be characteristic of the kind of child care typically available to most families in most communities. Another major issue had to do with timing of entry and particularly with infant care . . . .

A focus upon reunion behavior as a "window" on the security of the attachment relationship, coupled with the investigation of children from different socioeconomic strata and a myriad of child care experiences, leads me to conclude that there are too many findings linking more than 20 hours per week of nonmaternal care experience in the first year with increased avoidance of mother following separation, heightened insecurity, and subsequent aggression and noncompliance not to draw attention to the findings and raise concerns about their meaning. These developmental correlates, it must be acknowledged, are seen almost exclusively among children with extensive nonmaternal care experi-

ence, appear more probable in the case of boys and, as indicated above, may have as much to do with the child's experiences at home as with any in the child care setting itself.

There has been a tendency in the research literature on day care to selectively cite evidence consistent with a preexistent point of view—and I have been charged with this sin (Phillips, McCartney, Scarr, & Howes, 1987). I cannot deny the possibility that, as a point of view begins to crystallize, certain data may take on more meaning than do others. What I can point to, however, is a record of relatively objective analysis over the past decade. Although this analysis first led me and my colleagues to conclude that few risks seem to be associated with day care, nevertheless the record shows steady change and refocus (Belsky, 1984b, 1985, 1986, 1987; Belsky & Steinberg, 1978; Belsky et al., 1982; Bronfenbrenner et al., 1976). This refocus has drawn my attention to variation in the experiences and development of children in day care and to the need to distinguish care in the first year of life from that initiated thereafter. The change has been that risks seem to be associated with extensive nonmaternal care in the first year.

I know from experience that this is not a popular point of view within the develop-

© D. Michael Hostetler

mental sciences today. I also know that it is charged with being politically and ideologically driven. In my mind, there is no greater danger to a science of early childhood than the politicization of the research process. . . . Social policy is dangerous to the developmental sciences to the extent that it makes certain conclusions untenable or certain findings suspect. In point of fact, my reading of the literature leads to no inevitable or even necessary proposals with respect to public policy. Some people can—and undoubtedly will—read my pronouncements to mean that mothers should not go to work during their infants' first year. Others can—and conceivably should—be led to conclude in view of the poor state of day care in this nation (Young & Zigler, 1986) that the current evidence demands that more effort be made to provide parents with affordable, quality care and with greater freedom and choice regarding their day care decisions. It remains for each reader to infer, then, what the implications of this review are—to families, communities, and to policy makers. (Belsky, 1988)

Now that studies *are* being done in "everyday" infant care situations, skeptics' concerns are being well validated. In her research monograph on quality child care, **Deborah Phillips** writes:

Although the calls to move child care research beyond high-quality university-based centers have been heeded, substantial room for improvement remains. Studies of this type are all too rare.

Child care consists largely of unregulated arrangements. Pressures at the federal policy level threaten to expand the supply of child care without regard to regulation of quality. Many states retain numerous exemptions from regulations for church-run, part-day, or state-sponsored child care programs. And the unrelenting demand for relatively scarce forms of licensed care, such as center-based care for infants, implies that more children will be placed in nonpreferred arrangements while on waiting lists for the parents' program of choice.

In light of these trends, it is essential that deliberate steps be taken to include low quality and unregulated arrangements (which are not necessarily low in quality) in future studies of child care. Concluding that high-quality child care is good for children has a flip side. But until we can describe more fully the negative consequences of poor child care, this issue remains largely an abstraction, and policies that trade off quality to expand the supply of child care will persist. (Phillips, 1987, p. 122–123)

This last sentence implies that when we have enough accurate research on low quality child care, public policy will swiftly—or at least soon—change. Not only does this continue to avoid dealing with the issue confronting *average* families, but it may seem to some a glorification of the power of research findings. Many parents, practitioners, and public officials may believe that it will take a lot more than accurately "describing the negative consequences of poor child care" to cause Congress people and their constituents to overcome centuries upon centuries of convictions and assumptions about correct roles and duties for women, and about what those with money "deserve" and those without money "don't deserve." It's likely to take more than research to cause Congress and its constituents to become willing to alter all these years of negligence or strenuous resistance regarding the matter of budgeting on a nationwide basis for

1. paid parent assurance leave with job security;

2. comprehensive, intensive, extensive services and supports of all sorts, including job training and jobs, to families who need them in order to be effective parents, and

3. a full array of high-quality child care programs and providers, including homemaker/health aides, nannies, family day care mothers and center staff trained in developing our young children.

Throughout the centuries, common sense has informed us that TLC is better for babies than war, and when we have research it will document this fact. Yet we have never been able to secure the basics for babies, while in

© The Growth Program

1991 it proved possible in a few skinny minutes to get a billion dollars a day for war. Research will surely help, but personal political activism, voting wisely, and coalition building on the part of everyone who cares, is what's going to get us there—to nationwide child and family supports of all sorts, including child care of good quality, available to parents "for free," just as public school is.

About half of all American mothers of babies younger than a year are currently working outside the home, though some are working part-time. Most *can't* go home again: Two-thirds of the women who are employed are the sole support of their families or are married to men who earn less than $15,000 a year (Wingert & Kantrowitz,

1990). Many babies are cared for by the other parent, a relative, or an in-home sitter. Some are in child care centers. The proportion of infants in center care is growing, probably because more programs are willing to accept babies than were previously (Hofferth & Phillips, 1987). The most common caregiving arrangement for infants continues to be family day care. Most family child care is entirely unregulated. Even licensed or otherwise regulated family day care homes may or may not be good. This is true of day care centers that take infants, too. According to infant day care researcher Carolee Howes, most state regulations for infant care in centers and family day care homes do not meet NAEYC standards for quality [1989].

The more they argue, the less researchers of infant/toddler care seem to disagree. Even Alison Clarke-Stewart, who writes that there is no clear evidence that day care places children at risk, and is known as an endorser of "high quality" care, suggests that parents might consider working part-time when their children are young.

"I'll tell you what I think if you promise to keep me anonymous," says a gifted child developer and child care center director, whose program offers a great array of arrangements and schedules for infants, toddlers and twos as well as for older young children, and a variety of sensitive support services and useful resource and referral assistance, all in an attempt to cus-

Knowing that there are so many inferior infant, toddler, and two-year-old child care situations in this country should make child care professionals strive to bring quality up, struggle for government money to work with—to supplement what we already have—educate the public as to what to look for, and be very cautious in recommending full-time out-of-home care for babies.

Observing that about half of all mothers of babies younger than a year work outside the home also has a flip side: The other half stay with their babies, some for the joy of it, some because they can afford it and believe it's best, and some at great cost because they are convinced that extra care pays off by producing better people. Research has not confirmed that this is true.

tomize the program for the diverse needs of families.

Juanita says,

What we're looking at here is turfism; "If me and my clique of friend-colleagues didn't discover it, it couldn't be true." These late vintage "developmentalist" research people are not (contrary to what some of them seem to believe) the originators of *all knowledge* ever gathered about well-child development — the development of mental health, maturity, ability to cope constructively with adversity, and the kinds of happy childhoods that generate essential happiness throughout life, and *all knowledge* ever gathered about early life traumas and deprivations that have preceded severe problems some people have had in adolescence, adulthood, or midlife crises. There are other fields that specialize in the emotional side of people. They study these things, and have for a much longer time than developmentalist researchers. Psychiatrists, clinical psychologists, psychoanalysts, psychiatric social workers, nursery educators, the few pediatricians with additional training in parent/child psychology — they work *with* children and families. They treat dysfunctional adults. They get an understanding of factors in young lives that consistently cause havoc *later* in life. We know that the greater the number of unfortunate factors there are in the first years of life, the greater is the risk that the person will have troubles later. A great many people know what good mothering is and know that little kids need it and can see when it isn't being provided by caregivers. *And when it is.*

It's good this research is being done, but the way they bicker isn't helpful. The big value of arguing is that you become more and more sure of what you think; although you may not learn much if anything about what the other guy thinks and why. And some of them are so arrogant, they seldom write to *us* and when they do, they lecture us. They don't acknowledge that *we* are the expert developers of children, not *they*. They know only *facts*. We know how to work with children to produce nice people. I read it, but most of the teachers and directors I know blow them off exactly like they blow *us*

off — as know-nothings. Researchers would help those of us *who have* the children if they would start showing us some sincere respect.

For those in the research community who want day care people to take their word seriously, the feelings expressed by this director, feelings common in the field, are problems that need to be addressed.

➡️ **What are the implications for directors of infant/toddler programs and family child care providers of a baby's need for a lot of parent time?**

● We need to encourage families to bring their full-time children as late as is feasible, pick them up as early as is feasible, keep them home with a parent whenever a day or half-day of vacation or sick leave permits, or the sacrifice of half-a-day's pay is possible; and we need to encourage family members to either hang out or *help* out in the program around the edges of the babies' day in care, or during the parents' lunch break. The human variety, extra interpersonal

© The Growth Program

© The Growth Program

interactions, additional conversations, and added opportunities to engage an individual child in an activity especially appropriate for *that* child, are benefits to *all* the children in the child care setting.

Many programs do the opposite. They disapprove of parents who come late, and discourage parents from staying around. If we devote more of our time and attention to understanding and reducing (through reflection, reading, and discussion) tensions between caregivers and parents, perhaps we will be able to do a better job of welcoming family members into our hours with their children.

• We need to encourage parents to use our services part-time, and we need to enroll two children for one slot, at complimentary times (one child in the morning, one in the afternoon), or on alternate days, so we can *afford* to encourage part-timers.

Some child care centers and family child care providers do a super job of permitting parents to select the hours they need, and of fitting part-time children together so as to fully fill all spots. But too many aren't sufficiently responsive to families' scheduling preferences. It's true that complex scheduling adds to directors' work, but if we believe it's much better for babies to be in care only part-time, it may seem worth the extra effort.

• We need to share with parents the short-term and long-term reasons why young children benefit from ample good parenting, share readable, helpful books about very young children

and about strong family life with them, and brainstorm with them what they and their little ones can do together, and how to fit this into the nooks and crannies of busy lives.

How many programs do this?

➡ **What are the implications for policymakers and employers of a baby's need for a lot of parent time?**

In addition to suggestions already made, money should be made available to ensure that child care programs and providers are paid for the miscellaneous hours parents keep full-time children home. This would allow child care providers to give parents rebates on unused prepaid time, which would be an incentive to full-time employed parents to keep children home more. This would also allow child care personnel to encourage the practice, whereas now most of those who get paid by the hour can't afford to.

Leaders in "ordinary" rural, urban, suburban, Native American, African-American, Hispanic, Asian, and all other kinds of communities should arrange caucuses, hearings, and planning sessions—call them what you will—in which infant/toddler/two-year-old services and needs in each local community are considered and compared by parents and all relevant parties; and all the missing pieces are created, **with the younger-than-three-year-olds' need for ample good parenting as the centerpiece of the discussion.** All levels of local educators, social workers, nurses and other health personnel, child care providers

from all categories, all types of mental health professionals, service club representatives, employers, local authorities—all can add concerns, ideas, and resources to this community child care problem-solving effort, with a focus not just on coordinating existing child care services and creating new ones, but on figuring out how to support families in an effort to alleviate problems preventing effective, rewarding, and ample parenting of children under three. Who are the "leaders"? As child caring people, "the leaders are us."

➡ **What are the implications for teacher educators of a baby's need for the participation of her parent in her life in child care?**

Teacher education programs should devote much more time to practicums, problem-solving discussions, and reading about working with parents and the reasons for so many well-known tensions between parents and staff. (See Ellen Galinsky's "Why Are Some Parent/Teacher Partnerships Clouded With Difficulties?," July 1990, and "Parents and Teacher-Caregivers: Sources of Tension, Sources of Support," March 1988, for a thorough and sensitive discussion of this.)

There are major questions that have not yet been researched in addition to those already discussed. One of them is the question of "relentless" out-of-home, non-kin-care infancy through age eight versus this sort of care "intermittently." For example, is there any

---

Childcarers can unite and fight for every baby's right to time with parents. Quality time requires a quantity of time — with relaxed parents who can relate positively to their young children. Many parents who work full-time structure high-quality parenting into their family life. Others need our help. Many child care people creatively incorporate parents into their settings. Others don't welcome them. Are we campaigning for paid parental leave and working with employers to achieve flexible hours and better part-time possibilities?

Where Should Babies Be To Develop Optimally

difference between children who have been in full-time day care (forty/fifty hours a week) *continuously* from infancy through third grade (after school care, or before and after school care totaling — including the school day — forty/fifty hours a week) and children who were in full-time care during some seasons and some years, but were with a parent or other family member, or in their own homes with a caregiver, during other seasons and years? Probably far fewer children experience eight relentless years of full-time day care than experience day care intermittently.

III. *What arrangement is best for the individual child? Is there any particular circumstance that should be considered in selecting a child care setting for an individual infant or toddler?*

Derek is an unappealing two-and-a-half-year-old, or at least so say all the neighbors, relatives, and child care workers who've had contact with him, and there have been quite a few. His father feels this way too. "He's a wimp," Dad says of his wan son. Derek doesn't develop relationships, probably because no one person has ever taken care of him long enough or put enough into it for him to come to care about the adult. He doesn't talk to adults or make eye contact with them. He doesn't play with other children, or really play much at all. He's a sullen loner. Derek doesn't smile. He isn't "cute," and is not dressed in "cute" clothes. His nose always leaks long ropes of green mucus. He insists on pooping in his diapers.

Derek is in a family child care home. This would sound like a good idea except that the provider has two adorable, amiable, affable one-year-olds among her clientele, to whom the whole family and also the provider give most of their attention, admiration, and affection. The day care mother also has a new, very young baby, a heavy time consumer — and two of her own grandchildren, ages four and five. The four-year-old is extremely jealous of her gramma's involvement with the

Outstanding Staff Development Programs

Outstanding three- to four-day staff development programs for infant/toddler caregivers are offered annually by the Far West Laboratory, Bank Street College of Infancy Institute, and Syracuse University. Contact the following addresses and individuals for more information:

Far West Laboratory, The Center for Child and Family Studies, 180 Harbor Drive, Suite 112, Sausalito, CA 94965. *Contact:* Carol Lou Young-Holt, 415-747-0276.

Bank Street College of Infancy Institute, Bank Street College of Education, 610 West 112th Street, New York, NY 10025. *Contact:* Dr. Nancy Balaban or Dr. Virginia Casper, Co-chairpersons, Infancy Institute, 212-222-6700.

Syracuse University Quality Infant/Toddler Caregiving Workshop, College for Human Development, 201 Slocum Hall, Syracuse, NY 13244-1250. *Contact:* Dr. Alice S. Honig, 315-443-2757.

The Child With Poor Creative Coping Skills, Lack of Flexibility or Adaptability

In the child care world, we all have to handle and try to help individual little ones. Most toddlers and two-year-olds find *change* — transitions — difficult, *especially the change from parent to caregiver and vice versa,* but some children are really thrown for a loop by having to stop or leave, and tantrums ensue. Expert educarers and parents find that these are techniques that help.

If you find yourself with a child who has exceptionally poor coping capacity, you'll want a child care person or staff who can help your child by doing these things:

1. Keep it simple and predictable. Have routines. Have a routine song, chant, or some other cue to signify change.

2. Prepare the child. Give her a few minutes to get used to the new idea, the next event. This is time to shift gears.

3. Verbally walk the child through what will come next: "First we'll put these toys away. Next we'll go in the bathroom and wash our hands all bubbly and sudsy and clean. Then we'll have our yummy lunch." This is rehearsing.

4. If something out of the ordinary is going to happen, briefly explain, briefly state expectations, briefly identify the child's feelings, and briefly reassure the child that (whoever) will be with her. "We're going to the park. Tanya and (adult) are going to a new park with all the children. Tanya will slide on the slide. I know it's hard for you to go to new places, so I'll help you, (adult) will hold Tanya's hand."

5. For older two's who are still having trouble transitioning, add a preschool toy clock with moveable hands to all of the above suggestions. Point both hands at twelve. Say, "In two minutes, when this pointer is *here* (point to the two), we are going to . . . ." Move the hand in a few minutes and then show it to the child. The more the adult can remove himself from this procedure, the better it will work.

babies and takes her feelings out on Derek because he's irritatingly whiney, doesn't defend himself, and is not protected by the caregiver, who despises "tattletales."

Derek's day consists predominantly of being ignored, with occasional reprimands for soiling himself, "telling on" the bullying four-year-old, or "acting stupid." It would seem that Derek, of all children, needs a setting in which he's the youngest and "cutest," or the only child, who can be doted upon and emotionally nourished 'til he blooms, or to be in the hands of an unusually loving educarer in a family day care or center who can help him relate to other children and herself.

Colleen is almost three years old and already has three younger sisters. Her parents, probably wisely, think it important for her to be in a group of same-age children where she doesn't have to deal with any babies at all.

Gary is the gregarious twenty-six-month-old son of a two-mother couple. His parents agree that he needs men in his life. They searched until they found a center with an excellent male head teacher, then begged until they won a place in that particular teacher's group. (Before he turned two, Gary's mothers and several other families jointly hired a young man to take care of all three boy babies four hours a day, five days a week. Gary's parents both say that neither caregiver is remarkably good, but that both are good enough; their male caregiving style outweighs other variables, say all participating parents.) One mother states her belief that

You can never find everything you want in one child care setting. You have to base your choice on what's *most* important for *this* individual child.

Lin's mother died when he was eleven months old. The family feels that it's more important for him to be taken care of by one mother-like caregiver throughout his early years than to be in a stimulating setting. Their choices were the day care center in their town or a neighbor who cares for a small number of children and continues to take care of them before and after school once they get to kindergarten.

Rosaria is moderately mentally retarded and looks quite odd. She is also sometimes spastic. Many children and parents react to the leering and twitching of this 18-month-old girl with fear, thus they shun her. Rosaria's grandmother, who is her guardian, believes that the most important thing for Rosaria is that she be accepted by a loving caregiver who can allay the anxieties of others, and help them *help* this little girl. The grandmother likes one of the day care programs in her town best because the teacher used to work in Head Start, where she received special training in working with families and children with disabilities.

Janice tells us "My sisters and I have been extremely fortunate in finding a good day care center for our niece, Nancy. Her mother—our oldest sister—is really weird. She lives in cars, is always roaming from city to city on buses, and has no job. She doesn't provide any sort of suitable life for Nancy. She really neglects her horribly, leaves

---

The Wild Child

Some children are born with temperaments that cause them to be extremely active, restless, excitable, and tempest-tossed. Some children are made "nervous," fidgety, and "hyper" by stresses in their lives that produce in them a great deal of anxiety. Some children's tendency toward wildness is caused by a combination of *both* of the above. Whatever the cause, the expert parent or educarer understands that *prevention* and *early intervention* are the principles to go by. If you find yourself with a wild child, you'll want a child care person or staff who can help your child by doing these essential things:

1. Know the child. Think ahead—what's likely to be too much? How much will in all probability be enough? Manage the child's environment and experiences so that he isn't overstimulated or over-curtailed. (The very active child needs lots of opportunity for big muscle activity, ample outdoor time, and an outing a day; too much of the four walls will make him climb them.) Knowing that too much stimulation or too much boredom will rev this kid up past anyone's capacity to cope is *prevention*.

2. Watch the child. Spot warning signals that the child's behavior sends. Step in before the child's excitement level has escalated far beyond the limited self-controls any toddler or two-year-old can possibly have. Invite and distract the child into a calmer activity—a book to look at on a lap in a quiet corner, solo water play (usually a sure-fire soother), or a favorite tape to listen to. *This is early intervention.*

3. Stay calm. Stay neutral. Don't view the child as defiant. Don't get into a power struggle. Don't take the behavior personally. Adults who get emotional and yell and act like two-year-olds themselves aren't helpful as role models or as calming influences. A calm response defuses the situation, or at least avoids igniting it.

4. Give the child words for all this. Eventually simply using the words will help the child: "You're getting too excited (revved up, wild, out-of-control). It's time to stop this play and . . ." (Name a calm activity.) Be sure that you and the child both understand that you're *helping* him learn to manage his behavior (develop self-discipline): "I'm going to help you settle down. We're going to . . ." (State the calming activity you are going, together, to engage in.)

Most child care programs are one-size-fits-all style. That is never *high* quality.

her in cars, no health care, doesn't give her anything of her own to keep, like toys or books, but she loves her. But the authorities won't do anything.

"So me and my other two sisters convinced her to let us take turns taking care of Nancy. We all live in the same town. She's been staying with each of the three of us for a month each all year. We make a game of it so she'll feel loved: 'Who gets Nancy? Everybody wants Nancy! We have to share you, Nancy, we all want a turn with you.'"

"She probably doesn't understand the words, she's only 13 months old, but she understands that we want her, I know that. The great thing is this great day care center she goes to everyday, no matter which of us sisters she's with. They're great, they give her lots of TLC. They realize her need for a space of her own, and possessions. They have a special little area in the hallway for her 'to nest in,' the teacher says, and where she's allowed to keep lots of stuff."

© The Growth Program

One of our favorite family child care providers says:

There are only two things a person has to know about young children to be a great educarer:

1) the ages and stages and many, many ways in which all children of any one age are all alike, and

2) the necessity of getting to know and notice each child individually so you are able to respond to the many, many ways in which each child is unique.

Most child care programs are one-size-fits-all style. That is never *high* quality.

© 1991 Shia Photo

© 1991 Shia Photo

Every baby is different. What's good for one may not be best for the next. Insightful parents with choice take what seems best for the individual infant, toddler, or two into consideration, as well as other factors. Shouldn't every baby's needs be considered? Shouldn't every parent have choice?

What's the Best Thing To Tell a Parent-Abandoned Child (or a child who feels abandoned by a parent due to divorce or military service)?

Some toddlers and two-year-olds, who have been taken care of by their mothers or fathers, have been abandoned by this parent (due to parental immaturity, emotional instability, substance addiction, imprisonment, divorce, military service, or for reasons other than death. Sad to say, desertion — temporary or permanent or in the child's eyes — is not an unheard-of circumstance. In such instances, we need to make the child feel safe, build positive self-esteem, keep alive the possibility of the parent's return to a primary caregiving role, yet make no promises about what the future will bring.

1. Reassure the child from time to time, as frequently as seems appropriate, that a grown-up will always take care of her. Name yourself, other reliable caregivers, and regular friends and acquaintances in a rhythmic chant: "Emily takes care of little Linda, Mrs. Johnson (a neighbor) takes care of little Linda, Suzie (an older child) takes care of little Linda (etc.); everybody takes care of little Linda." Rocking the child on one's lap while sing-songing this message is very soothing.

2. Comment *casually* — and only occasionally — that the parent has some problems to straighten out, but loves the child. Exactly what the problems are need not be discussed. Every effort should be made to sound calm and to prevent the child from overhearing adult discussion about the situation, because it would certainly be misunderstood and anxiety-producing.

   Part of building the young child's self-esteem is to explicitly state that the child is a good child, and that *the parent's problems* are the cause of his or her disappearance from a caregiving role. A child whose parent is away in the military needs the same comforts as does a child whose parent has vanished from a caregiving role for any other reason. Infants, toddlers, and two-year-olds should be shielded from cruel realities as much as possible. Maybe the best thing to say is that the absent parent is away on a trip.

   Extra care should be taken to compliment this child, who probably feels unworthy of the parent's love (or, in her mind, why would she have been abandoned?), for every good feature and behavior, for every small competence or success. Ensuring that the child is surrounded by affection and appreciation will help mitigate the damage to her confidence and feeling of being a good person which an abandoned child always feels.

3. Don't burn bridges between the child and the parent. The parent may grow up, benefit from psychiatric treatment, be restored to herself/himself in a drug treatment program, be released from prison and return, become a participating parent once the fur stops flying from the divorce or when the child is older, or return from military service. Without saying anything untrue about how terrific the missing parent is if it isn't true, we can still avoid accusing the parent, or painting her as a monster, which we tend to do if a parent has gone off and left a child; of course *this* doesn't apply if a parent is in the service.

   Toddlers and two-year-olds can recognize photographs of their parents. Showing a photo and talking briefly about the parent in normal tones helps prevent the subject — and the child's confused feelings — from becoming a taboo topic.

4. Avoid promising that the parent will come back. The child must be able to trust his other adults, at least, and you don't really know if the parent will return. "She will if she can," and "A grown-up will always take good care of you," are helpful responses if the question comes up.

The more strengths we can build in the seriously harmed child, the better are his chances for suffering minimal permanent damage to his sense of self-worth, to his self-esteem.

The Frequent Weeper

Frequent, prolonged crying is a sign that something is wrong. It's an indication that the baby or little child's needs are not being met. The baby may be saying that she is being physically or sexually abused at home, or that a divorce is imminent. Her need to feel serene is not being met. The toddler may be telling us that his home lacks any semblance of predictability, routine, and rules because of adult drug or alcohol use, or because of parental mental unwellness. His need to feel secure is not being met. The two-year-old may be wailing dismay day after day as a way of reminding us that she is miserable from an as yet unrecognized chronic illness. Staff should pool experiences they are having with the frequent weeper. The caregiver or director should confer collegially with the baby's parents or guardian to compare notes and thoughts, and if necessary, advice from a skilled child psychologist or child psychiatrist should be sought so everyone involved can learn how to help this unhappy child. If a physical problem is suspected, a pediatrician should be consulted.

But the crying is not the problem, it's a *symptom* of the problem. In fact, the crying is a partial *solution;* there is medical evidence that tears release both tensions and toxins from the body. Because frequent weeping or shrieking and sobbing tends to be disturbing to other little children and is almost guaranteed to distress and annoy adults, the loudly crying child may have to be removed from the room. However, the caregiver's focus should be on comforting the baby and getting to the root of the problem, not on silencing the child.

There's a world of difference between a child who cries intensely but briefly after a physically, emotionally or socially painful experience, and a child whose constant tears of rage, anxiety, frustration, or grief are dramatic S.O.S. signals. We adults need to overcome our aversion to crying children and to allow them — even boys, which is much harder for most of us! — to cry it out. If something fundamental seems wrong, checking it out is more helpful than just trying to stop the sobs and dry the tears.

IV. *Usually, babies are part of families: What's best for the whole family?*

Where babies from neither optimal nor pathological families, but average families should be, at home with mothers, relatives or sitters, or in out-of-home child care settings, is a subject of great national debate. It will doubtless be one for decades, because, as we've been talking about above, it involves much more than what's best for baby. What we think is best for baby is in and of itself a mixture of fact and value-laden beliefs whose mysteries have neither been fully researched — because curiously, after 400 years of scientific research and well over 100 years of psychology, the "scientific" community has only recently become interested in what's best for babies — nor have these issues been resolved in other ways. They *can't* be for a generation or more 'til some long-term research and results are in.

There are also questions to consider such as women's and men's preferences, not just about who will take care of baby, but also about roles of women and men in society. Included are questions of gender equity in making the kinds of economic decisions that affect who "wants" to take care of the baby. The following considerations affect these decisions.

What does the mother want to do? What does the dad want to do? How does society promote or prevent their preferences?

Will most of the mother's wages or salary be paid if she stays home for six months, a year, two, three, or four years by taxpayer-funded full or three-quarter salary parent assurance leave? This significantly influences where many mothers of infants have to be, or feel they have to be. What if the father wants to be the primary stay-at-home parent?

Will the mother be seriously set back in her job or career by having chosen to stay home? "During the three weeks I was out, they promoted someone else who was exactly equal to me. What would've happened if I'd been out for a year?" "They didn't hold my job. I lost it, and also the pension plan I was

The needs of the whole family must be taken into account. To a large extent, except in unusual instances, what's least stressful and feels happily best for the overall family is best for baby, too.

vested in. When the baby was a year old, I started work at a different place. I had to wait another two years to get back in a pension plan." This kind of thing significantly influences where many mothers of infants have to be, or feel they have to be. The same is true for fathers:

I decided to stay home to take care of Danny 'til he was 18 months. I thought this was what modern dads were doing. But there I was, alone on the park bench for a year-and-a-half. I'm glad I did it. But people thought there was probably something wrong with me—a drinking problem or something. I had to start at a different job and a lower level. It definitely hurt my career. But it was worth it.

Will there be adequate, even *excellent* child care programs, even *options, conveniently* available to the mother—or the father if roles are reversed—if she elects to return to work part-time or full-time after six months, a year, two, three, or four years?

Will all these child care programs be affordable to her, regardless of her income? The average income for American women who are employed full-time is:

high school or less $15,806
some college $19,369
bachelor's degree $26,066

(See "Who Cares? Child Care Teachers and the Quality of Care in America" by Whitebook, Howes, Phillips, and Pemberton, in *Young Children,* November 1989, pp. 41–45 for more information.) If she doesn't have a husband, or former husband, who is earning a steady and sufficient income—many fathers are unemployed, or are only seasonally or episodically employed, or are employed full-time but only earn minimum wage ($7,300 per year)—and who is contributing enough of it to the household—some husbands earn but drink it up, gamble it away, etc.—

or if she is divorced and her former husband fails to make regular payments, this is all she has to live on, unless her family is helping her financially, a luxury not available to most single mothers. (According to the Organization for the Enforcement of Child Support in Reistertown, Maryland, only 25% of court-ordered child support is paid "as ordered.")

The Bureau of Labor Statistics says that 15 million of 63 million children, almost 1 out of 4, live in single-parent households:

● 42% of these 15 million children have parents who are divorced,

● 27% of the children have parents who never married, and

● 7% are the children of widows.

The Bureau of the Census has estimated that more than 50% of all children will spend at least some time in single-parent households. Almost 89% of the children in single-parent households live with their mothers, and about 11% with their fathers. Single-parent households headed by women are more likely to be poor than are other households with children. Nearly half of all households in poverty are headed by women. About 20% of children younger than three live with their mothers only.

The cost of high-quality infant/toddler care in many parts of the coun-

try is $6,000 a year. Can a woman living on $25,000 a year afford $6,000 a year for child care? Can a woman living on $15,000 a year afford $6,000 a year for child care? This is 40% of her income! And these are salary *averages;* many women earn much less than $15,000 a year. If these mothers get good care for their infants and toddlers, it's because they lucked into it. And the matter of women's low wages won't change significantly soon; look at this:

The National Commission on Working Women of Wider Opportunities for Women tells us that nearly 90% of jobs created between now and the year 2000 will be in the service sector.

● The low-wage, sex-segregated "pink collar ghetto" in which the majority of women work will be reinforced by the shift to a service sector economy.

● Five of the 11 occupations projected to create the largest number of new jobs over the next decade are now female-dominated occupations, with median weekly wages below poverty level (see table on p. 64).

And if the child care field expands, we will very likely have yet *another* growing, female-dominated occupation with median wages below poverty level; they are *now:* Child care workers' median weekly wages are $187.

All these factors strongly influence what mothers and fathers want to do. There are other factors. Is this a very young couple, eager to prove that both members are grown-ups who can hold jobs and earn? Sometimes to the young, the moment looks like forever: "As an adult, I want to work and earn," which means *right now*—there is no tomorrow. Is this a woman who has had a high-riding career for 15 years and will be nervously chomping at the

To be in their children's happy memories tomorrow, parents must be much in their children's lives today. Many parents are, even if they are both employed during their baby's first year.

A large part of attachment seems to be an instinctual tendency seen in primates and many other kinds of animals to keep vulnerable babies from becoming lost, thus dying. One hundred percent mother/baby proximity is not needed to ensure sound attachment.

bit if she spends 6 to 18 months at home part-time?

How much social pressure is a particular couple experiencing (or, conversely, how much freedom are they feeling) regarding adherence to rigid stereotypic descriptions of father's role and mother's role?

Whatever parents decide to do about all this, they should know that their values and characters are showing, and who they are is all but guaranteed to be the major influence among all the many influences that will determine what kind of people their children will grow up to be. Hence, a parent of good solid character and sound values as traditionally judged, if in good mental health, is very likely to turn out a similar sort of child/person.

Occupation	Number of jobs to be created 1986–2000	1987 % Female	1987 Median weekly female wages
Retail Sales	1,200,000	68.5	$192
Waitress	752,000	85.1	$178
Cashier	575,000	83.0	$183
Food Worker	449,000	78.5	$149
Nursing Aide	443,000	90.4	$212

Note: 1987 poverty-level income for a family of 4 was $11,611 or approximately $223 per week.

© 1991 Robert Maust

Are there other people in the family? What do they need?

There may be time in each week for two parents who have only one baby, and whose main interest when not at work is appropriate relationship with that baby, to give her what babies need for optimal development. But what if the parents are significantly involved with several *other* children, as well? Or frail and ailing elders? There are so many questions to ponder in relation to the simple (ha!) question you asked (?*@?) pages ago!

The matter of attachment has been of great concern to infant day care specialists. Will healthy bonds form between babies and parents?

Concluding thoughts

Young children—children and teens of *all* ages—need affectionate, supportive parent-child relationships. They need to be able to gain and store strength from their families. They need to learn how to relate well through witnessing and feeling positive relationships between members of their families. It helps if strong kinship networks exist with the extended family. For optimal development, children need opportunities to cooperate and be part of the work of operating a family. (Even two-year-olds can help with many kinds of chores.) Children need to be appreciated and enjoyed and to experience reasonable, democratic discipline. Children need to know that their parents believe in Good—which may be God, or some other way of conceptualizing the complicated and lonely

Even minimally adequate parents spend much more time with their young ones than do child care personnel, and many child care workers are good with babies, so physical separation for a number of hours a day would not seem likely to endanger attachment.

lifelong struggle to be our best ethical selves. Children need to know that their parents believe in effort, education, and other culturally acclaimed ideas; alienated parents generate alienated teenagers/adults.

To summarize our reflections on your question, let's get back to it, and add two final thoughts. **You ask if you should work away from home or not when the baby you expect is very young. Probably that's a less important question than these:**

1. How dedicated and creative can you be in ensuring that your young one gets a great deal of calm, content family life and firm, focused guidance in how to live "right" throughout infancy and on and on through adolescence and even into early adulthood, whether you work or not? Can you get up early enough to have a fat, relaxed chunk of time with your child before leaving in the morning? What else? It's unfortunate that there is such tension and condemnation between stay-at-home and work-away mothers. Many work-away mothers are part of strong families and make major contributions to creating great childhoods for their children. Conversely, we all know some stay-at-home mothers who don't provide optimal mothering. **To work or not to work may not be the key question.**

2. What is the quality of the human relationships you will have with the caregivers, and your baby will have in your absence? Child care programs that make mothers feel too left out

---

> ### How Soon Is It Realistically Likely That We Will Have "Good Enough" (Never Mind Optimal) Infant/ Toddler All-Day Care Available to Mothers of All Income Groups (Publically Funded As Needed)?
>
> #### Bettye Caldwell writes:
>
> As you know, I am a maverick on this issue. I know there is "a lot of bad care out there," as people love to assert, but I also know that there is a lot of good care out there. When I started in this field a quarter of a century ago, not a single state licensed center-based infant day care. That didn't mean that it didn't exist. It simply meant that no one paid any attention to it, monitored it, tried to provide training for those offering it. Now all states license it, monitor it in some way. And, though we don't have national standards, there is a healthy competitiveness among states to "match" one another in presumed quality indicators (try to improve ratios, frequency of inspection, etc.). I guess that what I am saying here is that infant care, as now represented in state licensing regulations, is OK for babies—provided there is fidelity between the regulations and what occurs in actual practice. (Personal communication, 1990)

What conditions of care promote sensitive, responsive best-friendship and deep love between parent(s) and child? Basic biological attachment, while essential, is not enough if strong, lifelong parent-child connections are the goal, but "to work or not to work" is not the central issue.

Where Should Babies Be To Develop Optimally

often lose their customers. Those forced by lack of choice to stay may take their resentment out on the child. Toddlers and twos are amazingly sensitive and responsive to the moods of parents and other caregivers. **If parents and caregivers are pleased with their lives, the child will probably be reasonably content too.**

References

Abbott, E. (1910). *Women in industry*. New York: D. Appleton.

Apple, M. (1982). *Cultural and economic reproduction in education: Essays on class, ideology, and the state*. London: Routledge and Kegan Paul.

Belsky, J. (1988). The "effects" of infant day care reconsidered. *Early Childhood Research Quarterly, 3*(3), 265–266.

Bernstein, B. (1971). *Class, codes and control, Vol. 1. Theoretical studies toward a sociology of language*. London: Routledge and Kegan Paul.

Bourdieu, P., & Passeron, J. (1977). *Reproduction in education, society, and culture*. Beverly Hills, CA: Sage.

Bowles, S. (1971). Unequal education and the reproduction of the social division of labor. *Review of Radical Political Economics, 3*.

Bowles, S., & Gintis, H, (1972). I.Q. in the U.S. class structure. *Social Policy, 3*, 65–69.

Bowles, S., & Gintis, H. (1976). *Schooling in capitalist America*. London: Routledge and Kegan Paul.

Brazelton, T. B. (1984). Cementing family relationships through child care. In L. Dittmann (Ed.), *The infants we care for* (rev. ed.) (pp. 9–20). Washington, DC: NAEYC.

Brooks, A. A. (1989). *Children of fast track parents: Raising self-sufficient and confident children in an achievement-oriented world*. New York: Viking.

Caldwell, B. (1990). Personal communication with author.

Chow, E., & Berheide, C. (1988). The interdependence of family and work: A framework for family life education, policy, and practices. *Family Relations, 37*, 23–28.

Collins, R. (1971). Functional conflict theories of educational stratification.

American Sociological Review, 36, 1002–1019.

Cott, N. (1977). *The bonds of womanhood*. New Haven, CT: Yale University Press.

Diamond, I. (Ed.). (1983). *Families, politics, and public policy*. New York: Longman.

Elkind, David. (1981). *The hurried child. Growing up too fast too soon*. Reading, MA: Addison-Wesley.

Elman, M., & Gilbert, L. (1984). Coping strategies for role conflict in professional women with children. *Family Relations, 33*, 317–327.

Galinsky, E. (1988). Parents and teacher-caregivers: Sources of tension, sources of support. *Young Children, 43*(3), 4–12.

Galinsky, E. (1990). Why are some parent/teacher partnerships clouded with difficulties? *Young Children, 45*(5), 2–3, 38–39.

General Mills, Inc. (1981). *General Mills American family report 1980–81; Families at work: Strengths and strains*. Minneapolis, MN: Author.

Gilligan, C. (1982). *In a different voice: Psychological theory and women's development*. Cambridge, MA: Harvard University Press.

Giroux, H. (1981). *Ideology, culture and the process of schooling*. Philadelphia, PA: Temple University Press.

Greenberg, P. (1969/1990). *The devil has slippery shoes: A biased biography of the Child Development Group of Mississippi—A story of maximum feasible participation of poor parents*. Washington, DC: Youth Policy Institute.

Guarendi, R. (1990). *Back to the family: How to encourage traditional values in complicated times*. New York: Villard.

Hofferth, S., & Phillips, D. A. (1987). Child care in the United States, 1970 to 1985. *Journal of Marriage and Family, 49*, 559–571.

Honig, A. S. (1990). Personal communication with author.

Horvath, F. (November, 1986). Work at home: New findings from the current population survey. *Monthly Labor Review*, 31–35.

Howes, C. (1989). Research in review: Infant child care. *Young Children 44*(6), 24–28.

Kagan, S. L., Powell, D. R., Weissbourd, B., & Zigler, E. (Eds.). (1987). *America's family support programs: Perspectives and prospects*. New Haven, CT: Yale University Press.

Kahn-Hut, R., Kaplan-Daniels, A., & Colvard, R. (Eds.). (1982). *Women and work*. New York: Oxford University Press.

Kamerman, S. (1980). *Parenting in an unresponsive society*. New York: Free Press.

Kamerman, S., & Hayes, C. (Eds.). (1982). *Families that work: Children in a changing world*. Washington, DC: National Academy Press.

Kanter, R. (1977). *Work and family life in the United States: A critical review and agenda for research and policy*. New York: Russell Sage Foundation.

Kessler-Harris, A. (1981). *Women have always worked*. Old Westbury, NY: Feminist Press.

Kohn, M. (1969). *Class and conformity: A study in values*. Homewood: Dorsey Press.

Kraehmer, S. T. (1990). *Time well spent: A father's advice for establishing a lifetime of closeness with your child*. New York: Prentice Hall.

Lein, L. (1974). *Final report: Work and family life*. National Institute of Education Project No. 3–3094. Cambridge: Center for the Study of Public Policy.

Miller, D. F. (1989). *First steps toward cultural difference: Socialization in infant/toddler day care*. Washington, DC: Child Welfare League of America.

National Commission on Working Women of Wider Opportunities for Women. (1989). *Women, work and the future*.

Pawl, J. (February, 1990). Infants in day care: reflections on experiences, expectations, and relationships—*Zero to three, 10*(3), 1–6. Arlington, VA: National Center for Clinical Infant Programs.

Phillips, D. (Ed.). (1987). *Quality in child care: What does research tell us?* Washington, DC: NAEYC.

Pleck, J., & Lang, L. (1978). *Men's family role: It's nature and consequences*. Wellesley, MA: Wellesley College Center for Research on Women.

Presser, H. (1988). Shift work and child care among dual earner American parents. *Journal of Marriage and the Family, 50*, 133–148.

Schorr, L. B., & Schorr, D. (1988). *Within our reach: Breaking the cycle of disadvantage*. New York: Doubleday.

Whitebook, M., Howes, C., Phillips, D., & Pemberton, C. (1989). Who cares? Child care teachers and the quality of care in America. *Young Children, 45*(1), 41–45.

Willis, P. (1981). *Learning to labor: How working class kids get working class jobs*. New York: Columbia University Press.

CHAPTER

4

What Is Curriculum for Infants and Toddlers in Family Day Care (or Elsewhere)? What Is the Goal?

QUESTION: I am a family day care provider. I keep infants and toddlers, too. I am not quite sure of myself. I like babies and little kids very much. I read about curriculum for infants. How much of all this do they need? I cannot do it all. What is most important?

True "curriculum for infants" is everything they experience indoors, outdoors, and in the community during their time with you. What the infants in your care really need is what children of this age at home with a parent or grandparent need. They need to develop self, pride in self (positive self-esteem), independent self, self-discipline. . . . They need to develop mental health. **A good "curriculum" for infants and toddlers is one that helps them become good people—people of good character.**

Notice needs and respond

Babies and young children thrive when people who enjoy them notice their needs, their attempts to express themselves, and the new things they proudly do. *They* tell us what's most important. It's so simple it's hard to believe, but merely carefully observing

Bryan E. Robinson

The "curriculum" an infant needs most is one loving primary caregiver, and other secondary caregivers who are also relaxed and pleased to give care.

an infant and responding sensibly is a great start. Is she lying there intently studying something? Then don't bother her. What are you teaching? Independence and industriousness. We are forever interrupting busy babies and then saying they're fussy or ornery or have short attention spans.

Friendly guidance promotes self-esteem.

Does this child seem sad? Imagine that you were sad. What might make you happy? A long, quiet snuggle, or gentle rock, or a back rub and a soothing hum from a loving adult? Something cheerful, playful, and fun? Or just a change of scene and something different to do? If we think of infants and toddlers as people and friends, it isn't so hard to notice what they seem to need or want and to help meet their needs and, within reason, satisfy their wants. We try to satisfy the needs and wants of close friends and we don't worry a bit about "spoiling" them. What are you teaching? Human kindness, respect for others, trust.

Prevent discipline problems by observing and responding (in time!)

A key to caring is realizing that each little cutie is a real person and must be responded to respectfully.

Observing and responding to the needs and wishes of creepers and toddlers often helps prevent "discipline" problems. It's the stitch in time concept. If a very young child is moving eagerly toward the exciting toy another is holding, how about anticipating the trouble-making snatch that will surely follow, and step in to offer an equally exciting toy? A game of patty cake or peekaboo can be the perfect prevention when baby is about to pull all the books off the shelf and it's almost time to go. Distraction. A wonderful invention! It is most useful when ap-plied by an adult who is observing the situation carefully, and who is *responding* appropriately. You're guiding the baby into good behavior without even mentioning it. (Waiting for "bad" behavior, and then punishing it with scolding or smacking, only produces angry children who are very likely to get back at their grown-ups later through defiant or whiny activity, or tense hitting and striking out at others.)

But here is a word of caution about the use of distraction, a suggestion from infant/toddler specialist and author Janet Gonzalez-Mena, "We must be careful not to use distraction to cut a child off from his feelings — sad feelings, angry feelings — until he has *experienced* them and we have acknowledged them."

Observing boredom and responding, by going outside to play, changing the scene, expanding the horizon, is something that skilled caregivers are good at. A flexible indoor/outdoor schedule that follows the childrens' leads and needs enhances the quality of child care. How about gazing together at the clouds, feeling the breeze on your cheeks and baby on his, giving baby a chance to crawl in the grass?

Novelty refreshes the spirits, and the great outdoors, be it beach or desert, snow or sidewalk, is full of novelties for eager young learners. Bugs, weeds, squirrels, ice, all of it is wonderful! Toddlers become alert to the environment outdoors in a way not possible inside where most things are predictable.

Notice and appreciate growth

Look and listen. So very often you'll observe that the young one in your care has learned to do something new again! Like us, infants, crawlers, toddlers, and children of all ages strive to feel competent. They try to do things. They struggle to succeed. They need and appreciate encouragement. You might say that part of the "curriculum" is built right into their bodies — learning to prop up on the arms and to hold up the head, learning to roll over, to sit, to rock the baby swing, to stand holding on, to walk holding on with two hands — with one, to walk without holding on at all (!), to run, to climb up onto and down off . . .

What are you teaching? All of this is part of your "physical education curriculum." Adults only need to provide safe space, time, permission, and expression of approval. The real reward for baby is achieving, but our approval is a nice bonus. At least it shows that we share the child's pleasure and are "on her side." Have you ever noticed how far afield a secure toddler will wander in your play yard, or in the park? The child is achieving independence and risk-taking where there's really no risk at all.

Let the little one lead; fit into the activity as a follower.

Physical fitness for infants

If you have time, you can play physical fitness games with babies **for a minute or two once or twice a day.** Move the arms gently in a rhythmic pattern. Make the legs "ride a bike." Firmly holding baby under the arms, boost her slightly above your face so she can laughingly look down at you. Hold the baby under the arms in a standing position on your lap and dance him briefly up and down. Encourage sluggish babies, but don't force them. For example, motivate the sedentary crawler by holding an attractive toy inches in front of him and see if he will creep to get it. Don't tease, though, if the baby appears to be frustrated. It seems pompous to call this "curriculum." These are the things most mothers have done for centuries. But it is part of what people trained as infant workers are shown how to do because all these activities in gentle moderation are good for babies. **Babies who are given enough freedom will do their own "physical fitness exercises"; these are the best kind.**

Toddlers are *very* physical and usually very sociable!

Toddlers are extremely physical people. They will happily, busily, play near each other, extremely pleased to have each other's company. Occasionally they will enthusiastically interact, working together on an activity of mutual interest. Sometimes they talk to each other. Often, they show great concern for one another—the need for a bottle that a friend is indicating, the need to be comforted after a fall. Of course, toddlers are individuals; a small percent are extremely shy, and are not a bit boisterous. All have personal preferences, but most like simple puzzles; cooking; feeding, bathing, and bedding dolls, and helping an adult dress and undress them; prolonged water play and play with dough or soft clay; and looking at appropriate books. However, after each round of quiet play alone or with a few playmates, toddlers get restless. They need action! A simple, safe indoor climbing structure will get lots of use. A hiding place to enter and exit (dozens of times in a row) will be popular. Toddlers enjoy jumping and engaging in lopsided, heffalump-style free-form dancing (to lively music). They love circle games such as "Ring Around the Rosy," clapping games, body parts games, and joining lustily in choruses of such songs as "Happy Birthday," "The Wheels on the Bus," and "Old MacDonald's Farm." Daily singing and dancing can add emotional sunlight to your program.

Toddlers look forward to vigorous outdoor play, a trip to the nearby park, or an outing such as a brief visit to the supermarket. The importance to the child's development (and to the family child care mother's sanity!) of spending lots of time outside—and outside of the program's four walls—cannot be overestimated. Young children need opportunities to explore the neighborhood and "the great outdoors" even if it doesn't seem so great to grownups. Alternating quiet play with active play is a must with this age group, and it *must* be the toddler who decides which it will be.

Curiosity equals motivation

Curiosity, too, is built into young children. Because babies and toddlers have a powerful, natural urge to look at it, grasp it, taste it, put it in and out, drop it and watch you pick it up, see it disappear and return, disappear and return, disappear and return (do they ever tire of this game?), all that we have to do is provide safe, simple household objects or toys, permission, some participation in their activities, and enthusiastic appreciation. Sometimes, the adult or older child just joins in. We let the little one lead; we fit into the activity as followers. At other times, we take the lead and initiate a small activity of the sort mentioned here, an activity that we know the child likes. We generally do this only when the baby is bored or needs distraction.

Pick-it-up games for practice

If you have time, you can play "pick-it-up" games with infants and toddlers. What appealing objects do you have around that babies can grasp, learn to put in and out of a container, and so on,

Nancy P. Alexander

Even as they get on their feet, toddlers need to be able to trust the friendly availability of their adults. The "curriculum" includes mastering independence, but it's important to know that "home base" hasn't vanished.

Patiently helping toddlers learn to take turns, to share, and to tell others what they need is teaching the beginnings of self-discipline. Self-discipline is needed in school and is part of strong character.

that are not objects they could choke on? Rattles, ring-stack sets, busy boards, nesting toys, plug-in pegs, or giant-size puzzle pieces, pick-up sticks, Tinkertoys™, twirling tops, push-and-pull toys, getting Mr. Teddy Bear to sit in his toddler-size high chair without sliding through or tipping it over — all are coordination projects that take a great deal of practice to learn. **The tricky part for caregivers is to assist but not to take over.**

Most adults remember all the work that went into learning to roller-skate, ride a two-wheeler, or swim. But do any of us recall the years and years of effort and practice that went into the steps leading to holding a fat kindergarten crayon and scribbling? (Scribbling, by the way, is an extremely important prewriting activity and every toddler should be encouraged to do it — preferably on a large piece of paper, not the wall.)

What kind of curriculum is this? What are you teaching through han-

dling objects together, hiding and "finding" the car keys, and all these "inconsequential" games? Small muscle skills and coordination, object recognition (later a *word* will be learned to go with each object), object permanence (objects and people exist even when you don't see them), and a sense of personal power (I drop it, you pick it up). **Perhaps even more important, the infant is learning human relationship. The two of you are making friends.** The baby is learning that two is a team, that friends are fun, that her choices are endorsed.

"But I keep reading . . ."

When we hear all this talk about *infant stimulation* and *curriculum for infants and toddlers* it's important to remember that the experts only got these ideas by observing what mothers who raise normally bright, functioning, happy children *naturally do*. Researchers do not create childrearing schemes. They observe, record, and disseminate what good parents *already* do. The extremely important contribution that researchers make to children is to identify what successful parents (parents of happy children with the characteristics that promise futures full of hope) *do* and pass it on to parents and caretakers who would like to ensure that they, too, are raising competent, confident, happy children.

"But don't they need these infant stimulation devices?"

No. Toy manufacturers have capitalized on the fact that a handful of highly ambitious people want to push their little children to make *themselves* look like superparents. (You can't blame the manufacturers; they will make what

people will buy.) A certain small segment of parents who have the mistaken impression that to maximize their infant's life they must commercialize it, surround their infants with overstimulation. (Other reasons for pressure-cooking young children were discussed in Chapter 3.) Most parents don't do this; they do what sensible parents have done for generations — provide a lot of *personal attention* and a normal amount of household activity and neighborhood outings while going out on errands or to Grandma's. Fortunately, many of the small percent of infants exposed to it ward off the overstimulation by taking in only as much as they can, and ignoring the rest of it.

Because toddlers are so impressively competent, and often astonish adults with cleverly creative use of language, it's oh so tempting to instruct them — to teach them colors, numbers, and other tricks to make us look like successful childrearers. Toddlers do not benefit from instruction. In fact they don't benefit from being interrupted. Chatting with toddlers about what *they* are initiating and involved in — extending their understanding of how the world works and expanding their language skills — *is enough*.

Sensitive human interaction is essential

The problem is that in understaffed infant/toddler programs, or programs in which adults are not sensitive to the emotional needs of our youngest children, young children do not get a *normal* amount of personal care and mental stimulation. It's urgently important to see that each infant/toddler care setting has an adult-child ratio that permits as extensive a personal involvement as the baby seems to need/want. One reason that many parents prefer family day care for their youngest children is that the small number of children being cared for, and the home-like environment, promote a mood of family-style interactions, which tend to be more intimate and tender than the school-style interactions so unfortunately easy to slip into in school-like environments. Staff training is very important too, because it steers adults in this direction.

> ### *Help Young Children Articulate Their Needs*
>
> Lucy is 19 months old. She is fretting. "What do you need, Lucy?" her teacher asks. "Need cracker," Lucy replies. "We're going to have crackers later," says the teacher. "Lucy will have a cracker later. Does Lucy need a hug?" "Lucy need hug. Lucy need read book." "OK!" the teacher says enthusiastically. "Let's have a hug and a lap and a story."
>
> Helping young children articulate their needs and helping them delay gratification are two aspects of toddler curriculum.

Bettina Bairley

Infants and toddlers benefit from a great deal of play time with a variety of materials and toys. They need ample time to play without adult interference. This is excellent curriculum for an infant/toddler program or any home.

each baby's eyes and to smile at him many times each day.

Here are some other ways you can communicate with even an infant younger than six months:

● Respond to the little uh-uhs, and dada, mama, and other cozy sounds, grunts, and gurgles the baby makes—or start a conversation of these sounds yourself

● Say the same words every time you do the same thing with the young child—when lifting him up, say "up-up-up"; when changing her, say "clean diaper"; when handing her the bottle, say "bottle"; when giving the rattle to the baby, say "rattle"; and so on

● When the baby shows understanding of certain action and object words like these, use whole ideas—whole sentences: "I'll pick Sarah up." "Should I pick Sarah up?" "Sarah wants me to pick her up." "Let's change Sarah's diaper." "Sarah needs a clean diaper." "Where is Sarah's bottle?" "Here's Sarah's bottle." "Sarah holds her rattle."

● Make entertaining noises, clucks with your tongue, the musical noise of tapping a glass full of water with a spoon, the noise of crushing paper, and so forth.

What are you teaching? Friendship, friendliness, that the world is a place that makes people feel good about themselves, and language.

The ability to learn a language is innate in the human species. We don't have to "teach" children to talk. Hearing language, **especially spoken directly to her,** lets the baby know which language to learn (or languages—one at home, and a different one, perhaps, in the child care setting), stimulates the learning, and sets an example of the many specific language conventions used by the socioeconomic group she's

There are also *parents* who are unaware of how important a great deal of personal relationship and *playfulness* with infants and toddlers *are*. Everything child caring people can do to interest these parents in playing and talking more with their very young children is a plus.

It's important to have a small variety of safe, simple, sturdy toys available to crawlers and toddlers. Some of them should be bright in color. It is not necessary, however, to break the bank for baby.

tunes that come into your head. Repeat a pair of rhyming words a few times over. Sit the tiny child on your lap or next to you, and turn the pages of a toddler book or of colorful preschool books, or a bright magazine, talking and listening as you go. For short periods, play tapes or recordings on which people are talking or singing. Play music boxes. Communicate with the children and coworkers around you through conversation and smiles. Chat and smile with your young charges, too. Remember to look into

Relate and communicate

Another very important thing that almost anyone who wants to can do with infants and toddlers is to talk with them. Baby coos and you do too. Sing. Sing whatever kinds of songs you know, or hum the bits and pieces of

When working with infants and toddlers, learn to talk out loud about each and every thing you do and they do. You are modeling language. Listen attentively, too!

What is Curriculum for Infants and Toddlers?

a part of. Children learn to use language as their families do (in restricted or elaborated form). If young children spend a lot of time in the care of others, they will learn some of *these* language forms, too, for better or for worse. (Young children's language development is discussed in Chapter 9.)

Talk with toddlers

Talking with toddlers is wonderfully helpful to them in developing mature language, a sense of respected and individualized *self*-connectedness to the parent or caregiver. A conversation with an 18- to 24-month-old may go like this:

Child (earnestly): Pillow. Lie down. Wipers. Diapers. Baby.

Adult: Yes, your baby put her head on the pillow. Your doll baby lies down very nicely.

Child: Wipers.

Adult: You're wiping her bottom with a wiper?

TV has almost no constructive place in infant/toddler programs. Very few programs are suitable for children younger than three. As background noise, TV can be inappropriately stimulating, thus destructive to the child's concentration, serenity, and self-discipline.

Child (very busy): Wipe butt.

Adult (expanding the child's thinking and creating further opportunity for language development): Are you the pretend mommy?

Child (smiling): Mommy. I [or the child's name] mommy.

Adult (wishing to extend this language development experience as far as comfortably possible): Do you like your baby?

Child: Yike baby. Baby c'ean. Baby diapers.

Adult: You're a good pretend mommy. You have a good baby.

Child: Baby s'eeping. Pillow. Lie down.

Adult: I see your baby is sleeping. Does she need a blanket?

Child: Need blanket. Here you go. Tuck.

Adult: Your baby is sleeping under the blanket.

Child: Un'er. Wake up!

Adult: Oh, I see! Your baby is sitting up!

Child: Sit up! Wake up! Morning.

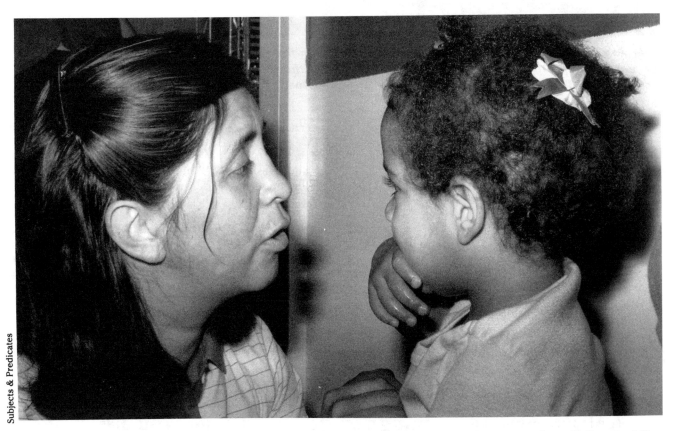

Chatting with each child throughout the day should be considered centrally important in an infant/toddler curriculum if language competence and later school success is sought.

Subjects & Predicates

Adult: Now what will your baby do?

Child: Befisk. Baby eat.

Adult: What will you feed your baby for breakfast?

Child: Cerool. Baby eat. [Child's name] eat cerool.

Adult: May I have some cereal?

Child (laughing): Feed [adult's name]. Feed [own name]. Feed baby.

The adult keeps this casual conversation going until the child loses interest, or until some unavoidable interruption interferes. This type of talk *is* stimulating to a language learner's thinking, but it isn't a gimmick that can be purchased. The valuable commodities in language development are interesting experiences — *something to talk about* — and the *time* of an interested person with whom to converse.

to ease him into sleep? What are you teaching when you let the little child feed herself some of her food and patiently put up with the mess, chatting and listening to her chatter throughout the meal? What are you teaching when you clean the baby's bottom with calm hands, calm voice, and no facial or verbal expressions of disgust? What are you teaching when you allow the toddler to choose between two shirts? Or set an example and demonstrate a great deal of friendly patience while guiding the child toward gradually using the potty rather than the diaper? What are you teaching when you wait for a dawdling toddler to get done "stirvin' in de bucket" (see the picture) and come to lunch?

Help Young Children Work Out Their Special or Social Problems

"Drew! Drew!" shouts 21-month-old Drew, hanging onto the toy doll stroller for dear life. The difficulty is that Marnie has latched onto the stroller and is frantically yanking it in the other direction. The adult says in a firm, friendly voice, "Drew, tell Marnie you're using it. Say, 'Drew is using it. Drew's turn.'" Turning toward Marnie and gently removing her grasp, the teacher says, "Marnie will have a turn with the stroller in a minute. Marnie will have the stroller, yes. *Now* Marnie can push the toy lawn mower."

Marnie will probably need the adult's company to become interested in anything other than what Drew has. Taking whatever time is necessary to help this toddler learn is teaching. Successful daily living is the curriculum.

The very young child who is overstimulated by unusually intrusive adults or by a loud, chaotic environment may cry a lot and be difficult to care for, or may excessively withdraw to tune out. To develop self-discipline, infants and toddlers require a calm human environment and leisurely, suitable routines.

Caretaking activities are curriculum

A critically important part of the "curriculum," of course, is the interactions that occur during caretaking activities such as feeding, burping, washing, diapering, consoling, toilet learning, self-dressing, preparing for naptime, and naptime itself.

What are you teaching when you tenderly hold a baby lengthwise against you, head on your shoulder? When you sit an infant on your lap facing you, talk with her, hold her carefully, and slowly raise and lower her to and from a reclining position? When you gently rub the back of a miserable teether, trying

If optimal opportunity in life is a goal, social behavior is a big part of the educational program

Helping our youngest children learn how to get along with each other cooperatively, yet hold their own, is surely a major educational endeavor. Parents do it with siblings. Family day care and other child care teachers do it with the children in their care. We must take time to understand the situation and to teach turn-taking, playing together in a twosome or larger group, and the ability to delay gratification. Success in school and in life depends upon these social skills. Episodes requiring the caregiver to teach these things are not

interferences to the curriculum; these are a core portion of the curriculum.

To the extent that an adult can guard children and guide them into positive social behaviors with a fairly child-proof set of rooms, a warm and cheerful attitude, clear expectations and explanations, help in understanding their own feelings and those of others, few cross words, and without threats or

---

The goal of "curriculum" for infants and toddlers is to build individual people, inch by inch.

---

hostile comments, or violence such as spanking, the adult is succeeding in providing a very fine infant/toddler curriculum. Infant/toddler curriculum *does* come in a box. But the best and most effective kind comes from the heart.

For further reading

Bos, B. (1983). *Before the basics: Creating conversations with children.* Turn-the-Page Press, Inc., 203 Baldwin Ave., Roseville, CA 95678.

Bredekamp, S. (Ed.). (1987). *Developmentally appropriate practice in early childhood programs serving children from birth through age 8* (expanded ed.). Washington, DC: NAEYC.

Dittmann, L. L. (Ed.). (1984). *The infants we care for* (rev. ed.). Washington, DC: NAEYC.

Family day care handbook. (1987). California Child Care Resource and Referral Network, 809 Lincoln Way, San Francisco, CA 94122.

Garrard, K. R. (1987). Helping young children develop mature speech patterns. *Young Children, 42*(3), 16–21.

Godwin, A., & Schrag, L. (Eds.). (1988). *Setting up for infant care: Guidelines for centers and family day care homes.* Washington, DC: NAEYC.

Gonzalez-Mena, J., & Eyer, D. E. 1989). *Infants, toddlers and caregivers* (2nd ed.). Mayfield Publishing Co., 285 Hamilton Ave., Palo Alto, CA 94301.

Gonzalez-Mena, J. (1986). Toddlers: What to expect. *Young Children, 42*(1), 47–51.

Honig, A. S. (1987). The Erikson approach: Infant-toddler education. In J. Rooparine & J. Johnson (Eds.), *Approaches to early childhood education.* (49–69). Columbus, OH: Merrill.

Honig, A. S. (1990). Infant/toddler education issues: Practices, problems, and promises. In C. Seefeldt (Ed.), *Continuing issues in early childhood education.* Columbus, OH: Merrill.

Honig, A. S., & Lally, J. R. (1981). *Infant caregiving: A design for training.* Syracuse, NY: Syracuse University Press.

Segal, M. (1984). *Birth to one year: Month-by-month descriptions of the baby's development with suggestions for games and activities.* The Newmarket Press, 18 E. 48th St., New York, NY 10017.

Stone, J. G. (1969). *A guide to discipline.* Washington, DC: NAEYC.

Weissbourd, B., & Musick, J. S. (Eds.). (1981). *Infants: Their social environments.* Washington, DC: NAEYC.

CHAPTER 5

How Does Good Character Develop?
Self? Self-Esteem? Self-Discipline?
Do We Have Anything To Do With It?

QUESTION: Many of my friends and I have teenagers. We talk about those that have "good character" and those that don't. They are either weak, completely unable to resist peer pressure, set long-term goals, get good grades, and so on, or we feel they have downright "bad" characters. Where along the way when we were rearing them did they develop character? Or were they born with it? These teenagers have such different personalities! To put it bluntly, they range from rotten to remarkable. Is this entirely due to luck or to parenting?

As a teacher of two-year-olds in a church-sponsored day care center, I sometimes wonder if I have anything to do with shaping these children's future character and their personalities. I would say no, I just look after them during the day, except that I am with them seven and eight hours a day, everyday. I know I can influence their self-esteem. Yet when they enroll they already seem to have positive self-esteem and lots of confidence, or low self-esteem and lack of confidence. As child care teachers, we read so much these days about self-esteem. When I used to be a family child care provider, I was *certain* I had a significant role in shaping those little people. Churches and synagogues provide more child care than any other auspice. We, of all people, are concerned about developing moral children, children of good character. What is *our* role in all this and how does it work?

The Growth Program

What is this little person's fundamental feeling toward the world? I'm inferior? I'm O.K.?

Although parents or guardians have the greatest influence on young children's personality, character, and moral development, as a teacher of two-year-olds, especially all day every day, you *do* have significant influence on the development of their character and personality. As a family child care provider, you did, too, of course. Here's how specialists in the subject believe it works.

From the moment of birth—expulsion or Caesarian removal from the uterus—an infant begins to experience "separateness from other." This ultimately leads to being a separate "self" (individual) and to having a positive or negative opinion of self (a positive or negative self-concept, which is a collage made up of judgments about various aspects of self). However, ideally, for the first three or four months, the infant is still very much and very often merged with the mother's and others' warm, soft bodies: being held snugly in a prone position on a lap and rocked; in a front pack moving rhythmically and comfortingly as the adult moves; in a backpack nestled against the grown-up's big body, bouncing gently around; being carried on a hip, football style, while the parent or other person goes about doing necessary duties; nursing or being cuddled, crooned to, and bottle fed; propped up perpendicularly against the adult's chest, getting a look at the world (if facing outward) or a belly warming or burping an air bubble

Personality, self, and character begin to take shape and take hold right from the start, and we strongly influence them.

to the tune of chuckling and cluckings from an affectionate person (if facing inward); or sleeping near a sleeping parent. (Barnard and Brazelton have edited a volume called *Touch: The Foundation of Experience,* 1990; it's quite a technical book, but it sure is convincing!)

Even as the infant experiences *not* being in contact with another's body, arms, et al., he or she benefits from a great deal of visual, tactile, and conversational togetherness. All this eases the shock of separating from the safe haven of the biological mother's womb and helps an *emotional* attachment develop where once the attachment was physical. Specialists in psychosocial development have understood this for a long time (for example, Erikson, 1950; Sullivan, 1953; Bowlby, 1969). More recently, infant researchers like Dr. T. Berry Brazelton have documented the details of how it happens. If you had babies this young in your day care home, you probably did the best you could to snuggle and hold them a great deal.

Sense of physical self as part of self-concept and positive or negative self-esteem

As a baby gradually becomes aware of the existence of his own separate physical feelings (hunger, satiation, pain, well-being) and then gradually realizes the existence of his body parts —here a foot, there a hand—and slowly gains the knowledge that this fascinating collection of pieces is an always-present, connected entity (his corporal self), he is evolving a sense of physical self (one basic aspect of self). "Senior babies"—babies nearing a year old and then graduation to toddlerhood—are getting good at correctly demonstrating the answers to, "Where's Rosie's nose?" "Where are Rosie's toes?" As this knowledge

grows, so grows Rosie's sense of physical self. The baby's attitude toward his physical self develops as he experiences his body and its performance, and as he processes and accumulates the reactions of primary and occasional caregivers to his body, body functions, body products, gender, and any physical anomalies or peculiarities he may have (a club foot, deformed hand, missing limb, distorted face, or condition such as cerebral palsy or spina bifida).

At a very young age an infant begins to assemble the images that become part of his *self*-image, concept of self, and assessment of self. Therefore, it's extremely important that, at the earliest date possible, parents and other care providers resolve problems they have with bodies, body functions, body parts, gender, and sexuality—their own, the infant's, or anybody else's— and physical exceptionalities.* What about the baby whose sourly frowning parent or caretaker usually looks at her (or her dirty diaper) with hard eyes, and whose dislike and disgust are obvious in the coldness with which she speaks—with each interaction the strength of her dislike becoming more apparent? Most people don't especially look forward to changing messy diapers; we mean a much greater than usual dislike and disgust. Won't this baby begin to feel that *she* is dislikable and disgusting? Adult disgust causes the baby or toddler to come to regard previously pleasurable activities (such as fondling his penis) shameful. Won't the child generalize this to a feeling of being ashamed of *himself,* at least in this one little way? What about the toddler whose father (though probably he would argue the fact) clearly

---

* *Note:* Gender development and sex education are discussed in the second volume of this three-volume set of books on character development in early childhood.

finds females ridiculous? How does this little daughter grow up feeling about her gender? Won't she feel guilty that she has annoyed and disappointed her beloved father by being the wrong sex? Won't she feel somewhat ashamed of her body, a body, she interprets, that displeases Dad? What about the little girl whose mother freaks out when the teacher says her daughter masturbates at nap time? What about the handicapped baby whose parents or caregivers typically look at her with faces full of misery and nerve-stirring foreboding? Won't this baby begin to feel that there's something deficient, defective, and shamefully wrong with *her* (her *self*)?

And as the self-image began, so it will in all probability grow on. It's hard, years later, for those trying to help to create a positive sense of self in a small child whose potential for positive self-esteem has already slunk away like a kicked cur. Positive or negative self-esteem accumulates from infancy onward. It's made up of many "droplets" that merge into a pervasive, persistent "mist" which infiltrates every crevice of personality. So every time you—as the family child care provider you say you used to be, or the center-based caregiver you are now—add to a baby's sense of well-being, one would guess that you've made a contribution toward developing "good character" in him.

If parents and caregivers are confronted with a difficult, "unlovable" baby or little child who, because of physiological or neurological problems at birth, displays distorted behavior that "turns them off," it's important that psychiatric advice be sought or an unfortunate cycle will soon be ricocheting ceaselessly between those involved. Some people are especially *attracted* to "pitiful" babies, but others have trouble loving them.

Some of the conditions that may understandably cause parents and other primary caregivers greater than average difficulty in bathing their babies with warming approval are:

● **visual impairments** (since the baby can't see you smiling at him, he smiles back only if you give auditory clues that you're there and that you're intimately interacting with him);

Difficult relationships in infancy can create and contribute to life-long self-esteem deficits.

There's more to character and self-esteem than a sense of physical self, and reaction to adult response to it. What is personality, and how does it hang together?

A lot is known about the development of each person's sense of self, personality, and character, although technical people, concerned with de-

able or grief is causing utter dysfunction, what about treatments and cures? For three-fourths of a century, psychologists have engaged in a massive amount of clinical work with unhappy, maladapted, or malfunctioning children, adolescents, men, women, and marriages. They have analyzed the prior and earliest experiences of millions of misfits. They have learned much of what can go wrong, where, and why as early development progresses, how it feels, and quite a bit about how to fix it. Their emphasis has been on diagnosing, intercepting, and correcting what's wrong.

Meanwhile, at infant and child study stations, in nursery schools and schools, hospitals, homes, and community programs of all sorts, "well child" developers and researchers have learned a lot about normal personality development, normalcy, maturity, and mental health, and about the factors and conditions causing *them,* as well as much about factors and conditions causing problems. Since the 1920s, trained nursery school teachers, especially, have had in-depth, long-term opportunities to get to know young children and their families. High-quality early childhood education has always involved a great deal of interaction with parents, so nursery school teachers, unlike other researchers, have been able to observe children "where they live"—at home, interacting with their families, and at school, interacting with a very fami-

---

Are we helping our babies feel good about their physical and sexual selves? About the body, its products, and its problems? This contributes to emerging self-esteem.

● **hearing impairments** (since the baby can't hear you speaking to her, she doesn't respond, and since she doesn't hear the language around her, her ability to sop up sounds and reproduce them herself—initiate verbal communications—is limited and delayed; to be fully responsive, she has to **see** you so she can realize the array of ways you are connecting with her nonverbally);

● **mental retardation** (since many of the baby's abilities are muted, she may be disappointingly less smiley, responsive, and "talkative"—more solemn and solitary—than adults expect and would enjoy; it may be necessary to invest more time and energy than the adult anticipated);

● **physical and motor impairments** (since the baby may be limp or too taut, may grimace instead of grin, or have any of many difficulties moving and communicating, adults may not get the favorable responses that help *them* respond favorably).

It's hard not to feel rejected under these circumstances, and rejected adults often tend to reject children.

tailed psychological workings, are eager to learn more. Some psychologists study animals, but many study people, who are very much more complicated. Psychoanalysts have studied people from the outset, so this branch of psychology, started by Sigmund Freud, with its derivative schools of thought, has been way ahead of the others in understanding personality development. Much of what these explorers in the depths of human personality development discovered and taught us earlier has been substantiated and elaborated on by developmental psychologists' and cultural anthropologists' research. What are the universals and the varieties of human personality and character? What variables can go wrong to create personality thwarting and warping, mental ill health, neurosis, pathology, and weak or "bad" character? What are the intricacies of human interaction between mother and child? Between father and child? Between siblings? How permanent are early affective and behavioral patterns? What is the ultimate human potential for productive, fulfilling functioning? When aberration is unendur-

---

Parenting Is Basic

● *Infants and Mothers* by T. Berry Brazelton
● *Toddlers and Parents* also by T. Berry Brazelton
● *Ordinary is Extraordinary* by Amy Dombro
● *Your Baby and Child* by P. Leach
● *Your Baby and Child from Birth to Age 5* also by P. Leach
● *Raising Good Children* by T. Lickona
● *A Mother's Work* by D. Fallows

---

liar parent substitute (teacher), and with peers.

With the exception of the psychotic illnesses and other physical givens, *the factors and conditions that cause mental health problems and "bad" character, and the factors and conditions that cause mental health and "good" character are usually human beings.* Some problems are obviously physical, but by far the most are parent-made, though "blame" is grossly inappropriate. Much that happens in parenting happens at a completely unconscious level. Some misfortunes are entirely beyond anyone's control—death of a parent, for example, which can be devastating to a very young child's psychological development. Sometimes parents are merely victims of *their* parents—perhaps they were emotionally unavailable and/or physically abusive. Parents may be the victims of the crushing strata of society in which they were born and raised. As far as an infant is concerned, adult caregivers and other human beings pretty much *are* the emotional, social, language, and intellectual environment.

While some researchers work at unlocking the genetic, chemical, and biological secrets that influence people, others—more and more in the past forty years—concentrate on understanding the process through which personalities are permanently contoured by their conditioning. People who specialize in creating good people focus on developing and strengthening children with sound mental health and good character. Psychiatric professionals use the word "character" in a specific way, but we can use it conventionally for *our* purpose—the purpose of thinking about developing the children we deal with. *Of course* you play a part in this if you're with the children so much—how could you think otherwise!

Personality is the fundamental point of view, the dynamic process of organized, patterned priorities and responses within a person, that deals with every level and every detail of his life. Personality is involved in a constantly fluid, maneuvering attempt to balance the physical, intellectual, and psychological instincts, needs,

and drives **inside** each of us, with pressures coming at us from **outside** people and other **outside** sources. A human being isn't born with personality. Babies are born with the capability of *developing* personality—self. (Language works the same way; babies aren't born talking, but they are born

---

Personality—self—is the coordinator of a complex system of inner and outer experiences and pressures.

---

with the ability to learn language, right from the start.) *Personality emerges from birth on,* because it becomes immediately necessary for the infant to develop some means of organizing and coping with the raw materials of which he's made and with the stimulating impressions coming at him from every side. He is largely genetically determined. Apparently, even his temperament is genetically determined. But every genetically determined factor

must be *applied* constantly. The infant needs a mechanism to manage the applications of these inner facts and conditions to continuously arising realities. Personality (self) is the liaison between inner "givens" and constant "situations" requiring coordination or decisions. Personality "decides" what to do. The infant is made of genes and chemistry and who knows what else. But all of these fixed factors are influenced by the baby's *feelings*, which, in turn, are influenced by people around him. *Personality filters and edits the perceptions of the infant's five senses.* It generalizes stimuli, and commits conditioning and reinforcers to memory, even though the baby is oblivious to all of it.

Personality screens all learning through the emotions and learns what's most relevant to it. All of the infant's experience is filtered through her emotions. She learns best by participating. If she only listens, she learns less than if she participates by *doing* something. And if she participates only by doing something, she learns less than if she participates by doing something vitally relevant to her, *something she chooses to do.* This is because her personality helps sort all of the obvious and the invisible demands and pressures placed upon her. To help her survive, her personality simply screens out those that it doesn't

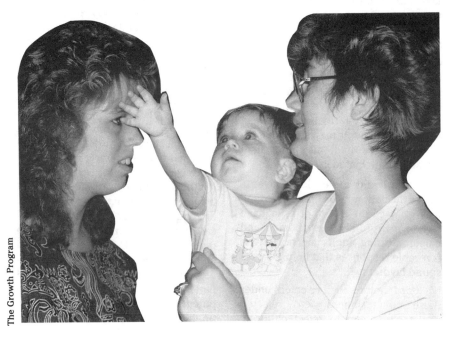

The Growth Program

consider top priority. *It sorts out those demands that are less relevant.* That's why crawlers, toddlers, and two-year-olds learn by leaps and bounds through exploration and self-initiated discovery, and much less through instruction. Personality "knows" the temperament the child was born with: excitable, calm, approaching, withdrawing, melancholy, cheerful, intense, relaxed.

As the baby grows, personality sifts the experiences thrust upon her: disease, disability, gender, poverty/wealth, education, accident, abuse, neglect, nutrition, physique, intelligence quotient, various possible gifts, behavioral difficulties resulting from factors beyond the control of the child, and relationships. Out of all this data collection and observation, the individual personality develops characteristic assumptions and behaviors. These form the essence of self that others recognize and that enable them to predict quite a bit about this individual child's likely actions and reactions. For example, we can guess with a fair amount of accuracy which of our children will be bold and which will hang back when we bring out a new activity. We can guess that Zoie will plunge in with pleasure and questions, and Jessie will fret and fuss and insist on being entertained by an adult who must engage in the new activity with her. Those of us who work closely with young children know them well; we know them as individuals. We know their unique personalities, even if they are still infants, toddlers, or only two years old, and even if, as they grow on, their personalities change to some extent.

Personality provides coherence to the whole swim of inner and outer experiences and behaviors. Personality is the coordinator. It develops styles of relating. It arranges a hierarchy out of pieces and parts and what needs to be done. When we feel ambivalent, personality determines what we will actually *do.* Usually, it eventually resolves conflicts so we can cope.

Personality screens all learning through the emotions, and learns what's most relevant to the individual.

Personality channels streams of ability and interest. It integrates strands and levels of self into a person sufficiently unified to function, and to function consistently. A personality, a person, is much more than a large collection of random cognitive skills, behavioral learnings, and feelings. Something holds all this together, acts as a magnet to attract certain kinds of information and to repel other kinds, works it all over, is the yeast that makes it rise, is the agent that converts some of it to something else new and creative and individual, the agent that decides when to take the initiative.

Personality is a system, a "self" system. Once it begins to emerge, form, and, as the child grows older, to gel, it becomes quite impenetrable and unbending. Because this is true, it's wise to *try*—to the extent that we have any control—to "grow in" the ingredients, learning thrusts, beliefs, and behaviors,—the characteristics—that are consistent with mental health, emotional maturity, and "good character." It is, conversely, unwise to inadvertently grow the wrong tendencies, and then to try to manipulate, punish, or psychoanalyze them into desired shape later. Ordinarily, except in cases of mental illness or finding itself in an extremely different setting which forces it to radically change its approach, personality is neither fragile nor flexible. Whether one attempts to ruin a healthy adult personality or mend an unhealthy one, one discovers that personality tenaciously, in some instances rigidly, retains its strengths, style, wisdom, weirdness, defenses, neuroses, and all. Personality is learned (in an elaborately complicated way, far too complex to go into here)

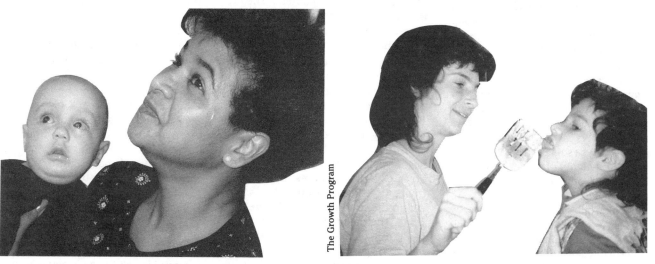

The Growth Program

The Growth Program

We influence the child's fundamental feeling about himself. The feeling may last a lifetime.

and, under normal circumstances, is extraordinarily difficult to unlearn, even in part. It's impossible to unlearn altogether. Personality has an amazing resilience hiding in its marrow bones. That's why, as parents and other caregivers, we need to take personality development seriously. We can develop academic skills later, but personality and character are developing *now*, for better or worse, whether or not we offer useful guidance.

Every personality probably forms a fundamental view of life in the first few years

Amazingly early in life, each personality apparently develops what might be thought of as a point of view. Personality takes a central and in many cases a permanent position to which it returns as it relates to any new person or situation for the rest of its life. Freud, the most famous pioneer in personality development research, felt that much in each personality's deepest dynamics has been formulated by age five, during the critical oral, anal, and oedipal periods. Erikson taught us that lifelong personality thrusts are powerfully influenced by a young child's learning of trust/mistrust in infancy and autonomy/shame in toddlerhood.

The nature of early *emotional* learning is thus urgently important. We all know adults, teenagers, even older children, with basic attitudes (personality positions) that cause them to miss out on many of life's joys. Character, personality, and self-esteem develop continuously throughout life, each stage of development and major life happening influencing them, but at each stage *earlier* learning and conclusions strongly influence what's learned and concluded *next*. To a degree, self-esteem fluctuates — we have good days and bad days. And each of us thinks more highly of some aspects of self and much less highly of other aspects. But it averages out to something — high, adequate, or low opinion of self. Although no one could say so for sure, by the age of three, a little child may already be trapped in an unfortunate cycle of low self-esteem. The child may be well on the way (unconsciously, of course) to feeling, therefore acting,

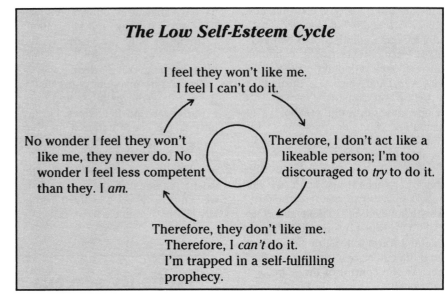

The Low Self-Esteem Cycle

I feel they won't like me.
I feel I can't do it.

Therefore, I don't act like a likeable person; I'm too discouraged to *try* to do it.

Therefore, they don't like me. Therefore, I *can't* do it. I'm trapped in a self-fulfilling prophecy.

No wonder I feel they won't like me, they never do. No wonder I feel less competent than they. I *am*.

therefore being, therefore having *reason* to feel basically bad or good about herself. For instance, a child may feel:

● **Hopelessly inadequate** (low self-esteem): There's no chance he can succeed or catch up; there's only pain and failure in trying. He decides he'll withdraw from, or cease entering, new and competitive situations. Apathy is his position, not trying, instead of risking the hard ball of anxious dread that forms like lead in his belly when he attempts to accomplish anything, including relationships. (Studies have shown that even babies only halfway to their first birthdays can have this conviction. They make no effort even to connect with their mothers. They're usually the babies of clinically depressed mothers or babies being raised in institutions.); or

● **Highly anxiously "inferior"** (low self-esteem): She's sure she's not as good as others; she's a loser. She suspects that others are always superior. But she'll valiantly, chin up, keep running along in the rear, and chipping in from the fringes. Anxious struggling, snared with a great many scary gray areas of nagging doubts, is her position. (As toddlers, people of this persuasion tend to anticipate failure, become frustrated and cranky when facing a challenge, and refuse to try the task until given a great deal of assistance and reassurance. People who feel this way about themselves fre-

quently sabotage their own efforts, en-*suring* failure.); or

● **Fiercely competitive** (low self-esteem): He thinks he's not as good as any other, so to defend himself from the pain of realizing this, he claims to be the best, must always be first, hurts and belittles other children to feel stronger and better than they, ignores adults, is ungovernable, appears to be shameless. He shoulders people out of the way, so to speak, and in general exhibits a "kiss off" attitude. He'll strive mightily to get what others have. His anger is always in search of a target. Authoritarianism, bullying, and demeaning others is his position. (If you've taught two-year-olds for any length of time, you may have met a few younger-than-three-year-olds with these tendencies yourself, but this attitude may not fully develop or fully reveal itself until a child is four or five.); or

● **Severely alienated** (low self-esteem): He knows he's no good, but you're no good either, and neither are others. He doesn't aspire to what *you* are and what *you* have. It turns him off. Nor does he want to be like the other children. He's estranged, disengaged. But he doesn't have confidence that who *he* is, and what *he* has, has value *either*, so he won't get involved in much of anything. He won't care. He won't commit himself to any heavy relationships. He experiences a gloomy feeling of foreboding. He is egocentric, resentful of being an outsider at the same time that he insists on being one, pessimistic, and self-dissatisfied. He sits cynically aside, acting superior but feeling *inferior*. His position is a feeling of distrust, loneliness, hopelessness. (You know adolescents like this. How did they get so alienated? At what psychological stage did serious problems crop up? Why was the child's personality unable to resolve them?); or

● **Equally "good," but not absolutely skilled and fulfilled, so motivated to grow** (positive self-esteem): He has both self-confidence and faith that those with whom he is interdependent are worthwhile, reliable, viable, and valid. The warm, private hiding place inside his experiences, roles, and relationships feels snug. He trusts others. He'll seek intimacy with one or some, and varieties of relationships with some or many. He'll care enough to know the needs of others, and thus will know enough to care constructively. He has had successes. He has met many challenges, and has been encouraged to go forward. His efforts have been appreciated. He'll risk new things, viewing them as opportunities, not as threats to turn against. His position is "I'm OK — You're OK" (Harris, 1967). Here, we think of the majority of toddlers and twos we know.

When we help infants, toddlers, and two-year-olds feel good about who they are during all the trivial details of our days with them, and when we help them feel safely cared for, we are ensuring that we're doing our best to give them a positive orientation to life. Usually, it's as simple as that. If more sophisticated treatment is called for, we can call for psychiatric consultation and can suggest to parents that they, too, seek professional advice.

No personality position is "free"; but some are less un-free than others

All of these positions are efforts to cope with interpersonal existence. *Existing* forces us to relate in order to avoid excessive loneliness, too much left-outness. Young children have a huge need to be included — in a family's routines and affection; by other

children's acceptance. Children's need for inclusion, approval, and affiliation motivates them to sacrifice many narcissistic pleasures and permit themselves to be socialized, difficult as that is. We humans never outgrow our need to be part of a herd. In a sense, *all* permanent core personality positions are servants to psychological survival. Thus, none can be considered "free." Yet some approaches to life permit more ability to see and compare alternatives, openness to change, intimate relationships, opportunities for achieving personal successes, and so forth, than others. These are the "free-*er*" personality positions. Parents can't raise children to be free; who in this world is fully free? Surely not you or me! But some people are free-*er*. Parents and other caregivers can raise children to be less or more free.

Most adults, barring miraculous happenings or remarkably successful psychoanalysis, keep their early childhood personality position, though it may go underground and not be obvious

Many, many features of a person's personality change as she grows, but apparently a deep-seated orientation is acquired exceedingly young. This can be ascertained by closely and extensively observing any child. Every child behaves with reference to his core point of view all day long. Observing a child and looking for the thread, or pattern, running through his behavior, usually will reveal his personality's fundamental point of view, though certainly not as clearly as the "portraits" just painted. Experts differ in their opinions about how permanent the core attitude toward life evident in early childhood is.

David, age 29 months, is almost always sure that one or another child or adult is trying to give him a hard time. Knowing a child over many years allows an observant adult to see tha pattern shift somewhat, and hide in the shadows, but — in many instances — continue. Do we believe that David will completely change in first grade? On high school graduation day? Or on his wedding day? Or does he grow on, always with his core frame of reference in tact? Maybe he *will* change; David is only a baby boy with

many developmental stages and conflicts yet to come, resolve, and grow from. However, unless his loved ones can help him develop a different world view, David *could* be the young man who says it's his friends' fault that he drinks too much, his girlfriend's fault that the relationship is on the rocks, and his boss's fault that he's failing on the job. There's plenty of time to help David if anyone pays attention to his slant on life.

Down deep where all learning is stored from infancy onward, the facts *and personality's interpretation of the facts* become imbedded and buried, become the invisible bedrock on which much future behavior is based.

As parents and child development professionals, many of us want to add healthy, happy bits and pieces of experience and solid, positive relationships to what gets buried and becomes the child's psychological and behavioral bedrock.

Expert parents, close friends of the family, and sensitive teachers of older twos can easily explain the consistent characterstics that probably add up to

● high self-esteem, or

● worrisome, questionable self-esteem

evident in the very small individuals they spend lots of time with. Descriptions of these children are featured in boxes on this and the next page.

How can adults foster positive self-esteem?

As caregivers, we aren't responsible for renovating the self-esteem in children in whom it seems to be sagging. But we are caring people, so we can be on the lookout for children who may be having difficulty feeling good about themselves, and in our work with all children can at least lean in a helpful direction.

➡ **Because a source of self-esteem is feeling that we can positively affect others,** caregivers can be careful to be promptly responsive to the child's needs, requests, and communications as frequently as possible, considering that we're busy with other things and other people, as parents and other caregivers have been through the centuries. We can really listen and comply when feasible. This is especially hard to do if the child in question is not a particularly pleasant child, but we are professional. We can usually rise to the occasion.

We can often ask the child's opinion on something suitably simple. ("Which tape do you think we should play?" "Do you think we should have cranberry or cherry juice today?") We can then take her advice, commenting, "That's a good idea."

➡ **Because a source of self-esteem is feeling lovable,** caregivers can make it a point to approach, snuggle, stroke, compliment, and briefly play with the child a number of times a day, regardless of how busy we may be, and how "un-cute" we may think he is. The less cute he is, the more he needs to hear how cute he is, and to become lovable, therefore, "cute." It's a challenge. It's our job.

➡ **Because a source of self-esteem is feeling capable,** caregivers can note the child's interest and ability levels and structure situations so he can surely succeed. When he succeeds, we can call attention to his success.

Parents and Caregivers May Not Use the Term Self-Esteem, but They Will Describe "Probably High Self-Esteem Children" Something Like This:

Some two-and-a-half-year-olds know what they want much of the time. They go off and do it. If challenged, they don't hesitate to insist on it, on getting their "rights," you might say. They're usually curious and eager to try new things. They assume they'll succeed. They tackle their tasks enthusiastically, and are proud of their many accomplishments. They get along reasonably well with peers—with give and take, as well as some tussles and tearful altercations. They assume that children and adults alike will like them, and generally seem to feel accepted (acceptable). Sometimes a small group of spunky children gets playing with such gusto, and seems so high, that their little hearts seem almost to brush the sky.

They engage in pretend play, using their knowledge of the world and expressing their feelings, both positive and negative, in the scenes they (loosely speaking) enact. They prefer lead roles to peripheral ones, but are quite versatile in the roles they can play, as long as the parts are *important* parts (no one will agree to be the pet, but one child will happily be the mother, the doctor, the teacher, the father, etc.). We see the *self* revealed, as the children exhibit their individual characteristics in play, yet these "high self-esteem" children have in common the fact that their play is usually positive, and they're seldom mean to each other, even though they may spank the doll or be a "cruel monster." Many older twos who have regular relationships in group care are amazingly skilled negotiators and are quite insightful about their friends' foibles, abilities, and proclivities, and are also quite forgiving.

Two-year-olds who (we're guessing) are developing a healthy sense of self-worth, can tolerate a moderate amount of frustration and a moderate amount of redirection from children, grown-ups, and tasks they're attempting. They are generally friendly and cheerful and their faces appear to be contented. They expect care and guidance from grown-ups. They come to them with their troubles, look them in the eye, confide, and (except when acting like the terrible twos we all know they can be) are quite cooperative. By almost three it's easy to see that each of these children feels like a good person, who tries to please beloveds and other caregivers out of love and an inner sense that it's the right thing to do.

In other words, they trust their grown-ups, their own autonomy (independent self), and their many competencies, including social competencies. They have confidence. Their self-esteem is sprouting delightfully.

("Tina, look what Nari can do! Did you know he could [throw a ball, flip his jacket over his head, put the pieces in the pail, get the doll to straighten its legs and lie down, complete the three piece puzzle]?"). In part, children get their cues about how to view a peer from the authority figures in their lives. If the teacher ignores or belittles a child, the children will. And if the teacher admires the child, the children will. (In some cultures children are taught not to stand out as individuals. In such an instance, adults can praise a *group* of children, who are *cooperatively* accomplishing something.)

Part of structuring a situation so a child can succeed is to remove from it children who will probably interfere or do the task better.

Another way we can help a child feel competent is to offer just the right amount of help. Too much and the child will believe we think him incompetent; too little and the child may feel we don't care about him.

Encouraging a child to be "culturally correct"—to behave appropriately in terms of *his* specific culture—encourages self-esteem.

Encouraging a child's language competence also encourages self-esteem. A child's self-esteem hinges on feeling competent in all age-appropriate and culturally expected dimensions.

➡ **Because a source of self-esteem is feeling listened to and accepted,** every time the child is trying to tell her something, the caregiver can try to pay attention and make every effort to understand the intended communication (too big a group decreases the possibility that a caregiver, however good, can do this). Engaging in frequent conversation with children helps them increase their ability to express their feelings and ideas verbally.

Sometimes (if it isn't offensive to families of the specific cultures *you* serve) it's useful if a caregiver squats down, looks the child in the eye, and paraphrases or extends what he said, instead of giving arguments or instructions.

If the child is complaining that Patrick tore his picture, say, "You don't think it was right that Patrick tore your picture. You're mad that Patrick tore your picture." Ask the child what he's going to tell Patrick. If another

---

Parents and Caregivers May Not Use the Term Low Self-Esteem, but They Will Describe "Possibly Low Self-Esteem Children" Something Like This:

Some older two-year-olds are slow to get involved, or seldom do at all, even in safe, familiar situations. They usually sit or timidly stand on the fringes, watching others or toying with something, looking rather unhappy. They don't seem to know what they want. They show little initiative. They don't join in with others, but neither do they have their own ideas. They don't exhibit vigorous parallel play, either. They seem indecisive. Some of them flit from toy to toy, not really playing with the toys at all—maybe just *claiming* each one "Mine! Mine!" or starting to play with the toy and then quitting when it frustrates them. These children seldom move far away from their caregivers. (As we who work with them regularly well know, *any* two-year-old does all of these things sometimes. We're trying to identify those whose *patterns* of behavior are cause for concern.) Some of these "possible low self-esteem" children are too docile. They don't stand up for themselves with other children—nor do they often oppose adults. If you try to involve these fringers, floaters, and roamers, they're reluctant and tentative in the way they use materials or approach a piece of equipment or group of children. They act as if they don't think they'll be able to do it or deal with it. Nothing ventured is nothing gained; these children experience fewer successes than those with what appears to be more robust self-esteem. Other children don't select the fringers, floaters, and roamers as playmates because they aren't good players—they don't participate heartily or add ideas to the project. When they *do* join others in pretend play, they are assigned the lesser roles. They don't know how to negotiate, so have to settle for what other children permit them in the way of inclusion.

Another type of behavior often seen in possible low-esteem children is hostile, aggressive behavior. Other children don't like to play with *them,* either, because they overassert, and are quite disruptive to the plot or the project. They are too obstinate for their peers to deal with, negatively obstreperous, and intolerant of others.

Both the timid fringer and the belligerent fellow give the impression of being oblivious to the groups' dynamics, and to the individuality of group members, which is quite the opposite of the sensitivity and sympathy socially successful older two-year-olds often display toward regular playmates. Some of the children on the social outskirts give the impression of being depressed; others seem tense, edgy and stressed. Some are loners, some are too passive, some are too good, and some seem permanently angry.

Children who may not be developing strong, positive, self-esteem don't turn easily to adults or other children when they need help. Instead, they may give up or disintegrate—strike out (or even bite) or howl. When an adult is talking to them, they tend to avoid eye contact. It's as if a direct look in the eye is a direct hit—too intrusive, too threatening. *All* two-year-olds refuse to obey sometimes, but the children we are sketching can be virtually unmanageable. Others in this group obey, but one senses they do so for fear of punishment more than from good-natured volition.

child is raging for no reason that you're aware of, help her express herself. Say, "It sounds like you're very angry. If you want to tell me about it you can." Probably she can't. She may be so upset because her mother is pregnant again—there was another baby last year, too—or because her parents had a screaming fight last night.

But the child can sense that you're listening to and accepting her even when you cannot solve the problem for or with her.

All activity (behaving and relating) seems to emanate from the core position

Many kinds of behavior in children and adults that at first glance appear inexplicable can be understood as personality's attempt to reduce tension and to establish a moment of peace *as defined by that particular personality.* The slightest change in situation will cause personality to "behave" *again;* to try again to adjust the interpersonal situation, or some other kind of situation, to a comfort point. **A person feels psychologically comfortable—non-anxious—when what's going on interpersonally is not threatening to the defense mechanisms that the individual personality has constructed to prevent itself from "knowing" (consciously) that which it finds too painful to know, and when the scene of the moment is consistent with the interpersonal "games" (getting along techniques) and situations which the individual personality has learned in order to help himself cope with the needs determined by his personality's core perspective:**

● I need to feel less than you (victim, loser, "inferiority complex");

● I need to feel better than you ("superiority complex");

● I need to feel equal to you.

In other words, a person—even a little child—who believes she's a victim, may not rest until she has caused somebody to "win," or victimize her in some way, leaving her the victim, the loser she "knows" she is. That's the role or position that feels familiar to her. At a nonconscious level, that's what she feels she deserves. Martina, for instance, invariably inserts herself into social situations with peers at moments and in ways that ensure rejec-

tion. She has an uncanny talent for creating situations in which she can honestly say, "They won't let me play." Social rejection is very hurtful to two-year-olds. Each episode further reinforces Martina's belief that she's unlovable and socially incompetent. In Martina's case, both are beliefs resulting from how she's treated at home.

(Another tendency of human behavior that operates in many "victim" situations—especially in child abuse situations—is personality's strong need to feel on top of things—effective with regard to affecting what happens to it. Therefore, children who *know* that they are victims, and will soon be victimized *again,* often *provoke* the abuse.* Apparently, personality feels less stress if it can predict when the abuse is coming (by provoking it) than if it's caught by surprise. Feeling completely helpless is a condition every healthy personality struggles to avoid. A child or adult who is emotionally paralyzed and cannot defend himself or take initiative on his own behalf is a badly damaged person. Severe, chronic child abuse can be one cause of such damage.)

To try to understand behavior exclusively in terms of what the individual knows intellectually about how to behave is futile, especially if the individual is younger than three years of age. What people know about "good" behavior comes from internalizing the "oughts" and "shoulds" promoted (or hidden and harbored) by parents and society. But behavior is not caused exclusively by one's conscience. Conscience instructs, but we don't always do what it says. Behavior is much more complicated than that. Besides, babies, toddlers, and two-year-olds don't even *have* fully developed consciences yet. Their consciences are still quite embryonic. Toddlers and twos don't remember the rules just because we've told them once or twice or two dozen times any more than people remember the rules of grammar in a foreign language until they have practiced applying them over and over. Furthermore, remembering the behav-

---

* *Note:* Learned helplessness is discussed in volume three of this three-volume set.

© Cleo Freelance Photo

ioral rule is far different from having the self-control (control of *self*) to implement it unerringly. Little children don't have full impulse control yet. While correcting each child's ill-advised behavior is part of a parent's and caregiver's job, we do it repeatedly and patiently and without much hope of regularly correct responses until a child is minimally eighteen months; usually much older. *Behavior* comes from a complex combination of conscious and unconscious factors and tensions engaged in an intricate balancing act aimed at accomplishing peacefulness, as interpreted by that particular personality and its point of view.

Personality can be thought of as having three major parts

1. The first is primarily unconscious, primitive, impulsive, self-indulgent, grabby, greedy, narcissistic, sometimes irrationally angry, maybe unacceptably aggressive, and usually anxiously in search of security and affection. As we who work with them every day are well aware, babies, toddlers, and two-year-olds often actually *act* in these ways. Before children develop self-awareness, self-control, and conscience, they act out what they feel. But even in a mature adult this is the once-upon-a-time-a-child segment of self. It's what remains of childhood in a dark, submerged layer of mind

throughout a lifetime. Classical psychoanalysis has called this untamed, impetuously vehement tyrant the **id.** Transactional analysts have called it the *child* part of a personality triad. Occasionally we get a glimpse of it, but usually only if we are pushed to extremes. For instance, if you become enraged at the driver on the road behind you because he's ceaselessly beeping at you, and you curse and scream, you know you're in the clutches of your "childish" self. If I feel I'm going to die because my boyfriend left me, I know I'm experiencing the abandonment anxiety so prominent in infant psychology. After the shock subsides, my mature self will recover control and I'll manage to survive.

Personality can be thought of as having three major parts.

Maturity has much to do with learning to channel, manage, and control this irrational, at times wildly emotional, portion of oneself, without losing other deliciously childlike qualities, such as wonder, joy, innocence, trust, spontaneity, creativity, and risk-taking. Self-awareness is the process of continually bringing unconscious childishnesses into the conscious mind, where they can be critically regarded, lovingly laughed at, and taught how to behave. Psychoanalysis is the process of delving into the unconscious, guided by a supportive, insightful, and extensively trained expert, to dredge up much of what's in there, haul it into the light of self-awareness, and teach it how to act in socially acceptable, personally constructive ways. Immature, neurotic, or seriously psychiatrically ill persons suffer, among other things, from *ids* that play naughty and terrible tricks on the other segments of their personalities, and with people they relate to.

As parents and other caregivers, one of the most important ways in which we can help each child build good character is to help her become

aware of her *id* feelings, accept them as part of her self, and in age-appropriate ways begin learning to manage them creatively, which is what sensitive caregivers do all day long as they gently socialize children. It isn't wise to make a little child feel so extremely guilty and ashamed of her unacceptably impulsive behaviors, greediness, selfishness, angers, fears, and insecurities that she feels forced to deny she's experiencing them by lying or repressing them beneath where conscious mind can learn to handle them effectively. On the other hand, children who are never put in a position of feeling *a little bit* guilty when they behave in unacceptable ways are not being given opportunities to master infantile, narcissistic *id* feelings and to feel proud of the achievement. Part of self-esteem — being proud of yourself — is knowing that you can control yourself — the part of self we're calling *id* — and can thus please your loved ones.

A child of almost three can exhibit considerable self-awareness and self-control — self-discipline. Adults can help each child achieve this without laying on guilt trips or shaming her.

Angela, about to be three, gives us an example of just how self-aware and restrained a mature, very young child can be. Her mother shares this anecdote about Angie, her twin Franchesca, and baby sister Nancy.

Angie and Francie were playing near a puddle, "making cakes." Francie ran to get some dry earth "to be the flour," fell, scraped her knee to bloodiness, ran sobbing to the girls' mother, and was sympathetically snuggled and rocked. Angie, seeing this, stood erect, held her head high, and bravely fighting the tears, rushed up the porch steps, into the house and into her mother's bed. In a moment, when Franchesca's serenity had been restored, the mother went in search of Angela.

She found her little girl sobbing in the safety zone of her mother's bed. Angie said, "I don't mind when Nancy sits on your lap because she's a baby, but when Francie sits on your lap I feel sad and angry." Remarkable! Typically, 35-month-old children do have some understanding of self and others

One part is the impulsive, self-indulgent, anxious, perhaps angry "primitive" part that the socialization process is intended to "civilize."

(story characters included), and good language to express it, but Angela is definitely advanced in this dimension of development. Many much older people wouldn't have been able to come up with this insight. A brief but deeply bonding hug and the mother's words — "I'm sorry you feel sad and angry. Sometimes people do feel sad or angry. I love Francie and I love you, I love you both, but you and I love each other very, very specially and privately, and that's just for us, right?" — quickly restored *Angie's* serenity, *too.*

Listening to, acknowledging, and accepting children's feelings is a good habit to get into if their emotional success in this particular culture is an objective.

A second part of personality is the "internalized parent"— the conscience.

2. A second part of personality is called, by some, the **superego,** or the *internalized parent.* This is **conscience,** the self-within-self that approves or disapproves. Parents, in part, parrot *their* parents. *Superego* is, in part, an absorbed parent. *Superego* not only records the *words and tones* of parents, but also their major and semi-invisible communications (*behavior* plus gestures, facial expressions, etc.).

Because there can be extreme inconsistencies between parental words and parental behaviors or nonverbal communications, the child's *superego* may get confused, conflicting sets of inscriptions about what he "ought" to be and do. Many of these conflicting messages originate in the *parents'* unconscious minds; so the parents don't even know they're transmitting them to be lodged for life in their children's *superegos*. To further complicate the matter, many children have *two* parents. *Both* are programming the child's *superego* with beliefs and behaviors that may conflict *within* each parent and *between* the two parents. Psychoanalysts believe the *parent* part of a personality to be much more complex than simply a "swallowed" parent, lodged in the psyche. It also includes negative reactions to parents, among other things.

Josh loved his usually loving mother, but she frequently beat him severely. She desperately wanted him to be good so people would view her as a good parent (so she would view her *self* as a good person). She also wanted Josh to be a good parent to *her* because she had never been drenched in the loving parenting each child thrives on. But Josh hated his mother as well as loved her, so he behaved dreadfully. He had *added* motivation to behave badly because, though his father told him (verbally) to behave, Josh could see from the grin on his father's face when he told friends about Josh's dastardly deeds that he was secretly pleased with his wayward two-year-old son. In other words, the father was *nonverbally* "telling" Josh that, to please Dad, Josh should misbehave. Josh's father had had very strict parents, and was quite a proper professional; probably Josh's defiant behavior was just what Dad had always secretly wished *he* could get away with.

Regardless of how complex the formation of conscience is, we all know that toddlers have little bitty budding consciences. At ages one and two, conscience consists essentially of learning to do what Mom says—of learning to get along with others. As the child grows through childhood, adolescence, and adulthood, a deeply entrenched and potent piece of personality that judges, moralizes, criticizes, condemns, censures, and directs him —conscience—grows too.

Adult self-awareness includes some conscious understanding of what's going on in this second segment of self, conscience. Sometimes part of psychotherapy's job is to remove this dictator from the pedestal it sits on in the unconscious mind, and to render it more harmless by exposing it to the light— which helps reveal it as the dictator it really is—and to the scalpel of reason. What a young child learned he should and shouldn't be and do may no longer be suitable when he's forty and times have changed. Or the conscience he was programmed with by excessively authoritarian parents may be much too strict, causing him constant self-doubt and self-deprecation. Because most people don't experience the luxury of extensive, high-quality psychotherapy, it's best to try to build appropriate consciences from the beginning.

Moreover, each child, even children only a year or two old, comes to her own conclusions about why she deserves to feel guilty or ashamed, which may be way off the mark, but which the child may carry with her—in her conscience—for years and years as a "truth" about some "bad" aspect of her *self*. Psychotherapy can bring these misinterpretations into the light of consciousness to be scrutinized and reevaluated.

Elsie, for instance, was a two-year-old who adored her mother, and who was tremendously motivated to make her happy—to be like her, to like what she liked, etc. When her baby brother was born, she was all set to be as happy about him as her mother was. But by the time he'd been around awhile, Elsie realized that he was a horrible intruder and she often hated him. Whenever she could, she hurt him. Though the parents had done everything the books tell parents to do, and, of course, soon figured out ways to prevent Elsie from hurting the baby, Elsie's parents couldn't prevent Elsie from putting two and two together and feeling guilty for distressing her mother and ashamed that (in this dimension) she wasn't the good girl she wanted to be.

We can't completely control how children interpret their experiences and how they judge themselves, but we can try to discipline them in kindly ways, which is the way to try to give them kindly consciences.

As parents and other caregivers, an important way in which we can help each child build good character and positive self-esteem is to help him become aware of his emerging conscience's expectations of him, ensure that these expectations and judgments are age-appropriate and reasonable, and help him learn to judge himself in a firm but kindly manner. A child of almost three has strong feelings about what's right and wrong and about what's fair and unfair. This is the beginning of conscience, morality, and ethical behavior. A child of almost three can understand that grown-ups expect a great many behaviors from him, but should not be burdened with severe or unattainable requirements, or with more requirements than are necessary to socialize him into his society.

3. The third part of personality can be viewed as the mature, adult piece, called the **ego.** Don't laugh—even at two, even at one-and-a-half, some children are much more mature and self-aware than others—they have strong **egos** for their age. The **ego** collects, processes, and files data coming in from *id* messages, *superego* messages, and from various outside realities and priorities. Even a young child's emerg-

---

The toddler has a budding conscience that grows with him to become a deeply entrenched, potent piece of personality that in later years judges, moralizes, criticizes, condemns, censures, and directs him.

The Growth Program

The third part of personality can be viewed as the mature, "adult" piece called the ego. It's primarily with the ego that skilled child developers — parents or other caregivers — work.

Babies, toddlers, and two-year-olds don't have fully developed consciences yet. Their consciences are still quite embryonic. Toddlers and twos don't remember the rules just because we've told them once, twice, or a dozen times.

ing **ego** has judgment from past experience and hopes for the future. It's the most rational section of personality, and also the most conscious. The **ego** is the self-aware segment of a self-aware person's personality. It's with the **ego** that a psychotherapist works. It's with the **ego** that a skilled child developer — parent or other caregiver — works.

During toddlerhood, children learn to walk, climb, run, throw, and master other physical skills that transform them from immobile infants into runabout, into-everything, powerful little people. **Astonishing mental gains also occur during the year between the child's first and second birthday.** One of them is **language,** another is the dawn of **self-awareness.** As they become able to recognize themselves in the mirror and in photographs, toddlers become able to recognize themselves as individual *people,* also. They become aware (conscious) of their past experiences (memories) and of themselves as *selves* — an individual, separate from others, but always

The Growth Program

After all, even two-year-olds are still very little people.

"me." Until this occurs, a toddler doesn't use the word "I"; he *can't,* he lacks the concept. As a child's awareness of self emerges, so do the assorted judgments he's been formulating about the fragments of self that have been coagulating into "me," and a sense of my *self* as a "good" or "bad" child, as a lovable or unlovable child, as a competent or *in*competent child. Self-esteem takes shape.

Another of the toddler's mental gains is the ability to **question authority.** The toddler's growing mental capacity makes it possible for her to question parental and other caregivers' instructions and expectations. But it's all very confusing to her: Though the toddler is instinctively driven by her psychobiology to separate from her caregivers, and though she increasingly resents their prohibitions and restrictions, she also loves and instinctively knows she needs them. One of the biggest jobs the toddler's **ego** has to accomplish is to

reconcile these opposites. During the emotional struggle, toddlers find themselves flung — startlingly and unpredictably — from feelings of great dependency and clinging, to feelings of great independence and omnipotence. Their behavior reveals these struggles. One minute they won't leave mom's lap, the next they refuse to cooperate, even if being offered a treat.

In the same way that the toddler practices walking, climbing, running, throwing, and other physical skills *until she masters them,* so she practices asserting herself, her separate-from-parent individualness, her autonomy, until she masters *it.* As a seasoned caregiver, did you ever think of all that obstinacy and contrariness this way? Just as she has become aware that she can put *spacial* distance between her caregiver and her self (but will still survive, and can always reunite), the toddler has become aware that she can put *emotional* distance between her caregiver and herself — by being "bad" (but will still survive, and can always reunite). Under normal conditions, a toddler or two-year-old has developed strong enough **ego** (self, separated, individuated, from parents) that she dares to be oppositional. Some children are shy or withdrawn and don't appear to be oppositional, yet are normal. Their "disobedience" and assertiveness may take the form of passive resistance — dawdling, for instance, or refusing to eat, or refusing to use the potty.

We worry about children this age who are too good.

"Herbert," the neighbor later said, "was too good. I never saw a 17-month-old boy who would be set on a chair and would still be sitting still right there an hour later when his parents took him away. He was a little, thin, frail thing, small for his age." After this toddler's death, the investigation revealed a history since birth of having been left in his crib for cruel and unusual lengths of time (for as long as a week at a time during the past year) while his mother, as she described it, "went out for a while with my husband." Both parents were crack addicts. After the neighbor called the police to investigate the two-week-long silence next door and a dreadful stench, and the autopsy had been completed, it was determined that Herbert had died of starvation. The first clue that all was not well in Herbert's life was that he "was too good."

As with any of the other new skills the normal toddler is picking up, the child wants to test her ability, in this instance to assert herself, over and over (and over and over and over until her parents are tearing their hair). **To put it simply, the toddler is working to master autonomy, just as she works to master her thrilling new physical skills.**

Some child developers (me, for example) think that in instances where this constellation of conditions exists, the more oppositional (defiant) the toddler tends to be, and at a younger age—perhaps 12 to 15 months instead of later:

- a very bright child,
- a very strong bond between mother and child,
- a very reasonable and understanding mother, and
- a child with a very intense temperament and a very powerful personality.

Those who believe this think that the very bright child catches on quicker than the average child to the possibility of defying The Source of Life and All Good Things, because the child's **ego**—awareness—matures younger. They suspect that the stronger the bonds (love, feeling of being "one," blurring of **ego** boundaries that occurs when any two people deeply love each other), the more strenuously the toddler must assert herself and protest her separateness; unconsciously, she fears that she may not *achieve* separateness. Some child developers see that the more reasonable and understanding the mother is, the greater the lengths the toddler must go to "get her goat," e.g., to get her to get the message: "I am *me*. I am not merely an extension of you. I do not always do as

you wish." And they see that children with intense temperaments and powerful personalities do *everything* more extremely than laid-back children.

Normal orneriness in young children (usually between 18 and 30 months but sometimes much younger) is *not* negativism, it's self-assertion. Nothing in child development is more important for success in the U.S. than the development of self, sense of self, sense of separate person-ness, sense of positive, activist, effective self. Self-esteem is rooted in achieving it. Parents and teachers of toddlers who appreciate the ever-strengthening individuality **(ego)** of these little people view toddler obstinacy very differently than do people who think of it as negativism or naughtiness and try to squash it. Parents tend to bear the brunt of difficult behaviors because toddlers are much more tightly bonded to their parents than to their caregivers, thus must strive harder to become separate selves. Besides, small children feel far more secure with even the "worst" parents than they do with other caregivers, so dare to "let their hair down."

It isn't wise to make a little child feel so extremely guilty and ashamed of her unacceptable behaviors that she feels forced to deny she's experiencing them.

As parents and caregivers, we need to understand and act on the understanding that two things can be true at the same time: The fact that toddlers need to be oppositional, doesn't negate the fact that parents and other caregivers need to set limits. One of the very things the toddler is trying to find out is, "Where are the limits? Where are the limits of my *self*?" The answer is, "The limits of *you* are where you bump into *me*—*my* needs and those of other people, you bumptious child, you. You have the right to be yourself. And the rest of us have rights too." At this point, swoop, scoop, and without a tantrum (on our part) we remove the toddler and redirect her to something as similar as we can find. (If she was throwing a hard object at her brother's head, we give her a soft ball and a safe place to throw it.)

Repeated, repeated, and repeated firmness, permeated with friendliness and fairness, is *the* essential ingredient of "teaching" self-discipline.

Teaching involves us in many a moral dilemma, and one of them arises here: What about children from other cultures whose parents do not have standard American childrearing goals and are absolutely against the idea of autonomous, assertive children?

Many of us work with parents and children from other cultures. Parents may have powerful objections to our teaching their children characteristics that are "wrong" for *their* cultures. For example, Southeast Asians (Vietnamese, Cambodians, Laotians, and Hmong), who have immigrated to this country in large numbers, usually strongly disapprove of independent, self-reliant behavior in children. Parents discourage such characteristics. They train children to subjugate egocentric feelings and behaviors and to feel and show unquestioning obedience to parents and other authorities (caregivers and teachers among them). Shaming children so they will not bring shame to their families (through unacceptable behavior, low grades, etc.) is a prominent childrearing technique.

We are child developers and "know" what's best for young children. We also know that a cardinal rule of our profession is to respect and work with parents. Hence the dilemma.

The answer—though far from easy—is to create as many opportunities as possible for parents and staff to get to know each other *socially,* and to become acquainted with each others' cultures by viewing and discussing films together and discussing customs in general. The Vietnamese culture is not exactly the same as the Cambodian culture, which is not exactly the same as the Laotian culture, which is not exactly the same as the Hmong culture. People with a high literacy level are not exactly the same as people with a low literacy level; urban people are not exactly the same as rural people; and so on. Learning about various aspects of each culture through in-service workshops and the informal approach and by developing personal relationships can often facilitate a workable reconciliation of differences. High on the list of helpful hints about working with parents from diverse cultures are

● to hire some staff *from* that culture, and

● to compromise to some extent.

Working with Southeast Asian parents brings another complication: Typically, parents do not believe that they "should" participate actively in their children's programs and schools, and they *expect* teachers to discipline their children as severely as is seen fit.

In startling contrast to the too-strict, inappropriately authoritarian, downputting, spirit-crushing adult, we have the absurdly overpermissive adult. Read what one intelligent mother and Waldorf educator writes about learning to be firm:

Most children are over-indulged, whether from love, insecurity or mistaken ideals. With a second or third child, there just isn't time to indulge her every whim, and life has to become more rhythmical and orderly or mother won't survive. With my first child, I fell into the philosophical pit of not wanting to be authoritarian, and chaos reigned until I realized that I could (and should) insist on

right behavior. This needs to be done with calmness rather than anger, but with absolute certainty that the child can and will learn what is expected. It is appropriate that parents be guardians and guides (less charged words than *authorities*) and help children in the process of becoming pleasant as well as bright three-year-olds! Your children unconsciously trust you to know more about becoming adults than they do. Because their **ego** is not yet fully incarnated, you must provide the **ego** for them (that is, the source of wisdom and responsibility that holds them and keeps them from getting "out of themselves"), just as an effective teacher does this for an entire class in school (Baldwin, p. 101)

Mature adult **ego** is able to balance the mental health need to be autonomous and assertive within the boundaries determined by the child's culture, with the mental health need to respect other individuals, groups, and society, and to live relatively harmoniously and empathetically with them. In our culture, and most in the world, many females are brought up in ways that cause them to have more difficulty with the former, and many males are raised in ways that prevent them from developing the attitude and interpersonal skills required to do the latter with individuals of *both* genders.

When parents and caregivers practice strengthening a child's character by showing respect and further opportunities to develop his existing strengths, it's the ego they're relating to and strengthening

The **ego,** or most grown-up piece of self, flexibly and intelligently responds to realistic facts of the present.

● Whereas the *id* (child) part of the self system is much concerned with what it wants, wishes, demands, fantasizes, would deem fulfilling, and feels impelled to dump on others,

● Whereas the *super-ego* (internalized parent, conscience) part of the self system focuses on what "they" say I *should* be, *who* "they" say I should be, *how* "they" say I should live, and so on,

the **ego** concentrates on probabilities, possibilities, and positive action. It translates and applies instructions from the past and yearnings for the future to the current situation relatively *appropriately.* If the instructions in-

Urine, Feces, and Sense of Self

One of the many things that's happening as the **ego** (sense of self and, hopefully, *pride* in self) develops is the toddler's awareness of what's *outside* his body and what's *inside.* If he likes his body, he's likely to like the products his body makes (urine and feces). Yet—how bewildering!—though nobody asks him to give up his foot, "they want me to give them my poop!" More confusing even than that is the fact that once he gives them this interesting part of himself, they trash it—they flush it. If all goes gradually, with encouragement, and without excessive criticism, the toddler or two-year-old slowly moves from delighting in diaper-type messiness to being pleased that he can achieve one more of the competencies that are such an important part of his self-esteem—bladder and bowel control.

Major internal conflicts between *id* and **ego** go on at this time in the toddler's life. In many instances, major *external* conflicts between child and parent or other caregiver go on too, as the child struggles to decide how he will best gain gratification—by doing what comes naturally *(id),* or by doing what he deems wisest, all things (including winning adult approval) considered **(ego).**

Shaming the young child with regard to toilet learning behaviors usually backfires. Because his understanding of what is him*self* and what are expendable *products* from his body is still blurry, he may learn to be ashamed of toileting accidents *and of himself.* We are working so hard to create positive self-esteem in the child that we wouldn't want to *lower* it by shaming him and having him misinterpret or exaggerate what we're shaming him about.)

scribed on the child's *superego* by his parents are limiting to his potential to be a free person, as defined by his culture, the child's **ego,** if healthy and strong, tries to break their spell as he grows up. Mature **ego** is the creative coper.

When a normally nicely behaved toddler or two-year-old disintegrates before our very eyes, appearing to become an irrational lunatic, when we exchange glances expressing disbelief and throw our hands up in dismay, when we say the child "has lost it," we're dealing with a situation in which the child's **ego** (mature self) has temporarily "disintegrated," has temporarily lost control, and *id* feelings are running the show. The child *has* "lost it"; she has lost control of herself. The sensible, self-aware part of herself has been briefly overcome by *id* feelings too strong for her newly evolving **ego** —inner controls—to restrain. The dam of self-control (self-discipline) has burst. Exhaustion, extremely emotional experiences, and over-stimulation can cause **ego** to lose control, but so can less dramatic situations. We can't always see the cause.

As their parents and other caregivers, one of the important ways in which we can help toddlers, and two-year-olds build good character is to relate to their *mature* self as much as possible—trusting it, talking to it, endorsing and encouraging it.

More about the development of conscience

Conscience—the internalization of parental and other adult expectations, policies, procedures, ideas of right and wrong, and morality— *self discipline*— develops throughout infancy, toddler-

hood, and the child's third year, as well as after these years. During the second half of the first year, babies usually become quite cooperative with adults about adhering to familiar routines (e.g., "the right way to do it," the adult's expectation). The baby will usually plop his head down when put in bed, start to play when placed in the playpen, sit contentedly in the car seat when buckled in, etc. This compliance indicates that the baby is aware of the adult's feelings, and that the adult's assumptions are becoming the baby's assumptions. The senior baby (nine to twelve months) has learned *motivation* to win adult favor— "to be good"; both needed and fun things, like passing a toy back and forth, come through cooperation and communication. The crawler recognizes that behavior which previously brought reprimands is prohibited. This recognition indicates the beginning of memory and of the process of "swallowing" the grown-up so he or she can become an internal instead of external guide. But a one-year-old is nowhere near ready, yet, to regulate her own behavior! She may be dimly beginning to get the idea, but she definitely doesn't yet have control of all aspects of self! (As a matter of fact, do any of us ever?)

However, throughout the child's *second* year, *external conflict* (fighting about the "right way" to do it) *gradually becomes internal conflict*—a battle between the child-self and the more adult-self (the part that will eventually evolve into conscience) *within.* Toddlers tell themselves "no-no!" They're concerned about peers in distress, and may try to help them.

Many classic and neo-Freudian psychoanalysts have studied and theorized about conscience (morality) since the 1930s (for example, Anna Freud,

Fenichel, Rapaport, Hoffman, Kennedy, Rest, Yorke, Kopp, Damon, Klinnert, Sorce, Emde, and Buchsbaum all have studied where the human self-control mechanism, conscience, and the internalization of "good" and "bad" morality, come from, and how). Helen Buchsbaum and Robert Emde write:

We propose that propensities for moral internalization are strongly biological, but require facilitation and direction through accumulated experiences within the infant-caregiver relationship. . . . [We] have found that by 2 years, children normally show clear evidence of the components of moral development. (1990, p.131)

Here is a situation in which expert parents and caregivers have known a truth denied for years by theoreticians and researchers. While we have known that older two-year-olds know a lot about what their grown-ups believe is right and wrong (empathy and cooperative responses are good, opposition to adults' policies and procedures is bad) and have a fairly good, if still primitive, set of preliminary self-controls, psychoanalysts insisted until very recently that this could not be so until after "the resolution of the oedipal conflict" (age five), and Piagetians told us that it couldn't be until approximately age seven! There is some danger in developing a theory based on observing a small sample of children—usually in a highly artificial lab setting where the richness and variety of children's behavior and interpersonal relations can't be seen —researching its validity in a self-fulfilling prophecy way, writing it in textbooks, and teaching it to students as a doctrine of our profession. When students memorize authors and their theories, they may not truly observe and think about individual children.

Shaming children is the opposite of encouraging self-esteem and is not necessary in helping children develop strong conscience

Shame is a powerful feeling. If experienced severely, it's rarely forgotten, and recurs, carrying almost as heavy and painful a charge each time, even years later. Experiences of feeling deeply ashamed and humiliated are not uncommon among people's earli-

---

One of the most important ways in which we can help toddlers and two-year-olds build good character is to relate to their mature self as much as possible — trusting it, talking to it, endorsing and encouraging it.

One of the dangers of expecting unrealistic "performance" from a child is that her superego may begin making more and more unrealistic perfectionist demands of her "self," so she almost always feels she is falling far short of her ever more idealized self. She will feel ashamed of herself even if no one shamed her.

est memories. To feel ashamed as a person older than three is to feel exposed; someone disapproving (parent? teacher? peers? imagined audience? conscience?) is seeing a secret side of us—is seeing *inside* us, and is seeing something disgusting.

Many parents, teachers, and other children (*especially* siblings) shame young children. The gist of the taunt always amounts to trying to make the child feel incompetent. This becomes partially internalized as "What I think of myself compared to" ("You should be ashamed of yourself!") and *superego* (conscience) kicks in. Society reinforces many sanctions. Mommy may have said it first, but it then becomes, "What will the neighbors think?" A child may even be told (or an older person may sense on her own) that God knows everything she does *or even thinks*. If self-discipline and self-esteem are the goal, we want children to look at their behavior and evaluate it, but we *don't* want them to judge themselves too harshly or unrealistically, or to believe that they are failures.

A younger sibling may do this to himself even if no one does it *to* him. For example, Jeffie felt very inferior to his four- and six-year-old brothers because at two-and-a-half he couldn't speed around on a trike like brother Mike, or run as fast, express himself as well, pump his legs to make the swing go as high in the sky, or read like brother Steve. Throughout his childhood, Jeffie felt ashamed of what he viewed as his deficiencies—he *never* was able to do what his always ahead brothers could newly do.

Adults can't be responsible for how a child misjudges himself, or to whom he compares himself, but we can be sure not to contribute to his unfair self-evaluations and feelings of shame.

When shame is too overwhelming, the person experiencing it does not allow herself to feel it. Without being aware of it, she wraps it in layer upon layer of protective padding, then hides it beneath cleverly camouflaging beliefs and behaviors. Thus a child, adolescent, or adult who feels deep shame about himself in some secret place within may behave shamelessly, as if he doesn't care what anyone thinks. The attitude and actions are like military feints or mother sandpipers faking broken wings and racing away from their eggs or baby birds to mislead the predator. The person is protecting himself from feeling shame so great that he fears it would disable him if he faced it. He's protecting himself from people who, if they sensed his problem, might dangle it in front of his eyes, like a dead and rotting rat, forcing him —horrified—to face it. A person who must spend a great deal of emotional energy protecting a hidden part of self from the watchful eye of self-aware self **(ego)** and from the judgmental view of conscience *(superego)* does not have the emotional energy available to power initiative, purposefulness, and enthusiasm. Overall personality and interpersonal relations are harmed. However, if conscience is reasonable, resilient **ego** doesn't concentrate on defending itself. It can allow into self-awareness some feelings of mild guilt and shame.

If the achievement of mental health and other successes in the mainstream American culture is the goal, it isn't a good idea to make a child feel frequently or deeply ashamed. He will sometimes make himself feel that way, even if his grown-ups avoid ridiculing him and confine themselves to firm limit-setting—and we *must* set firm limits wherever we feel they should be. But it's one thing to say, "You can't race around this room and stand on the chairs. We don't allow it," and quite another to say, "You're giving me a headache. You're such a naughty girl. You should be ashamed of yourself. One of these days you'll give me a heart attack." We want toddlers and twos to begin to feel *occasional* regret for having done something wrong ("I'm disappointing someone I care about"), *mild* shame ("I'm not proud of myself when I do this"), and enough self-criticism and remorse to make them hesitate for a moment before doing it again—but not so much that they don't *dare* do it again. The child will probably do it again many times, but each firm, fair reprimand adds to his growing wish to exercise self-control —and eventually he usually will. This is called self-discipline. In mainstream American culture, **excessive shame prevents appropriate adaptation to life, including appropriate, balanced self-discipline.**

For better and for worse, mental health includes accepting "self" as is

Each of us has an image of ourself as we would like to be—as we wish we were—as we would be if we could be. It's usually a little (or *more* than a little) idealized—too good to be true. On the other hand, each of us has secret knowledge of the worst side of ourselves; each of us knows of undesirable traits, indiscretions, nasty habits, and sins of which we are "guilty." We may exaggerate *this* side of self too, and feel guiltier than is really necessary. But as long as a person is aware of his idealized self *and* not-so-hot self, and doesn't allow either one to get out of hand (in other words, as long as the **ego** can keep a balance between the two and a sense of reality), all is well.

How Does Good Character Develop?

Applying the Principle of "Disciplining Without Shaming" to a Difficult Behavior—Biting

Is it normal for toddlers and two-year-olds to bite? Why do they do it? What should we do when one child bites another? As one of the rare pediatricians who is sophisticated about psychological and social aspects of child development (not just about physical aspects of child development) explained to a poor, suffering mother, "Biting in toddlers and two-year-olds is not 'average'—most *don't* bite—but it is 'normal'; at least one out of ten *does* bite, so you can't consider it *ab*normal." Biting in preschoolers is more alarming than biting in one- and two-year-olds, but biting *at any age* must be consistently and unmistakably discouraged from the first episode.

A mistake that many adults make through which they unintentionally invite biting is playing pretend "gonna eat you up" games. Adults should assiduously avoid biting games with babies and other young children. As every caregiver or parent who has had to deal with a prolonged bout of biting is keenly aware, biting is an extremely serious problem because it's

- terrifying to the child who is bitten (while being bopped is not);
- enraging to the victim's parents;
- a behavior that can take over like a virulent virus—a behavior that can swiftly "infect" an otherwise lovely child's behavior with peers to the point where he or she simply can't be permitted within arm's length of other children;
- frightening to the biter to feel so powerful—and so out of control;
- **very** hard to prevent or cure, certainly without enough adults to assign one to the biter as a non-stop guard who blocks each unexpected and lightening quick attempt to bite (and sometimes is accidently bitten in the process);

- extremely distressing to parents and other caregivers.

In group care, biting has to be stopped as soon as humanly possible; it can't be tolerated.

There are different kinds of biters. **There are babies who take an experimental bite** out of mother's breast (shoulder, hand, etc.). Often a sharp, startled "No!" accompanied by pulling the flesh and the baby apart—perhaps repeated on a few more occasions—puts an end to the painful practice. Teething babies need lots to bite on as well as prompt, clear signals not to bite people. Adults must never laugh about this. If they do, they give a mixed message and can expect to be bitten again.

There are toddlers and twos who become utterly frustrated in an interaction with a playmate, and, lacking adequate language, negotiating techniques, and self-control to satisfactorily solve the problem, lean over and chomp the other child's cheek or arm. This may be a reflexive reaction to frustration. The child honestly may not have meant to do it, and may be startled by what he did and by everyone's shocked reaction. Usually one or all of these approaches together works:

- react very disapprovingly (but not harshly);
- immediately comfort and care for the victim and the victim's wound; and then
- carefully and colleaguially explain to the biter that—
  —biting *hurts very much,*
  —(name) *can't bite,*
  — *biting is not allowed* because it makes friends *so sad,*
  — *biting is not nice,*
  — *biting is a no-no,* if (name) needs help, *go to a grown-up, we will help you* (state the problem get a turn with the . . . , or whatever).

Several such episodes usually end

the biting. With this type of language-lacking, impulsive biter, it's important for the caregiver to intervene **quickly** and also to *(1)* **watch for signs of rising frustration,** *(2)* **teach the child to recognize his feelings,** *(3)* **teach the child suitable words to express feelings or to get something.**

A third kind of biter is the child who feels threatened. The child believes she or her rights are endangered and bites in self-defense. Another child may indeed be provoking her. The group may be large, the child small, and the whole scene just too much. The approaches just listed, combined with ensuring that she, her rights, her possessions, and so forth, are safe, generally are effective. The insecure child who doesn't know what to do with her feelings needs a great deal of help in recognizing and managing them.

Of course, if the child *really is* in danger due to violence in the home or immediate neighborhood, or war, empty reassurances won't be enough. Endangered children are terribly fearful and insecure for good reason. The only thing that seems to help in desperate circumstances is a strong, reassuring adult who shields and shelters the child as much as she or he can from the horrors, practices the most developmentally appropriate child-rearing possible under the circumstances, and maintains a warm, loving relationship with the child in spite of all.

A fourth kind of biter is the power biter. Probably the smallest number of biters can be described as power biters. All children need to feel a sense of personal power. Preventing biting includes responding promptly to the bite-prone child so that he feels interpersonally effective (powerful); helping him learn effective interpersonal skills with peers so he can influence them without resorting to biting; offering him many choices so he perceives himself as a person with the power that competencies bring; and encouraging him to develop and use the power of language.

Biting brings instant and dramatic results. If the child is trying to get a grown-up's attention, biting gets it. If the child is trying to get another child's attention, biting gets it. Therefore, *giving* the child attention and assisting him in winning the attentions of peers when he *isn't* biting somebody reduces the child's tendency to bite for attention-getting purposes. It's easy to think that the power biter, who smiles at his success while the bitten child shrieks and bleeds, is malicious. Indeed he may be. Some children are very angry. For whatever reason, some children do seem to have a "mean streak." But this is uncommon, and even if it were the case in a particular instance, angry adults make angry children, so a calm, educational child guidance approach is most effective if solving this behavior is our objective, rather than getting revenge on a "bad" child.

The first time a child bites, the caregiver should casually mention the incident to a parent, find out if biting has occurred elsewhere before, and informally discuss the approach that was used in the program on the day of the incident to discourage the behavior. The parent may be distressed and should be comforted. The caregiver's attitude can be collaborative: "Don't worry, we're in this together, we'll solve it." We encourage the parent to take a firm stand with regard to biting if it happens at home.

If this and the other methods already mentioned don't work, and the biting increases, an adult must be assigned to stand so close to the child, and keep such a close eye on him, that she or he can jump in at a moment's notice and intercept a bite. **Biting is such an effective method of getting someone's attention that each time an essen-** **tially powerless young child bites and senses the powerful weapon she has stumbled upon, the behavior is strongly reinforced.** Therefore, the goal is to prevent the child from experiencing any reward, including the "reward" of enjoying dominance over another person, by preventing a bite from occurring. Every intended bite must be intercepted. This may mean that the likely biter is told he or she can't play near (so-and-so), but must play (this) far away so we can keep (so-and-so) safe. "It's my job to keep children safe; I can't let you hurt her by biting her." Besides being there to intercept any forthcoming bite, alertly standing by gives the caregiver an opportunity to discover the child's pattern. What signals us that the child is about to bite?

If the biter has had success of any kind as a result of this behavior (at home, in another setting), our problem in stopping it is worsened. Overpermissive parents fail to teach their children "limits" and self-discipline. They have inappropriately low behavioral expectations for their children, and the children oblige by not having high standards for themselves. They don't know any better because they haven't been taught any better. Overprotective parents, while not in general overpermissive, always want to give their children the benefit of the doubt, so do not transmit unmistakable messages about the unacceptability of biting. In either instance, we must help parents understand the great disservice they do their children: They are ensuring that children and adults will shun their child, leaving him lonely and in danger of developing low self-esteem in the social domain.

Sometimes when a young biter (hitter, kicker, scratcher) is in group care, the *group* can be mobilized to help the aggressive child overcome the undesirable behavior. The teacher assembles the children around her and says confidingly and soberly, "Mary Ellen has a very big problem, and I want to know if everybody will help her. Do we all want to help her?" (The children will chorus, "Yes!") When Mary Ellen is being a *big* girl, she never, ever, ever bites (hits, kicks, scratches) *anybody*. But sometimes she forgets, and hurts somebody—she bites (hits, kicks, scratches) somebody. "Do we like it when Mary Ellen bites?" (The children will chorus, "No!")

The teacher turns to Mary Ellen and says, "The children don't like it when Mary Ellen hurts them. We want Mary Ellen to be a *big* girl, not a biting (hitting, kicking, scratching) girl. Can you be a big girl, Mary Ellen?" (The child will say "Yes.")

Turning to the group again, the teacher asks, "Who will help Mary Ellen be a big girl?" (The children will chorus their willingness to help.) "O.K.," says the teacher, "If Mary Ellen looks like she's getting upset, say, 'Don't bite, Mary Ellen! Remember! Be a big girl! *Talk* about it.'"

Teachers who have tried this technique are amazed at how eagerly and earnestly a group will attempt to help a peer "be big," and how appreciative and responsive the individual with the problem behavior will be. Using the strength of *positive* peer pressure to help a child is often effective. **This approach should be used only in conjunction with the other approaches discussed here.**

Biting—and other unacceptably aggressive behaviors such as hitting, kicking, and scratching —can be converted to verbal negotiations, cooperation, turn-taking, and so on by firm, kind, consistent, *patient* adults, working as a team. As the toddler and two-year-old learn to become socially competent, their self-esteem is enhanced. Learning age-appropriate self-discipline increases pride in *self*— self-esteem. Gently teaching good-enough behavior is not taking time from the curriculum; it's an essential element in the *core* curriculum —character development.

However, one of the dangers of expecting unrealistic "performance" from a child is that her *superego* may begin making more and more unrealistic perfectionist demands of her "self," so she almost *always* feels she's falling far short of her ever more unrealistically idealized self. She will feel ashamed of herself even if no one shamed her. All her life, she denigrates herself. She may project this self view and feel that parents, teachers, peers, and supervisors are denigrating her. This can get very discouraging. The safest course of action for parents and caregivers whose goal for each child is mental health is to help each child behave in a good enough way most of the time, applauding a few exemplary episodes, forgiving a few unfortunate transgressions, and always putting into words what's going on in these dimensions.

It's also important to help toddlers and two-year-olds accept their oppositional, "naughty," fearful, and angry feelings and behaviors as part of self. They shouldn't have to invent a fantasy friend, to whom they attribute all their furious emotions and acts (although some will anyway!). With language comes the danger that a child will only discuss — eventually only be *aware* of — his idealized, ultra-socialized, "veneer" self — a *false* self — and will repress (forget) all "*id*" and disapproved aspects of self, unconsciously coming to view this "unmentionable," "bad" self as his only *true* self — "the real me." Winnicott was the first psychoanalyst to wonder whether a *false* self might arise from the process of socialization and the advent of language. Bowlby (1969/1990, vol. 3) and Stern (1985) both speculated that language acquisition makes it possible for a child to be persuaded (by beloveds, other caregivers, and playmates) that he is someone other than the self he felt (through his emotional and sensorimotor experiences) he was. The child may begin to believe that his false, perfect self is *him*. Feeling that he's expected to be perfect, and expecting *himself* to be perfect, yet knowing he isn't, he may develop deep shame about who he wrongly believes he really is.

We frequently contribute to a child's misunderstanding of himself, or falsifying of self, without realizing it. "Say you're sorry. Jake is sorry he hit you." (Jake is *not* sorry.) "Mira, get out of the mud! Mira doesn't want to get her lovely dress dirty!" (Mira doesn't care a bit if she gets her lovely dress dirty.) And of course our famous line, "We're all friends here," which denies the intricacies of the many different relationships among the children in any group.

Two-and-a-half-year-old Emeralda, for example, loves her mom, knows her mom is happy about nine-month-old Terry, but increasingly resents this brother who crawls into and interferes with everything she's doing. It helps Emmy accept her negative feelings as a legitimate aspect of her *self* to hear her mother acknowledge and allow them — put them in words, and not appear dismayed by them: "I see you're angry at Terry. He's bothering you." "I guess it makes you mad to see me busy nursing Terry when you need me to snap your teddy's coat." Protecting the child from having real reason to accumulate unmanageable amounts of anger is also important: "I'll take Terry out of your way. He can play in his high chair and watch us." "I helped you fix a bed for your teddy before I sat down to nurse Terry. Soon I'll be finished and I'll help snap teddy's coat."

Skilled caregivers informally pass insights and pointers along to parents. Skilled parents try to share insights with caregivers, but many of the latter have an aversion to partnerships with parents — in spite of their words — so don't listen.

Sense of self compared to others — learning to live with diversity — at infant, toddler, and two-year-old developmental levels

We don't develop a sense of self in a vacuum, or just within the family's dynamics. Each person — even if merely one and two years old — contrasts himself with all sorts of other people. We are alike and different in many ways.

Children are smart in different ways from one another. Observing each of them carefully as they go through their days with us, and conversing with their families about their special interests and abilities, will reveal that some two-year-olds have unusual language and thinking ability, some have a surprising talent for figuring out or grasping mathematical concepts. Some have

---

Are you aware of each child's family situation (adoptive, interracial, cultural factors, religion, socioeconomic)? Do you actively include endorsing remarks, resource people, outings, books, foods, etc., in your daily program?

Young children's "selves" are still very much merged with those of their parents or guardians. If we send out negative nonverbal vibes about a child's parent, or make negative remarks, the child feels disparaged. This is not good for her self-esteem.

---

amazing spatial awareness for their age, some are unusually sensitive about music, rhythm, and movement, and some have exceptional small-motor abilities. Some children—even though not yet three years old—astonish us with their interpersonal skills, and some are extraordinarily insightful, like Angela a few pages ago. We want to encourage all children to feel confident and to develop competence in all dimensions, but we can also assist children in appreciating specialties they or others may have.

One's race, obvious physical anomalies, ethnicity and culture (which in some cases includes religion), socio-economic status, and family composition are important aspects of *self*, hence of self-image. By three years of age, and in many instances much sooner, children are keenly aware of family composition differences, race and body differences, and the more obvious ethnic and cultural differences (Katz, 1982; Ramsey, 1987; Derman-Sparks, 1989). Soon after, if not earlier, children become aware of glaring socioeconomic differences.

There are only two things about people who appear to be different in any way that babies, toddlers, and two-year-olds need to learn from their grown-ups:

● To feel good about family composition, race, body, ethnic and cultural, and socioeconomic aspects of self; and

● To feel good about family composition, race, body, ethnic and cultural, and socioeconomic aspects of other people they meet.

What do we do? We continuously act in accordance with our overall philosophy of encouraging each child to accumulate positive self-esteem-building encounters in any and every dimension including, specifically and directly, experiences relating to his and other people's

● family format
● color
● physical or ability differences
● cultural habits
● language or dialect
● socioeconomic status, etc.

This is considerably easier said than done, because, as we all know, these are value-laden subjects. They are touchy, sometimes volatile.

Diversity in family composition is difficult for many caregiving adults to accept because it threatens entrenched, heartfelt hearth and home beliefs

Many expert practitioners find that children whose families are "different" are aware of it—and sensitive on the subject—before they are aware of other kinds of differences. Probably this is because very young children's selves **(egos)** are still so merged with their families. The distance between toddler and parents is not great. The boundaries of the toddler's **ego** are not obvious; the toddler's **ego** is amorphous and amoeba-like, frequently merging briefly back into the parents—typically the mother. Therefore, if an outside authority figure seems suspicious, skeptical, or disapproving about a child's family (because the parent is a single parent, because the parents are a different race from the child or from each other, because the child has two mothers who live as a married couple, or for any other reason), the child, still quite egocentric, perceives that the adult is questioning his or her OK-ness, and suffers tinges of self-doubt.

Many people forget about non-stereotypic families as they work and talk with little children everyday. Therefore, they say things that omit or violate the adopted child, the child living in a reconstituted family with "his, hers, and theirs" children, children of never-married mothers, and so on. Many people don't believe that a non-stereotypic family is an O.K. family. Many people, for example, still firmly hold to the notion that all **divorced families** are "broken." They make no distinction between *acute divorce* (a sharp, often painful changing period) and divorce a year or more ago (no longer transitioning, a new family format "chapter" in ever-evolving family life). Therefore, they don't see that some divorced families are suffering, others are happily recovering and healing, and yet others are just normal families; "divorced" is simply one of many descriptive words applicable to them. Biased observers view with pity, without looking at individual situa-

tions, all children living in divorced families. Because of their basic attitudes about divorce, these adults are not able to genuinely convey to each child in the group—whenever a casual, conversational opportunity arises—that a divorced family may be as "O.K." a family form as any other. **The toddler or two-year-old living in a divorcing or divorced family slowly but surely picks up negative vibes about her family (e.g., about an aspect of her *self*), and is drip-by-drip formulating negative self-esteem with regard to the family dimension of self.**

What can we do? Besides monitoring ourselves in this regard, we can include among the books we read to our two-year-olds books about the vicissitudes of family composition. We need books about co-parents who live in two different homes; a mother (or mother

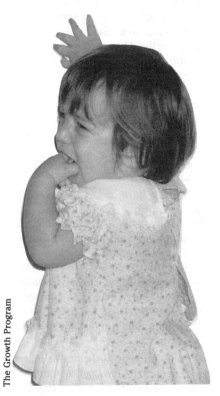

The Growth Program

One of the biggest jobs a toddler's ego has to accomplish is to reconcile two opposites: the need to separate from loved, needed, and respected adults in order to develop autonomy, and the need to be deeply and affectionately connected to them. The dual urges can cause some stormy scenes!

animal) and her children where no mention is made of a father (for children who don't know their biological father, like Willy, whose mother is single, or children whose father is no longer in the picture and who don't have another father); books about a father (or father animal) and his children where no mention is made of a mother (for children who don't know their biological mother or whose mother is no longer in the picture, and who don't have another mother like Mary, whose mother abandoned her,); and books where the "parent" is a grandparent, like Shantele, whose mother has lived in another state to go to dental school since Shantele was a few months old. These are not stories about parents separating, or visiting daddies, or tragedy. This type of book simply presents an eminently satisfactory unconventional family. For example:

I Know I'm Myself Because (mother only);

Oh Lord, I Wish I Was a Buzzard (father only);

"More, More, More!" Said the Baby: 3 Love Stories (mother only, father only, grandma only);

Are You My Daddy?; Are You My Mommy?; Grandma and Me; Grandpa and Me; Daddy and Me; Mommy and Me; Ten, Nine, Eight (father puts daughter to bed); and *A Man Can Be* (two fathers).

Children who hear these stories learn that there are all kinds of O.K. families — without a lecture from us or an awkward silence when a child says something about a "different" family. We comment whenever it fits into the conversation that each family is different and there are all kinds of families.

The younger the child, the more of her*self* is simply how she sees her family reflected in the eyes of important others.

Many people aren't acquainted with, so don't feel comfortable with, biracial families (mom is white, dad is black; dad is white, mom is Asian; or the parent is white and the child is Hispanic, etc.). So they avoid the subject with children. They act colorblind. It's best to openly and pleasantly comment on these facts, **but only after asking the parents how they prefer to have the matter handled.** If you aren't experienced in this area, you may want to read an article entitled, "Are You Sensitive to Interracial Children's Special Identity Needs?" (Wardle, 1987). There are almost no books for children younger than three that show interracial families, but many books for toddlers and preschoolers show people of various races in the pictures; having these books around to look through with a few children at a time is better than nothing. Several useful titles are: *Babies; Friends;* and *Colors Around Me.*

Probably the hardest family format for teachers to accept in a matter-of-fact manner is the gay or lesbian family. Most caregivers probably "don't believe in" two-mother families like Susanne's, but there are more and more of them, so if you haven't had one in your program yet, you may very well one of these days. What we believe is right is one thing, and our obligation to be professionals who contribute to each child's self-esteem in every dimension is another (Clay, 1990).

It is circle time at the Happy Baby Childcare Center. Little three-year-old Susanne is sharing with her class her latest visit to the zoo. "Well, Mama said that monkeys are smarter than us and Mommy said that they are very friendly." The teacher pauses and then asks, "Susanne, did you go to the zoo with your mother and grandmother?" Susanne says, "No, I went to the zoo with Mama and Mommy!" The teacher is clearly bewildered and would like to clarify for herself who Mama and Mommy are, but the rest of the children in the group are becoming restless. She leaves her questions for another time. . . .

Susanne represents one of the increasing numbers of children of lesbian parents in the country. . . . According to Hoeffer (1981), there are approximately 1.5 million lesbian mothers who reside in a family unit with their children, most of whom were born to mothers who had previously been in a heterosexual relationship. In addition, there is a growing trend toward artificial insemination among lesbian partners who wish to become parents. To illustrate, 150 children were born to lesbian mothers last year in the twin cities of Minneapolis-St. Paul, Minnesota. . . .

While the Koepke and Hare study cannot be generalized to the whole lesbian population, it does offer a limited profile of lesbian families. This sample of ninety-four women represented middle- and upper-middle-income families. In the majority of couples, both women worked outside the home. Average family income for the total sample was $55,687; average income for couples with children was $60,294. Overall, this was a highly educated group of women: 45% held a four-year college degree, 27% held a master's degree, and 13% held a Ph.D., a J.D., or an M.D. The couples had lived together for an average of five years, and the average number of children for parenting couples was 2.3. . . .

The academic program of most preschool teachers does not prepare them for variant family forms, like Susanne's, which currently exist in this country. It is vital that teachers have a heightened awareness and sensitivity to diversity in family structures in order to create the best learning environment for all children. (Hare & Koepke, 1990, pp. 20–21)

Susanne is older than two — she's three — but as has been said, two-year-olds are very sensitive to what people think of their families, and many "Susannes" are in child care settings at two. Two-year-olds are also very sensitive to the concepts of alike and different. They don't want to be so different that there isn't someone in their situation in the group or even in a book! So far, we've seen no good book about two-mother families, but sooner or later there's bound to be one. **Two-year-olds are very sensitive to inclusion. They feel that something is wrong with them if their form of family is never referred to in conversation, circle time, story time, or by playmates. Like all other children, these children need to hear their families validated.**

Our feelings on these sensitive subjects are contagious to the impressionable children we care for

Instead of hushing childen when they stare and make "embarrassing statements" about these facets of their friends and classmates, we join the conversation, smilingly adding interested and appreciative comments. Thus, each child receives an "I'm O.K., you're O.K." message that allows each to feel good about her family's configuration and color(s), the racial and other special aspects of herself, and so forth. Each affirming incident adds to the accumulating and solidifying dimensions of her positive self-esteem. Each such incident also adds to the child's embryonic good or accepting feelings about disabilities, race, religion, and other special aspects of those with whom she may come in contact.

Very young children are strongly imprinted with the deep-seated attitudes and feelings of those nearest and dearest to them. Therefore, if a parent or caregiver suddenly frowns, abruptly reprimands, and tries to change the subject, children sense our disapproval, fear, and discomfort; because they identify so intimately with their parents or guardians, they absorb these attitudes and feelings into themselves. One child learns that people who are "different" are people to pull away from. (Colin won't sit next to Jimmy at lunch because Jimmy is dark brown.) Another learns that *he* is "different," and that there is something

very alarming about that! (Jimmy learns that dark brown is uninviting and frightening to Colin who is *light* brown.) With our frowns, reprimands, and sudden subject changing, we have taught *both* children unfortunate "lessons."

What can we do? **If we support children's curiosity as we support it in all other areas of exploration and inquiry, the children sense that difference is a natural part of everyday life.***

What else do we do by way of communicating feelings that can help toddlers and two-year-olds gradually grow good feelings toward others? We make sure that we try to chat with *all* children, say encouraging things to *all* children, spend time with *all* children, and hug *all* children as equally as is feasible. Research has shown that teachers tend to neglect children who appeal to them less, which sometimes includes "foreign looking" children. (Translation: "children who look different from the children in *my* family.") Even babies and one-year-olds read our body language and facial expressions, as well as our tone, and soon, our words. If we avoid, hence discriminate against children in the group we care for, on the basis of family type or shape, race, disabilities, culture (which can include religion, where religion is a way of life), or socioeconomic status, few two-year-olds will miss it, although they are unlikely to have the least idea why you "don't like" certain children. By the same token, however, **when we take care of young children tenderly, try to understand and empathize with their needs, and are fair to one and all, we transmit these "good germs" too; we are "teaching" fairness and thoughtful responsiveness to others.**

Note: Dealing with diversity of all sorts is discussed in greater depth in volumes two and three of this three-volume set of books.

This cluster of behaviors is the opposite of biased discriminatory behaviors.

One- and two-year-olds are busy examining and classifying everything, why not what color their acquaintances are? Why not who has one arm and who has two?

It's developmentally appropriate for one- and two-year-olds to notice similarities and differences. They "notice" whether people are familiar or strange to them. They care about routines being "the same," and become discombobulated when schedules and procedures are "different." A great deal of their free play pertains to sorting and fitting activities (this shape is the same as that shape and that's why this piece fits into that slot). With all this in mind, it shouldn't surprise us that two-year-olds often stare at people, *especially at a person who looks different* (skin color, wheelchair, leg brace, stooped and wrinkled). It shouldn't surprise us that two-year-olds often comment on the fact that a classmate's family appears to be very different from the generalities they are just now learning about what a family consists of. (One child has no mother? Why, what do you mean? I'm just learning that *every* child has a mother!) With a two-year-old's primitive stage of mental development in mind—she's focusing on *like* and *unlike*—the following true story shouldn't shock us:

Two-and-a-half-year-old Katie is in the bank with her mother. On the far side of the large, marbled lobby, she spots Clyde, a neighborhood friend of hers, a clerk who works at the supermarket. He's African American. Delighted to see him, and suddenly noticing a detail about him which had escaped her before, the color of his skin, she shouts for all in the lobby to hear, "You look like chocolate!" Stunned silence falls as all banking transactions stop. Everyone stares in horror at the child, the man, or the mother.

Do you have posters, pictures cut out of magazines, pictures reproduced and enlarged from children's books, etc., showing children and adults with special needs?

How Does Good Character Develop?

Mercifully, Katie's mother is quick on her feet. Smiling warmly at the man, she loudly says, "Yes, and chocolate is your favorite thing, isn't it!" To which Katie immediately responds, racing across the expanse of the seemingly endlessly big lobby into Clyde's arms, "Yes, and Clyde is my favorite friend!" Laughing, Katie's mother walks straight to Clyde, and putting her hand on his arm says so everyone can hear, "Well, if *that* wasn't the most embarrassing thing that ever happened! Luckily, you and I know that Katie loves you and loves chocolate, and intended a compliment, and was just saying what she's seeing, the way two-year-olds do!" The three strolled out of the bank hand in hand, the two adults feeling that they were co-survivors of a devastating problem in our society, racial tensions.

Young children are often much more matter-of-fact than are adults.

Brian was playing with Brad. Brad said, "Where's your other arm?" Brian said, "I have *this* arm." Brad said, "But where is your *other* arm?" Brian said, "This is my arm." Brad said, "Oh." The two continued to play and the subject didn't come up again, it had been settled.

Unfortunately, most of the books showing young children and adults with disabilities are *about* disabilities. What we're looking for is, *good literature* about children's issues and activities that simply *include* children with special needs. But better than books, anyway, are *people* of as big a variety as we can mobilize to participate in the daily lives of the children we care for.

Our feelings about socioeconomic class and educational levels come through in subtle if not in blatant ways. We look *up* to some parents. We look *down* on others. Children sense this. It shows when we make eye contact with and address certain parents more frequently than others, and seek their advice, while to others we *give* advice. It shows in the tones of our voices. It shows when we seat ourselves near some parents, but not others. It shows when we teach conventional "lessons" like the names of the rooms in a home and talk about the "dining" room, and a bedroom for each person or two persons.

Our feelings about religion come through, too. Except in child care programs sponsored by other religions, it's generally assumed that all participating families are Christian. It's more than a matter of Christmas—we need to become at least superficially familiar with religions represented in our child care settings (and country), and keep their highlights in mind as we spend our days with young children. Children don't find religious diversity hard:

Noam Yitz and Celia, two advanced players, are playing pretend. Noam Yitz says, "You be Haman, and I'm gonna shake the grogger at you because you'e so bad." "Yeah!" Celia shouts gleefully (although she has no idea what Noam Yitz is talking about; it's the story of Purim, isn't it?")

Noam continues, "You be Queen Esther. You have to have the feast."

"O.K.," Celia agrees. Being a queen sounds good. She makes her contribution to the plan,

"And you can be Donder and Blitzen." (Aren't they two of Santa's reindeer?)

Becoming sensitive to concerns about diversity is difficult but ever so possible.

*　　*　　*

Families have more influence on children's character, self-esteem, and self-discipline than anyone else. But as more and more American infants, toddlers, and two-year-olds spend more hours a day developing in the care of family day care providers, caregivers in centers, and in-home caregivers (because they continue to develop regardless of where they are), we have correspondingly more and more influence in shaping them. It's primarily through our relationships and conversations with children and their families that we do this, although the routines, activities, and friends we offer play an important part in it. It isn't necessary for every caregiver to know theories and research results, although ideas like those in this chapter are very interesting to many people and can enhance our confidence that what we're doing and believing makes sense to others, expert in their own way about young children, less directly than we, but equally validly. Learning what theorists think and researchers find can increase caregivers' self-esteem as they become ever more professional child developers, and can sometimes provide insight and direction when we feel baffled.

When society unveils and bestows its awards and rewards, parents and other caregivers are usually left unlaurelled; but while we work for better wages, benefits, working conditions, and the respect of our country for what we do, we can take great pride in our work: We contribute significantly to the mental health and good character of our nation's future citizens.

In the next six chapters—chapters 6 through 11—we take a detailed look at child development during the first, second, and third years of life, ages three months to three years, with emphasis on what we as caregivers can do to optimize it.

Michael D. Sullivan

Some important sources of self-esteem are feeling that we can positively affect others, feeling lovable, feeling capable and competent, feeling listened to and accepted.

For further reading

Adams, P.L., Milner, J.R., & Schrepf, N.A. (1984). *Fatherless chilren*. New York: Wiley.

Ainsworth, M., Blehar, M., Waters, E., & Walls, S. (1978). *Patterns of attachment*, Hillsdale, NJ: Erlbaum.

Arend, R., Grove, F., & Stroufe, L.A. (1979). Continuity of individual adaptation from infancy to kindergarten: A predictive study of ego—resiliency and curiosity in preschoolers. *Child Development, 50,* 950–959.

Asher, S.R., & Gottman, J.M. (Eds.). (1981). *The development of children's friendships*. New York: Cambridge University Press.

Asher, S.R., & Renshaw, A.D. (1981). Children without friends: Social knowledge and social skill training. In S.R. Asher & J.M. Gottman (Eds.) *The development of children's friendships*. (pp. 273–296). New York: Cambridge University Press.

Bandura, A. (1986). *Social foundations of thought and action*. Englewood Cliffs, NJ: Prentice-Hall.

Barnett, M.A., King, L.M., Howard, J.A., & Dino, G.A. (1980). Empathy in young children. Relation to parents' empathy, affection, and emphasis on the feelings of others. *Developmental Psychology, 16,* 243–244.

Basch, M. (1983). Empathetic understanding. *Journal of American Psychoanalytic Association, 31,* 101–126.

Baumrind, D. (1971). Current patterns of parental authority. *Developmental Psychology Monographs, 4* (1, part 2).

Brazelton, T.B., & Cramer, B.G. (1990). *The earliest relationship: Parents, infants, and the drama of early attachment*. New York: Addison-Wesley.

Bridges, K. (1931). *Social and emotional development of the preschool child*. London: Routledge & Kegan Paul.

Collins, W.A., & Gunnar, M. (1990). Social and personality development. In M.R. Rosenzweig & L.W. Partner (Eds.), *Annual Review of Psychology, 44,* 387–416.

Coopersmith, S. (1967). *The antecedents of self-esteem*. San Francisco: W.H. Freeman.

Corsaro, W.A. (1985). *Friendship and peer culture in the early years*. Norwood, NJ: Ablex.

Curry, N.E., & Bergen, D. (1987). The relationship of play to emotional, social, and gender/sex role development. In D. Bergen (Ed.), *Play as a medium for learning and development* (pp. 107–132). Portsmouth, NH: Heinemann.

Damon, W., & Hart, D. (1982). The development of self-understanding from infancy through adolescence. *Child Development, 53,* 841–864.

Dunn, J. (1988a). *Beginnings of social understanding*. Cambridge, MA: Blackwell.

Dunn, J. (1988b). *Normative life events as risk factors in childhood. Studies of psychosocial risk: The power of longitudinal data*. New York: Cambridge University Press.

Eckerman, C.O., Whatley, J.L., & Kutz, S.L. (1975). Growth of social play with peers during the second year of life. *Developmental Psychology, 11*(1), 42–49.

Eder, R.A., & Mangelsdorf, S.C. (in press). The emotional basis of early personality development: Implications for the emergent self-concept. In S.R. Briggs, R. Hogan, & W.H. Jones (Eds.), *Handbook of personality psychology*. New York: Academic.

Erikson, E. (1950). *Childhood and society* (2nd ed.) New York: Norton.

Escalona, S.K. (1968). *The roots of individuality*. Chicago, IL: Aldine.

Fallows, D. (1985). *A mother's work*. Boston, MA: Houghton Mifflin.

Gerson, K. (1986). *Hard choices: How women decide about work, career, and motherhood*. Irvine, CA: The University of California Press.

Greenspan, S., & Greenspan, N.T. (1985). *First feelings: Milestones in the emotional development of the child*. New York: Viking.

Harris, A.T. (1967). *I'm O.K. — You're O.K., A Practical Guide to Transactional Analysis*, New York: Harper and Row.

Harris, P. (1989). *Children and emotion*. Cambridge, MA: Blackwell.

Hartmann, H., Kris, E., & Loewenstein, R.M. (1941). Comments on the formation of psychic structure. *The Psychoanalytic Study of the Child, 2,* 11–38.

Hetherington, E.M. (Ed.), & Mussen, P.H. (Series Ed.). (1983). *Handbook of child psychology: Vol. 4. Socialization, personality, and social development (4th ed.)*. New York: Wiley.

Higgins, E.T., Ruble, D.W., & Hartup, W.W. (Eds.). (1983). *Social cognition and social development: A sociocultural perspective*. New York: Cambridge University Press.

Hoffman, M.L. (1983). Affective and cognitive process in moral internalization. In E.T. Higgins, D.N. Ruble, & W.W. Hartup (Eds.), *Social cognition and social development*. New York: Cambridge University Press.

Isaacs, S. (1933). *Social development in young children*. London: Routledge & Kegan Paul.

Izard, C.E., Kakan, J., & Zajonc, R.B. (Eds.) (1984). *Emotions, cognition, and behavior*. New York: Cambridge University Press.

Johnson, A., & Szurek, S. (1952). The genesis of antisocial acting out in children and adults. *Psychoanalytic Quarterly, 21* 323–343.

Kagan, J. (1981). *The second year. The emergence of self-awareness*. Cambridge, MA: Harvard University Press.

Kubie, L.S. (1958). The neurotic process as the focus of physiological and psychoanalytic research. *The Journal of Mental Science, 104*(435).

Lamb, M. (Ed.). (1986). *The father's role*. New York: Wiley.

Lewis, M., & Rosenblum, L.A. (Eds.). (1975). *Friendship and peer relations*. New York: Wiley.

Maccoby, E.E., & Jacklin, C. (1974). *The psychology of sex differences*. Stanford, CA: Stanford University Press.

Mack, J.E., & Ablon, S.L. (Eds.). (1985). *The development and sustenance of self-esteem in childhood*. Madison, CT: International Universities Press.

Mahler, M.S., Pine, F., & Bergman, A. (1975). *The psychological birth of the human infant*, New York: Basic.

Matas, L., Arend, R., Sroufe, L.A. (1978). Continuity of adaptation in the second year: The relationship between quality of attachment and later competence. *Child Development, 49*(3), 547–556.

Mecca, A.M., Smelser, N.J., & Vasconellos, J. (1989). *The social importance of self-esteem*. Berkeley, CA: University of California Press.

Mintzer, D., Als, H., Tronick, E.Z., & Brazelton, T.B. (1984). Parenting an infant with a birth defect: The regulation of self-esteem. *Psychoanalytic Study of the Child, 39,* 561–589.

Mordock, J.B. (1979). The separation-individuation process and developmental disabilities. *Exceptional Children, 46,* 176–184.

Murphy, L.B., Mintzer, D., & Lipsett, L.P. (1989). Psychoanalytic views of infancy. In S.I. Greenspan & G.H. Pollock (Eds.), *The course of life, vol. I, Infancy* (pp. 561–642). Madison, CT: International Universities Press.

Neugebauer, B. (Ed.). (1987). *Alike and different: Exploring our humanity with young children.* Redmond, WA: Exchange Press.

Patterson, J.G., DeBarsyshe, B.D., & Ramsey, E. (1989). A developmental perspective on antisocial behavior. *American Psychologist, 44*(2), 329–335.

Piaget, J. (1952). *The origins of intelligence in children.* Madison, CT: International Universities Press.

Piaget, J. (1954). *The construction of reality in the child.* (M. Cook, Trans.). New York: Basic.

Prescott, E., & Jones, E. (1967). *Group day care as a childrearing environment.* Pasadena, CA: Pacific Oaks College.

Resch, R. (1979). Hatching in the human infant at the beginning of separation-individuation: What it is and what it looks like. *Psychoanalytic Study of the Child. 34,* 421–444.

Rosenberg, M. (1979). *Conceiving the self.* New York: Basic.

Rothbaum, F., & Weisz, J.R. (1989). *Child psychopathology and the quest for control.* Newburg Park, CA: Sage.

Smetana, J.G. (1984). Toddlers' social interactions regarding moral and conventional transgressions. *Child Development, 55,* 1767–1776.

Spitz, R. (1965). *The first year of life: A psychoanalytic study of normal and deviant development of object relations.* Madison, CT: International Universities Press.

Sugarman, L. (1986). *Life-span development: Concepts, theories, and interventions.* London: Methuen.

Thomas, A., & Chess, S. (1977). *Temperament and development.* New York: Brunner/Mazel.

Tolpin, M. (1971). On the beginning of a cohesive self. *Psycholanalytic Study of the Child, 44*(2), 112–119.

Vaughn, B., Kopp, C.B., & Krakow, J.B. (1984). The emergence and consolidation of self-control from 18 to 30 months of age: Normative trends and individual differences. *Child Development, 55,* 990–1004.

Vygotsky, L.S. (1978). *Mind and society: The development of higher psychological processes.* Cambridge: Harvard University Press.

White, B.L. (1985). *The first years of life* (rev. ed.). Englewood Cliffs, NJ: Prentice-Hall.

White, B.L. (1988). *Educating the infant and toddler,* Lexington, MA: Lexington Books.

Wickes, F. (1972). *The inner world of childhood.* New York: Appleton-Century.

Winnicott, D.W. (1965). *The maturational processes and the facilitating environment.* Madison, CT: International Universities Press.

Woodcock, L. (1941). *Life and ways of the 2-year-old.* New York: Basic.

References

Baldwin, R. (1989). *You are your child's first teacher.* Berkeley: Celestial Arts, P.O. Box 7327, Berkeley, CA 94707.

Barnard, K., & Brazelton, T.B. (Eds.). (1990). *Touch: The foundation of experience.* New York: Bantam.

Bowlby, J. (1969/1990). *Attachment and loss.* (three volumes). New York: Basic.

Brazelton, T.B., Koslowski, B., & Main, M. (1974). The origins of reciprocity. In M. Lewis & L.A. Rosenblum (Eds.), *The effect of the infant on its caregiver* (pp. 49–76). New York: Wiley.

Brazelton, T.B. (1974) *Toddlers and parents.* New York: Dell Press.

Brazelton, T.B. (1983). *Infants and mothers.* New York: Delacorte Press.

Buchsbaum, Helen K., & Emde, Robert N. (1990). Play narratives in 36-month-old children. Early moral development and family relationships. In A.J. Solnit, P.B. Neubauer, S. Abrams, & A.S. Dowling (Eds.), *The psychoanalytic study of the child* (p. 131). New Haven, CT: Yale University Press.

Clay, J.W. (1990). Working with lesbian and gay parents and their children. *Young Children, 45*(3), 31–35.

Curry, N.E., & Johnson, O.N. (1990). *Beyond self-esteem: developing a genuine sense of human value.* Washington, DC: NAEYC

Damon, W. (1988). *The moral child.* New York: Free Press.

Derman-Sparks, L., & The A.B.C. Task Force. (1989). *Anti-bias curriculum: Tools for empowering young children.* Washington, DC: NAEYC.

Dijs, C. (1990). *Are you my daddy? A pop-up book.* New York: Simon & Schuster.

Dijs, C. (1990). *Are you my mommy? A pop-up book,* New York: Simon & Schuster.

Dombro, A. (1988). *Ordinary is extraordinary.* New York: Simon & Schuster

Erikson, E.H. (1950). *Childhood and society.* New York: Norton.

Fenichel, O. (1945). *The psychoanalytic theory of neurosis.* New York: Norton.

Freud, A. (1936/1960). *The ego and the mechanisms of defense.* New York: International University Press.

Hare, J., & Koepke, L.A. (Winter, 1990). Susanne and her two mothers. *Day Care and Early Education,* 20–21.

Isadora, R. (1990). *Babies.* New York: Greenwillow.

Isadora, R. (1990). *Friends.* New York: Greenwillow.

Kagan, J. (1984). *The nature of the child.* New York: Basic.

Katz, P.A. (1982). Development of children's racial awareness and intergroup attitudes. In L.G. Katz (Ed.), *Current topics in early childhood education* (pp. 17–54). New York: Teachers College Press, Columbia University.

Kennedy, H., & Yorke, C. (1982). Steps from outer to inner conflict viewed as superego precursors. *Psychoanalytic Study of the Child,* 37, 221–228.

Klinnert, M.D., Campos, J., Sorce, J.F., Emde, R.N., & Svejda, M.J. (1983). Social referencing. In R. Plutchik & H. Kellerman (Eds.), *Emotion,* vol. 2 (p. 57–86). Orlando: Academic Press.

Kopp, C (1982). Antecedents of self-regulation. *Developmental Psychology,* 18, 199–214.

Leach, P. (1989). *Your baby and child.* rev. ed. New York: Bantam.

Leach, P. (1978). *Your baby and child from birth to age 5.* New York: Bantam.

Leach, P. (1986). *Your growing child.* New York: Bantam.

Lickona, T. (1985). *Raising good children.* New York: Bantam.

Ramsey, P. (1987). *Teaching and learning in a diverse world: Multicultural education for young children.* New York: Teachers College Press, Columbia University.

Rapaport, D. (1967). A theoretical analysis of the superego concept. In M. M. Gill (Ed.), *The collected papers of David Rapaport* (p. 685–709). New York: Basic.

Rest, J.R. (1983). Morality. In P. Mussen (Ed.), *Handbook of child psychology,* vol. 3. (pp. 556–629). New York: Wiley.

Ricklen, N. (1988). *Daddy & me.* New York: Simon & Schuster.

Ricklen, N. (1988). *Grandma & me.* New York: Simon & Schuster.

Ricklen, N. (1988). *Grandpa & me.* New York: Simon & Schuster.

Ricklen, N. (1988). *Mommy & me.* New York: Simon & Schuster.

Sorce, J.F., & Emde, R.N. (1981). Mother presence is not enough. *Developmental Psychology,* 17(6), 737–745.

Stern, D.N. (1985). *The interpersonal world of the human infant.* New York: Basic.

Sullivan, H.S. (1953). *The theory of psychiatry.* New York: Norton.

Wardle, F. (1987). Are you sensitive to interracial children's special identity needs? *Young Children,* 42(2), 53–59.

Williams, V.B. (1990). *"More, more, more," said the baby: 3 love stories.* New York: Greenwillow.

CHAPTER

6

For Infants, Toddlers, and Twos, Keep It Like Home (But Not Like a Boring Home): The Job of an Optimal Home Is Building "Good Character"

QUESTION: We think babies and toddlers whose mothers have to work, or *really, really* want to work full-time, deserve a home-style first few years, even if they cannot be home.

We try to be like relatives, like each child's extended family. Family day care mothers have always been viewed as kin, and have always cared for the babies. We have been family day care providers and are using the model here in the center. Each caregiver in an infant room has three babies. There are only two caregivers and six babies in one infant room. We have a *second* infant room with another two caregivers and six babies. To keep it close to home-like, we don't want 12 infants living and sleeping in one room.

Twice a week, at one point in the morning, the caregivers "take their babies visiting"; sometimes they're all in one room for 30 or 45 minutes, sometimes in the other. The other three days, everybody gets belted into our "six-pack" baby buggies (six-seater strollers) and we go for long walks, talking with the children about everything they're seeing along the way. In the afternoon, we all play outside with the older kids, the toddlers. If it's raining, the babies get to visit in "the big kids' room." We don't have any instruction.

We are interested in other suggestions for making our program unlike "a program." We want it to be like home. We are also concerned that these children might get bored shut up in this place with us day after day.

Mixing the ages for part of each day is a good idea. Many homes have children of more than one age in them. In those that don't, very young children who spend their days at home with their mamas are often taken to play with friends' or neighbors' children, or to a twice-a-week play group with ones,

Subjects & Predicates

twos, and threes in it. Mixed-age grouping is one of the great advantages of family child care homes, if the children get along well together. Babies learn so much by observing children just a notch or two older than they. Toddlers (12 to 24 months) learn by spending time with two-year-olds (24 to 36 months), and two-year-olds learn by spending time with three-year-olds. **Encouraging the children to mix is much more educational than "teaching them things" would be** (this is obviously your philosophy). The infants' interests and motivation are being stimulated in nature's way. The back and forth visiting undoubtedly offers exciting variety to your children, too, a treat to anticipate.

You're also wise to keep your babies **separated** from the runabout toddlers much of the time. Older toddlers, at least, if not the youngest ones, often "teach" babies. Babies earnestly try, try, and try harder to comply. This can be overstimulating and quite stressful

to them. When they succeed in doing what their admired toddler teachers are painstakingly attempting to teach them, they glow, they crow. **But when they are unable to succeed, they feel inadequate.** Babies benefit from the enriching variety of being with older children for part of the day; they also benefit from time

- with peers only, where they are more likely to feel equal,
- alone with one adult, so each can feel special, and
- completely private, each infant to himself, to absorb, digest, and recover.

As to toddlers and twos, much as they typically get a kick out of babies, they also find babies a bother. Babies get into their purposeful projects. Toddlers need time to *them*selves, and so do two-year-olds, many of whom are much more mature than the wobbling toddlers. Two-year-olds *also* need time away from three-year-olds, who are much more able and therefore push two-year-olds to the limit. This is challenging for part of each day, but two-year-olds need to retreat for significant periods of time each day as well.

Babies have a built-in urge to learn; they learn a lot through practice

Actually, for generous portions of each day, your babies will not only entertain themselves if you set things up appropriately, but will learn and learn and learn while they play right in their own infant rooms, sometimes with people, sometimes solo. They will learn

in all "domains": physical, social, intellectual, and psychological, without you even struggling to memorize a zillion bits of jargon. **We need to remember and remind parents and staff: Everything a baby succeeds in learning on her own adds to her emerging sense of positive self-esteem and love of learning.**

Three- to six-month-olds learn a lot about . . .

Moving

They roll over, sit, move their legs and feet in fancy new ways. Exercise becomes a source of great enjoyment to them. Do you have a variety of mats, pads, rugs, and other surfaces of differing textures and colors in differing locations in your room for the babies to lie on while they **spontaneously** "work out"? Do you sometimes serve as a human trampoline for your babies, holding their bodies below their arms and allowing them to bounce up and down on your lap? They're practicing walking, as well as playing a glorious, gleeful game with you.

Looking

They love to look at facial expressions, those of the other babies and yours. They like looking in mirrors. Do you have low, unbreakable mirrors on the wall, and small mirrors with handles they can pick up and peer into?

A secure baby feels accepted and lovable. This feeling is an important part of self-esteem.

Babies of this age like to look at large simple pictures. Some mothers and caregivers buy or make (cut out, glue to heavy paper, and laminate) large picture "boards" for babies to handle and examine.

Probably you have out-of-reach bulletin boards displaying simple, colorful things familiar to children of this age, and shelves at adult eye level containing interesting special objects, which you can tour individuals past in your arms, chatting as you go. Variety, variety, variety, **but within the security-building familiarity of your room and your arms.**

How about a shoebox full of photos of loved ones for each six-month-old baby, which occasionally comes out for inspection? Many babies can soon recognize the picture of each of the special people in their lives.

Some programs and family child care homes borrow "great art" from their libraries and change it each month. They show it to the babies. You can't start teaching aesthetic appreciation too early, if by "teaching" you mean placing beautiful things in babies' environments and happily noticing them together.

Babies of this age adore small objects (but we must beware of the kind they can swallow and choke on). They study small objects with remarkable perseverance. They also like to grasp and hold objects so as to look at them.

Do you have some bouncy canvas "Sassy"™ seats, or other types of infant seats that your children can lie slanted in, so they can look at everything going on in all parts of the room? Canvas seats on sturdy bent wire bases are best

because baby's every move makes the seat gently rock her. Three- to six-month-olds are good lookers. In a busy home or child care program, they have a great deal to look at and they appreci-ate all the action (maybe more than the adults do).

But not all babies can see. If you notice that an infant never makes eye

---

Babies learn incredible physical things with no instruction. While they learn, positive self-esteem is growing from two sources:
pleasure in prowess
pleasure in our pleasure at their prowess

---

contact with anyone and doesn't reach for nearby objects, suspect a visual impairment. Staff should compare notes. The person closest to the parents will need to ask if they have noticed this too and suggest that the situation be brought to the pediatrician's attention for further guidance.

Even if a baby is blind or has seriously impaired vision, it's important for parents and caregivers to do all of the things suggested here, conversing with him constantly in order not to deprive him *additionally*. Nature is already depriving him of a certain amount of sensory learning. Like any baby, the baby with a serious disability needs to develop a strong ego. We can help (Fraiberg & Freeman, 1964).

Our society virtually abandons families of "exceptional" children — children with visual, hearing, speech, language, orthopedic, psychiatric, or other special situations. At the time when parents, newly discovering that their beautiful baby has a serious disability, are feeling shock, guilt, fear, anger, and the disruption of their dreams, it's critical that as child care professionals, we don't turn away from them and their baby because we are uncertain, uncomfortable, and maybe even afraid. Families of special needs children want and deeply appreciate comfort and support, and urgently need to see us take the lead in ensuring that their babies get as much as is feasible of everything the other babies are getting.

Listening

They thrive on hearing us talk to them. Look a baby in the eyes and talk only to *this* individual little person. It's helpful to babies if we speak slowly and clearly. Most expert parents and care-givers automatically do this because they know they're speak-ing with a person from a foreign place who does not yet know our language. By now these babies know sad, happy, and angry voices. (Hopefully they don't hear angry adult voices in *your* place!).

They pay attention to all the voices and sounds in the room. They get a great kick out of all sorts of sounds. It's educational for them to hear the clock tick, the phone ring, the sound of footsteps approaching! . . . and it's fun for them to hear themselves make a variety of sounds, chuckles, and "speeches." Babies love to make funny sounds with their mouths, or with objects in their mouths. Like

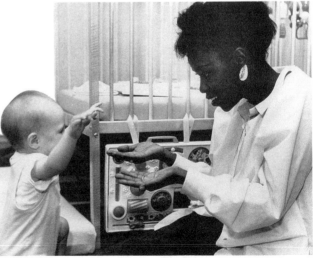

the rest of us, babies three to six months of age like to hear themselves talk.

Do you ever play listening games with your babies? For example, tap-tap-tap on something they can see for a while, then scritch-scratch-scritch sandpaper with a fingernail, wind and rewind and rewind a music box or musical animal, and so on.

Here we have a word of caution, however. A child care setting for babies, toddlers, twos, threes, or fours without enough toys, equipment, suitable activities, caregivers, conversation, and the variety offered in enriched family life can cause children to be depressed and to appear dull, or to grab, clutch, and refuse to wait for a turn or to share. These conditions interfere with the healthy self-esteem a child should be building at this age if mental health is the goal.

But the opposite is often seen too: A child care setting (especially a model center or lab school situation) with too many toys, too much equipment, too many adults can also be very detrimental to positive self-esteem. Staff, participating parents, visiting prospective parents, invited resource people and specialists, student teachers, and perhaps even researchers all milling

around bothering babies, bombarding them with dialogue and with one-on-one "cognitive activities," enveloping them in constant commotion and cacophony that children cannot escape are just too much for babies to cope with. (Overstimulating commotion and cacophony can occur in a very inferior program, too, where there are too many children, where caregivers yell at children and constantly gab together, and where noise is more prevalent than programming.) Many children become overstimulated, hence, in the common parlance, "hyper." The snatching, scratching, and biting begin! Certain children, those who can't stand so much auditory and other sorts of stimulation, are considered "bad."

One of the worst things parents and educarers can do is label babies, children, and teen-agers "bad." Children will very likely incorporate the label into their self-concept, which cannot possibly contribute to their **positive** self-concept, to **self-esteem.**

Anyway, as we were saying, babies learn a lot through listening.

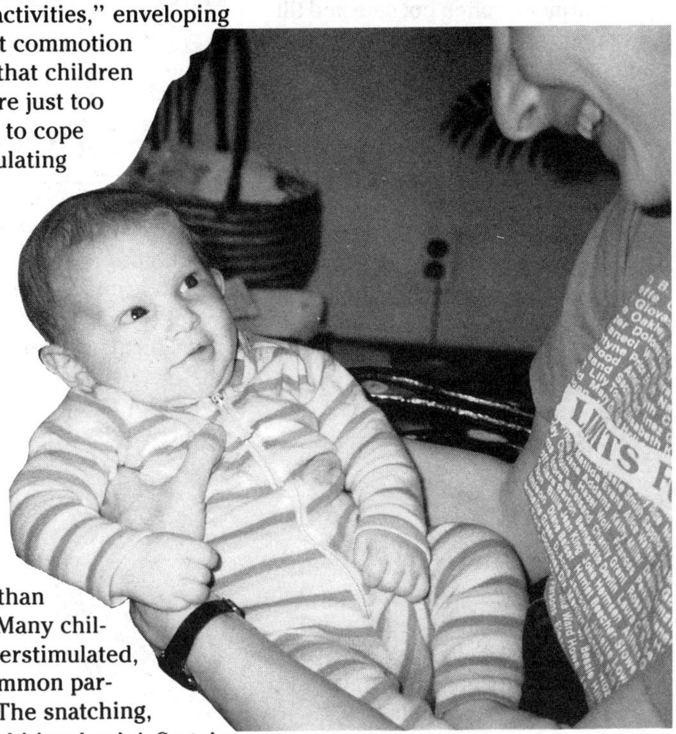

The Growth Program

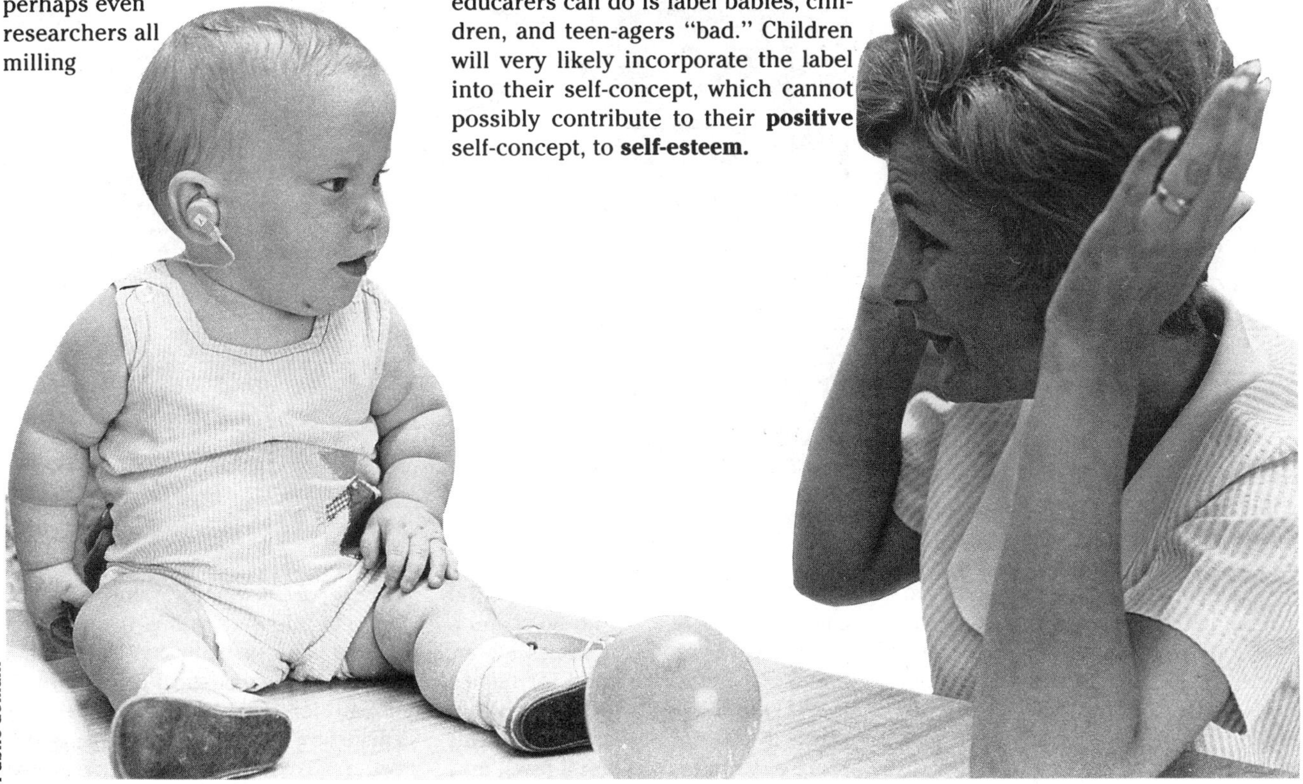

Public domain

But not all babies can hear. Some children have mild or moderate hearing impairments, often not detected till they enter school. Watch for babies who don't respond to your voice, who don't turn their eyes to find a sound, who don't enjoy noisy toys, and who don't make the baby sounds your other same age babies do. **The admonition given above about how to help avoid further sensory deprivation of visually disadvantaged babies also applies to hearing impaired babies.** So does our strong encouragement to staff to befriend the unfortunate family that must struggle with the heavy emotional and financial burdens that usually come with exceptional children.

Touching, holding, and handling

These activities take a lot of time and practice. At this time in their lives, infants wave, shake, hit, and pat with their arms; play with their hands and feet; lift almost everything to their always exploring mouths; and can spot something and go for it . . . at least with their arms and hands. Babies of this age are generally in a good mood and, as you well know, are tons of fun to be with.

*We need to remember and remind parents and staff: Everything a baby succeeds in learning **on her own** adds to her emerging sense of **positive self-esteem** and love of learning.*

Six- to nine-month-olds practice and refine what they have already learned, plus learn more about . . .

Moving

They figure out how to get into sitting positions and not topple over even when they turn around to see what's going on, begin to wiggle backward or forward or both (Is it belly up and rest on your propped up arms? Or is it belly on the floor and swim with the arms? Where do the knees go? It takes lots of trial and error to get it together.), and to crawl. One home-like thing we can do is delight in each baby's fresh accomplishments and share these joys with parents.

Like any baby, the baby with a serious disability needs to develop a strong ego.

Child care programs (family day care homes and center-based) have a great advantage over homes when it comes to keeping crawlers safe and out of trouble: They are *designed* for people this age, whereas homes are designed for adults. Parents need to do a great deal of childproofing in order not to have an over-

© 1991 Rick Reinhard

whelming number of no-no's. Child care places have a *few* no-no's, and a *few* no-no's are good for babies. (A few no-no's at home are good for babies too.) **From the beginning of their mobility, it's OK for babies to know that there are limits (but just a few), and**

that grown-ups' judgment is to be trusted and lived by. Babies do not feel less loved and do not develop low self-esteem when we set a *small number* of sensible boundaries that we *kindly* and *consistently* and *clearly* enforce. This is the beginning of self-discipline.

But not all babies can get around. We need to be grateful if the babies we care for are beginning to move around and get into everything. Many babies *cannot* due to physical handicaps caused by neurological or orthopedic impairments. Some disabilities are caused by brain-to-muscle linkage disorders, like those involved in epilepsy and cerebral palsy. Other disabilities, such as missing limbs, are caused by congenital malformation or injury, injuries often involving car accidents.

Sometimes parents need to enroll sick babies in child care: babies that have sickle cell anemia, asthma, cancer, or congenital heart disease, for instance.

Child care workers, including, of course, family day care mothers, may be the first to notice developmental delays. Mental retardation may be the reason for the delay. Mental retardation may be genetic, or may be the re-

sult of mother or infant malnutrition, illness, or brain injury, again, often from car accidents. **Appallingly, in 1989, not one state required special education (special educare) to be provided in the critical years from birth to three, although we know very**

well that early and accurate diagnosis is needed if we are to make the best of a bad situation.

Low-income families' special needs infants are not uncommonly *additionally* stranded by helping services,

which may indeed exist, because the family's necessary focus on survival (possibly complicated by language, unemployment, and low education level barriers) prevents them from learning about, or being able to take advantage of, them. Bafflingly—because it's *more expensive and less good for children*—low-income families are not infrequently forced to institutionalize children in order to be eligible for financial assistance.

Looking

By examining tinier and tinier particles with greater and greater intensity, babies learn about *depth*. (But they lose interest in a toy that's covered up; as far as they're concerned, out of sight, out of existence.) Babies are developing attention span when they spend their time examining things. **It's foolish to interrupt them; we all believe attention span is important.**

Listening

Babies recognize the sounds connected to familiar activities and people. They know people communicate with sounds. Isn't it interesting how they watch your mouth when you talk, as if through studious looking and listening your meaning might become clear? One of the most valuable things you can do with your babies is chat with them about *everything*, even very ordinary care activity.

Babies like music and have favorite songs. Older babies may even hum along. You probably have a nice collection of high-quality lullaby and other music cassettes you can play for a child who touches the tape player indicating that she wants music. The more we en-

Even older babies can sense when we mean business. They respond by calming down and doing what we want done. However, high-tension bodies or voices, angry or cold tones, and physical violence toward babies undermine our objectives. In a cold, angry emotional climate babies don't learn self-discipline, they learn stress, fear, and anger, all of which are likely to cause them to behave badly. All this is not good for mental health.

courage our babies to *initiate* activities, the better we're doing at helping them develop *initiative,* a characteristic we all believe in. Do you sit on the floor with a baby, or plunk one in your lap, and sing songs together?

Touching, holding, and handling

Babies can now transfer things from hand to hand, and have some judgment about how *heavy* things are. No doubt you spend hours playing "Hand-It-To-Me, I'll-Hand-It-To-You" with each baby in your family-style group. Do pairs of babies play this game with each other? By now, babies can squeeze, scrunch, crumple, scratch, fold, rub, smack, whack, poke, twist, and so on. Treat your children to balls of crunched paper. A floorful is fun, with babies moving around amidst the crackling poofs of scrunched paper. How about sponges, both dry and wet?

Among all the other things that tantalize and tempt babies to squeeze, scrunch, crumple, scratch, rub, smack, whack, poke, twist (and bite) are other babies, especially their eyes. *We start gentle discipline, which we expect soon to grow into* **self-discipline,** *here.* "No! We don't [poke eyes, bite people]. Here's something you can [poke, bite]."

- An immediate, calm, **firm** response is essential if we expect to be effective.

- We never permit a child **of any age** to hurt another person **of any age.**

When babies hurt each other, there's no anger or hostility, just curiosity and lack of judgment. Babies don't understand that what they're doing hurts.

- In addition to close supervision and immediate, decisive intervention, setting a good example is important.

If we smack babies—or bite them "to teach them how it feels"—we're setting the opposite example than we should be. Teaching "be gentle," and *being* gentle ourselves, is a better way.

Touching, holding, and handling are major learning activities at this time of life. Speaking of holding, do you sometimes allow a baby to hold his own bottle to feed himself while you keep him company? Such independence! And again, *we need to remember and remind parents and staff: Everything a baby succeeds in learning* **on his own** *adds to his emerging sense of* **positive self-esteem** *and love of learning.* But a baby who needs and wants help holding the bottle, and concomitant cuddling, deserves to get these needs met.

Nine- to 12-month-olds can really get around!

Moving

These older babies can crawl speedily and in a well-coordinated way. Crawling is no longer a trick to practice; it's a slick rapid transit system. Now all the things the baby could only gaze at from her fixed position are accessible! And most babies are intent on "accessing" them! Everything is fascinating, no less so if forbidd' Selma Fraiberg graphically describes this phenomenon:

Parents who want a fresh point of view on their furniture are advised to drop down on all fours and accompany the nine or ten month old on his rounds. It is probably many years since you last studied the underside of a dining room chair. The ten month old will study this marvel with as much concentration and reverence as a tourist in the Cathedral of Chartres. Upon leaving the underside of the chair he pauses to wrestle with one of the legs, gets the feel of its roundness and its slipperiness and sinks his two front teeth into it in order to sample flavor and texture. In a number of circle tours around the chair at various times in the days and weeks to come he discovers that the various profiles he has been meeting are the several faces of one object, the object we call a chair.

Every object in his environment must be constructed in this way until its various aspects are united into a whole.

The world he discovers is a vast and intricate jig-saw puzzle, thousands of pieces

Parents and other primary caregivers are in an excellent position to detect visual, hearing, neurological, or other impairments. Early diagnosis by medical experts and intervention by specialized professionals are critical.

scrambled together in crazy juxtaposition. Piece by piece he assembles the fragments into whole objects and the objects into groups until he emerges with a fairly coherent picture of the tiny piece of world he inhabits. At eighteen months he has even begun to give names to some of the objects. This learning of the first eighteen months is a prodigious intellectual feat. No wonder every parent thinks his baby is a genius. He is! (Fraiberg, 1959, pp. 53–54)

This simple but extremely important concept is what in his exceptionally hard-to-decipher prose Piaget is telling us about how **young children construct meaning through their senses, body action, and experiences** (Piaget, 1936/1952, 1937/1954).

To see a flight of stairs is to scoot up it. Do you have carpeted steps staff can stand watchfully on while climbers practice their thrilling new skill? How about furniture your children can pull themselves up on and walk around holding? Do you have time to let each person who's ready hold your hands and take a teeny walk unsupported? Most do walk between 10 and 16 months. Lots of padding, pillows, and reliably sturdy furniture to hang onto help at this time. Learning to walk involves more falls and perils than learning to ski. We can soften the necessary bumps and blows with thick carpeting and calm sympathy.

For a marvelous description of this fabulous new age of locomotion, what it's all about physically and psychologically, read the beautiful passages

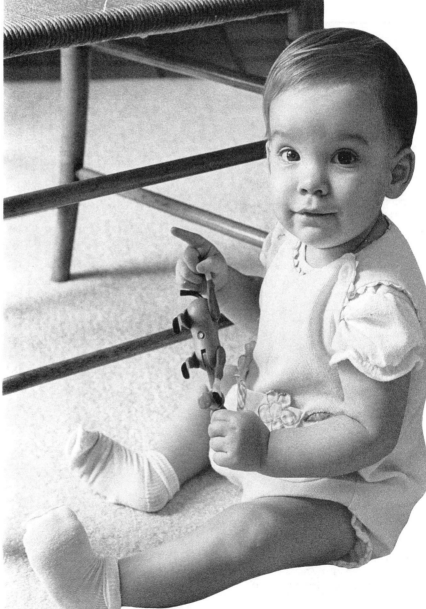

(under *"Senior" Babies Discover Their Autonomous and Solitary "Selves"*) reprinted from *The Magic Years* written by Selma Fraiberg that start below and continue through p. 115.

Looking

"Senior" babies—babies in this age bracket—enjoy sharing a book with someone who can help turn pages and name objects. **This is the perfect time to start "teaching" motivation to read: Enjoy book after book with each baby perched or snuggled on an unhurried lap, labeling pictures as you go.** This should rarely be done in a group, and never when a schedule says book time, but preferably when a *baby* says book time by bringing you one. Babies may be more concerned about practicing their finger dexterity by turning the pages than they are with hearing us label the pictures, but that is all right.

Babies by now are learning that objects don't cease to exist when they vanish from sight, so they love disappearing games; more about disappearing in a moment.

Babies nearing a year have learned a tremendous amount about the meaning of their primary caregivers' facial expressions, postures, and gestures. Effective parents give clear strong physical signals that are easy for babies to see: smiling face and hands reaching, inviting, open for play; frowning face, hand moving swiftly to make a "stop" sign indicating "stop what you're doing" . . . body language is the first language human beings learn. Body language consistent with *spoken* language so no mixed messages are sent is a major piece of how we teach **self-discipline**.

"Senior" Babies Discover Their Autonomous and Solitary "Selves"

. . . Like all geniuses this baby works indefatigably at his discoveries. He is intoxicated with his newfound world; he devours it with every sense organ. He marvels at the bit of dust he picks up in his fingers. A piece of cellophane, a scrap of foil, a satin ribbon will fill him with rapture. He revels in the kitchen cupboards, pursues the hidden treasures of drawers, wastebaskets and garbage cans. This urge for discovery is like an insatiable hunger that drives him on and on relentlessly. He is drunk with fatigue, but he cannot stop. The hunger for sensory experience is as intense and all-consuming as the belly hunger of the first months of life. But this baby, navigating toward his first birthday, or charging ahead into the second year, has almost forgotten his belly. He can do without your nourishing custards, your little jars of pureed vegetables and strained liver. He refuels briefly, bangs on the tray of the high-chair for release, and is off again on his grand tour.

What drives him on? What is the source of this energy? A most exciting new psychological development, no doubt, but what mother has time or energy to contemplate it? For the mother of this dynamo has grown lean and hollow-eyed as she pursues him all over the map. And just at the point that she feels *she* needs two naps a day, this indefatigable globe trotter makes it very clear that *he* is not interested in any naps, thank you, he just has a little too much work to do. The mother of this child will naturally be little interested in these developments from a psychological point of view and will be heartily excused if she prefers to skip the next few lines, or even abandon the whole project and turn to a book of science fiction.

Nevertheless, it *is* an exciting development, a marvelous transformation in energy and goals. Energy that once was centered exclusively on the satisfaction of body needs is now released in part for the pursuit of goals outside the body in the objective world. The hunger that once was exclusively body hunger has been transformed into a voracious appetite for the world. Love that centered first in the mother who satisfied body needs has expanded and ramified to embrace the ever-widening horizons of his world.   The baby is in love with   the world he has discovered through his mother's love, and he behaves like those intoxicated lovers in songs and verse who find that the whole world has been transformed through love and the most common objects are infused with beauty.

This analogy may strike us as somewhat extravagant, but it is not a bad one at all and has a sober, scientific backing. For babies who are deprived of maternal care, babies of sterile institutions, are not attracted to objects; they do not find pleasure and excitement in discovery. They possess the same sensory organs as other babies, they learn to sit up, to crawl, to walk. But since human objects have given them no pleasure, there is no pleasure in the world outside their bodies. Such babies remain, for an alarmingly long time (and sometimes permanently) on the psychological level of the young in-

© 1991 Florence Sharp

Listening

These babies can hear so well and have heard so much that they can copy our sounds. They understand quite a bit of what we say (including their names and the names of all familiar people, body parts, objects, events, and activities). They often try to do what significant people in their lives ask them to. If they don't follow simple directions, it's quite normal, they are not even a year old yet! If they do, it's an early stage of **self-discipline:** *Wanting to please (first loved ones, later yourself) is the basis of the healthiest kind of* **self-discipline.**

Touching, holding, and handling

When holding their own cups, senior babies are able to lurch a few sips to their waiting lips without spilling all the liquid en route. Those who have been encouraged to practice are, of course, more proficient. Babies are also fairly proficient at finger-feeding and spoon-feeding themselves. They used to know that spoons were intriguing, shining objects. Now they know what to do with them. This is an example of infants' remarkably rapid progress during their first year toward comprehending what everything is and is for. However, wrist control is in short supply until 15–18 months, so tippy spoons and spilled juice will be common long after expertise in finger-feeding has been established.

You know that cognitive growth (the evolution of understanding) occurs as infants and toddlers play (and learn *while* they play). You probably provide educational tools (as well as the variety you say you seek to offer) by frequently bringing out your pots with lids, allowing the opening and shutting of certain cupboard doors, boosting and toting babies so they can operate

---

(Fraiberg, continued)

fant. The body and the body needs remain the center of existence for them. It appears, then, that the miraculous achievement of the normal infant, the movement away from body-centeredness to object relationships is not just the product of biological maturation but the achievement of the human family through ties of love.

Lois Main

Locomotion and the solitary self

If we look closely at two lines of development in the last quarter of the first year we find a paradox. Around the same time that the baby demonstrates his strong attachment to his mother, at that period during which he can hardly bear to be separated from her, he is already beginning to leave her! He is starting to crawl, and with the beginnings of independent locomotion the ties to the mother's body are loosened. After a few weeks spent in straightening our mechanical problems (many babies start off in reverse gear and nearly all of them find their bellies touching bottom), this baby cuts his moorings and goes steaming off for new worlds, leaving his mother with an empty lap.

But how can we account for the paradox? He moves toward the mother and away from the mother in the same period of development! And if the ties to mother are so strong, if anxiety at separation is so pronounced during this phase, why should he not remain in the safety and close intimacy of his mother's arms? Why should he go off for reckless adventure, to be trapped in the dark cave under the sofa, to be assaulted by capricious lamps and obstinate tables? If you or I should go off to explore strange territory and find ourselves slugged by unseen villains at every turn, we'd prudently retire to our homeland, after which the most persuasive travel agent could not lure us through his front door. But this adventurer is stopped by nothing. He pauses briefly for first-aid after a collision that raises an egg-sized lump on his head, he allows his mother to stanch the flow of blood from his nose, he is cheered by a kiss and a few moments in his mother's lap, and then he is off again to risk another duel with the lamp, another skirmish with the temperamental chair.

You don't have to encourage him. You don't have to offer him any incentives to lure him on to new achievements. This is a self-starting, self-perpetuating mechanism. I once watched an eight-month-old girl for three weeks as she subdued an obstinate tea-cart. She could climb on to the lower shelf of the cart, but the cart perversely moved when she did. After days of futile trials, she finally learned to tackle the tea cart from the back which rested on wooden gliders instead of from the front which rested on wheels. Now she was on it. But how to get out? It was too large a drop to climb out of the cart and her pride was hurt if she was helped out of the cart. She usually fell on her face through any of her own methods of debarkation. But several times a day she set out for the cart, solemn and determined. As she started to climb on to the lower shelf she whimpered very softly, already anticipating, we your light switches (what a powerful feeling! no pun intended), and setting up for water play. Why are little ones so addicted to water play? Is it, again, the feeling of empowerment that appeals? Water (and sand) are so responsive to a child. Do you set out plastic buckets or basins on plastic sheets (if outdoors is out), and provide washcloths, soap, things that float, and things that sink? Does this type of activity enthrall your little people for hours? Research has discovered that

between 9 and 18 months, infants spend almost half of their waking hours inspecting and manipulating objects. The physical environment becomes a laboratory in which the infant labors to enlarge her understanding of the laws that govern experience. Objects are the equipment for her ceaseless experiments. (Chase & Rubin, 1979, p. 206)

Because they have finally learned to let go (earlier they could intentionally pick up and hold, but not intentionally let go), babies of nine to 12 months love to play "Drop It" and to throw things down. They are discovering gravity, the satisfying noises things make when they fall, and other Scientific Facts. You are quite likely among the infant care experts who tie some toys to cribs, highchairs, and playpens and show babies how to pull them back after they've pitched them.

● When *you* return what the baby has dropped or tossed, she learns that she can influence people. This social skill is a good thing to learn.

● When the baby *herself* fetches back what she dropped or tossed, she learns that she can initiate happenings, and she can see that some of her own simple needs and wants are taken care of. This independence is a good thing

---

(Fraiberg, continued)

felt, the danger of getting out and the inevitable fall on her face. Her parents tried to discourage her, to distract her to other activities. It was too painful for grown-ups to watch. But if anyone interfered she protested loudly. She *had* to do it. And finally at the end of three weeks she discovered a technique for backing out of the cart, reversing the getting-in method. When she achieved this, she crowed with delight and then for days practiced getting in and getting out until she had mastered it expertly. From this point she moved on to more daring ascents, climbing a few steps of the staircase, then a few more, and a few more, till the staircase became a bore. She tackled chairs, any kind of chair, undismayed by those that teetered and collapsed on her.

The urge to climb, the urge upward, was so powerful that no obstacle, no accident could deter her.

All this activity is leading to the establishment of the upright posture. The crawling baby learns to pull himself up to a standing position and begins to maintain this position for longer and longer periods. It will be many weeks before the baby stands alone briefly, many more weeks before he takes his first independent steps. It all unfolds as inevitably as an evolutionary process. But consider the hazards that attend each phase of this process, the bumps, the spills, the perilous falls. When we consider it, the child's achievement of the upright posture is truly heroic.

What impels him? A powerful drive that urges him upward, the legacy of those remote ancestors who cleverly learned to balance themselves on their hind legs in order to put the front paws to work. It is a biological urge that is largely independent of environmental influence. Curiously enough, even some of the unattached babies of poor institutions seem to learn to sit up, to crawl, to stand and to walk at approximately the same ages that family-reared babies do, while we recall that in other developmental areas that are dependent upon strong human ties for incentive, these institutional babies were severely retarded. And this striving for the upright posture is so powerful that it impels the child forward even when he repeatedly experiences dangers and body injuries and the surrender of maternal protection that necessarily accompanies each of these stages in independent locomotion. In fact we should observe that the means for overcoming the anxiety are identical with the means for producing it. It is through repetition of the experience of crawling, climbing, standing up right, walking, that the hazards are finally overcome and the successful achievement of these goals gradually diminishes the anxiety.

As the child moves toward the upright posture his personality undergoes a change. The average overworked mother is not aware of a personality change as such but of certain difficulties in maintaining the old routines. Changing the baby's dia-

© 1991 Janice Mason

to learn, too. *Being able to function well independently is another ingredient of healthy self-discipline and self-esteem.*

Helping families with special needs children, and their children, develop positive self-esteem is part of our work

Due to an assortment of serious disabilities, many infants and toddlers cannot function as independently as others. Caregivers in "ordinary" family day care homes and infant/toddler child care centers don't have special training in how to maximize the capability for independence that each child with serious impairments has and the positive self-esteem resulting from it. However, there are important things we can do:

1. Accept special needs infants and toddlers in our programs. There are three broad categories of programs for exceptional babies: parent-child programs, hospital programs, and developmental day care programs.

● Parent-child programs use the home as the therapeutic setting and help parents strengthen the child's potentials. These programs provide training, materials, and activities that address the individual little one's special needs.

● Hospital programs provide comprehensive services in day care situations. Included are clinic care, physical therapy, nutrition, social services, and infant education as individually prescribed. Parent participation is required.

● Developmental day care offers comprehensive services in a regular child care center or family day care home. There may be many children there not identified as having a serious disability.

(Fraiberg, continued)

pers, which used to be a one-two-three operation, has turned into a performance that ideally requires two assistants. First, you catch your baby. Then you put him on his back to change him. He protests loudly. Unpin the wet diaper and sing his favorite little ditty with two diaper pins in your mouth. In a moment your baby has wriggled free, made an expert turn and is sitting upright grinning at you or crawling off in another direction. Repeat step one. Give him a toy to hold, and work fast, because there he is, *up* again!

What's happened? A few weeks ago he found your singing enchanting and it took this or very little else to keep him quiet on his back for the thirty seconds required to change a diaper. But now the moment his spine makes contact with an under-surface, a hidden spring is released and up pops the baby!

It has to do with establishing the upright posture. He can't tolerate being flat on his back and passive, and is impelled by the most irresistible urge to upright himself, the same urge that sends him climbing and pulling himself up, over and over all day to the point of exhaustion. It is an inner necessity, having more to do with defiance of gravity than defiance of the mother.

We can test this in other areas, too. Not so long ago he went peacefully off to his naps or his night's sleep, dozing off in his mother's arms before he reached the bed. But now, however, groggy he may be, he is likely to protest furiously at the moment he is put

down in his crib, and he summons all his reserves of energy to upright himself, pulling himself up at the bars of the crib the instant after you have put him down. Now admittedly this is not a clear-cut example since the baby at this stage also hates naps and bed-times because they mean separation from loved persons and all the pleasures of his new-found world. But there is this other element, too, and one that recurs so frequently in one context or another during this phase of motor de-

velopment that it is worth considering apart from other factors for the moment: Motor activity is so vital to the child of this age that interference, restrictions of this activity even through another biological process, sleep, is intolerable to him.

We must remember, too, that the child experiences a certain amount of anxiety in connection with these adventures in loco-motion and that activity, in itself, is one of the means by which he masters motor skills and masters anxiety as well. His behavior is not unlike ours, as adults, when we

© Cleo Freelance Photo

Why should we accept infants and toddlers if three kinds of special programs exist, plus residential programs? Because *none* of these types of program exist in a great many communities. Where they do, they are often full. And, as with anything else, the fact that it *exists* doesn't guarantee that it's any good. Moreover, research shows that parents of *young* children with special needs tend to prefer that their children mingle with mainstream children. What a rejection for families, who already feel isolated at a time like this, to be told that we will not accept them!

2. Work closely and cooperatively with the families of special needs infants and toddlers. Parents need help in facing and learning the facts about their child. They need help in *getting* help: from their pediatrician and from a variety of agencies and resources. Child care professionals can keep on hand an up-to-date file of resources. Caregivers and on-site child care administrators can keep careful records on successes and difficulties each baby is having and share the detailed data with parents. This helps the family learn facts and face facts. We can help

the family with the turbulent emotions surrounding the subject of their exceptional infant. We can ease (or inflame) parents' adjustment to the baby. The sooner they can accept, support, and love the baby, the sooner "all that can be done" will begin happening. **Without love and encouragement, no amount of brilliant medical procedures and educational interventions will give the child positive self-esteem.** Caregivers can be supportive friends to families as they struggle with doctors, nurses, and social workers, many of whom are said to be notor-

(Fraiberg, continued)

begin to learn a new sport, like skiing, that involves a certain amount of risk. The novice skier may feel the full measure of his anxiety when he gets his skis off and mentally reviews his hazardous first attempts. He feels impelled to get back on his skis, to go over his lesson, repeat it again and again until he has mastered the technique and mastered the danger. At night he cannot fall asleep. He is skiing in bed, and his muscles go through all the motions involuntarily as the events of the day are mentally repeated.

The baby mastering the skills that lead to establishment of the upright posture behaves in much the same way as the novice skier. He feels compelled to repeat the activity hundreds of times until he has mastered the skill and mastered his anxiety. He often reveals that he is having difficulty "unwinding" when we put him to bed for his nap or for the night, and if you peek into his room while he is settling down to sleep (or unsettling down for sleep), you may see him, groggy and cross-eyed with fatigue, still climbing and pulling himself upright, collapsing momentarily with weariness, then exerting himself for another climb. He repeats this over and over until finally he cannot lift himself even once more and succumbs to sleep. One set of parents discovered their eight-month-old daughter climbing in her sleep on several occasions during this mastery period. At eleven or twelve at night they could hear soft sounds in the baby's room and upon entering

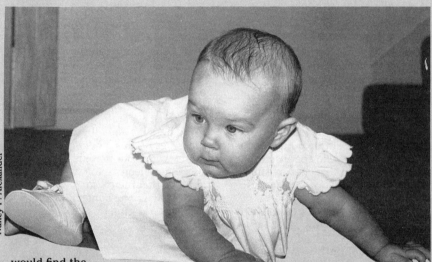

Nancy P. Alexander

would find the baby standing in her crib, dazed and dimly conscious, too sleepy to protest when she was put down in her bed again. When the art of standing was perfected, the baby gave up practicing in her sleep.

The first time the baby stands unsupported and the first wobbly, independent steps are milestones in personality development as well as in motor development. To stand unsupported, to take that first step is a brave and lonely thing to do. For it is not a fear of falling, as such, that creates apprehension in the child of this age. He takes these little spills and bumps with good grace. But it is the fear of the loss of support that looms big at this stage. Until this point he has employed contact with another human body or a stable piece of furniture for his exercises in stand-

ing or taking steps. We notice toward the end of the supported period that the baby is actually using only token support, the lightest touch of his mother's or father's hand serves as "support" while actually his employing his own body fully for balance. But he is not yet ready to let go of the symbolic contact with mother's body, the supporting human hand. When he does let go for that first step it is usually for another visible or known means of support, another pair of hands, a nearby chair or table. And when he *really* lets go, many weeks later, and takes a half dozen or so steps on his own, he often retains symbolic contact in a comical way. I know one small girl who bravely toddled forth clasping her own hands together, hanging on to her *own* hand. You will notice

iously insensitive to parents' feelings. But caregivers, too, need **support and training** in order to help special needs infants and their families.

3. Reduce the bias our society has against people with disabilities. Only by exposing all children to children with various disabilities and of various races, types of families, socioeconomic levels, ethnic and religious backgrounds — *and only by dealing directly with fears and other feelings each of us has*—will we combat the cruel prejudices in our world. Only when we acknowledge and appreciate the worth of all people on this diversity-filled planet can the chance for equality exist for all children.

Conquering abandonment anxiety is part of the curriculum

Apparently there's also a strong psychological motivation for the determination babies in this age range exhibit to drop things and see them retrieved (or retrieve them themselves), to fit things inside of other things and watch them come out (or get them out themselves). It's the same psychological reason that they've played disappearing games with devout attention since the age of approximately six months. *They are dealing with the idea of disappearing loved ones.* They're struggling with their basic human fear of abandonment:

We must remember that a child who lives in a world of vanishing objects perceives his human world on the same basis. It is not only glasses and key-cases and Teddy bears that have no existence when he cannot perceive them. Mothers and fathers, loved persons, are subjected to the same primitive reasoning. They appear and disappear in a

(Fraiberg, continued)

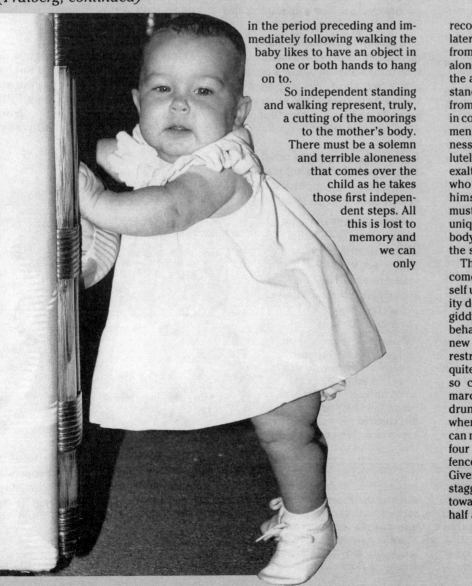

Nancy P. Alexander

in the period preceding and immediately following walking the baby likes to have an object in one or both hands to hang on to.

So independent standing and walking represent, truly, a cutting of the moorings to the mother's body. There must be a solemn and terrible aloneness that comes over the child as he takes those first independent steps. All this is lost to memory and we can only

reconstruct it through analogies in later life. It must be like the first dive from a diving board, or the first time alone at the wheel of a car. There is the awful sense of aloneness, of time standing still, that follows the spring from the board or in leaving the curb in command of the wheel. In such moments there is a heightened awareness of self, a feeling of being absolutely alone in an empty world that is exalting and terrifying. To the child who takes his first steps and finds himself walking alone, this moment must bring the first sharp sense of the uniqueness and separateness of his body and his person, the discovery of the solitary self.

The discovery of independent locomotion and the discovery of a new self usher in a new phase in personality development. The toddler is quite giddy with his new achievements. He behaves as if he had invented this new mode of locomotion (which in a restricted sense is true) and he is quite in love with himself for being so clever. From dawn to dusk he marches around in an ecstatic, drunken dance, which ends only when he collapses with fatigue. He can no longer be contained within the four walls of his house and the fenced-in yard is like a prison to him. Given practically unlimited space he staggers joyfully with open arms toward the end of the horizon. Given half a chance he might make it.

(Fraiberg, 1959, pp. 124–126)

ghostly fashion, like dream people. And, unlike the furniture of the objective world, these human love objects are necessary for the child's existence and his inner harmony. Until one has proof of the permanence of these loved persons, certainty that they have a substantial existence independent of one's perception of them, there will be disturbing feelings at times when these loved ones are absent. This does *not* mean that the child between the ages of six months and eighteen months lives in a state of constant anxiety. And it does *not* mean that parents must be constantly with a baby to give him reassurance. There are healthy mechanisms at work within the child's personality to reassure him. He can even make excellent use of his magic thinking during this period to assure himself that disappearance is followed by return; a loved person goes away and comes back. But since this magic belief doesn't always work—mother won't *always* be there when he needs her, can't always magically appear with a bottle when hunger is imperative, will sometimes be out for the evening when the baby wakens—the magical theory of disappearance and return will frequently break down. At such times anxiety—a mild anxiety or a very strong anxiety—will appear.

Unless this anxiety is very severe and pervasive, really disturbs the healthy functioning and development of the child, we do not need to be alarmed. It diminishes normally in the course of the child's development. And here is the practical application of the theory we have been discussing: As the child gradually constructs an objective world—a stable and coherent world in which appearance and disappearance, comings and goings, are subject to their own physical laws—he acquires an intellectual control over his environment that helps him to overcome his anxiety at separation. When you know that a mother and a father are substantial persons who cannot evapo-

rate, who may be hidden from the eyes like the objects in the games we described and yet exist, the temporary absence of loved persons can be managed with far less anxiety. (Fraiberg, 1959, pp. 51–52)

Specialists studying the human organism's central nervous system explain that babies are biologically unable to remember at very young ages, and that's why beloveds (and other things) seem to them to have disappeared when not visible.

Child care programs need strong policies urging parents to participate in "separation education" and in general

A group family day care provider whose beautiful work is described in the highly recommended, highly readable book *The Good Preschool Teacher: Six Teachers Reflect on Their Lives* (Ayers, 1989), says

"When parents come and see my home, it looks like such a wonderful place to visit, so many interesting things to do, so inviting. . . . All I commit to, and what I work on, is that children will feel okay here without their parents, that they'll be able to acknowledge the difficulties and still participate fully in life here. That's the whole program." . . . When Chana interviews parents, she describes why separation is such a critical issue for young children. She discusses the tension between connectedness and autonomy, and she gives them materials to read. "We expect more than a change of clothes from parents. We want

people to be prepared to spend enough time here in the beginning to allow the child to feel comfortable, we want photographs and tapes from home, we want to create a comfortable bridge for kids. We do home visits and we do small groups of kids visiting each home during the year. Of course, people interpret it differently. Some people do it in the way we had hoped they would, others say, 'But I have to be some place at 10 o'clock and I hope my kid isn't one who needs more time!' " (pp. 45–46)

● Parents should not be permitted to "disappear."

● An explanation of what's to happen should always be given to babies: "Mommy's going out now. Mommy will come back and get [name]. [Name] will take care of [name]."

● Parents should be urged (ahead of time) to leave immediately after giving their children this goodbye statement and a goodbye hug.

What does each staff member do to help babies separate trustfully from beloveds?

Nancy P. Alexander

In your child care center, what do you do to help your babies cope with "abandonment" by their vanishing loved ones, besides playing Disappearing/Reappearing games and You Drop It, I Get It games?

Strongly encourage families to launch babies, toddlers, and twos gradually. The most important ways to help babies *and all young children* trust adults other than family members enough so that they aren't hampered from reaching out to friends and to learning by overwhelming feelings of fear of having been abandoned (perhaps forever — how is a baby supposed to know?) are

● **to have a family member stay with them during a longish launching period of two-hour visits and half-day**

Charles N. Estes

sessions when they first enter the child care situation and

● **to have the family spend small amounts of time with the little one in the program frequently thereafter.**

Building trust builds positive self-esteem, confidence, and eventually self-discipline. You cooperate with those you trust and who make you feel good about yourself.

One mother we know told us that a center she planned on sending her 12-month-old daughter to would not agree to let her stay on the sidelines the first day. "What did you do?" we asked. She replied, "I forfeited the deposit and firmly told them what I thought of their lack of understanding of what is of utmost importance in developing trusting babies. Leave a trusting baby who can't grasp explanations alone with 'strangers'? Terrify her? Pull the rug out from under her growing confidence? Never! It wasn't easy, but I found another center that was sensitive to young children. And wouldn't you know: It cost more."

Hildegard Adler

Stop, look, listen, and make every effort to understand what a baby is trying to tell you. Among other reasons that 6- to 24-month-old infants and toddlers may be tense about the possibility of being approached, talked to, even touched and taken care of by unfamiliar people is that they've learned to communicate expertly with the people who regularly tend to them; **Unfamiliar Others haven't the least idea what they need or want to convey, or misunderstand the emerging language of the toddler.**

Take time to help children feel at home. Sensitive child care workers spend a great deal of time helping infants and toddlers who are deeply attached to their parents cope with separating from them. Some young children cheerfully let family members go each day or *most* days if they've been

launched in a leisurely manner with family remaining with them during the first few days. For example, 27-month-old Lindsay first visited her child care center with her mom for an hour and a half after nap. Several days later, she and her mom visited for a morning. Her mother explained she was going to go away for a little while, left while Lindsay lunched "at school," and returned to take her home. The following week, Lindsay started attending the center for full eight-hour days, three days a week, without incident.

Some very young children show mild or even considerable distress day after day when adult departure time draws nigh. There are babies who are so deeply distressed about separating from loved ones for so many days that unless having them in child care is absolutely unavoidable, many child development experts would advise against it. Difficulty separating

feelings — frequently *ambivalent* feelings — and help them talk over the situation. The family child care provider, the program director, or an empathetic staff person may want to discuss with mothers who

has been left, the primary caregiver should sympathize and snuggle the child, or keep her near for security building purposes, but should remain calm. Identifying too much with the baby's misery and grief can alarm her further; she'll feel that there's truly something to fear — even this adult is upset. Expert teachers have found that it helps some young children if we avoid looking directly into their eyes; apparently, this is perceived as too intrusive. The caregiver can, at intervals of five minutes or so, try to entice the child into playing with a toy, or into a tempting activity. But if this is to no avail, and just provokes loud wails, the baby should be allowed to stay on the lap or the hip as long as she needs to.

Even after each baby has adjusted to this new aspect of his life, group care as part of his usual week, he may panic if his primary caregiver is out of sight. With the ability and *realization* of this ability to leave trusted and necessary adults comes anxiety about being left. Kindly caregivers understand these real infantile fears (they don't ridicule and speak of crocodile tears). They generally take a child or two who feels this way everywhere with them.

Some educarers find it helpful to record five minutes of **calming parental conversation on a cassette** ($5 or less), one per baby, during the first day a child is in attendance *with the parent.* Subsequently, several times a day, when the parent *isn't* there, caregivers play each baby's tape for him. He feels in contact with his best beloveds. One program requests **close-up snapshots of a few of the baby's favorite people** when the applicant is accepted. The staff laminate the photos, punch holes in them, string colorful yarn through the holes, and have this amulet ready for the baby to wear when he starts in the program. Encouraging "lovies," "cuddle bankies," or other **"transitional objects,"** as a comforting item

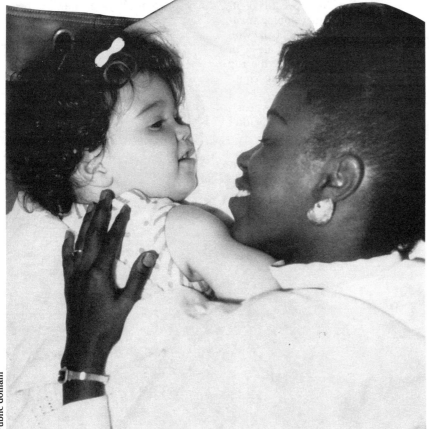

from loved ones is *not* necessarily a symptom of a child's immaturity or of *parents* who are having trouble separating, although it may be either. Difficulty separating *may* just be a "symptom" of people who love each other very much, or a telltale sign that the child care setting isn't providing as high-quality an experience as the child's home is!

Take time to talk with parents about feelings. Some parents feel guilty about leaving their infants and toddlers all day, even in good care. (Other parents *don't* feel guilty.) Parents may show their troubled feelings by being critical of the caregiver, or by having a lot of difficulty *leaving* each day. Some parents may prefer to sneak out when their child isn't looking. Skilled caregivers are aware of parents'

are suffering too much at leave-taking time whether they might prefer (be able) to stay home with their babies another six months or year. Most will want to keep the child in care; the decision has been made. However, **directors and parents should explore this question when parents first visit a program before enrolling a child.**

After an unhappy baby, toddler, two-year-old, or older young child

Babies and children who trust their parents and caregivers trust their judgment and cooperate with them (i.e., behave well).

Without love and encouragement, no amount of brilliant medical procedures and educational interventions will give the child positive self-esteem.

from home is called in our trade, usually helps. (Of course, a baby or toddler would never be expected to share her "nightie-night duck" or other anti-loneliness object.) At a dull moment, do some Peek-a-Boo antics. Duck out of sight behind anything, or flip a towel over your face. "Hide" only for a second. This activity is of particular delight to babies struggling with vanishing objects (6 to 12 months), and to babies and toddlers worried about the return of a loved one. **See the relief in the little one's face when you reappear after hiding!**

Some recommended readings on separation, written for both staff and parents, are Jeannette Stone's *Teacher-Parent Relationships* (1987), Kathe Jervis's *Separation* (1987), and Mary Renck Jalongo's article "Do Security Blankets Belong in Preschool?" (1987). Also recommended are Dr. Joseph Stone's three wonderful kibbutz films showing how separation can be eased by well-trained caregivers (*metapelets*) and because of the strong friendships so evident between caregivers and mothers. **Friendship between families and caregivers reassures infants and toddlers.** Many family child care providers tell us that a sizable proportion of the babies they care for are those of friends and neighbors; that one reason the friends and neighbors choose them is the friendship between them—it's good for the little ones.

Parents of infants and toddlers should be encouraged to participate with staff in all caregiving activities involving their child

Staying for 15 or 30 minutes when bringing the child in the morning, coming early at pickup time, or coming for lunch creates leisurely overlap with chances for information-sharing chats, and builds the baby's trust in the team

that takes care of her. Infants and toddlers don't like confusion and transitions, but if they're old pros in child care, Mom or Dad coming for lunch and leaving again is as it would be if the child were at home and a family member went out, came home, and left again. Nursing mothers may want to come at prearranged times to feed their babies. Good child care programs give parents choices about the starting and ending hour each day; even if most parents visit several times a week, there will probably not be too many adults around at any one time.

Shulamit Gehlfuss

An infant/toddler program should be thought of as a parent/child program. Dr. T. Berry Brazelton discusses this:

Strengthening the family should be the major priority of any program directed to the care of infants from birth to two years. In the face of increasing problems for all nuclear families in our culture, and with some awareness of the dynamics of these problems, we must see the period of infancy as an opportunity to reach young families. This time is inevitably a period of increased stress for them, and one in which their dependency needs press them to reach out for help. We can especially see what a major role an organization could play in early diagnosis and prevention of potential problems for families at risk.

In *all* families in our present cultural confusion, supportive and preventive services are needed. Young parents would be better able to provide optimal conditions for the early development of their children if information about infants' developmental needs and supportive services for their own needs were available. . . .

The relationships between families that revolve around the center make it a potential focus for a kind of communal living, which could conceivably replace what we have lost from having given up extended family life. There are parent-child community movements beginning with this concept in mind, cementing peer families, elderly groups, and young children who are not related but who become included in such centers as if they were. The gains for three generations in such models are obvious and may surmount the interpersonal pressures that have driven generations of families apart in our society.

The opportunities for reinforcing good childrearing practices for modeling and teaching strengths, which seem appropriate to the child and parents under stress, are great in a center where this is a priority.

Daytime care of young children is one of the most demanding jobs in our society. Unless the day-to-day care is coupled with an emphasis on care of the family as its ultimate goal, centers for young children could conceivably do more harm than good. That just must not happen.

(Brazelton, 1984, pp. 9, 18–19)

Keep It Like Home: The Job of an Optimal Home

Having readable articles available for parents to borrow from the center or family day care home may help parents understand the child development philosophy embedded in and entwined around every casual, caring, adult-child interaction.

Talk, talk, talk with babies

One of the most important ways educators in child care programs can model themselves after optimal homes for babies is to converse with them constantly. By the end of the first year, a great many babies say words. Somewhere between 14 and 18 months, most babies have come to understand that words represent objects, actions, people, and so on. They begin to suspect that anything they can point to has a word to go with it, so they test this hypothesis by pointing to one thing after another, endlessly asking, "Wha dis?" Many expert parents and caregivers find that the babies with the earliest and most competent language:

● have been talked with and sung to a lot,

● have been listened to and responded to when they communicate, and

● have a strong sense of self (ego), high self-esteem, and a strong identification with a dearly beloved, all of which combine to cause the baby to assume that "if it can be done, and if *you* can do it, I can do it too."

These are usually the first talkers, the babies who talk well early. Other babies may have these blessings and *not* talk well early, for other reasons; but those who do talk early generally fit the above description. Talk with babies all day long. Speak in normal sentences and use simple words.

Without instruction, you're teaching these babies the beginnings of positive self-esteem

All through the day, right while you're providing this lovely home-like variety of physical, social, and cognitive experiences for each individual child in your charge, you're "teaching" positive **self-esteem** and **self-discipline.**

Infants Are Individuals

It's important for all of us who care for children to understand *how* they all learn and the ages and stages they all pass through. At the same time, we need to remember to consider each child as an individual.

As Bank Street College infant/parent specialist Judith Leipzig illustrates so poignantly in the following excerpt, *infants are individuals.*

Jane was an 11-month-old baby that I once worked with in an infant-toddler day care center. She was thought of by the entire staff as a "fussy" baby. We tried everything that calmed the other babies, but nothing satisfied or quieted her. I would often sit by her crib, rubbing her back for long periods of time, while she lay wide-eyed and obviously very tense beneath her blankets. It was not until the possibility of Jane's very high sensitivity to stimulation was suggested to us that we began to really see her. The combination of her low threshold for all kinds of stimulation and the almost constant noise, talk, and confusion in the center combined to make her very uncomfortable. When the staff considered the possibility of this extrasensitivity we began to develop techniques for helping Jane. Whenever things got particularly noisy or hectic in the center, we would try to remove her from the eye of the storm —either by taking her to a quiet corner, or actually out of the building for a walk. If Jane was upset, we would no longer rock her, sing to her, pat her—these were actions which were contributing further to her feelings of being overwhelmed. Instead, we would face her away from the action, hold her on our laps with our arms gently still around her. We learned in time to provide Jane with a few things to look at rather than an array. Within a week of our really beginning to look at Jane's needs, her behavior and attitude drastically changed. She was no longer a fussy baby most of the time. When Jane was given the space she needed, both in terms of noise level and actual physical space, and when she had some control over the amount of stimulation that was coming in, she behaved in a very different way. Jane no longer was overloaded with stimulation, and so she was able to project herself into the fray. She began to actively seek out social interaction with children and staff, and explore the physical surroundings with obvious pleasure.

I've thought a lot about what might have developed for Jane had we not recognized her individual needs. Her intelligence and her delightful interest in the world and her desire to engage it were getting all mixed up with her feelings of being overwhelmed. The adults around her did not respond to her with the same pleasure we felt for the happily responsive babies, since she wasn't particularly nice to be around. Also, no matter what we did for her, she just wasn't a rewarding baby to please, so that while we certainly did not neglect this child, we didn't automatically initiate or continue interactions with her. Jane was losing out on so much. Without the help and insight of caring adults, a baby like Jane, stuck in a noisy, visually chaotic day care center for 40 hours a week, could grow into a child and an adult who carries around deep feelings of alienation, rage, and impotence. Much of this could have been avoided by the significant adults in her life looking for and recognizing her individual characteristics.

Babies and toddlers on the other end of the continuum—that is, kids who really need a lot of stimulation to engage them, might also suffer greatly in a busy program. These children are much more vulnerable to the not particularly tuned-in caregiver than infants who all by themselves are receptive to environmental stimuli. These babies require a lot more work on the part of the adults to engage them in play, to help them get noticed, and to explore the world. They are at risk for getting lost, for going unnoticed more often.

. . . Understanding the concept of individual differences in temperament and style from birth gives us a valuable lens through which we can see and learn about the children in our care, and as a result enrich the care we give them. (Leipzig, 1988, p. 41)

There are many babies and small children like Jane. Most child development specialists would strongly urge the parents of such a child to choose a less stressful child care arrangement than a *center.*

The child learns to feel good about herself through the practice and mastery of each new *physical* skill. This contributes to her respect for herself (**positive self-esteem**). She learns to feel good about *herself* through *your* enthusiastic, approving reactions to her practice and her mastery of each new physical skill. She learns to feel good about herself (**positive self-esteem**) through literally thousands of satisfying *interactions with you*. She is beginning to realize that she can respond to you in ways that win your smiles. She is beginning to realize that she can initiate a relationship with you in ways that enable you to know what she wants so you can respond in ways that win *her* smiles.

She learns to feel good about herself (**positive self-esteem**) because she senses that you enjoy being with her. You take time from your duties and from doing for your group, just to *be* with her—to watch the raindrops slide down the window pane, to look at the bug and laugh together. You like her. So she likes herself. The younger the children, the more their views are your views. A young child absorbs and believes the judgments of the major people in her life. To very little children, parents and significant others are godlike. Their opinions are believed to be infallible.

The infant/toddler/

An outstanding home or child care program does much more than "keep children." Adults encourage self-esteem and self-discipline in infants and toddlers. This is an important part of what we call "character development."

preschooler/primary grade child will like himself only as much as we like him. We are the mirrors in which he sees himself—his self-image. It takes time to make anyone—a child, a baby—feel cherished. Special needs children need our time and our cherishing as do all children we care for. It takes time (and a very small number of babies per staff person!) to truly *see a child,* not merely "watch the children."

Each baby in your child care program is learning to feel good about herself through gradual awareness of the pieces and parts of her life, and that they all make sense. She feels that she comprehends. She feels cognitively competent. She feels smart. She feels good. She senses that *you* think she's smart. She feels even better, she feels the same glow of having her "superiors" give public recognition of her abilities, efforts, and successes that an employee feels if her boss compliments her work in front of others.

This child is developing a firm foundation of positive self-esteem, the cornerstone of mental health and maturity.

Without lectures and threats, you're teaching those babies the beginnings of self-discipline

The baby learns to wait a minute cooperatively (**self-discipline**) when you, an always reliable, trustworthy giver of care, are briefly busy, and say, "Wait a minute, I'm [doing this or that], and then I'll [do whatever the infant is signalling she wants]," *and then do respond very, very soon.* The baby

Francis Wardle

learns to be responsible and do what she says she will do (**self-discipline**) because you are setting an example of reliability and trustworthiness; *you* are behaving responsibly toward *her.*

The baby learns to go along cooperatively with your program's policies, procedures, personally preferred ways of doing things (**self-discipline**) *because you expect her to, and because you firmly, in a superfriendly way, guide her in desired directions.* Slowly, she begins taking pride in doing things according to your definition of "the right way." **She's behaving in a disciplined way, not because she fears you, but because it makes her feel good "to be good." This is surely a giant step toward being self-disciplined and toward positive self-esteem!** "Exceptional" children need the same gentle guidance and firm limits all other children need.

Sensible Standards of "Good Behavior" (Developing Self-Discipline) for Babies

1. Assume that if infants over three or four months of age cry during times when you expect them to be awake, they're *telling* you that something's the matter. Try to sleuth out what it is. Try to make the infant more comfortable, or briefly entertain her. (We all get bored or lonely once in a while).

Don't assume that babies cry and fuss a lot. All babies cry *occasionally*, but comfortable happy babies do not cry a lot. Don't assume that "it's good exercise for babies' lungs" to cry.

2. Assume that if infants over three or four months of age often cry during times when you expect them to be falling asleep, sleeping, or playing quietly in their cribs around the edges of sleep, you're not being clear and consistent enough about your sleeptime expectations and routines.

- Sleeptimes should be scheduled in accordance with what adults **observe** are the natural tired times for individuals. If a few babies in a group program just don't get tired when the others do, you can talk with their parents about possible sleeptime changes at home, you can assign one adult to have private time with the non-sleepers, or you can let them hang out with staff as they do chores and enjoy time off. Those who aren't tired can be put down *last,* which, in a group care setting, may be as much as half an hour later. Babies need cribs to contain them and to convey the message "This is a sleeping place. Therefore, this is a sleeping time."

Don't assume that babies regularly cry at bedtime. Tired babies do not usually cry when put in cribs at predictable, customary times. (There are exceptions to everything! *Any* baby will cry once in a while, or during a difficult week. Don't assume the worst; you can get her back on schedule.)

- Sleeptimes should predictably follow a specific preceding activity (such as lunch). They should involve a set sequence of "lead up" activities (for example, diaper changing, individual lap-sitting and book-looking, a bottle and a cuddle, a little song, affectionate covering in the crib, and a lullaby tape in the background).

Don't assume that babies will keep fussing for more time, and that kind adults are supposed to give in. Emotionally and socially satisfied babies usually accept adult judgment that the enjoyable routine has run its course and now it's crib time.

- Sleeptime schedules should allow for shorter and longer nappers, with minimum and maximum lengths.

Don't assume that an individual baby will sleep the exact same length of time each day. **Don't assume** you have to jump and acquiesce if baby decides 25 minutes is a long enough rest today. **Don't assume** you have to wake up a big sleeper at a fixed time just because the others are up. And **don't assume** you have to let a baby sleep all day when you know it will wreak havoc in family life tonight.

Note: Behavioral standards differ in different cultural groups. Almost all child development specialists would agree that these are reasonable standards if they suit you and children's parents. If not, negotiate until you all agree.

3. **Assume** that older babies who know what spoons and forks are for will try to use them, and will be very messy eaters; that they will eat many foods with fingers and by fistful; and that cup drinkers will spill rivulets and streams of liquid with each effort.

Don't assume that infant diners need to fling, drop, sling, and pour their meals overboard. Without anger, exasperation, or the sound of a threat in your voice, say, "Are you finished? I'll put your [food, drink] away if you're finished, and get you down." If the act is repeated, wipe the baby off while pleasantly engaging in running commentary, and let him crawl off to play.

4. **Assume** that mobile babies can learn to adhere to a few no-no's. Babyproof *to the maximum feasible extent,* and then teach limits.

Don't assume that the baby is king of the castle: Grown-ups and others live there too, and this baby has to learn to accept a limit on his freedom from the beginning of mobility. Be firm. Be physical. Move the baby away from the no-no as you pleasantly explain the rule.

5. **Assume** that a baby of any age will seek your attention if she needs it. **Assume** that attention span is something to promote. If a baby is busy, don't bother him. Do something else, watch, or join in, **allowing the child** to initiate at almost every step of the play.

If she's busy, **don't assume** she needs you. **Don't assume** that your ideas of what activity she should do are more important than hers. Don't intrude, overwhelm, and interrupt with your own agenda. Infants and toddlers don't play just to kill time. When they play contentedly, they learn contentedly.

The baby learns to treat and use objects reasonably appropriately (**self-discipline**) because *you* do, and because you give her information ("Hot!" "Sharp!" "Too tippy!" "No throwing toys!") and clear, consistent, *firm* behavioral guidelines ("Babies don't touch hot, no-no, hot *hurts* babies"; "Knives are for grown-ups. No. Babies don't touch sharp knives. Sharp *hurts* babies"; "People sit on chairs. Please sit down. Chairs are too tippy to stand on. You need to sit down right now." "Toys [sand, water] are for playing with. We don't throw toys [sand, water].")

Abundant attention, affection, and appreciation are absolutely necessary to the development of mental health, but after the infant's second or third month, more is needed.

Most of all, the word *home-like* suggests lovingness. An excellent home may offer dozens upon dozens of activities and a wealth of variety, but the most important thing it offers is unconditional love. We cannot expect caregivers to love other people's babies unconditionally (which is the chief reason that many child development specialists don't think infants and toddlers should spend the majority of their weekday awake time in out-of-home care). But we *can* expect professional educators to connect warmly with each little person many, many times a day, to make that child feel valued and worthy. It isn't sufficient to say, "I love these babies." The question is does each child in my care *feel* loved by me throughout our trials and tribulations together, throughout all that long time we spend together?

We mustn't let an essential ingredient of a baby's well-being — parents — be missing!

"In spite of all this, I just don't think infants and toddlers should be in out-of-home child care more than 20, 25 hours a week at most. Something's missing," says an expert mother we know.

"What?" we ask. "What's missing?"

"Parents," she promptly replies. "Parents are missing."

We need to collaborate closely every day in as many ways as are feasible

Our focus must be on lovingly developing good people — good character.

with parents. Indeed, they must be our partners. This is easy to actualize in settings such as yours where your goal, you told us, is to be like relatives to the infants and toddlers in your care — to be like extended family.

* * *

Whoops! You were asking about ways to make programs home-like, and ways to provide variety, in settings for infants, toddlers, and twos, and in all these pages we've only had time to talk about infants! We hardly got to toddlers and twos, just touched on them briefly! Well, isn't that just the way it always is when you work with this age group! These children are so busy that they keep *us* so busy we never get through. We touched on toddlers, but we'll just have to wait to talk more about them till the next chapter; they, too, are so busy growing, developing, and learning language, physical competencies, and so much more that they deserve a chapter all their own.

For further reading

Brazelton, T.B. (1983). *Infants and mothers: Differences in development* (rev. ed.). New York: Delta/Seymour.

Caldwell, B.M., & Stedman, D.J. (Eds.). (1977). *Infant education: A guide for helping handicapped children in the first three years.* New York: Walker.

Connor, F.P., Williamson, G.C., & Siepp, J.M. (1978). *Program guide for infants and toddlers with neuromotor and other developmental difficulties.* New York: Teachers College Press, Columbia University.

Escalona, S.K. (1968). *The roots of individuality: Normal patterns of development in infancy.* Chicago: Aldine.

Greenspan, S.J., & Greenspan, N.T. (1985). *First feelings: Milestones in the emotional development of your baby and child.* New York: Penguin.

Honig, A. S. (1982). Intervention strategies to optimize infant development. In Aronowitz, E. (Ed.), *Prevention strategies for mental health.* (pp. 25–55) New York: Neale Watson.

Lewis, I., & Sparling, J. (1979). *Learning games for the first 3 years.* New York: Walker.

Murphy, L.B., & Moriarty, A.E. (1976). *Vulnerability, coping and growth.* New Haven, CT: Yale University Press.

Ramey, C.T., & Trohanis, P.L. (Eds.). (1982). *Finding and educating high-risk handicapped infants.* Baltimore: University Park Press.

Spock, B.M., & Rothenberg, M.B. (1985). *Baby and child care* (revised). New York: Dutton.

Thomas, A., & Chess, S. (1977). *Temperament and development.* New York: Brunner/Mazel.

Viorst, J. (1987). *Necessary losses.* New York: Random House.

References

Ayers, W. (1989). *The good preschool teacher: Six teachers reflect on their lives.* New York: Teachers College Press, Columbia University.

BoPeep Productions. (1988). *Doing things* [Videotape]. Eureka, MT: Author.

Brazelton, T.B. (1984). Cementing family relationships through child care. In L.L. Dittman (Ed.), *The infants we care for* (rev. ed., pp. 9–20). Washington, DC: NAEYC.

Chase, R.A., & Rubin, R.R. (Eds.). (1979). *The first wondrous year.* New York: Collier.

Fraiberg, S. (1959). *The magic years: Understanding and handling the problems of early childhood.* New York: Scribner's.

Fraiberg, S., & Freedman, D.A. (1964). Studies in ego development of the congenitally blind child. *The Psychoanalytic Study of the Child, 19,* 113–169.

Jalongo, M.R. (1987). Do security blankets belong in preschool? *Young Children, 42*(3), 3–8.

Jervis, K. (Ed.). (1987). *Separation: Strategies for helping two to four year olds* (rev. ed.). Washington, DC: NAEYC.

Kendrick, A.S., Kaufmann, R., & Messenger, K.P. (1988). *Healthy young children: A manual for programs.* Washington, DC: NAEYC.

Leipzig, J. (1988). Seeing children as individuals. *Day Care & Early Education, 16*(2), 41.

Piaget, J. (1952). *The origins of intelligence in children.* (M. Cook, Trans.). New York: Norton. (Originally published in 1936)

Piaget, J. (1954). *The construction of reality in the child.* (M. Cook, Trans.). New York: Basic. (Originally published in 1937)

Stone, J.G. (1987). *Teacher-parent relationships.* Washington, DC: NAEYC.

CHAPTER 7

Respecting Toddlers and Twos, Respecting Teachers, Respecting Parents

QUESTION: Some people on my staff are somewhat sullen. They dole out the activities I ask them to, but without enthusiasm. We have the usual problems of absenteeism, turnover, and so on. We cannot pay better wages because ours are working class and rather low-income parents and they can't pay higher fees. We await the day when the federal government will subsidize child care the way it pays most of each child's K—12 school needs. Parents would not be able to send their children to public school if the government did not pay just about the entire amount of the tuition. I believe that is the way it should be with child care for people who want or need it.

I am particularly concerned about our toddlers and two-year-olds. We do not take children under 18 months, so these are our youngest groups. The greatest difficulties the staff have are keeping the class involved in each activity, lining up to move from one activity to the next, and disciplining the children. Teachers get so frustrated trying to keep the children in order that the time-out chair is always occupied. I cannot make over each staff member, and I have a few churlish, childish ones. What are the most important things to look for when hiring replacement people, something I always seem to be doing? Please keep in mind that I cannot afford to hire well-trained people. Most of the people available to me do not have much college, if any.

Not every expert (outstanding parent, outstanding family child care provider, and outstanding group care person) would agree, but many would probably say that in your circumstances the most important hiring criteria, beyond health, reliability, and so on, are:

1. Caregivers who enjoy children *of this age.*

2. Caregivers who have intuitive-type temperaments that enable them to be "good with" *little* children. They "have a way with" *this* age group. They seem to be able to tune in to the needs of most toddlers: They're *in tune* with toddlers and two-year-olds.

3. Caregivers whose preferred pace is slow. As noted toddler authority Magda Gerber says, "Slow down. Most caregivers are always too busy. You have to unbusy your head and unbusy your body." This requires caregivers to have a calm disposition as well as protection from too many duties.

4. Caregivers whose self-esteem is adequate, or even above average, and who are not excessively angry human beings.

People are priority: Hire people who "have a way with" children of this age; then you can help them learn to handle the different situations you mention

Although there is evidence that caregivers who have benefitted from relevant courses in child development and from sensitive staff development generally do a better job than those with no training, there isn't a large body of research about

● the superiority of caregivers who enjoy the age group they work with over those who dislike the age;

● the superiority of caregivers born with intuitive temperaments over caregivers who are more cerebral or stiff in their style;

● the superiority of caregivers with a slow style over those who are in a hurry to get through the day, or in a hurry for the child to learn the next thing;

● the superiority of caregivers with good self-esteem over caregivers with low self-esteem;

● the superiority of caregivers with normal levels of negative emotions

Marilyn L. Nolt

If you hire people who genuinely enjoy children and who themselves are in good mental health, you can usually help them learn to observe individual children, respond appropriately, and work with small groups.

over those who harbor huge reservoirs of

—hate and hidden anger (those who are stone-faced and hard in their relationships —really, *lack* of relationships—with children), or

—anxiety and crippling fears (those who are so consumed and constricted by their own emotional situation that they can't focus fully on each child).

There is no great focus on these criteria on the part of early childhood education researchers. Many seasoned practitioners, however, will agree:

● Delighting in children of the age they work with makes an immeasurable difference in the kind of care adults give.

● Book learning, while important, does *not* cut the mustard past a most minimal level without "the magic touch" ("mother wit," intuitive sensitivity, interpersonal creativity, and responsiveness to children).

● Enjoying a leisurely pace, so babies, toddlers, and twos can take their time to discover and "be," is a much more

important ingredient of good caregiving than is the desire to "stimulate" (interrupt) them throughout each day.

● Positive self-esteem helps caregivers be "adults" rather than be childish and threatened by independent or dawdling or oppositional one- and

because their own overwhelming emotions impair their interpersonal relations.

We also know from experience that adults who have never resolved the issue of independence vs. dependence in their *own* lives, and adults who need children to be dependent on them, often dislike the headstrong behavior toddlers typically display. (The same people may be good with *babies*.) Of course people who hire can't know this in advance, but discussing during the interview the applicant's feelings about, and understanding of, one- and two-year-olds' frequent oppositional and sometimes seemingly irrational behavior is a wise idea. Infant/toddler specialist Alice Honig adds,

Hire people who weren't *shamed* a lot in their own childhoods—otherwise toddlers who suck thumbs, masturbate, eat snot, etc., evoke *old* shames. (1990)

Hiring intuitive, mentally healthy people usually works out best

As was said in Chapter 1, you're far better off in terms of staffing if you start with the right stuff. In programs for young children, people are priority— they are much more important than what many people call "curriculum," meaning canned activities forced on children, ready or not, interested or not. **Above all, seek and find people who "have a way with children." Directors often find that if a caregiver likes little children, "has what it**

Showing respect for our teachers precedes expecting them to show respect for children and their parents, especially if the teachers are people who have previously received little respect in their lives.

two-year-olds, and be open-minded regarding guidance from the director or the credentialed early childhood teachers who may be in the program.

● Excessively angry or excessively anxious adults are not able to reach and react to each child appropriately

takes" (intuition), feels good about herself as a person, and has average mental health (is not excessively angry or anxious), she is willing and able to learn—may even be *eager*— through directed child observation and discussion, reading, accessible materials, looking at and talking about staff development videos, attending workshops and conferences, and visiting interesting programs within driving distance. Conversely, if a caregiver doesn't like the work, doesn't "connect" with children of this age, has low self-esteem, and is either seething with inner anger or shackled by serious anxieties, or has a problem with control versus "letting go," she is likely to learn little or nothing from staff development opportunities. Or, as a head teacher tells us,

She may *learn* it, but she is unlikely to be able to *do* it. Children don't care what you *know*. They respond to what you *do* and what you *are*; what kind of a human being you are.

Training is important, but as you yourself have said, you can't make over each staff member. If you hire the right kind of people it won't be too hard for you to help most of them *learn* not to *try* "to keep the class involved in each activity," "to line the children up," and "to discipline them." More about these issues in a minute.

This is an area where the experience of a generation of on-site staff development specialists, common sense, and cross-over findings from mental health research, and employment and training areas other than early childhood education can give us direction, whether or not there is as yet a body of formal research data on the subject in the—narrowly speaking—early childhood education field.

To reduce the matter to the bare bones, people whose own self-esteem is OK (so they don't have to prove that they are powerful by "putting down" babies), and who resonate to children's struggle toward "personhood," can be helped to work in ways that almost always show respect for toddlers. **Each child forms evaluative estimations of each aspect of self from within. The younger the child, the more her primary adults' level of self-esteem is contagious to her. This is because it's hard for many adults** who lack self-confidence and self-appreciation to help generate the same in babies and young children.

No doubt we are in agreement that the "character" and personality of a caregiver and the quality of the relationship between caregiver and child are of far greater significance than are the specific art or other "activities" provided in a child care center. It goes without saying that it's incredibly difficult to hire good, permanent people at the low-level salaries we are limited to due to the need to keep fees affordable to families and the lack of federal subsidies to fill the gap. But **it's a fascinating fact that some directors are better "character judges" than others, and seem able, quite frequently, to hire good caregivers, even if they don't stay forever.**

The *controlling* individual values conformity in children. This person will function most comfortably in a highly structured program that puts adherence to a schedule above allowing toddlers to complete absorbing activities. Children often bear the brunt of anger and resentment when such caregivers find their beliefs in conflict with the policies of a center valuing appropriate development of autonomy. Such a person may not recognize the coercive quality in her personality, and those traits may not surface during an employment interview.

On the other hand, the *passive,* anxious-to-please individual may

> A person's positive self-esteem results in large part from being respected. This is as true of toddlers (and of their teachers!) as of anyone else. If at all possible, hire people who respect themselves, children, and parents.

Faith Bowlus

Gently but firmly guiding little children toward the development of good character is more important than "instructing" them, or forcing them to join in activities.

shrink from making independent decisions in situations calling for adult intervention and guidance. Such a person might find it difficult to function in a loosely structured program that requires creative responses based on mature judgment. These traits are often easier to spot in an employment interview, and they can be easier to modify through supervision and encouragement toward independent handling of children.

Interviewing potential caregivers can be compared to setting out on a journey to an unknown place: It's probably a little easier if you have a map to suggest what you may want to look for. One director said

I look for just-out-of-high-school-or-college students who "love children," and youngish, still energetic grandmothers who have enjoyed intensive grandmothering. I get them to pledge a few years of their lives. I'd rather have enthusiastic people who turn over rather than dull, dead permanent people. Then I invest time showing them "how we do it." The seasoned people get a small pay increase and change of title and become trainers of *new* people.

Disagreements among teachers and teachers, teachers and parents, and parents and parents may be legitimate

Well-trained child development specialists agree on just about all basic principles of how adults and infants, toddlers, and two-year-olds can live most comfortably and effectively together, but there are also areas of significant, *legitimate* disagreement. There will be disagreement between skilled parents and capable caregivers, too. **Disagreements are usually in value-laden areas of behavior, and closely relate to people's conscious or nonconscious child-rearing goals.**

For example: One expert believes that distraction is almost never a good idea because its purpose is to stop children from feeling their feelings. Another believes that children should be allowed to feel their feelings and should be given help in interpreting, expressing, and accepting them, but that

"enough is enough," and that even babies need help in learning how to "keep things in perspective," and to "recover." Both understand the importance of validating and tolerating feelings. Both are reasonable viewpoints. The former indicates a hierarchy of values that puts feelings above all else. The latter indicates a hierarchy of values in which appreciation of feelings and self-control are about equal. Neither of these philosophies harms the development of positive self-esteem in a baby. "And *I* think distraction is *wonderful* with toddlers about to embark on foolish or dangerous activities without much thought as they so often do!" adds Alice Honig (1990). Discussion of potential areas of disagreement like this one during prehiring talks will probably pay off. It lets you know that the applicant's philosophy is just too far from yours, or it sets the stage for further dialogue during your ongoing staff development work.

Having enough staff and/or recruiting, training, and supervising teen volunteers, parent volunteers, and older volunteers — men as well as women — makes it possible for each caregiver to do better, and for each child to get enough individual attention.

Nancy P. Alexander

© 1990 Jeffrey High Image Productions

Teachers of toddlers and two-year-olds should be encouraged to observe and enjoy individual children. Hire people who like children, then show them how to observe and respond.

Another example: One expert parent (i.e., a parent who has raised some children into adulthood who have "turned out well" in all dimensions customarily included in the global label "mentally healthy," or who, in spite of significant life crises or hardships, which may include disabilities the child has had, has raised the child into an adult who is in much better shape as a human being than might have been expected "under the circumstances") believes that crawlers and one-year-olds (toddlers) should almost never be "contained" because exploration, leading to self-reliance, risk-taking, and independence—extremely important qualities—is all-important. Another equally expert expert believes that crawlers and one-year-olds need only a small amount of utterly unfettered freedom, that they should usually be held—should virtually live on laps—or be kept in pens, strollers, or seats next to their actively engaged grownups and older children, because interpersonal relations and cooperative activity are

far more important than endless independence, which, the latter expert believes, tends to lead to loneliness and disregard for others. Good caregivers may disagree here, too. Culture and socioeconomic status will often significantly affect views in this area.

The first of these experts believes that a wide variety of toys and activities are essential for optimal intellectual stimulation, which hopefully will promote success in school, whereas the second expert doesn't think unusually high academic achievement is necessary, and values creativity more; she prefers the "less is more" approach to purchased toys—buy less and children will invent more. They will play games that use their bodies in many ways, and use natural materials such as sticks, mud, stones, and water. Both understand the importance of warm interaction between chatty adult and little person. Both are reasonable viewpoints. The former probably instills in children the idea that their adults are product oriented, as well as that they very much value independence. The

latter may convey the concept that friendship and creativity are greater values to grownups.

In neither case will the little child's self-esteem be lowered or made negative, but to some of us it seems sensible to "take the cue from the kid," as a fine caregiver we know phrases it, "pick them up or put them down according to the clues they give you." In either instance, the caregiver's values will have only a limited effect on the individual infant; for better or for worse, **the child's family's values will usually predominate.**

A center director stresses:

Nothing is more important than a thirty-day trial period. First the interview. If I'm interested, I ask the applicant to try a morning with us, "to see if you like it"; we pay her. Then, if it looks good, I hire, explaining that we have a one-month trial run "to see if we're going to be happy together."

Enough staff, a critical quality variable, is also essential; without enough adults you can expect that teachers will herd flocks of children, rather than spend the day, family style, with individual children and small, usually spontaneously formed clusters

We doubtless also agree that having *enough* staff is critical if we aim to give good care to young children. How can a caregiver be expected to do "the max" for each individual child if she can scarcely locate him in the crowd? It's obvious to any expert mother—and *should* be obvious to those at all levels who determine child care policy and regulations—that a person can care more and be more promptly generous with the care she gives an infant, toddler, or two-year-old if she isn't exhausted, distracted, or absorbed in other duties. This is especially true if

Toddlers and two-year-olds are in Piaget's (1937/1959) sensorimotor stages; they learn through all senses and by using their whole bodies. Their self-esteem is enhanced by physical triumphs.

the adult is attempting to deal with a raging tiger of a toddler, or a two who refuses to do as tactfully told to; or the little girl who doggedly keeps on doing it when courteously asked to stop; or the constantly cranky, crotchety kid; and any others who require a saint's patience. How can a caregiver be expected to be leisurely and appreciative when she must ceaselessly rush hither and thither to accomplish all her responsibilities? Except for the geniuses of our genre — and there *are* some — unpaid caregivers (mothers) and paid caregivers can be more sensitive and responsive to the babies they're taking care of if

● they have fewer children to care for;

● they each have a co-caregiver with whom they regularly or often work at least for short periods, and with whom they generally get along (for a family child care provider this may mean the occasional collaboration of a friend, older child, mate, mother, or other);

● the environment is set up suitably (few dangers, considerable convenience for caregivers, many toys, soft and hard surfaces, places for privacy, space for gross motor activity, etc.) and is aesthetically pleasing (pleasing environments are soothing to moods; environments that are displeasing, dark, cluttered, ugly, and crowded are stressful to adults and toddlers alike);

● health and hygiene is good so grownups and children alike *feel* well;

● temperature and noise are controlled so nerves aren't frayed;

● they have help with the housework;

● they are not on duty too many hours in a row; and

● *their* needs are met, too (in the case of nonparents, this means respectable pay, benefits, a nice staff lounge in the center or getaway place in the family day care home where the provider can take a break while children nap or a helper supervises them).

Even with absurdly tight budgets there are things that can be done to avoid overloading caregivers too much:

1. **Work hard to establish meaningful parent involvement and the participation of regular volunteers** from high schools, colleges, service clubs, programs for elderly people, churches, and other potentially promising places. Of course, volunteers have to be screened, trained, and supervised, and should be assigned suitable duties as individually appropriate. (A book that will help you work with *older* vol-

© Bm Porter 1990/Don Franklin

C & W Shields

The "program" in a center, home, or child care home should take place largely outside. The "curriculum" in a center, home, or child care home should consist largely of exploring the environment — discovering the exciting ordinary objects and experiences that surround us every day. What these are will somewhat depend upon where you are. Keep in mind that to the young child "the ordinary is extraordinary"!

unteers is *Young and Old Together* by Carol Seefeldt. And an article that may give you an idea to follow up on is "Young Teens Help Young Children for the Benefit of Both."

Some infant/toddler specialists disapprove of bringing volunteers into care settings for such young children because very young children don't immediately feel at home with people who are strangers to them. Other specialists think that the benefits brought to one and all by more helping hands, one-on-one friendship, and variety are well worth the effort. An effort must be made to allow each individual child to study the new person as long as he likes before any approach or direct contact is made.

The most successful method of integrating a new person into a relationship with a child is to busy the visitor for a few minutes with a task 10 or 15 feet from the child, allowing the child to watch and to be given a few fragments of information about the "stranger" from the lap or the "safety circle" of a familiar adult, whether parent or other care provider. Next, the visitor comes closer, but does not directly confront the child. The adult places an interesting toy or object *between* himself and the toddler. This serves both as a protective barrier (from the toddler's viewpoint) and as an invitation to indirect "dialogue." It's an invitation because the typical toddler is curious and eager to examine everything that piques her interest. The vol-

unteer chats with the child's security person, not with the child, and plays with the toy, talking as he plays. Very shortly, most toddlers will involve themselves. It's important to remember that toddlers and two-year-olds prefer the familiar and the predictable, and to make choices and feel in control. So we wait until the new volunteer has become a little familiar and a little predictable, and permit the *child* to choose when and how to reach out, thus feeling in control of this "threatening" situation.

2. **Pay an older child or teen-ager minimum wage to come in several times a week to clean designated places and objects.** The drudgery escaped by a staff person will improve that person's morale, as well as permit her more time for direct interaction with children or time off to refresh and rejuvenate. A director says:

And you'd be surprised how much two-and-a-half-year-olds can and love to do to help. Mine consider it a special treat to wash all the toys and equipment in sudsy water while a staff person washes things in disinfectant solution twice a week. Of course an adult—usually a volunteer—works *with* them, and ensures, among other things, that the liquid doesn't go in the mouth. There's nothing two-year-olds love better than water play, but equally important, I consider it critical for each child to learn to help those who need help. These kids get a great

Respecting Toddlers and Twos, Teachers, and Parents

kick out of hearing and saying that the babies and toddlers aren't old enough to wash their own toys, so "the big kids" are needed to do it for them. Then everybody will have safe, healthy toys to play with. (Obviously, adults would not offer this chore to children who will surely suck the wet toys or drink the cleaning solution.)

3. **Get together with directors from all area family and center-based day care programs (a family child care provider is the director of her program) and discuss the need for *all of you* to raise fees in order to pay for an extra full- or part-time person to relieve regular staff members.** Then work with staff and parents to help everyone understand the "trilemma":

The Trilemma

good caregivers,
and enough of them
=good program

Quality care can't be provided without quality caregivers, and quality caregivers can't be attracted and retained without adequate pay and/or adequate working conditions. Show respect for your parents and staff by giving each group an opportunity to understand each other's perspective. (Some relevant materials you may want to read, share, and discuss are listed on this page). **Showing respect for our teachers precedes expecting them to show respect for children and their parents, that is, to encourage children to be individuals, rather than to regard them as a "class."**

Many mothers who are employed outside the home prefer that their toddlers be in family day care rather than in a day care *center*, because so many of these factors can be present in a family day care home. These homes, if licensed, have only a family-style number of children; for example, in some states, there can be no more than six with one adult, and only one or two of the children are toddlers or two-year-olds. Sometimes the family day

care provider's husband, mother, or friend, an enrolled child's parent, or an older child in the group helps out. A family child care provider emphasizes

My older after-school children — 10, 11 — are like junior parents to the small children. They love to prepare the snack, read stories, play baby games, push the toddlers in our baby swing or in a stroller out in front. . . After nap, the little children can't wait till the big ones come "home" from school. I think it's wonderful for the school-age children to be needed and to develop their nurturing skills.

The "classroom" may be most of the caregiver's home, her yard, the neighborhood, and the greater community (recreation center, library, swimming pool, etc.). Wise family day care providers "take care of themselves," by

getting out with the children regularly, and from time to time having a sub so they can "recreate."

Ongoing, "do-it-yourself" staff development helps a heap

Courses in parenting or caregiving help adults live in developmentally appropriate ways with little people, whether offered as an ongoing, on-site staff growth program (Greenberg, 1975) or off-site, for example, at an area high school or college. Such courses help center staff and family day care provider alike. Dr. Honig says:

I feel *strongly* about the importance of "book learning" about the Eriksonian battles and seesawing between dependence and new fierce urges (even absurd ones!) toward au-

---

Resources You May Want for Your Staff and Parents

Brochures:

National Association for the Education of Young Children. *NAEYC position statement on nomenclature, salaries, benefits, and the status of the early childhood professional.* Washington, DC: NAEYC. #530

National Association for the Education of Young Children. *The full cost of quality in early childhood programs.* Washington, DC: NAEYC. #537

National Association for the Education of Young Children. *Where your child care dollars go.* Washington, DC: NAEYC. #545.

Articles:

Galinsky, E. (1989). The staffing crisis. *Young Children, 44*(2), 2–4.

Galinsky, E. (1989). Is there really a crisis in child care? If so, does anybody out there care? *Young Children, 44*(5), 2–3.

Marx, E., & Granger, R.C. (1990). Analysis of salary enhancement efforts in New York. *Young Children, 45*(3), 53–59.

Modigliani, K. (1988). Twelve reasons for the low wages in child care. *Young Children, 43*(3), 14–15.

Morin, J. (1989). We can force a solution to the staffing crisis. *Young Children, 44*(6), 18–19.

National Association for the Education of Young Children. (1987). NAEYC position statement on quality, compensation, and affordability in early childhood programs. *Young Children, 43*(1), 31.

Phillips, D. & Whitebook, M. (1986). Who are child care workers? The search for answers. *Young Children, 41*(4), 14–20.

Video:

Whitebook, M., & Morin, J. *Salaries, working conditions, and the teacher shortage.* Washington, DC: NAEYC. #811.

tonomy that each toddler goes through. The toddler wants to merge with the loved one(s) and be taken care of, to be obedient —but is also a small person whose ego strength and sense of self bud so bravely and fiercely (albeit sometimes foolishly and exasperatingly). (1990)

An important part of any staff development endeavor is a group effort to solve a real problem caregivers are experiencing. The education director of a group of family child care homes reports

At the end of each meeting, I get someone to volunteer to bring us a problem next time. Usually, they are behavior problems. If the provider *has* no problem, she reads something from our little "library" and presents the topic to us. Then we discuss it.

It boosts self-esteem to know that you are trusted to be capable of sharing knowledge and advice, and of wishing to grow professionally. Infant/toddler specialist Rose Bromwich emphasizes the fact that caregivers should be encouraged to really get to know individual children — to observe, to develop a close relationship — because it's much more pleasurable for the adult than to be in charge of a *herd* of children. Dr. Bromwich believes that this is so rewarding to many childcaring people that it may relate positively to the retention problem: Being really connected to individual children may cause a caregiver to want to stay in the job.

As soon as the majority of people on a staff have some new child development or early childhood education understandings, they can present them, and lead a discussion about them, at a parent meeting. **Sharing learnings with parents, as staff people are exposed to them themselves, is a wonderful way to include parents in the program**—to show respect for parents. Moreover, as staff teach what they just learned, they reinforce it in their own minds.

Another idea that works is to have a fundraiser, or to solicit contributions from area businesses, so you can **send two staff people from the center each summer to a week-long infant/ toddler workshop,** such as those identified in the box on this page. Sending *two* people is better than sending *one*, because the two can support each other in trying out some new things and in leading sharing at staff meet-

You Can Create Your Own Staff Development Program Using Available Media Training Materials

Here is a resource you can't afford to miss!

Infant-Toddler Caregiving:

An Annotated Guide to Media Training Materials

Alice S. Honig, Ph.D and Donna Sasse Wittmer, Ph.D

This document was developed as part of the Infant Care in California Media Training Development Project by: The Center for Child & Family Studies, Dr. J. Ronald Lally, Director, Far West Laboratory for Educational Research and Development 1855 Folsom Street, San Francisco, California 94103.

The *Annotated Guide* is part of a concerted effort by the California State Department of Education's Child Development Division and Far West Laboratory for Educational Research and Development's Center for Child and Family Studies in collaboration with many organizations and institutions throughout the nation to upgrade the quality of care provided to children under three. It represents the first attempt to survey and record all the videos, films, filmstrips, slide cassette programs and audio programs currently available that were developed for the specific purpose of training caregivers of children under three.

Selected to do this work were Drs. Alice S. Honig and Donna S. Wittmer, two experts in infant care known for their bibliographic work for ERIC of the printed training materials for infant and toddler caregivers. Because the rental or purchase of video and filmstrip material is often quite expensive, Drs. Honig and Wittmer were asked to write extensive annotations of the materials they reviewed, and to comment on the materials' usefulness to various audiences. This technique was used so that the reader could make an informed decision about appropriate use of a particular video or filmstrip before an actual viewing. I feel that they have accomplished this task quite nicely, and in so doing have made an invaluable contribution to the child care profession and specifically to those who have as their responsibility the selection of training materials for infant and toddler caregivers.

Of course the *Annotated Guide* does not include information on all media materials currently available. A list of all materials viewed in preparation of this document can be found in the guide. The materials selected from that list for annotation have been judged by the reviewers to have content worthy of your attention. At present, the plan is to update the *Annotated Guide* every two years so that quality materials missed by the first review process and materials newly created will find their way into the guide. These revisions will be made available as they are produced.

ings. The first time you do this, be sure that you, as director, are one of the two who go, so you can be in on what's happening, and on transmitting what you learn to your staff. (What is taught in these brief staff development programs will support the ways of working with children that you believe in.) **Many family child care providers close, or have a substitute, for two to four weeks in the summer so they can replenish themselves through vacation and professional development experiences.** As you and your staff become comfortable with these learning experiences, raise some extra money; invite a few *parents* to go with you.

How many programs show respect for teachers in all these ways? A book you may want to read and talk about at one of your get-togethers is *A Great Place To Work* by Paula Jorde-Bloom. Some of these things are beyond the control of an individual child care program. We must unite in teacher and family day care provider associations, and in other advocacy groups, to work on them. Another book to read and discuss is *Speaking Out: Early Childhood Advocacy* by Stacey Goffin and Joan Lombardi. Get your parents to join you in advocacy efforts. Working side by side for a good cause really builds solidarity! Leaders in most individual child care programs could do more than they *do* do for staff if they put their minds to it, including encouraging parents to join the team.

Good supervision is central if your goal is to help your staff to grow toward appropriate practice with children. Do you have a clear philosophy, and clear policies and procedures that every staff person and parent has in writing? Have you discussed them with everyone involved? Does everybody pretty much agree; is there a good team feeling? How do you work on areas of disagreement and difficulty? Do you have regular planning meetings with your staff during which you encourage individuals to participate in program-wide decision making, as well as working out plans for parent meetings, small informal outings for the children, and fresh activities? Above all, are you, as manager, fair about the distribution of unpopular duties? Pay? Pay increases? Fringe benefits? Giving encouragement and compliments? The figure on this page shows what it takes to create and maintain a healthy work climate. We all know how much easier it is to *read* something like this than to *achieve* it, but every effort you can make to move toward the creation of a healthy work climate is likely to help your situation.

Why? **Because only when each individual staff member feels fully respected can you progress in your effort to get her to show respect for each individual child, and therefore to stop expecting children to be a group moving as one body through a series of predetermined activities.**

When we think about it, we realize that a big part of a person's positive self-esteem results from being respected. This is as true of toddlers (and of their teachers) as of anyone else. And surely we agree that we deserve respect for our *own* needs, too. If your staff is not interested in hearing about the importance of developing positive self-esteem in young children, maybe they *will* be interested in talking about how to make the job *easier*. Now let's spend some time talking about that!

Ten Dimensions of Organizational Climate

Dimension	Definition	Related Research
Collegiality	Extent to which staff are friendly, supportive, and trusting of one another. Measures the peer cohesion of employees and the esprit de corps of the group as a whole.	Goodlad, 1983 Little, 1982 Moos, 1976 Zahorick, 1984
Professional Growth	Degree of emphasis placed on personal and professional growth.	Fullan, 1982 Joyce et al., 1983 Kent, 1985
Supervisor Support	Strength of facilitative leadership that provides encouragement, support, and clear expectations.	Fleischer, 1985 Purkey & Smith, 1982 Silver & Moyle, 1984 Zigarmi, 1981
Clarity	Extent to which policies, procedures, and responsibilities are clearly defined and communicated.	Moos, 1976 Pettegrew & Wolf, 1982 Schwab & Iwanicki, 1982
Reward System	Degree of fairness and equity in the distribution of pay, fringe benefits, and opportunities for advancement.	Adams, 1971 Nash, 1983 Stern, 1986 Whitebook et al., 1982
Decision Making	Amount of autonomy given to staff and the extent to which they are involved in center-wide decisions.	Fox, 1974 Neugebauer, 1975 Whitebook et al., 1982
Goal Consensus	Degree to which staff agree on the goals and objectives of the center.	Fox, 1974 Silver & Moyle, 1984 Wilson et al., 1984
Task Orientation	Emphasis placed on good planning, efficiency, and getting the job done.	Moos, 1976 Nash, 1983
Physical Setting	Extent to which the spatial arrangement of the center helps or hinders staff in carrying out their responsibilities.	Phyfe-Perkins, 1980 Prescott, 1981 Steele, 1973 Weinstein, 1979
Innovativeness	Extent to which the organization adapts to change and encourages staff to find creative ways to solve problems.	Berman & McLaughlin, 1978 Fullan, 1982 Jorde-Bloom, 1986b Young & Kasten, 1980

The Growth Program

Children: our investment in the future

Buy appropriate low-cost materials about infants, toddlers, twos, and programs for them. Allocate paid time several times a week for staff people to read and discuss brochures, booklets, and books of their choice in a comfortable staff room. Perhaps a staff member per week can make a short, simple presentation to the others. Through discussion, you and your caregivers can solve many of the problems interfering with the quality of your program.

Arranging for a developmentally appropriate program reduces discipline problems and transition problems as well as indicates respect for children

To begin with, you can duck out of the difficulty you mention of "keeping the class involved in each activity" and do away with "lining up to move the group from one activity to the next" *by offering a home-style play day in which, within few parameters, each child **chooses** what she or he will do.* The very best toddler programs offer children many choices, so it wouldn't be just "making do" if you changed to this approach, too. In the kind of home that turns out terrific children with high self-esteem, strong self-discipline, and what we call "good character," we

often find that each young child chooses what he will do **in the realm of play** from dawn to dusk, *but there are a wide variety of excellent choices, through any and all of which the child will learn.* (Please don't misunderstand. The child does not decide *everything,* just how she will use her play time, which should be a high percentage of her waking time.)

Some structure will automatically be provided by the framework of the day in your center or in a family child care home:

● Arrival time (the time no one can come *sooner* than — it's best if arrivals are spread over a broad period of time so caregivers can **help each child become established,** and can **cordially coordinate with the person who has delivered the child).**

● Indoor playtime with a special art, science, cooking, music, or movement activity offered to **individuals who want to join in.**

● Perhaps a 45-minute outing for a small group of children and a caregiver.

● Outdoor playtime (many of your special projects can be done *outdoors* —**outdoor playtime can be most of the day).**

● Snack (snack is a good outdoor activity, too).

● Story **for people who want to listen.** (See Chapter 9 for a short discussion about toddlers and twos who *don't* want to listen.)

● Indoor playtime with a special art, science, cooking, music, or movement activity offered **to individuals who want to join in only.**

● Perhaps a 45-minute outing for a small group of children and a caregiver.

● Lunch.

● Preparation for naptime.

● Naptime.

● Outdoor playtime.

● Indoor playtime with a special art, science, cooking, music, or movement activity offered to **individuals who want to join in.**

Baby Games

A favorite activity for babies in happy homes is playing simple games with grown-ups and older children. Launching into a playful activity like a suitable giggle-producing game *at a time when you can see a baby isn't busy* is also a way to add variety to your babies' days. Do you use rhymes, songs, and games like those on this page? Most babies older than three months enjoy them.

> Pat-a-cake, pat-a-cake, baker's man.
> Make me a cake as fast as you can.
> Prick it and pat it and mark it with a "B,"
> And pop it in the oven for [baby's name] and me.
> Say "pop" in a lively voice and make a shoving-it-into-the-oven motion.

> Knock at the door (tap the baby's forehead)
> Peep in (lift his eyelid).
> Lift the latch (tip his nose up).
> Walk in (lay two fingers on his lower lip and let them "walk").

> B-A-Bay
> B-E-Bee
> B-I-Bye
> Bay-bee-bye.
> B-O-Boh
> B-U-Boo
> Bay-bee-bye-boh-BOO!
> When you say "BOO!", touch foreheads with the baby.
> Crawl on the floor with the crawling baby. Play "I'm Gonna Get You!" and "Can You Catch Me?" Each "play" culminates in a hug. Be prepared for shrieks and squeals of happiness.

Toddlers and two-year-olds are in Erikson's (1963) stage of emerging autonomy. They are struggling to evolve individual selves, independent of parents and other primary caregivers, and so need a great many opportunities every day to do it their way. Their self-esteem is enhanced by doing it their way.

- An outing, perhaps to the park, store, or library.
- Story time (though "story time" is almost *any* time!).
- Pickup time.

Further structure is provided by the fact that each child is NOT free to hurt other children, their feelings, or their projects. From the toddler and two-year-old viewpoint, interference in "doing what comes naturally" is nearly constant, even when grownups intervene only when essential to help children solve social problems. See Chapter 11 for details.

Everything except this skeleton framework for a child care program day, and alert staff intervention to assist *each* child in understanding where his play partner "is coming from", and in controlling his impulses, aggression, etc., can be optional for each child. Surely, envisioning an enriched home as your model — instead of an elementary school "class" — should prevent many staff-child hassles, and thus many "discipline problems." This approach to programming and scheduling is not new and radical; this has been the traditional nursery school way of working with two-, three-, and four-year-olds since about 1917! According to authoritative national early childhood organizations such as the National Association for the Education of Young Children (NAEYC) and the Association for Childhood Education International (ACEI), *this is still the recommended,* "ideal" way to work with groups of young children. If you decide to update to this approach, you'll be in good company!

Avoiding most "group times" with toddlers and twos shows respect for their growing autonomy

It's hard to gather toddlers and young two-year-olds into a group, and nearly impossible to keep them there. It's also extremely inappropriate. Each toddler is totally busy learning to become a competently functioning *self*, an individual. **Becoming a competently functioning individual comes before learning to become a competently functioning *group member.***

If several toddlers or twos spontaneously congregate like a flock of penguins to investigate what a caregiver is doing (maybe playing with a toy? making a salad? pasting pretty paper?), to watch the service repair person, to check in on the story a staff member is reading to someone, so be it. It's not developmentally appropriate, however, to hustle, cajole, and chide toddlers and twos toward chairs, expect them to remain quietly seated for ten minutes while a teacher distributes materials, and then to perform in a conforming manner. At *most,* young toddlers (12 to 21 months) should be gathered into a group only for lunch or

You can duck out of the difficulty you mention of "keeping the class involved in each activity" and do away with "lining up to move the group from one activity to the next" by offering a home-style play day in which, within few parameters, each child chooses what she or he will do.

Nancy P. Alexander

© Bm Porter 1990/Don Franklin

CHAPTER 7

to go somewhere, and older toddlers and twos (21 to 36 months) should be invited but not compelled to attend music or story group for five to ten minutes. Some may stay much *longer;* we're talking about *expecting* them to stay much longer. Even snack time doesn't have to be an occasion when everyone is expected to sit down all at once. Two children per day can be invited to help prepare the snacks and snack table, and another two children can have the privilege of inviting each member of the group to have a snack when ready. Two is often a sensible number of children to select because two can talk together (natural language development), and take turns (social development), while you work. On the other hand, this is also a splendid time to enjoy and get to know any one individual child. **You can set an example for your staff by working with the children in these ways yourself, and you can also make this approach to teaching the topic of frequent staff development discussions.**

Toddlers and twos should be *expected* to move around about their business — which may or may not include arriving at and plunging into (literally) an art or cooking activity an adult is sharing with stray children

who show up, or which may or may not include joining in to hear a story being read to another toddler who asked to be read to. This certainly doesn't mean that children wander aimlessly all day, and teachers sit around ignoring them!

Games for Toddlers and Twos

Ring around the rosy
A pocket full of posy
Ashes, ashes, we all fall down.
(Hold hands and walk
  in a circle.)

Of course staff is very busy luring floaters and roamers into tempting activities if they seem too scattered for too long. **Even music time can be something the adult just wordlessly starts doing; some children come to get involved and others don't.**

This is how exemplary early childhood and infant/toddler teacher education programs (Bank Street, Sarah Lawrence, Vassar, Pacific Oaks, Syracuse) teach teachers to teach. This is how exemplary early childhood programs *do* teach:

Instead of summoning everyone to sit down (which, because we're dealing with small people whose *job* is to separate from us and *not* to do what we want, will cause at least several toddlers to go off in the opposite direction) and *instead* of keeping the little wigglers waiting while we dish out art supplies or whatever, the teacher simply sets up a suitable art project (pasting bits of tissue paper onto construction paper, for example, or stirring paint), *starts doing it herself,* and welcomes any child who wishes to have a turn. Eventually, a child (or three) who hasn't yet come over and asked for a turn can be invited to enjoy the fun. **To choose not to join in one particular activity is a fine and respected choice.** The same approach to snack is preferred by many care providers.

Instead of insisting that everyone sit in a circle so music time or story time can start, *just start.* When you begin playing galloping music on the piano or tape, a herd of heavy-hoofed "horses" will soon be loping laughing laps around you. **Never mind if some toddlers choose not be horses; it's a legitimate choice.** You do not have to pretend to be a horse at age two to grow into an adult of good character. When you sit down in a cozy spot with some comfortable-looking space around you and begin reading a fascinating story, a cluster of eager listeners will soon be nestling in next to you clamoring to see the pictures. A child "won't" come? Who cares? **To choose not to hear this story on this day is an OK choice.** If a particular child almost *never* comes to look at a book with a grown up, his grown ups can devise quiet opportunities to enjoy at least a *page* of a book with him alone several times a day.

Instead of requiring that all the children collect together and engage in an activity you have selected, circulate, and join a few children in an activity *they are busy with.* **Fit in.** Describe what you see them doing. Comment appreciatively ("I see Juana is wearing the cowboy hat." "Jerome, you look so nice in those big work boots. Are you playing family? Is this your dinner over here?"). Add an idea. ("Maybe you would like to use this real pot to cook in.") Play for several min-

utes. ("May I have some soup, too?") Go away and visit another cluster of toddlers or an individual child. **Fit in.**

NOTE: *You can offer exactly the same mix of active and quiet activities in all "subject areas" on this basis: Schedule a caregiver to keep moving through suitable activities, but don't schedule the children—let them come and go at will.*

ANOTHER NOTE: Studies and experiences show that temperamentally, physically, and behaviorally less appealing children receive significantly less attention from staff than do the *most* appealing children. Dr. Bromwich suggests that caregivers be encouraged to consider it a challenge to carefully observe and specifically engage in relationships with the least tended children in the group. Parents, too, sometimes neglect their least attractive child. They can be helped to become better friends with the child they find least special. Every child needs to be treated as a special individual, whether at home or in out-of-home care.

YET ANOTHER NOTE: Because of the family home environment and the multiage group, family day care providers, usually mothers or grandmothers themselves, are less inclined to "instruct" toddlers and twos—another plus for family child care homes!

ONE MORE NOTE: As you start trying out these sophisticated ways of working with children, plan staff meetings to discuss these methods. Encourage each staff member to share feelings and opinions.

A FINAL NOTE: A fine way to help teachers develop "ownership" of new methods and philosophies is to support them in leading parent meetings to introduce parents to these modern

ways. Again, you're showing respect for parents, as well as winning some of them over to "your side" as far as child-rearing ideas go.

Games for Toddlers and Twos

London Bridge is falling down
Falling down, falling down,
London Bridge is falling down,
My fair lady.

Build it up with sticks and stones,
Sticks and stones, sticks and stones,
Build it up with sticks and stones,
My fair lady.

(*Two children hold their arms up and hold hands to form a bridge under which others walk while all sing.*)

Good timing: A sign of a caregiver in tune with children

Timing and tempo are everything. Adults who are truly in tune with toddlers and two-year-olds sense exactly when to introduce something new (and when not to), and allow all activities to occur at exactly the pace the children seem most comfortable with. In many cases, the difference between a high-quality toddler program and a poor one is not the activities. The activities may be identical—timing makes the difference. **In the less good program,** *the activities* **rather than the children are respected.** Each activity is dished up. The children, as one unit, are expected to engage in it. **In the better program,** *the individual child rather than the activity is respected.* When one or more children are ready, at the optimal moment, the activity is

launched. Children may participate *if they choose to.* Their individual wishes are respected.

One caregiver may move slowly through the activities planned for the day. Other caregivers observe and assist free-playing toddlers, from time to time suggesting to an unbusy or unhappy child that she "go see what Ms. Martinez is doing over there with the tape recorder (or paints or drum)," or offering a quiet, private moment. Who needs a few private minutes with a calm adult? *Every* child during the course of the day. *Every* child needs to feel specially sought out, *special.* In addition, private time can be very valuable for the dangerously passive loner, withdrawn like Wynetta, who is usually overlooked; and for the "bad" child like hyper Henry, a bubbly boy who needs many opportunities to be appreciated for his ingenious ideas and ingenuous personality. Or, **caregivers may take turns throughout the day busying themselves with activities suitable for toddlers.** Take it from our expert toddler teachers: Most toddlers will sooner or later want to join in. Their incurable curiosity and innate need to imitate propel most children of this age into participation if peers and dearly beloved adults appear to be enjoying themselves.

Here again, though, is the matter of individual differences. Rosie can entertain herself with puzzles, blocks, and construction sets of all sorts for an hour at a time. Lindsay lasts for several minutes, at most. But Lindsay can expand upon a dramatic play "story" she's spinning for great lengths of time. The problem is not short attention span for either child—it's that unobservant adults constantly interrupt to present "an activity." Why do they do this? Don't they notice that these children are busy? Don't they appreciate

---

Toddlers and two-year-olds, according to many theorists and expert practitioners, are in a stage where feeling lovable, appreciated, and personally powerful is of primary importance. Their self-esteem is enhanced by feeling loved, admired, and like a VIP.

Everything except this skeleton framework for a daily child care program and alert staff intervention to assist each child in understanding where his play partner "is coming from," and in controlling his impulses, aggression, etc., can be optional for each child.

the developmental values of play? **Here is another important discussion topic for you and your staff.**

Encouraging toddlers' independence and physical development promotes their self-esteem

If caregivers work *with* toddlers rather than against them, "discipline problems" nearly disappear. Toddlers were not designed to do much group sitting, or sitting upon command. At the core of quality child care and learning "program" for toddlers, whether it takes place at home, in the home of a family child care provider, at a center, or somewhere else, are physical activity and free choice. Making choices and choosing freely should be encouraged. Ability to make choices sharpens thinking skills and leads to self-discipline. **A great deal of a toddler's positive self-esteem comes from feeling competent in "decision making" and**

Don't the extraordinary accomplishments of 12-to-36-month-old babies deserve our admiration and respect? Being admired and respected develops self-esteem.

in all areas involving physical skill. Feeling personally powerful is an urgent need toddlers and twos strive to meet. A toddler's positive self-esteem also largely comes from feeling lovable, huggable, and appreciated. At *this* age (roughly 12 to 24 months), the child's self-esteem is influenced more by these things than by her perceived socioeconomic level, race, etc.; however, with bright, socially sensitive two-year-olds, this may not be true. (See Chapter 5 for more about this.)

Toddlers not only exercise their newly found independence, but also practice their big and small muscle skills, increase their knowledge base, and learn to "manage" their environ-

ment by doing a lot of wandering around, often carrying things large and small, or fetching things you might wonder why they want. This is why a variety of toys and other miscellaneous household objects of varying sizes, textures, colors, and shapes— especially things to put in and out, snap, or stack; toys they can push or pull; big and little balls to carry, roll, and throw; and things older people use (lunch boxes, pots and pans, books, magazines, pads of paper, envelopes) —is helpful to development. The greater the variety of things to play with, the more toddlers learn about the nature and properties of things we take for granted, and the less soon they get

---

More Baby Games

This little piggy went to market,
This little piggy stayed home.
This little piggy had roast beef,
This little piggy had none.
And this little piggy said,
"Wee! Wee! Wee!" all the way home.

Gently squeeze each toe in turn, and end with a poke on the tummy. Say the rhyme over and over, sometimes in silly voices, always with a smile.

All around the cobbler's bench
The monkey chased the weasel.
The monkey thought 'twas all in fun—
POP goes the weasel!

For this one, sit the baby on your lap facing you. When you say "POP," lift the infant high off your lap.

Note: Do *not* use the violent nursery rhymes riddled with child abuse ("There was an old woman who lived in a shoe; she had so many children, she didn't know what to do. She fed them on broth without any bread and whipped them all soundly and sent them to bed."); nursery rhymes in which adults show strange neglect of babies ("Rock-a-bye baby, on the tree top, when the wind blows, the cradle will rock. When the bough breaks, the cradle will fall, and down will come baby cradle and all."); or the fairy tales that transmit gender bias from generation to generation ("The Sleeping Beauty" and "Cinderella" are examples).

Just because a nursery rhyme is traditional does not mean we must mindlessly use it. Many are perfect. Let's choose them.

---

bored; that is, *the longer is their attention span*—something we strive to develop. Two-year-olds tend to be much more settled players, capable of sustained play. We're speaking of *one*-year-old toddlers. **Reading and sharing practical experiences with each other about the differences between one-year-olds and two-year-olds would make several interesting staff development sessions.**

Adults experienced with toddlers, twos, and preschoolers find it wise to bring out new toys or materials when boredom is becoming evident and, at the same time, to remove some of the currently unused ones, which will make a fresh appearance another week when they are of renewed interest. Paradoxically, perhaps, **attention span is not increased by trying to make young children pay attention. Providing engrossing activities and enthusiastic encouragement of personal choices is the best way to develop the attention span.** Toys are not removed as punishment; they are removed and temporarily replaced by others only as a way of refreshing play spaces. Another trick of our trade, this one for getting a hard-to-involve child interested in playing with a toy, or for distracting a child from a tug-of-war with another child over a coveted item, is to start playing with a toy yourself. This technique always draws toddlers like a magnet. You can teach your teachers these techniques. Their "discipline" problems will be reduced if they become good at using these tried and true methods.

Toddlers practice running—in brief bursts of awkward, semi-unstable enthusiasm. Children of 18 months or so practice walking backwards, dancing, and jumping, as well. By two-and-a-half or three, most children can *aim* the ball

Respecting and helping a toddler or two learn how to hold her own, yet get along well with others, is developing her self-discipline.

being thrown, kick a ball to a selected destination, jump in place, run, and climb well. "I couldn't used to climb this rope ladder down backwards, but now I *can*," Jasmine proudly announces. (If Duke tried to do it, he'd fall off. He may be older, and he may be a boy, but individuals differ widely. Appreciating the differences is more helpful to the development of each child's self-esteem than is applying developmental formulas and other stereotypes.) Many older twos can pedal a correctly sized trike. Some can do these things sooner. Kelly could ride a trike expertly at 15 months.

Of course, children who have lots of practice and lots of encouragement have a great advantage over those whose adults restrict, restrain, and ceaselessly criticize. They are free to bloom when they're ready. (Children given fewer chances to practice in toddlerhood seem to catch up in the later years of childhood, assuming that they are given the opportunity *then;* but children encouraged to become competent as early as their own inner timer indicates that they are ready to do so will feel positive self-esteem in this highly self-valued area: *competence.*) This is why very young children, to do best and be easiest to live with, need to be in wide open spaces, indoors and out, several times a day. (Besides, stir-crazy kids don't behave well. Pent up energy explodes their precarious ability to self-regulate.) Because of their innate need to practice the basic gross motor skills of walking

© 1990 Jeffrey High Image Productions

If several toddlers or twos spontaneously congregate like a flock of penguins to investigate what a caregiver is doing (maybe playing with a toy? making a salad? pasting pretty paper?), to watch the service repair person, to check in on the story a staff member is reading to someone, so be it. It's not developmentally appropriate, however, to hustle, cajole, and chide toddlers and twos toward chairs and expect them to remain quietly seated for 10 minutes while a teacher distributes materials and then to perform in a conforming manner.

and running—not to mention their *built-in motivation to learn* by seeing, hearing, touching, and handling new, everyday things in the world around them—toddlers like going for walks (if, as toddler specialist Janet Gonzalez-Mena says dryly, "the adult isn't too goal oriented"—toddlers taking walks are not directional; they seem to go all ways at once). Toddlers drift and stray, and find fascinating treasures such as a half-sucked throat lozenge, or a mostly smoked cigar butt. One of the most obvious things about toddlers is their fondness for mobility.

Toddlers are "on the go" most of the time. In fact, the toddler who has just become mobile has been compared to an adolescent who has just received a driver's license. Both want to cruise, to move around in space because it feels so good to finally be able to do that independently, without assistance from anyone. (Stonehouse, 1988, p. 47)

Games for Toddlers and Twos

Row, row, row your boat
Gently down the stream
Merrily, merrily, merrily, merrily
Life is but a dream

(Children sit on the floor and row their boats, leaning way back, and pulling way forward.

Practicing mobility is closely related to developing autonomy

Toddlers practice climbing—on and off all manner of climbables (and *non*-climbables, as safety-oriented adults see it), and up and down everything (including a suddenly discovered flight of stairs, one reason they have to be within view *at all times*). Toddlers'

need to practice climbing is why it's a good idea to supply toddler play rooms with soft armchairs, surrounded by large pillows; low platforms and steps, carpeted or made of smoothly rounded plastic with no sharp edges to crack heads on; low furniture and equipment with railings; low climbing and sliding equipment and ramps placed on carpet if indoors, or bark mulch—maybe a gently sloping hill if outdoors. Most toddlers are tireless explorers. They spend most of their waking time investigating the world around them (and that's why they are so competent when they are two or three!).

Although "autonomy" is highly valued in certain circles, particularly in this country, in all fairness we must mention that independence is not "worshipped" and believed to be so urgently important by people in all cultures—Italy, for example, and many Central American countries—or by all cultural groups *within* this country, Moreover, it has been found that toddlers who are lovingly reared, but not offered many opportunities for autonomy, catch up physically soon after, when, at an older age, they're given the chance to practice all these skills. It *is* likely, though, that encouraging early autonomy "tells" the toddler that it is a valued aspect of character, one to which he's supposed to aspire.

Have you ever asked the people you know who don't realize the value of play to consider these ideas?

● Many of the adults who think young children are wasting time when they walk, run, jump, and so on are the very same adults who put quite a bit of pressure on the very same children only a few years later to practice similar skills (soccer, baseball, football, and other sports).

● Practicing walking, climbing, running, throwing, pushing, pulling, and

---

A Few Books and Articles You and Your Staff May Enjoy Reading

Dombro, A. L., & Wallach, L. (1988). *The ordinary is extraordinary: How children under three learn.* New York: Simon & Schuster.

Honig, A. S. (1985). Research in review. Compliance, control, and discipline. *Young Children, 40*(2), 50–58; *40*(3), 47–52.

Jones, E. (Ed.). (1979). *Supporting the growth of infants, toddlers and parents.* Pasadena, CA: Pacific Oaks College.

Jones, E. (1986). *Teaching adults: An active learning approach.* Washington, DC: NAEYC.

Lurie, R., & Neugebauer, R. (Eds.). (1982). *Caring for infants and toddlers: What works, what doesn't* (Vol. 2). Redmond, WA: Child Care Information Exchange.

Marzollo, J. (1977). *Supertot: Creative learning activities for children one to three and sympathetic advice for their parents.* New York: Harper & Row.

Miller, C. S. (1984). Building self-control: Discipline for young children. *Young Children, 40*(1), 15–19.

Miller, K. (1984). *Things to do with toddlers and twos.* Chelsea, MA: Telshare.

Tempestuous toddlers and two-year-olds need caring adults to keep them physically and emotionally safe, and to offer support and guidance as they learn to cope with uncooperative objects, "undesirable" situations, unyielding peers, and grown-ups' "unreasonable" demands.

Respecting Toddlers and Twos, Teachers, and Parents

so on are toddlers' and preschoolers' sports.

● We all get self-esteem from feeling physically competent, athletes especially. Think of each little child as a person busily building self-esteem.

Once again, encouraging your staff members to think and talk about these ideas would probably be a professionally developmental experience for some of them. And then, repeat the meetings with parents. Parent growth is important too.

Toddlers and twos also need a great deal of practice to get their small muscles to do what they want them to do. Even before one year, many babies clumsily feed themselves finger foods and eat from a spoon. They waveringly lift, hold, and sloshily drink from a cup. They like to help fumblingly undress and dress themselves, though they may get garments on in strange and skewed ways. Clever caregivers consider all these caregiving activities curriculum. They take time to include the child's tempo (slow), level of skill development (low), and interest (very, very high) into the period of time scheduled for the activity (lunch, getting ready for sleep, getting dressed to go out or home). They take time to converse about each detail with the child, to look into the eyes of an earnest toddler jabbering unintelligibly, to listen intently, and to respond respectfully to the child, thus building language; the child's ability to communicate (part of self-discipline); rapport, affection, and respect between child and adult; listening skills; and the child's understanding of *her* life and *her* world (anything farther away is too abstract for most toddlers).

By one and a half, many toddlers love to help adults with whatever chores they're absorbed in and love to *play* that they are adults (dressing up, preparing and serving food, taking care of babies, shopping, zooming toy vehicles around the room, sidewalk, and sandbox). They like to paste and scribble (scribbling is an important prerequisite for writing). Eighteen-month-olds enjoy rhythm instruments, moving to music, simple games such as "Ring Around the Rosy," "London Bridge," or others included in this

Ellen Galinsky

Each toddler is totally busy learning to become a competently functioning self, an individual. Becoming a competently functioning individual comes before learning to become a competently functioning group member.

chapter, and turning the pages of board books and (disposable) magazines (the pages usually rip). Many babies of this age enjoy hearing rhythmic rhyming jingles like the one in the box (over and over!). They may have some degree of bladder and bowel muscle control.

By two years old, toddlers can do simple puzzles (three to six pieces); string big beads; and use felt marking pens, fingerpaint, low balance boards and planks, Caroline Pratt unit blocks and the transportation toys and small furniture, people, and animal figures to go with them. The originality and creative thinking we're seeing now, will serve the child—and community she lives in later as an adult—well. Many two-year-olds are almost fully able to control bladder and bowel functions. Of course, some are not, and they should never be made to feel bad about it. Among other things, this is a matter of muscle maturity. (See "Thoughts on Diapering and Potty Training" for one caregiver's account of how toilet learning happens in the program she works in.) Prepare for some puddles!

By 36 months, many children can stay dry all night. And some cannot. Many can put on most of their clothes

If you don't respect someone, can you expect that person to respect you?

(but cannot button or tie), enjoy a greater variety of very simple, *noncompetitive* games, for example, simple board games like Lotto™, and *short*, involving group times. Many can pedal tricycles. By the age of three, almost all American children have learned to use the toilet, and a great many, if they are good friends who frequently play together, are capable or long periods of cooperative dramatic play. When toddlers and twos play pretend, it's obvious that they're *playing*. But what begins as imitating their grownups becomes part of the child/adult's personality: The toddler who nurtures his ted-

---

Games for Toddlers and Twos

(A child sits on your jig-jogging lap, while you say this old rhyme.)

Jockety jog, jockety jog,
Over the hills and over the bog.

Jockety jog, jockety jog,
Many a mile this day I've trod.

Jockety jog, jockety jog,
I'm the milkman's horse, old Naggetty Nogg.

Jockety jog, jockety jog,
My master's name is Reuney K. Rogg.

Jockety jog, jockety jog,
I'll bear him safe through all this fog.

Jockety jog, jockety jog,
I'll not stumble over that log.

Jockety jog, jockety jog,
Over the hills and over the bog.

Jockety jog, jockety jog,
Safely home through all the fog.

Jockety jog, jockety jog,
Safely home, Reuney K. Rogg.

Jockety jog, jockety jog,
Safely home, old Naggetty Nogg.

---

dybear, tending to his needs for feeding, bedding, and riding around in the stroller, will probably become the father who does the same for his son. (Well, at least we can hope so.)

Toddlers and two-year-olds learn a great deal through sensory experience

This is why ample time each day to play in sand, or gravel, or with play dough, or water—or all four—plus other textured materials is very educational for them. Watch the attention span of a toddler washing dishes! And how one- and two-year-olds love to paint walls and fences with big brushes and buckets full of water! Little children learn through hearing "insterding" noises, as a two-year-old friend says (translation: "interesting") and discussing them; seeing interesting sights and discussing them; smelling interesting scents and discussing them; and tasting interesting tastes and discussing them. The pleasure and educational value of most experiences enjoyed by young children are enhanced through conversation (not interrogation) about them.

Toddlers and two-year-olds are learning to feel personally empowered.

So they need opportunities

● to use materials that respond to their manipulations, including sand, gravel, play dough, and water;

● to manage the use of their time, making many, many choices during each play period;

● to take charge of their own toileting with (sincere) encouragement and (friendly) guidance from grownups; and

● *to practice skills that prove how powerful they are,* such as making swings go back and forth, hoisting and lugging large blocks to and fro, and causing riding and rocking toys to go.

This is why well-balanced riding horses with wheels and stable bikes with and without pedals are basics in a good toddler program. The opposite of personal empowerment is the conviction that nothing one does matters, that it's all up to fate anyway. Personal empowerment permits a person to take charge of her life.

The Time-Out Chair

You mention the time out chair. While it may occasionally be necessary to take a child aside to cool off, calm down, and regain his control and composure, the time out chair as generally used is an example of negative discipline. The teacher dictates, the child doesn't get to use his emerging self-disciplinary skills. Conforming is the goal, not understanding. For more about the time out chair see "Guidance and Discipline: Teaching Young Children Appropriate Behavior" by A.S. Clewett in *Young Children, 44*(4), 26–31.

Toddlers and twos have unlimited curiosity and a tremendous urge to become competent. Therefore, they very often attempt to do things that they can't do (fit the puzzle piece in, dress the doll, string the bead, get into or out of a piece of clothing). This is one reason an adult should usually be available. Adults can't always concentrate exclusively on toddlers, and much of the time toddlers can be expected to play resourcefully near adults. When is it OK to continue doing a duty or chore of some sort, and when should one stop to meet a toddler's need? A parent or teacher skilled in toddler development has fine-tuned sensitivity as to how long to let the earnest toddler *try* to do it (we want to foster attention span and perseverance) before the experience becomes too frustrating (we do *not* want the tykes' days to be filled with failures). If we aspire to assist toddlers in *learning,* we do not *teach*—meaning *instruct*—we hone our observational skills and sensitivities so that we have a sixth sense about when to step in with a helping hand or a suggestion and when not to. We become experts in "reading" the frustration signals children send. Toddlers *can* solve many problems if we encourage them, but some they can't solve. Is it fair to ignore a child's mounting frustration until he can't control it anymore and becomes

---

whiny, or takes it out on other children, and then punish him? Ignoring toddlers' frustration during play is asking for trouble. When his frustration level rises too high the toddler loses his fragile ability to regulate his behavior and falls apart, often in antisocial ways. As a toddler learns to trust that one well-intentioned, interested adult is usually there to help and is almost always fair, he learns to respect adults. *When an adult treats a child with respect, the child does the same, turn and turn about.* This doesn't mean that adults are expected to be toddlers and to play with them nonstop.

Toddlers, and two-year-olds too, have to learn many limits, and one of them is that adults are sometimes busy "for a few minutes." Caregivers are paid to be available to the children in their care. They should be given a small enough group of children, encouragement, and not too many related duties, so that each child gets quiet, personalized time, and all children feel that their caregiver is usually available to them. (Caregivers also need decent breaks in an attractive "grownups only" staff room—but we've already emphasized *that*.) Parents and caregivers can't stand by full-time, but they can make themselves more or less available to their toddlers, depending as much upon how much of a priority they think it is as on how busy their days are. An expert in toddler educare (a term invented by the distinguished infant care specialist Bettye Caldwell) is not an instructor, but a sophisticated facilitator—an educarer (a term created from Caldwell's *educare* idea by

Children of this age are definitely characters, but what kind of *character* are you trying to help them develop?

the distinguished infant care specialist Magda Gerber).

If toddler play is so important, aimless as it may appear to the uninformed person, it's important not to interrupt it frivolously. There are sometimes real reasons to stop the toddler or two-year-old in the midst of what she's engrossed in. Toddlers frequently show lack of judgment about what is wise or unwise to do. The day is full of routines, such as meals and naps, and other people occasionally have needs that clash with the young child's. However, it's usually possible to find natural stopping places where a child has come to the end of one activity and is cruising around in search of the next, as children of this age do move from one thing to another rather frequently.

Is it really essential that the two who is happily painting at the easel be forced to stop to go to "the next" activity? Couldn't the child catch up with the others in a few minutes? We're trying to show respect for these children, and to teach attention span.

Encouraging toddlers' and two-year-olds' social development promotes self-esteem and self-discipline, too.

Inner controls develop slowly. We know that babies and young toddlers don't have them. When they want something another child has, or want the other child to do something— or to *stop* doing something—or are angry, toddlers and twos communicate *physically*. They grab, hit, scratch, bite, and so on. Or they communicate with *"nonverbal sounds"*; they cry, howl, fret, and so on.

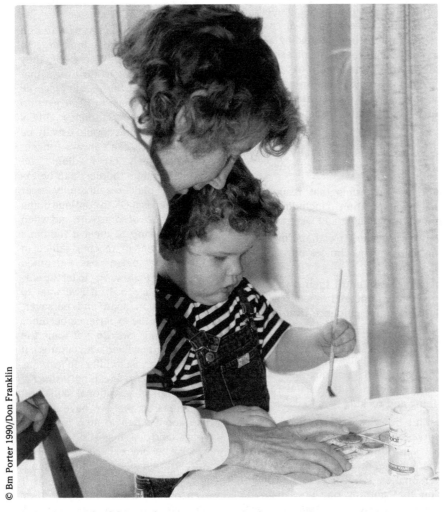

© Bm Porter 1990/Don Franklin

Set up a suitable project—an art project, perhaps—and just start enjoying it yourself. Curious toddlers and twos will begin to arrive.

More Games for Toddlers and Twos

Here we go round the mulberry bush,
Mulberry bush, mulberry bush,
Here we go round the mulberry bush,
Early in the morning.

This is the way we wash our clothes,
Wash our clothes, wash our clothes,
This is the way we wash our clothes,
Early Monday morning.

This is the way we iron our clothes,
Iron our clothes, iron our clothes,
This is the way we iron our clothes,
Early Tuesday morning.

This is the way we scrub the floor,
Scrub the floor, scrub the floor,
This is the way we scrub the floor,
Early Wednesday morning.

This is the way we mend our clothes,
Mend our clothes, mend our clothes,
This is the way we mend our clothes,
Early Thursday morning.

This is the way we sweep the house,
Sweep the house, sweep the house,
This is the way we sweep the house,
Early Friday morning.

And now we play when work is done,
Work is done, work is done,
And now we play when work is done,
Early Saturday morning.

(Children circle, holding hands. Then they scrub their clothes, make ironing motions, etc.)

All aboard for Boston,
All aboard for Lynn,
Baby better watch out,
Or she's gonna fall in!

Play this game with the child sitting on your lap facing you. When you say "fall in!" dip the child backwards, till her head is near the floor and thrill her with an upside view of the world.

The farmer in the dell,
The farmer in the dell,
Hi ho, the derrio,
The farmer in the dell,

The farmer takes a wife,
The farmer takes a wife,
Hi ho, the derrio,
The farmer takes a wife.

The wife takes a child,
The wife takes a child,
Hi ho, the derrio,
The wife takes a child.

The child takes a nurse,
The child takes a nurse,
Hi ho, the derrio,
The child takes a nurse.

The nurse takes a dog,
The nurse takes a dog,
Hi ho, the derrio,
The nurse takes a dog.

The dog takes a cat,
The dog takes a cat,
Hi ho, the derrio,
The dog takes a cat.

The cat takes a rat,
The cat takes a rat,
Hi ho, the derrio,
The cat takes a rat.

The rat takes a cheese,
The rat takes a cheese,
Hi ho, the derrio,
The rat takes a cheese.

The cheese stands alone.
The cheese stands alone.
Hi ho, the derrio,
The cheese stand alone.

(Children hold hands and walk around in a circle. More than that is too complicated for most children this age.)

She'll be coming round the mountain when she comes.
She'll be coming round the mountain when she comes.
She'll be coming round the mountain,
She'll be coming round the mountain,
She'll be coming round the mountain when she comes.
Toot, toot!

She'll be driving six white horses when she comes.
She'll be driving six white horses when she comes.
She'll be driving six white horses,
She'll be driving six white horses,
She'll be driving six white horses when she comes.
Whoa, back! Toot, toot!

Oh, we'll all go out to meet her when she comes.
Oh, we'll all go out to meet her when she comes.
Oh, we'll all go out to meet her,
Oh, we'll all go out to meet her,
Oh, we'll all go out to meet her when she comes.
How do! Whoa, back! Toot, toot!

And we'll all have chicken and dumplings when she comes.
And we'll all have chicken and dumplings when she comes.
And we'll all have chicken and dumplings,
And we'll all have chicken and dumplings,
And we'll all have chicken and dumplings when she comes.
Yum, yum! How do! Whoa, back! Toot, toot!

She'll be wearing red pajamas when she comes.
She'll be wearing red pajamas when she comes.
She'll be wearing red pajamas,
She'll be wearing red pajamas,
She'll be wearing red pajamas when she comes.
Scratch, scratch! Yum, yum! How do! Whoa, back! Toot, toot!

(Are you all driving your white horses around the mountain? Can you say, "toot, toot!"?, Let's go out and meet her! Should we wave "hi"? I'm eating my chicken and dumplings. Are you eating your chicken and dumplings? Are you wearing your red pajamas?)

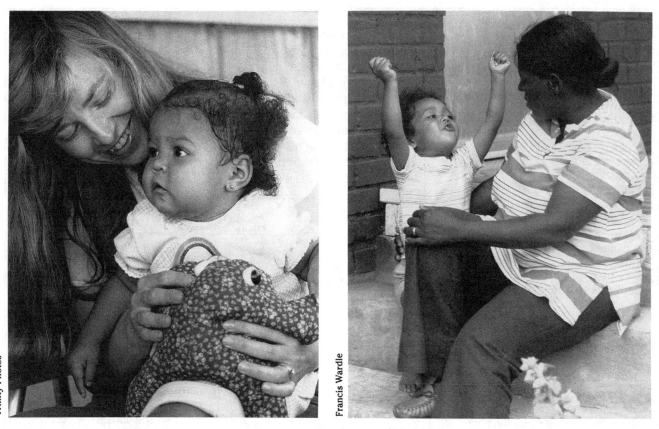

Trinity Photos

Francis Wardle

One caregiver may move slowly through the activities planned for the day. Other caregivers observe and assist free-playing toddlers, from time to time suggesting to an unbusy or unhappy child that she "go and see what Ms. Martinez is doing over there with the tape recorder (or paints or drum)," or offering a quiet, private moment. Or, caregivers may take turns throughout the day busying themselves with activities suitable for toddlers, and taking turns helping children who are not involved in the particular special activity being offered.

As teachers, **one of the most important jobs parents and other caregivers have is to teach social skills, how to get along, how to communicate needs and wants with words instead of physically or with mere noise.** We don't expect children to know how to share, take turns, handle anger, and solve problems amicably through the use of language (explaining, planning). But many excellent parents and practitioners *do* expect that providing guidance as children laboriously *learn* how, rather than *lessons,* is a core of our "curriculum."

How much guidance to provide is one of many areas of disagreement among good caregivers. Some people believe that if children are about equal (one is not a known "bully," one is not always being victimized) they should frequently be allowed to "fight it out," **if nobody is hurting anybody.** Other

people believe that this is OK *on a rare occasion,* but that **children really aren't learning better ways to work things out through this "laissez faire" adult approach because adults are neglecting to provide guidance.**

A toddler teacher tells us
Until they're two, I give a one sentence explanation to each child of what the other one wants. I look at Michelle and say, "Zeke wants to finish playing with this roadgrader, he isn't finished yet." Then I turn to Zeke and say, "Michelle wants to play with the roadgrader, she needs the roadgrader when Zeke is finished." Then I politely

stand guard so that "rights" are protected all around.

But when they're two-and-a-quarter or two-and-a-half or nearly three, depending on the maturity level, I say, "I'll hold it while you guys figure out how you can share it or take turns." The solutions they come up with are hilarious! I just stand there holding it, smiling, till after a while they come up with an approach that works, or they lose interest and go off happily to do something else. It works fairly often.

This method of helping very young children learn to settle disputes shows respect for their primitive abilities to

Very young children's sense of time is quite biological — hungry, tired. . . . Beyond this, they have little understanding of time.

do so, but balances it with the belief that one of the roles of a caring adult is to take time to provide gentle, careful guidance.

Toddlers are learning that they affect others

We want them to develop an image of themselves as people who affect others *positively*. We want each child to grow into feelings such as these:

"I have good ideas that lead to fun for my friends and myself."

"I am a kind person who can make other people feel better."

We *don't* want young children to develop an image of themselves as people who can affect others only negatively, by harming them, by destroying their property or projects, or by hurting their feelings. Many adults who have never been able to affect others positively affect them in negative ways—through physical or verbal abuse, through crime, or in other antisocial ways.

A trick of our trade for getting a hard-to-involve child interested in playing with a toy, or for distracting a child from a tug-of-war with another child over a coveted item, is to start playing with a toy yourself.

Thoughts on Diapering and Potty Training

We don't change our toddlers lying down. We go into the bathroom with them and let them entertain themselves washing their hands with running water and lots of soap while we sit or kneel near them and change them standing up. We find it easier to clean kids' bottoms when they aren't lying on them kicking us, and it is easier on our backs. This avoids the arguments that occur when you try to make active, assertive toddlers lie still. It makes diaper changing time a treat for the children to look forward to; one- and two-year-olds love nothing better than playing with water and slippery, bubbly soap (they also love to look at themselves in the mirror we have over the sink, and this is good for them, too, because they are studying their self-image). It also encourages the handwashing habit, which is very important, of course; this way they also see *us* setting an example when we wash *our* hands after changing each child.

Potty users are using potties at the same time with another teacher. This motivates diaper users in the right direction. If they start showing interest, staff pick up on it. We ask if a child would like to go pee, go poop, go potty, or go to the bathroom like so-and-so is doing. Our girls usually show interest at a younger age than our boys, around 24 months, some sooner. Many of the boys are still in diapers when they move up to preschool at 2.9 years old. This is OK with everybody. Many of our children are first children or "onlies," so most parents look to us for guidance about when to start potty learning and how to go about it.

When a child indicates readiness, we keep her in diapers, but we take her to the potty about every half hour. This is not a big deal. We never argue with a child about it if she doesn't want to go. If she succeeds, we show mild approval, but we don't make too big a deal out of this, either (making potty training a big deal just gives a kid a great issue to fight with you about). When the child keeps the diapers dry, we suggest training pants. We call them potty pants. Some children start to realize when they have to go soon after they are wearing potty pants, some catch on months later with many accidents in the meantime. We are very casual about all this. We often start them in pairs. We mention penises and vaginas. All this encourages natural and pleasant attitudes toward bodies, and helps these toddlers learn what a boy is and what a girl is, gender identity. We usually start the boys sitting down. Later, we show them how to pee standing up. One of our mothers had a good idea: She floats a piece of toilet paper in the toilet and asks her son if he can pee on it. We now do this for boys.

We never pressure children about staying dry. They get to wear underpants when they can almost always keep the potty pants dry.

Alice Hoben
Waverly Oaks
Child Development Center
Waltham, Massachusetts.

Respecting Toddlers and Twos, Teachers, and Parents

Francis Wardle

An important source of personal power for toddlers and twos is successful interactions with others

We want children to feel that they can make their needs, wants, and ideas known. We don't want them to feel that no one respects their ideas even enough to hear them out. We aren't attempting to raise victims or wimps or smolderingly angry or deeply depressed adults. This means that people who care for little children must devote great patience and much time to helping them develop the ability to put their feelings into language and, at the same time, to develop self-discipline. The better children can express themselves, the better we can expect them to control physical violence and screaming because they have more effective ways to communicate.

* * *

Toddlers and two-year-olds learn faster and more when allowed to regulate their own learning. Their mental processing takes longer when given directions. Therefore, hurrying learning backfires; children learn less well.

Maturation is an amazing feature of nature. We want to allow young children to unfold as naturally as possible, each at his or her own pace, with as little pressure and instruction as is possible. But "growing up good" requires guidance as well as opportunities to explore, discover, flounder, and learn through trial and error. **Sense of self develops through maturation. But whether the emerging child judges her evolving sense of self positively or negatively is not an automatic matter of maturation.** Positive self-evaluations are largely a reflection of what the child's primary people think of her. **Good character does not merely mature either, it needs a little tender loving shaping.** Adults responsible for children, be they parents, educarers, or caring others, generally benefit from extensive discussion:

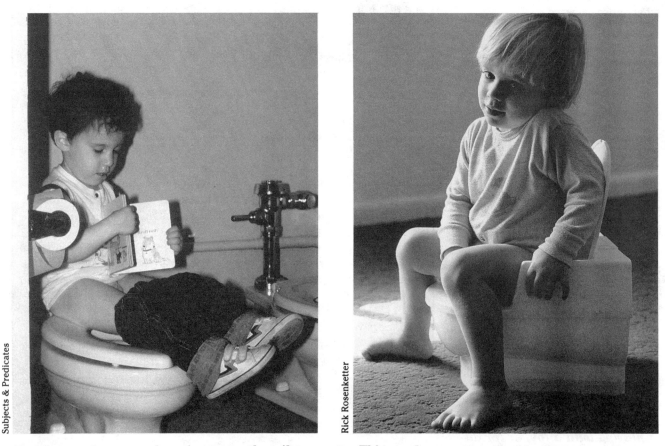

Subjects & Predicates

Rick Rosenketter

Toddlers and twos are learning to use the toilet or potty. This can be a matter of achieving personal power (over bladder and bowel functions), or can be a matter of "me against you." If you let it be the latter, the child will win.

Feeling personally powerful is an urgent need toddlers and twos strive to meet. "Look at me! I'm way up here! I have to hold on tight, I'm very dangerous!" "Look what I can do! I can breathe the blocks down!"

What kind of people are we trying to shape? What characteristics do we like to see in grownups? What do we know about children of this age? What can we learn through reading, watching videos, inviting area child development specialists in to work with us? And how do we best help children *of this age* become the best people possible?

References

Erikson, E. H. (1963). *Childhood and society* (2nd ed.). New York: Norton.

Gerber, M. (1987). *Respectfully yours.* San Francisco: Far West Laboratory for Educational Research and Development.

Goffin, S. G., & Lombardi, J. (1988). *Speaking out: Early childhood advocacy.* Washington, DC: NAEYC.

Greenberg, P. (1975). *Staff growth program for child care centers.* Washington, DC: The Growth Program.

Honig, A. S. (1990). Communication to author.

Jorde-Bloom, P. (1988). *A great place to work: Improving conditions for staff in young children's programs.* Washington, DC: NAEYC.

Piaget, J. (1952). *The origins of intelligence in children.* (M. Cook, Trans.). New York: International Universities Press. (Original work published 1937)

Piaget, J. (1954). *The construction of reality in the child.* (M. Cook, Trans.). New York: Basic. (Original work published 1932)

Seefeldt, C. (1990). *Young and old together.* Washington, DC: NAEYC.

Shine, J. & Campbell, P. (1989). Young teens help young children for the benefit of both. *Young Children, 44*(3), 65–69.

Stonehouse, A. (1988). *Trusting toddlers: Programming for one- to three-year olds in child care centres.* Australia: The Australian Early Childhood Association, Inc.

Toddlers and two-year-olds are learning to feel personally empowered. The opposite of personal empowerment is the conviction that nothing one does matters, that it's all up to fate anyway. Personal empowerment permits a person to take charge of her life.

Games for Toddlers and Twos

Go round and round the village,
Go round and round the village,
Go round and round the village,
As we have done before.

Go in and out the window,
Go in and out the window,
Go in and out the window,
As we have done before.

Now follow me to Boston,
Now follow me to Boston,
Now follow me to Boston,
As we have done before.

Go in and out the window,
Go in and out the window,
Go in and out the window,
As we have done before.

Now go and pick a partner,
Now go and pick a partner,
Now go and hug your partner,
As we have done before.

Now run and leave your partner,
Now run and leave your partner,
Now run and sit in a circle,
As we have done before.

(We slightly alter this one to meet our needs. Play the game where there's a table children can crawl under-and-out-of, or where there is something else to go in and out of while singing "in and out the window."

Start with the children sitting in a circle. Stand and walk in a circle when singing "round and round the village." Then the window, as described. Follow (the leader — the adult) "to Boston." Each child "picks" the child next to him; you may be playing this game with two or four children. Make sure hugs are gentle. Finish up sitting as at the beginning.

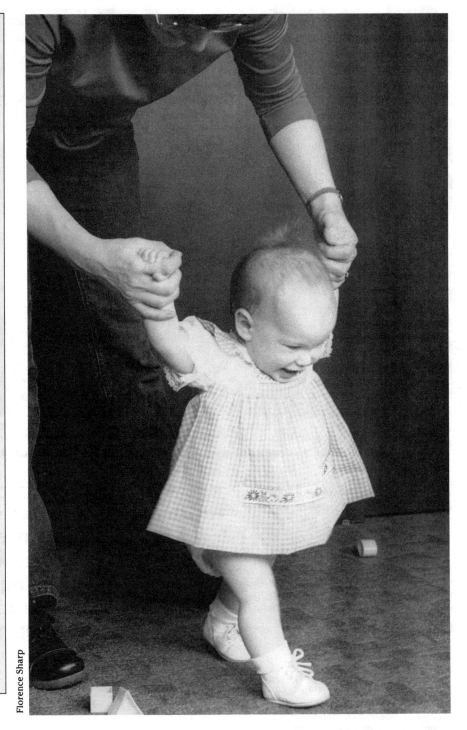

Florence Sharp

CHAPTER

Toddlers' Oddities Often Are Evidence That "Self" Is Getting Organized

QUESTION: Last year I was transferred from the preschool class to the toddler group. Toddlers do so many odd things, and sometimes they behave so badly!

For example, I lost the top to the diaper rash cream tube and heard about it from a 14-month-old fellow for a week. I was taking several children for a walk. We passed a tree that had been cut down. Branches were on the ground, and some chunks of chopped wood. A 22-month-old talked about "the broken tree" like a broken record.

One 17-month-old child will not nap without her pajamas on. With her pajamas on, she lies right down and dozes off. Another child of 21 months insists on being read to while she sits on the pot, which she *asks* to do and *loves* to do.

When MARGIE's family moved, her mother nearly went nuts. Margie, who is two, would not go to sleep, and when she finally did, she woke up screaming and would not go back to sleep; would not play and entertain herself; burst into tears about every tiny thing throughout the day; and *bit the moving man*, shrieking, "Dat man takin' my crib!" The mother asked our advice about disciplining this incredible kid.

JUAN is fanatically neat. He bosses us around, tells us to put away whatever we get out, and will not let the children take toys from their shelves!

We took our toddlers to a public wading pool. TIMMY was totally happy splashing and laughing with me till I ducked under and popped up with my normally curly hair plastered to my skull. Then he seemed to be terrified of me. He became hysterical. Another teacher had to take him. It reminded me of the fit FRANNIE threw when the staff put on Halloween masks last fall. You would have thought we were murdering her. And when we have subs at our center, half the class goes into total tailspins!

BARBARA JEAN used to love to splash and play in our own little toddler wading pool. One day she saw me undo the plug and drain it. Ever since then, swelter as it may on these scorching summer days, two-year-old Barbara Jean refuses to get in. If pressed, she howls. Ian goes cheerfully down the cement steps to the play yard until he gets to the fourth step. Then he stops and whimpers. Eventually, after a great deal of cajoling, he takes a giant step over a hairline crack in the concrete, and, with great relief and pride, as if he has just jumped over the Grand Canyon, he plods down the rest of the steps. KEIKO becomes hysterical when she scrapes her knee, nicks her finger, or scratches herself—anything that brings blood brings howls.

I do not like so much orneriness in children. Sometimes all these situations I am telling about grow into full-blown tantrums. Why are toddlers so bad?

Because all behavior is *caused* by something, it's frequently possible to play detective and figure out the cause of your children's peculiar doings and sayings. The job of behavioral detective is made much easier by a good understanding of child development.

Helping toddlers get mentally and emotionally organized

Take the case of the tube top and the case of "the broken tree." Toddlers are trying hard to sort out the cacophony of sounds, sights, objects, textures, tastes, facts and happenings, smells, rules, causes and consequences. *You* would be too if you suddenly found yourself standing on Mars, surrounded by a wild commotion of clamorous sounds (including a strange and constant foreign language), thrilling sights, fascinating objects, tantalizing textures, exotic tastes, unbelievable facts, a whirl of weird happenings, compelling smells, a barrage of bewildering and inconsistent rules, all coming at you at the speed of light and without rhyme or reason (while irritated Martians towered above you, expecting you to handle it all calmly and correctly and, above all, to hurry up).

Cognitively, toddlers are trying to comprehend the astonishing new world around them

Toddlers' world is quite a bit more cognitively, emotionally, and socially complicated than the one each child

We need to realize that the apparent rigidity toddlers tend to display when we deviate from what they're accustomed to is frequently more worry than stubbornness. They are just striving to make sense of what's going on in their lives. With this in mind and in our plan of action, it's easier for us—and toddlers!—to cope. Another word for good coping is self-discipline.

only recently inhabited (a uterus). Toddlers are struggling to understand their lives by mentally organizing each aspect and mastering concepts of how each thing works or is meant to be.

The first boy you speak of has seen grown-ups take off and put on his diaper cream tube top innumerable times. He's a bright boy, and has learned that diaper cream tubes are meant to have tops. A tube without a top is incomplete, "wrong," not The Way It's Meant To Be. It's disturbing. Until the tube top is located and tight-

ened to its tube, this child remains restless and uneasy. The same is true of the felled tree. In his short life, this boy has seen many, many trees, hundreds of trees, millions and billions and trillions of trees (well, almost). They stand up, tall and tremendous. Here, now is a shocking situation!—a violation of How It Is, of reality, of one of the facts of life that a guy can really count on. It makes a fellow feel very insecure. Until the child has processed and understood this new possibility—that a tree can

appear in a form unlike the usual form—he feels intellectually jangled and unsettled.

Though she could not explain it herself, part of a toddler's emerging self-esteem comes from sensing herself as mentally competent

If you've ever known an elderly person who's "losing it," you have seen the painful confusion, discouragement, depression, and anger that accompany the feeling that one is *not* on top of it— the awareness that one is mentally less than competent. Toddlers seems to feel this way too. Each infant and toddler is an individual. Some have a greater need to sort out their world and to see things function "the right way" than others. However, by 18 months or thereabouts most children are very interested in how things work and in how they are meant to be. Mature toddlers focus on these concerns quite a few months earlier. Intellectually gifted children also tend to care more about keeping track of how everything is "s'posed to be" at a younger age than other toddlers. However, **all toddlers are sticklers for seeing that the things in their world act properly.**

A possible cause of frazzled, disorganized toddler behavior leading to what adults perceive as "discipline problems" is the feeling of being overwhelmed by a chaos of objects or people that don't look like and do what they are supposed to.

Here's what caregiving adults can do: Comment frequently on things that are normal: "Today we *have* the top for

---

Toddlers are struggling to understand their lives by mentally organizing each aspect and mastering concepts of how each thing works or is meant to be. To do this, toddlers struggle as hard intellectually as they struggle physically to master a great many large- and small-muscle skills. Feeling competent in many areas usually results in better self-discipline because less frustration lurks, ready to boil over.

Fear of loss of identity, of identity confusion, of being lost in the group — these are common human concerns. Feeling that self is safe is part of feeling secure.

your diaper cream tube. That's good!" "This tree is standing up the way trees usually do." This reassures the toddler that indeed his growing concept that things make sense and are predictable is on target. When the toddler brings up something that's alarmingly different from what he expects ("Top yawst! Top yawst!" "Twee bwoke!"), laugh, agree, say, "*That's* funny! Trees should stand up." This gives the child a supportive companion as he hits this startling pothole on his novel intellectual journey toward comprehending his immediate world.

Feeling mentally competent is part of the ability to remain calm, and the ability to remain calm under duress is part of **self-discipline.**

About the child who will not sleep without pajamas: Is this really orneriness? Is this a discipline problem? Or are you furnishing us with another example of toddlers' strong need for things to function "the way they're s'posed to"? Probably the child's parents have always put pajamas on her before putting her to bed. **She has developed a habit. We all love our habits. We lean on them for comfort. Habits are our security blankets.** The child has learned to look for the clue that sleeping time will now start. The clue is climbing into those pajamas. Pajamas are her cue to snooze.

Here's what you can do: Tell her that at home children get into their pajamas before they go in their cribs, but at the center (or at the family day care home the child goes to), people just take off their shoes (or describe whatever naptime customs your program has) before they go in their cribs. Make a little jingle out of these "right ways to do it":

At home, pajamas on, at the center, shoes off.

At home, pajamas on, at the center, shoes off.

The child will feel that you understand her conceptual dilemma, a dilemma jeopardizing her newly acquired idea of how one knows it's time to sleep. Possibly you will want to share this with the child's parents and suggest that they chant the same refrain to their daughter, and discuss the two different ways to go to sleep, "the home way" and "the center way." Thus authorized to develop a new naptime habit at the center, the child will probably quickly do so. Then be sure to alert naptime staff people to the necessity of taking off the shoes or whatever you have trained the toddler to expect, so you don't find that you've "lied" to the trusting child.

See if the same principle works with the book-addicted potty person. Ask the child (and the parents) if book-looking and story-reading always accompany potty-sitting. Most likely this is the home routine. It's not at all a bad idea to make toilet learning time a happy time to which the child looks forward. The child has developed the habit of expecting an adult to enjoy a book with her during this sedentary activity. She feels deprived of her regular treat when you, busy as you undoubtedly are, resist reading to her. Most

© Cleo Freelance Photo

Think in terms of comforting a disoriented toddler rather than in terms of disciplining and controlling.

> **It's our goal to help toddlers feel that they are *intelligent*, that they *do* understand. Tricking them is counterproductive, as is laughing at them. Feeling intelligent is part of healthy self-esteem.**

likely this sharp disappointment makes her angry. Moreover, because the story is part of her cuing system, she may feel that her ability to do what will please you—eliminate in the potty—is impaired. Her anger rises, fuelled now by anxiety. **It all becomes too much for her new and still fragile self-discipline skills and she explodes into a tantrum.**

For a delightful example of how a kindly caregiver can on some occasions yield to the idiosyncracies of young children, and how complicated it is to balance all the idiosyncracies of all the children in group care, read this anecdote told by a family day-care provider:

. . . I cleaned up the kitchen as Karen took the children to nap. This is Barbara's job. She has always managed naptime from the day we started working together. Naptime for her is twelve little bodies sleeping on twelve little cots, cozy with their assortment of books, cuddly toys, and blankets. Naptime for Karen that day was twelve little bodies going wild in the main playroom, crawling over and under the cots, throwing things, some reading—it was true—but Jason and Barney throwing their cuddly toys at each other and screaming.

When I walked into the playroom that day, Ana was standing on her cot, her pants down, showing everyone her 'litteris. I have never seen a little girl who loved her vagina more. I just stood in the doorway and looked at her and then at the rest of the kids. Children crowded around me. "Joanie, can I?" "He hit me. He hit me!" "No, I did not." Karen said to me, "Where's the—" as she set up the last few cots. "Whose sock is that?" I said as one flew through the air and hit the wall. "Jason! If you don't—"

It was then that I remembered Barbara had left me a list of instructions. Just yesterday I had stuffed them arrogantly into a drawer. I didn't need instructions. Now I ran to the hutch in the other room to find them. When I returned, believe me, I followed them to the letter.

Dear Joan,

1. Take the phone off the hook.
2. Ask each child to show you which cot he or she sleeps on (Barbara knew that even with a map I'd never get it right). Put Bev and Christopher in cribs.
3. Ask toilet trained children if they need to pee. If they say, "No," you are to ask them to "go to the toilet and see if pee will come out."
4. As you ask about the toilet, go around the room and remove shoes, asking about removing socks. (Some prefer to sleep with their socks, it seems. None in the current group need to sleep with their shoes on, so don't bring that up as a possibility.)
5. Make two milk bottles and two apple juice bottles and warm Barney's soya milk formula by adding hot water from the tap to the refrigerated three ounces of soya concentrate that is in a bottle on the refrigerator door shelf. Sally and Jason get the milk bottles. Mary and Nate accept only apple juice.
6. *Before* you prepare the bottles and *after* the children are settled (toileted, shoes off, and covered up) put on the *Fox and Hound* record on low volume #3.
7. Give those who use them their bottles and ask aloud to the group if they are all set. If they are not, do as they ask to settle them. Bramble hates what she calls "squishy pillows." If she's unhappy see if she took the wrong pillow and let her exchange it for a "nonsquishy" one as she doesn't like it to be called a "hard" one. We know the opposite of squishy is harder or firmer, but she won't accept another pillow if it's been called either hard or firm. So if she looks unhappy ask about the exchange as she may not want to tell you that that's what it is about.
8. Now lie down between Joel and Derek's cribs. Pat Joel on his back softly while looking into Derek's eyes. Derek will lie still and go to sleep quickly if you keep eye contact with him. If you lose it he'll get up. Lie him back down and soberly tell him to go to sleep (*don't* smile) and keep watching his eyes until they close. Once they are closed, keep watching as he some-

times is only testing you and they'll pop open again. He is really sleeping when he is breathing regularly and is not sucking his fingers rhythmically.

9. Mary has learned that I need to put these two to sleep before I can tend to her. Remember that she is waiting for you to lie beside her once these two are asleep and don't skip doing this even if she is snoozing because she'll know if you did it or not and if you didn't she'll wake up at 2:00 and cry because you forgot her. If she's awake just lie beside her but don't touch or pat her. She hates that. Stay there till she sleeps. If she's sleeping lie down beside her anyway for *at least five minutes*. Take my word on this one, Joan. If you don't, she'll be brokenhearted and if that's not enough to keep you there remember that when her heart is broken she cries *very loudly* and *for a very long time* and EVERYONE WAKES UP!
10. It should be about 1:15 by now if all has gone well. Look about. If anyone is still awake lie next to them *but* don't talk to them, touch them, or in any way make eye contact. You don't want to communicate anything that they may want to respond to in the way of conversation. Your nonverbal message must continually be: go to sleep . . . go to sleep. To get this to happen you must think it over and over in your mind. You are there but not available. Got it? Now that everyone is sleeping you can lie on the couch and sleep too. You'll need it.

Love, Barbara

At 2:00 P.M., only forty-five minutes behind her schedule, all the children were sleeping. Barbara's instructions were perfect. As I watched these sleeping little ones that I had put down with Barbara's love and caring, I marveled yet again at the depth of this well that is Barbara's love.

I walked over to the bookcase for a magazine to read on the couch when Bramble began to stir. This wasn't in the plan. I quickly pulled a cot over to hers and laid down next to her, hoping that this would be enough to send her back, although to be frank, I had visions of twelve children waking up and crying around me. Where are you, Barbara? (Roemer, 1989)

> **Be sure substitute teachers are familiar to children before the subs take charge.**

Any disruption of the toddler's newly forming world view is disturbing. This is why toddlers need routines.

Major disruptions of a toddler's world are highly stressful

Margie's close-to-complete collapse of self-discipline during the move indicates how traumatic the dismantling of her world was for her. This isn't a discipline problem, it's a problem of finding the best way to reassure a temporarily terribly distressed child. Margie's anxiety level was so high at the destruction and disappearance of everything familiar and friendly that she wasn't able to maintain the self-discipline she had already developed in her extremely brief life. This self-discipline normally enables her to focus on examining, using, and playing with her toys for quite long periods of time; to play pretend about issues that are on her mind till she works them through; to handle her angers and frustrations through waiting and words; and to recover control of herself rapidly after an occasional short circuit of her recently achieved complex set of self-disciplining skills.

Think in terms of helping and comforting disoriented toddlers, rather than in terms of disciplining and controlling. Think how *you* would feel if you looked up one day and strange men were snatching all the special possessions you had been taught were untouchables, cramming them into cartons, ruthlessly rupturing the room arrangement you had believed was forever, and marching casually out with your TV. Probably the feeling a shocked toddler experiences upon discovering that his home has been turned upside down is analogous to the devastated feeling you would have if you walked unsuspectingly into your home and found that is had been vandalized and burglarized. Even under less dramatic circumstances than vandalism and burglary, adults feel frazzled. When everything in the house is topsy-turvy, everything at work is at sixes and sevens, and the bills are piling up, though few of us bite anyone, at least physically, many an adult has been known to snap at the mate, sit

down and cry, or even whack a child. **Caregivers can help parents feel more empathetic to their difficult toddlers at atypical moments like these.** Other highly stressful experiences for a toddler would be the arrival of a sibling, divorce, and so on. These situations are discussed in other chapters.

As was said, part of a person's self-esteem comes from feeling that we understand how our world is organized and how it works. **This child's self-** discipline will return when her world appears to her to be under control again.

Appreciation of the toddler's anxiety is more important than is disciplining in these instances

We need to realize that the apparent rigidity toddlers tend to display when we deviate from what they're accustomed to is frequently more worry than

---

What You Can Advise Parents To Do in Advance of Moves

1. Explain to the toddler or two-year-old, in the simplest possible, often repeated refrain, that you're going to take *all* the toys, and *all* the food, and *all* the clothes and [name each important and favorite item] to a new place (describe it and name it) and that [child's name] will play with it, eat it, wear it, sleep in it, look at it, listen to it, and so on (name each item) *again*! **Toddlers are enormously reassured by repetition.**

2. Start this only a few hours before you do it. Too much lead time does *not* help very young children adjust; it alarms them and places too complicated a cognitive burden on them. They think that they're expected to comprehend, remember, and cope and they feel bad when they fail to be able to do it. This is often particularly true of exceptionally intelligent children. It appears to many who work with gifted young children that how intelligent they *feel* they are influences — positively or negatively — their self-esteem more strongly than normal children's perception of their intelligence influences theirs.

3. If the new home is nearby, driving past, pointing it out, and commenting on desirable features may help. Make the home familiar, rather than the move a big deal.

4. Do as much dismantling as possible — *all* of it, if feasible, while the child is out with a family member or is at her regular day care. The "destroying of the nest" seems to be especially devastating to toddlers' idea of how "the world is supposed to be": safely familiar and predictable.

5. Remain serene throughout the move (ha-ha! It's a good *goal*, though). Prepare to provide the distraught little child with lots of extra laps, lullabies, healthy snacks, or favorite routines during the traumatic days of unsettled living. Expect the child to sleep badly for a week or two, and count your blessings if night crying doesn't occur.

6. Include the toddler in *unpacking*, putting away, setting up — in short, **include the toddler in building a new nest.**

---

stubbornness. They're just striving to make sense of what's going on in their lives. With this in mind, and in our plan of action, it's easier for us—and toddlers—to cope. What we have in these situations is not discipline problems, it's surging intellectual development. Although nowhere near two years old yet, the toddler has come an amazingly long way toward organizing the welter of experiences that continuously besiege her. **Virtually any disruption of the toddler's newly forming world view is disturbing. This is why toddlers need routines. Any change in routines, just as any change in the way a familiar object looks (the broken tree), should be explained to the child.** Doubtless, the toddler will want the explanation repeated several dozen times, as you would, if something critically important to you were being explained in rapidly, carelessly spoken Latin.

Figuring out Juan's overzealous insistence that you put everything in its place, his refusal to let children take toys from "where they're s'posed to be" in order to play with them, and his way of scolding the grown-ups when they spill may reflect his stage of intellectual development. His behavior may be the reaction to a compulsively neat, over-controlling parent; or perhaps to too stern, too strict, and too soon potty using. But just as likely, it's another example of what we're talking about: a toddler's need to feel that his world is organized, so he can feel that his thinking and understanding are organized. **The security of knowing what's coming next builds self-esteem and self-discipline, the capacity to control oneself.**

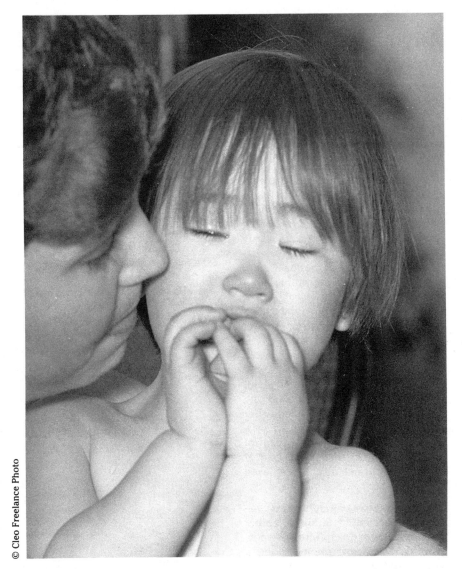

© Cleo Freelance Photo

The toddler is not sure whether the slick-haired silhouette in the swimming suit or the skeleton face advancing toward him is you or who, and of what he is expected to do. So he cries in fear and confusion. The greater your efforts to console him the harder he howls. Putting his worries into words can help him reorganize his thinking. Reassurance about what's real is also required; teasing is mean.

The security of knowing what's coming next builds self-esteem and self-discipline, the capacity to control oneself.

Here's what you can do: Establish and maintain comfortable, developmentally appropriate routines. Slowly, simply, patiently, and repeatedly (if requested to) explain deviations from this routine. Also, agree with Juan that each thing has its place (name the item, name its place). "But sometimes we take (toys, etc.) *out* of their place to *use* them!" (smile). "And when we're finished, we put them back! You're right!" "Yes, Juan, we try not to spill. But if we spill, we wipe it up. That's OK, we wipe it up." Juan's idea of "what's s'posed to happen" can be expanded.

Helping toddlers get socially and emotionally organized

No wonder Timmy became terrified when you emerged from the water looking like a different person. No wonder Frannie freaked when you transformed yourself into a cat or

Becoming psychologically organized is crucial to higher level thinking processes.

ghost or whatever your mask made you look like. Why so? Because Timmy and Frannie are not at all sure you are still you. You look mighty like a stranger. Again, what we're seeing is admirable intellectual development. These toddlers have come to trust you. They *know* you: how to bring you an especially intriguing toy and entice you to play with them; how to bang on the highchair and call "Mo! mo!", causing you to deliver more tasty tidbits for them to devour; how to test and annoy you till you tartly say "No!"; how to hang grinning and chattering on your leg till you hoist them up for a hug and a refreshing aerial look around the room.

It's alarming when a trusted adult appears to have been replaced by a monster

On many levels, the toddlers we take care of regularly *know* us. They know how to woo and win our love, patience, and favors. They know what we mean and often cooperate when we set boundaries verbally. ("Thank you for showing me my pocketbook. You can put it back now. That pocketbook is just for me.") They know we know they're pretending when they cook us hot soup and cold "eythcweam." They know that if they lovably tell us what they need we're likely to comply ("Need a cuddle").

Now, suddenly, the person so well known, liked, and trusted by the toddler has vanished (hasn't she?) and a scary stranger has taken her place (maybe?)! The mysterious newcomer (or is it you?) acts intimately, evidently assuming a prior relationship (but maybe this *is* you). The toddler is not sure of whether the slick-haired silhouette in the swimming suit or the skeleton face advancing menacingly toward him is you, and he is unsure of what he is expected to do. So he cries in fear and confusion. The greater your efforts to console him, the harder he

howls. (It's not very consoling to be approached by a huge monster trying to get you in her clutches, claiming she just wants to "hug you"). Toddlers study and memorize the faces, laps and hugging apparatus, scents, eyeglasses, and so on, of the people they love or care for.

But they don't yet have complete confidence in their memories; is this who I think it is, or am I mistaken? Very often what they *think* they know (for instance, that tubes have tops, trees stand tall, pajamas are put on prior to sleeping time, people read to people who sit on potties, *you* have a mop of curls, *teachers* do not have faces like monsters and ghosts) proves untrue. How can a 19-month-old gal guarantee

to herself that her memory serves her perfectly? (*Younger* babies don't fear the unfamiliar because their central nervous systems haven't developed enough for them to fully understand that something *is* unfamiliar! — Kagan, 1984)

An important part of helping toddlers get socially and emotionally organized is to allow them to attach to one or two primary caregivers, thus enabling them to trust, to be understood, and to have influence upon someone "important."

Here's what you can do: Put the toddler's worries into words: I'm (name). I look funny without my glasses (with my wet hair, with my beard shaved off, etc.), don't I? Soon I'll put my glasses on again (dry my hair again, etc.). You can help me." Prove that you are you by saying, "Does (name yourself) look funny? I am (name), but I look funny because my hair is wet. It will dry. Then I'll look like (name) again. Hair can be dry, hair can

---

Here's What Caring Adults Can Do if a Sub Is Needed

1. Have the same substitute often enough that she's known to most of the children. Other children will be calmed by the calm of those who know "the stranger."

2. Before a new substitute takes over a group, pay her for half-a-day when you are there *too*, so she can at least superficially get to know the children and the children can at least superficially get to know her. (If you are a family day care provider, your regular assistant, a friend who regularly drops in, or a parent well-known to the group may be your sub.)

3. Put name tags on the children throughout the sub's visit and duty, so she can speak to them personally, and they will feel less loss of identity.

4. Introduce each child individually. Say, "[Name] will take care of you today."

5. Ensure that familiar staff people are present throughout the first half day with a sub and after that are in and out, on and off.

6. Provide something special for the sub to give the children near the beginning of the day, for instance a healthy snack treat.

7. If you know in advance that a sub will be coming, send a note home: "In the morning, please tell your child that a different teacher (name) will be taking care of him today at the center. Name the familiar people (list), including his favorite children. Name his favorite toys. Explain that these people and things will be there, and so will (name the sub)."

Taking these steps *for each child* will enhance the coping skills of each child, hence self-discipline.

As she progresses from 9 months toward 18 months, the older baby (young toddler) achieves much more organized behavioral and emotional patterns, achieves self-discipline. Some of this progress is caused by biological maturation; much is caused or not caused by us.

be wet. That's funny!" Helping toddlers develop a sense of humor is a good way to help them learn to be copers. So much for your alarming wet hair.

As to masks, **here's what you can do:** Keep them away from toddlers. Masks almost always frighten toddlers, hence are no fun. This is true of many preschoolers, too, and even some five-year-olds. You have to be very sure of what can be real and what can only be fantasy to think fake horror is fun, and many children are not altogether able to make that distinction during their preschool years; almost *none* are when only toddlers.

Of course, the substitute teachers at your center cause "half the class to go into a total tailspin." Infants and toddlers feel comfortable with familiar caregivers, and *only* with familiar caregivers, for reasons discussed in this chapter: They feel understood by these people. They trust these people. They know what to expect from familiar caregivers, so can predict what they will do or expect. Thus, even older infants, and toddlers of every age, can feel mentally competent and confident. Feeling mentally competent and confident includes having control over a number of *things*—possessions, body processes, *and information* (who will take care of me?). **Feeling competent and confident promotes both positive self-esteem and the capacity for self-discipline.**

With help, toddlers usually soon learn to accept disruptions and exceptions as an expected part of life

Getting emotionally and socially organized is a major ingredient of developing self-discipline. Typically, toddlers who experience mildly dis-tressing differences and disturbances in the familiar people, places, and routines of their lives make a rapid recovery with a little adult help. **Grown-ups who react to toddlers' dismay as supportive friends help toddlers quickly regain their composure (self-discipline).** Gradually toddlers learn that temporary disruptions, exceptions, and so on are part of a comfortable pattern of living. Being able to tolerate change and being somewhat flexible are important "emotional skills" in this day and age. Our society is exceptionally complex, and one of the few things we can count on is constant change.

Here's what Stanley Greenspan, noted practicing psychiatrist and chief of the Clinical Infant and Child Development Research Center at the National Institute of Mental Health, says on the subject of getting emotionally organized:

The transition from babyhood to toddlerhood takes place gradually between the ages of nine and eighteen months. During this time, your new "little person" is developing so many skills, activities, and behaviors that you may at times want to say, "Stop! One at a time!" It is also a phase when the more flamboyant skills your baby learns—crawling, standing, and walking—may overshadow the immense gains in overall social and emotional development that are also occurring. These gains could be even more important for understanding your

Francis Wardle

The fact that toddlers know how things should be, and notice when they're not that way, is evidence that the central nervous system has matured sufficiently for retrieval of memories to take place.

baby's development at this age than his or her motor accomplishments. The emerging ability to piece together many small activities and emotions into a pattern, known as the ability to organize, is crucial to the development of higher-level thinking and planning. Becoming more "organized" in behavior and emotion is the major challenge facing your toddler. (Greenspan & Greenspan, 1985, pp. 83–84)

The Greenspans' *First Feelings: Milestones in the Emotional Development of Your Baby and Child* (1985) is a book that many people who live or work with children of this age will want to read.

Helping toddlers learn real and unreal

The cases of Barbara Jean refusing to get in the play pool and Ian's great difficulty surmounting the tiny crack in the steps are a slightly different problem in the toddler's effort to mentally and emotionally "get it together."

These are cases of faulty (not yet understood) spatial relations. In her superb classic about the oddities of early childhood and the reasons for them, *The Magic Years,* Selma Fraiberg, expert among experts, discusses, in her engagingly literate, graceful writing style, just such situations:

I recall the story of a two-year-old girl who developed a morbid fear of ants. She cried out in terror when she saw one because, she said, the ants would eat her up. Her parents were completely baffled because the same little girl would cheerfully put her fist in the mouth of any big dog who came up to greet her and never accused even the most ferocious animal in the zoo of a wish to eat her up. It was weeks before the matter was cleared up. The child's grandmother remembered that one day when she opened the kitchen cupboard she discovered some ants. Mimi, the two year old, was in the kitchen when grandmother threw up her hands in alarm and said to the cook, "Those ants are here again. They will eat everything up!"

In the marvelous world of the two year old, if there are ants that will eat *everything* up, they will eat up a little girl, too. Problems of relative size do not enter into the matter. Grandma herself seemed horrified by the prospect and the housewifely commotion in the kitchen over the appearance of the ants must have struck the little girl as an entirely suitable reaction to the prospect of being devoured by ants.

In the small child's Brobdingnag all things are possible. Healthy, good-sized boys and girls around the age of two years are said to disappear down bath-tub drains. Impossible, you say. Very well, so you say. But just to be on the safe side, the two year old intimates, he'd rather not take a bath today.

Well-equipped modern households in Brobdingnag keep a monster in their closets. When hooked up to an electrical wall outlet it inflates with a deafening roar and sucks everything in its path into its chromium-plated jaw. "It's nothing dear. Only a vacuum cleaner!" *Only* a vacuum cleaner. Dear Lady, I can only hope that one morning you will rise from your bed and encounter a roaring iron monster twice your size, steadily eating a path toward you, its monster guts shrieking with the labor of unspeakable digestion. I can only hope Madam, that you will ignore the sales talk and take to your heels.

The panda's eye has fallen out. An empty socket and the first glimpse of the cotton entrails that pull out easily now in an urgent, sickening search. And suddenly the panda is a flaccid sack and horror spreads over you. The panda is no more. He is a nothing, and for the first time the thought comes to you that *you* could lose your stuffing and become a nothing. "Never mind, dear. Don't cry so. We can get another panda." "NO! NO! NO!" And no words can be found in this new tongue, the English language, to tell of the dreadful secret tugged from the bowels of the panda.

So the world of the two year old is still at times a spooky twilight world that is closer to the world of dreams than the world of reality. As in a dream, a little boy in a respectable and prosaic middle-class family encounters a mechanical monster in his living room that pursues him with eager jaws and terrible noises from its belly. As in a dream, a little girl splashing with joyful abandon in a porcelain bath tub observes the water sucked thirstily down the drain and sees herself suddenly, horribly, sucked down the drain into the void. It is in dreams that we encounter the ants that can devour one little girl and her grandmother and the cook as well. Dream people may take off for "Yurp" by poising themselves on the front

Toddlers and two-year-olds are very wary of the unfamiliar. This includes familiar people or things that have changed. Safe people and simple, sound explanations help.

David Gladstone

lawn, flapping their arms and ascending without effort.

In time, these monsters, these man-eating ants, devouring drain pipes and flying humans will be relegated to the attic, so many useless acquisitions not easily disposed of, but happily forgotten. They will rarely emerge in broad daylight in the after-years of reason. They become the attic debris, the useless, forgotten, dusty souvenirs that turn up in dreams bringing with them astonishingly the same horror, awe, grief and helplessness of the original experience.

The dreamer wakens and the merciful thought comes to him "It's only a dream!" The sense of reality rolls over him like a tide and gives him back the safe years of distance from these dark and terrible events. But the child who lives mid-way between the world of magic and the world of reality does not see that one world excludes the other: the two worlds exist side by side; reason is not affronted by the appearance of a monster in the living room or cannibal ants in the cozy kitchen. The sense of reality is not yet strong enough to judge and exclude phenomena from the picture of the real world. (Fraiberg, 1959, pp. 124–126)

(The Magic Years is a book that no one who works with young children should miss. One way caregivers benefit from the delightful descriptions of children birth to six years, and from the author's path-finding insights, is to ask one staff member to read a chapter and lead a discussion of key points with others. Portions of the book may be read aloud. Everyone learns and enjoys when using *The Magic Years* as a staff development centerpiece.)

Self-awareness and self-control are part of good character.

Keiko is another example of a child's lack of understanding about real dangers and improbable, unlikely, or downright *unreal* dangers. Keiko correctly believes that blood is precious, and that when it all gushes out of a person, the person ceases to be. But Keiko doesn't yet realize that the *size* of the opening through which blood is escaping in the case of a scraped knee, nicked finger, or ordinary scratch, is not such that it is possible for a significant amount of blood to pour out of her body. **Most toddlers are afraid when they see blood seeping out of themselves. A second reason for the anxiety here is this: they fear that their new found *self* is leaking out.**

Many toddler oddities are evidence that "self" is getting organized

Between 9 and 18 months, toddlers learn a great deal about the purposes and predictability of objects, procedures, systems, and people. The learning, of course, continues for years. **In the process, children also learn flexibility, originality, and humor — if parents and other major caregivers provide the basic routines and other "samenesses," and if they help the toddler understand the possibility of exceptions and change and the**

humor in life. For another three or four years *after* 18 months, young children continue not to understand a great many things that adults assume. They need our sincere attempts to understand and alleviate their concerns. They need to know that we are supportive friends. **Understanding young children and providing guidance toward self-discipline should be our goal, not controlling and disciplining them.**

For adults who enjoy young children, to live with a toddler is sometimes a misery, and it's entirely normal for adults occasionally to find themselves at their wits' end. But living with toddlers is generally a joy. There are difficult moments and difficult days, but for adults who take the time to understand them, most toddlers are not dreadfully difficult, they are utterly delightful.

References

Fraiberg, S. (1959). *The magic years: Understanding and handling the problems of early childhood.* New York: Scribner's.

Greenspan, S. I., & Greenspan, N. T. (1985). *First feelings: Milestones in the emotional development of your baby and child.* New York: Penguin.

Kagan, J. (1984). *The nature of the child.* New York: Basic.

Roemer, J. as told to Austin, B. (1989). *Two to four from 9 to 5.* New York: Harper & Row.

CHAPTER 9

Why All This Emphasis on Chatting With Children? Developing Language: Another Aspect of Self-Esteem, Another Route to Teaching Self-Discipline and Promoting Good Character

QUESTION: I work in the toddler and two-year-old room of a corporate-sponsored child care program. We have a visiting education director. She urges us to talk with the toddlers, and listen to them. In my family and neighborhood, people don't talk and listen to young children; it simply isn't the custom. My friend works in the infant room. Talking to babies seems even sillier to her than it does to me.

Most practical articles and books about child care talk about the importance of looking into a child's eyes, answering the child, singing, looking through books and talking about the pictures with children, explaining everything during the day in simple terms, saying little rhymes and playing baby games, helping them learn how to express their feelings and wants in words, speaking politely to them, making jokes with them, and so forth. I took a course about language development, but all I got out of it was that theorists use jargon and argue a lot about who's right when common sense suggests that they all have a piece of the truth.

Children all over the world have always grown up able to talk, unless they have hearing, mental, or other special problems. Why, suddenly, all this business about having conversations with them? This book emphasizes this too.

You're entirely correct that the average child will learn the language spoken in his or her family and community simply because the ability to learn language is rooted in the biological nature of human beings. As the child's body and mind mature, so does the ability to understand and speak a language. Which language? Naturally, it will be the language spoken all around the baby/child, complete with dialect, accent, and details specific to the family's socioeconomic group. Whether or not people consider themselves language models, they are "demonstrating" a language (or *two* if they're bilingual), with a particular dialect or accent, pronunciation style, vocabulary, set of cadences and idioms, and are saturating the little human being in it. Whether or not they think of it that way, these people are providing a total immersion language learning lab. Children imitate and practice by babbling away much of the day in a specific manner that changes with their maturational developmental level. Whether or not people have ever heard of (or believe in) behaviorist theory, they naturally "reinforce" certain of the sounds babies, one- and two-year-olds utter—by responding to them, admiring them, and repeating them—and "extinguish" those sounds that don't "mean" anything to them—by ignoring them, thus decreasing the probability that the child will keep "saying" them after a few years of just enjoying making sounds and weeding out the ones that "don't work." What you say is true; in many cultures and socioeconomic groups, adults don't attend to what little children are saying to them, and don't have conversations with children, yet words and even grammar somehow unfold and are absorbed (probably some of each). The children develop normal language.

The central theme of this *particular* book is not how children achieve normal development. **The central theme of this particular book is what concerned parents and other caregivers can do to assist infants, toddlers, and two-year-olds in achieving optimal self-esteem, self-discipline, mental health, and good character.** Your education director's reason for encouraging staff to chat with children is probably that she's trying to aid you in making your program a high-quality program. One sign of a high-quality family child care or center setting is that adults have lots of pleasant interactions with each child, *including language interactions*. Yes, language will develop without special attention or intervention. Yet there is much we can do to enhance it. You mention many such things in your opening remarks. Because possessing excellent language skills is basic to so many kinds of excellence in life — including reading and *interpersonal* success — if we're

Note: The second volume in this series by Polly Greenberg, *Character Development: Encouraging Self-Esteem & Self-Discipline in Three-, Four-, & Five-Year-Olds,* includes an in-depth chapter on language development.

aiming high all around in our child developing work, we have to consider it important to facilitate language development.

Why do young children need language?

The development of language — first nonverbal, then verbal — is an essential element in infants', toddlers', and two-year-olds' constant efforts

● to connect in warm and mutually trusting ways with appreciative parents and caregivers — to develop a feeling of inclusion, a basic human need,

● to cause parents, major caregivers, and other miscellaneous people around them to respond to the signals and grins the little ones give — and, soon, to their words, phrases, and sentences — in order to develop a feeling of personal effectiveness,

● to create sense out of their surroundings — to develop confidence in their ability to comprehend — to develop confidence in their intellectual competence,

● to coordinate and control to some small but swiftly increasing extent the "*id*" part of their personalities (the purely emotional, volatile, not yet socialized part) — e.g., to use words instead of claws to get what they want (or they would soon be ostracized from the human community),

● to become separate selves, autonomous people capable of stating

their needs and of other communicative competencies,

● to become competent members of their cultures and communities (families, ethnic groups, child care programs, etc.), able to understand instructions, express ideas and feelings in accordance with the cultural customs of those around them; become able to get peers' and grown-ups' attention and cooperation; become able to assist in comforting peers and adults appropriately, and

● to connect with siblings, cousins, little friends and neighbors, and regular baby friends in child care settings.

As they grow older, children need language for additional reasons, but these are the reasons that children younger than three need words and other communications skills.

Caregivers can encourage natural language development

Language is part of so many fundamental efforts infants, toddlers, and two's are engaged in that it's easy to foster language competence while providing routine care, observing play, and facilitating general psychological development. We've mentioned each of the following threads of "what babies are doing" emotionally, socially, intellectually, and physically — and how we can promote them — in one or another chapter of *Character Development: Encouraging Self-Esteem and Self-Discipline,* some of them many, many times. We've underscored

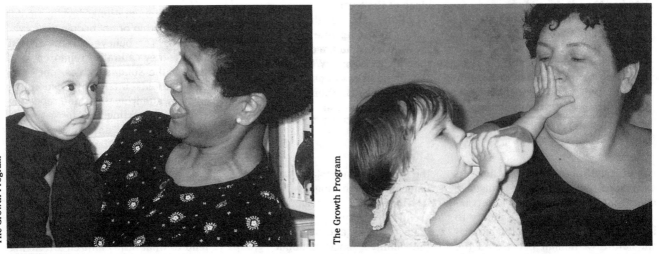

First, babies and their primary caregivers — if normally tuned in to one another — develop sophisticated nonverbal language systems. Another argument against frequent staff turnover!

- how important it is to develop a close mutually trusting relationship with each of our infants, toddlers, and two-year-olds — including returning their coos and chirps, babble and jargon, and early efforts to use words (usually nouns and verbs because they're more concrete than words like "is" and "the," as is the thinking of our very youngest); we repeat babies' coos, chirps, and simple words; we include singing and reading as we live with little ones,

- how supportive it is to a baby's emerging sense of self to observe each baby and respond promptly to its expressed (or mysterious) needs in an effort to enable the child to feel personally effective and respected; to look directly into the eyes of a toddler or two when she speaks to us; and to answer helpfully and courteously,

- how effectively we can encourage senior babies, toddlers, and two's in their earnest and continuous effort to make sense of what's going on, and to feel intelligent (intellectually on top of it),

- how clearly and cleverly we can help them in their effort by naming, explaining, and commenting (e.g., soon, from his beaming face we can see how smart fourteen-month-old Hurant feels when one adult says to another, "Let's take them out for a walk," and Hurant runs and climbs in the stroller. By confirming his understanding — "Yes! We're going in the stroller!" — we encourage the child to *try* to understand),

- how supportively we can strengthen the child's **ego** as it valiantly struggles from birth on to establish control over *id,* to accommodate to the onslaught of socialization required to become part of any of the world's cultures while still developing autonomy and pride in self,

- how firmly but gently our guidance is required as the child slowly learns to solve social problems with language rather than with sobs, screams, or scratching,

- how patiently we toil, teaching each child to use words by translating into language what we are doing, and about his everyday play activities (e.g., "I'm washing Adas's face with warm water and a wash cloth. Here, Ada, do you want to wash Adas's face?" "Jemal is using his spoon so well! Jemal is eating

mashed potatoes with his spoon." "I see you're making a ball with your clay. What will you do with your ball, roll it? Mush it some more? "); most effective parents and caregivers put a great deal of time into helping each infant, toddler, and two-year-old become communicatively competent,

- how enormously much of our time with senior babies, toddlers, and two-year-olds is taken up with teaching them how to be socially competent, much of which involves learning to listen to and talk to other people.

(See *Language* in the Index to locate all these discussions.)

The bottom line regarding language is this: A child would not need — so probably would not be genetically psychobiologically programmed to learn — language if she did not live in an interpersonal context — if human beings were not social creatures and did not live in groups. This fact offers us parents and other caregivers a ready-made opportunity to help children learn language as we interact with them, play with them, and show interest in what they're doing, asking logical open-ended questions to stimulate in them thoughts of more things they'd like to say. Young children are tremendously motivated to learn language by their emotional need to be part of the human family.

The growth of *language* competence in very young children is entirely entangled with the growth of their *emotional* competence (maturity, ego development) and the growth of their *interpersonal* competence. If as caregivers we observe carefully, respond warmly and reliably, encourage autonomy, encourage self-discipline, enrich the environment (including with lots of listening and talking to), encourage competencies of all developmentally appropriate kinds, and encourage self-pride, most children's language will progress well. For most children, language just happens. For some children it comes early and very expertly in part because they are taken seriously, listened to, and conversed with frequently throughout the day.

When the youngest infants study our faces, listen intently and watch our every move, they're learning language

Then, near their first birthdays, babies begin attempting words. Of course they talk about things that are very familiar, or are favorites.

(listening skills, how to coordinate the sounds they hear with the mouth, facial expressions, and body language that go with the sounds, familiarity with the rhythms, cadences, and syntax (grammar) of the language spoken by their families. Of these aspects of language acquisition, Jerome Bruner says, "syntax is, perhaps, the most mysterious for . . . it constitutes a highly intricate and inter-dependent set of rules in every language" (p.18). When a baby smiles or looks interested, distressed, startled, surprised, enraged, pleased, disgusted, displeased, afraid, sad, avoiding, wary, joyous, petulant, anticipating, bored, coy, anxious, or confident, he is communicating. When a baby, toddler, or two-year-old accepts the invitation we give by holding something out to him, and extends his arm to reach for it, and grasps it — or offers *us* something — he's engaging in reciprocal communication, the back and forth give and take that are the foundational pattern of conversation — human dialogue; he is learning language. When senior babies, toddlers and two's point at something they want or want us to notice, they're "talking" — learning language.

Unless they have hearing impairments, certain kinds of learning disabilities, mental retardation, or some

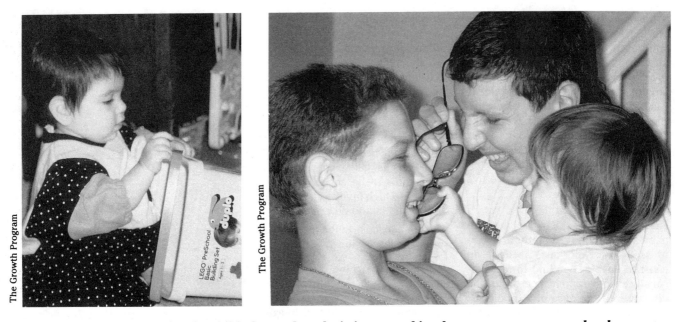

The more we converse with the child about what she is interested in, the more we encourage her language.

other special circumstance, children begin saying words at around twelve months of age—certainly by twenty-four months; most toddlers go through a sudden word spurt at about 18 months. Children have to have a working knowledge of the world before they have *enough* knowledge to need to label it. They have to have a concept—an idea—before they have enough motivation to talk about it. Although the writings of child language researchers are full of protestations that toddlers don't learn their first words from those that their grown-ups say, but that, instead, their early words name things meaningful to them in their own lives, this would seem to most caregivers a very academic argument. Of course toddlers talk about objects, then actions (walk, ride, climb) that are most meaningful to them—that they experience frequently and as significant in their daily lives; why would they bother to try talking about anything else? *All* of us talk most about what interests us most, and about the daily trivia in our lives ("I'm going to take a shower now," "Please pass the peas," etc.). But it doesn't make sense to think that babies aren't *also* imitating the words their grownups use to label these objects and actions; how else would they know to attempt to say "bottle" (baba) instead of to try calling it a "zlach" or a "kurzu?" So the more we converse with the child about what

the child is interested in, the more we encourage his language.

We model language by saying the same things over and over and over, and naming the same objects, as we go through our routines with children. We're modeling the grammar of our culture or subculture (for example, Chinese or BEV—Black English Vernacular), as well as vocabulary. Most people who live and work with young children spontaneously simplify their language, stripping it of confusing and cluttering extras, and coming straight to the point.

We refine the child's pronunciation by accepting the language she gives us (not correcting her), and then pronouncing the word correctly as we repeat her communication back to her by way of confirmation: "Yes Sal can have some milk." Sal had asked for "mim." Language learning is interactive—it takes at least two people for progress to occur—one to try it, the other to respond to it (reinforce it) and refine it so it becomes possible for folks other than the tuned in mother or father to understand it.

We expand the child's shorthand communications toward sentences in the same manner; the caregiver repeats *almost* what Sam said: Mom plays back, "Sam says, 'I wanna see doggy.'" Sam had said, "I wanna doggy," but had intended to communicate that he wanted to *see* the dog

standing just outside the gate of his caregiver's home.

We negotiate each communication with the toddler and two. Jerome Bruner points out that mothers, fathers, and other caregivers

. . . often do not know what their children have in mind when they vocalize or gesture, nor are they sure their own speech has been understood by their children. But they are prepared to negotiate in the tacit belief that

something comprehensible can be established. (1983, p. 86)

Conversing with very young children is something of a joint problem-solving process. Communication always occurs in a context—the child is eating, trying to open something, looking at something, feeling tired, feeling constrained—so a combination of using context clues and trial and error usually solves the problem. As in any learning, a child progresses faster if challenged at the frontier of what she already knows and knows how to do than if merely left to mature. This is why educators at every level offer

learning experiences and opportunities, and do not simply provide food and water and wait till children mature into adults. Caregivers can watch for language delays and collaborate with parents as needed.

Usually language comes easily and naturally to young children, it just happens, as we said, because the ability to learn it is rooted in each infant's biological makeup, as is the ability to learn a wide variety of other mental competencies (thinking skills, comprehension). Hence we have the psycholinguistic theory of language development.

But some children, for many reasons, experience serious delays in language development. Caregivers will want to talk tactfully about the child's language development with his parents, *after ensuring that the parents have observed other same-age children in the group, and have realized that their child's language is significantly less developed.* Parents and caregivers need not be psycholinguists, but *do* need to notice children who don't seem to be progressing as expected, in case evaluation by a suitable specialist is called for. Normally, by the time a baby reaches her first birthday she

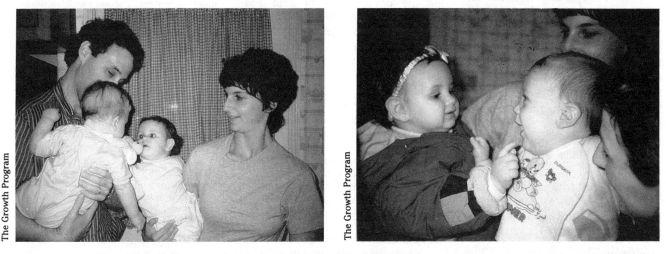

When babies spend their time in language-rich environments (where adults converse with each other and with them, and read to them), their language is being encouraged. Many infants, toddlers, and two's who are together regularly become good friends. They develop very effective communication techniques, including verbal language.

Why Chat With Children?—Developing Language

A child would not need (so probably would not be genetically psychobiologically programmed to learn) language if human beings were not social creatures that live in groups.

- lets caregivers know what she needs them to do or to give her, and protests if they don't (effects their behavior), and
- gets, and for a while keeps, caregivers' attention because she seeks inclusion (social interaction, affiliation, relationship, communication, to become involved in a joint activity).

Can language acquisition research and theory help caregivers?

Reading and taking courses in any and all segregated subjects pertaining to child development deepens our understanding and enjoyment of our work, so it's probably a plus that you took the language course. Language experts have been disputing for two centuries exactly *how* humans acquire language. They believe that knowing the origins of language acquisition is of paramount importance. Undoubtedly it *is* to academics who devote whole careers to this specialty. However, our "career" is developing children, and the only things we *really* have to know about language acquisition are

1. how to "say" what little children are seeing, doing, and needing and encourage them to do the same,

2. how to listen attentively and respond appropriately,

3. how to notice when language isn't coming along within a normal range, and

4. how to work with colleagues, parents, and specialists (if needed) to help children with language delays or special problems.

Researchers and theoreticians who have specialized in language acquisition (Chomsky, McNeill, etc.) have agreed for many decades that human babies are born with an innate ability

to learn language — whatever language is spoken around them. Piaget pointed out that although the human species' intellect is psychobiologically programmed to mature through stages of thinking (from concrete to symbolic), *it's activated and challenged by running into challenging experiences at the frontiers of its capacity that cause it to react by assimilating new information and accommodating thinking and behavior to it.* In exactly the same way, researchers and theoreticians (Bruner, for example) tell us, the human species' language learning capability matures through stages of readiness but is activated and challenged by running into experiences that challenge it to understand or to use more language. To a degree, being aware of the major findings of research and theory in all special aspects of child development can help caregivers. As caregivers, we have to blend splintered knowledge together and balance it, because *our* expertise is in helping whole children develop in *all* dimensions, with emphasis on the development of high self-esteem, sensible self-discipline, and good, strong character **(ego).**

Writing in "Zero to Three," the bulletin of the National Center for Clinical Infant Programs, Prizant and Wetherby point out:

When caregivers describe the communicative behavior of infants and toddlers, their comments frequently suggest the close link between the development of communication and language in the early years and the growth of socioemotional competence. Unfortunately, researchers have begun only recently to integrate socioemotional and communicative perspectives on development. The extensive body of research on communication and language development has given little consideration to socioemotional development — the growth of a child's ability to experience and express a variety of emotional states, to regulate emotional arousal, to establish secure and posi-

tive relationships, and to develop a sense of distinct, capable self (Prizant and Wetherby, 1990). Similarly, research on socioemotional development has rarely considered the impact of emerging language and communicative competence on child's socioemotional well-being and social competence.

The fragmented picture of early development that has resulted from such separated lines of research hampers not only our intellectual understanding of young children, but also our efforts to assess and assist infants and toddlers at developmental risk. Recent literature on language and communication delays in young environmentally at-risk children, and on the co-occurrence of emotional and behavioral disorders and communication disorders in older children clearly points to the close relationship of these aspects of development. Yet assessment approaches continue to chart isolated developmental strands or domains. And fragmented assessments all too often lead to disjointed intervention strategies. (p. 2)

Lewis, an internationally known specialist in the psychology and sociology of speech, explains:

A child is born a speaker and born into a world of speakers. To recognize this is of the utmost importance for our understanding of the growth of language and its place in human development.

The linguistic growth of a child in his social environment moves forward as the continued convergence and interaction of two groups of factors — those that spring from within the child himself and those that impinge upon him from the community around him. The growth of many other creatures has, of course, this dual character. Where a child's development differs is that he is so much more richly endowed with the potentialities of speech and that he grows up in a social environment permeated by symbolization, the most potent form of which is language. (1963, p. 13)

This is why we encourage parents and other caregivers to chat with children. In many mundane ways during our days with little children we support and encourage their language development — or neglect to.

References

Bruner, Jerome. (1983). *Child's talk: learning to use language.* New York: Norton.

Lewis, M.M. (1963). *Language thought and personality in infancy and childhood.* New York: Basic Books.

Prizant, B.M., & Wetherby A.M. (September, 1990). Assessing the communication of infants and toddlers: integrating a socioemotional perspective. *Zero to Three, 11* (1), 1–12.

CHAPTER 10

Laughing All the Way: Using Fun-Filled Friendship As Part of Developing Self-Discipline in Young Children

QUESTION: In our program, we have children from two- and three-years-old and up. As I see it, education is serious business, and school is a serious place. Several of my colleagues laugh and play with the children in our child care center. I am concerned that this will develop the wrong attitude toward discipline. What do you think about this—humor versus discipline with young children of any age?

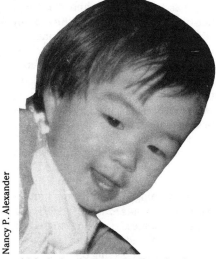

Nancy P. Alexander

Having fun together is not necessarily the opposite of discipline. **Many parents and teachers use humor, good humoredness, and humoring as** *part* **of discipline, particularly as part of preventive discipline.**

A key to good discipline is the fact that a child cares what people think of him. If he doesn't *care* what you think of his behavior, you lack major leverage in *influencing* his behavior.

If you want a child to care about your opinion of him, you need to ensure that he likes you. Usually, we do not make strenuous efforts to please people we don't like. Having a good time together on a regular basis is an important way that people develop friendships—mutually caring relationships, a logical aspect of which is that each person wants to please and be approved of by the other. Having a good time together includes being sensitive and responsive to each other's needs and moods, having plenty of meaningful things to do and discuss, and just plain having fun—laughing, joking, enjoying each other.

In a friendship between adult and young child, the adult is the tone setter. It's up to the adult to set an example of sensitivity and responsiveness. Over time, the child will learn to do the same. It's up to the adult to provide, or encourage the child to initiate, meaningful things to do and discuss. It's up to the adult to pick up on fun the child launches, to play in the same way, and to allow time for laughing, joking, and enjoying each other.

A key to the kind of discipline that enhances self-esteem is developing a happy, fun-filled friendship with each child. This creates in the child motivation to be approved of by you, so results in better behavior.

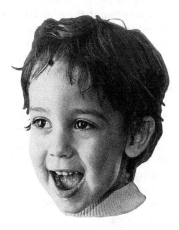

Ellen Levine Ebert

Different social classes tend to use different styles of humor. Humor can be used to expand upon children's ideas of what's funny, and to gently guide behavior, or to shame and subdue.

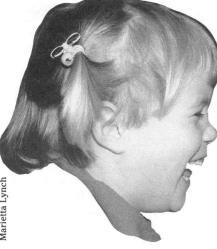
Marietta Lynch

Francis Wardle

What do young children think is fun and funny?

To find out, all we need to do is watch them, and then go along with them — join in.

Two-year-old Peter is making cakes, "and another cake and another cake and another cake." He's grinning as his diapered bottom jogs back and forth between his oven (an upside-down table) and the adult to whom he is presenting his lovely (invisible) cakes. To join in the fun, all the adult has to do is welcome a twinkle into her eye and a smile onto her face and say, "*I'm* making cakes, *too*—bigger cakes and bigger cakes and bigger cakes." Her arms show bigger, bigger, and yet bigger. Peter is delighted. His imagination has been recognized and appreciated. We all enjoy having our ideas recognized and appreciated. Moreover, as he knows he's making believe, pretending, joking, he knows that the adult is also, and this pleases Peter. What greater compliment is there than to be copied?

Three-year-old Carmen is bending down, peering through her corduroy-clothed legs, laughing uproariously at the view. When she pops upright, people and furniture are restored to their normal appearance — what power Carmen has to disarrange and rearrange her world! When the smiling adult silently imitates Carmen, Carmen is thrilled. Her lead is respected, her game is admired, her play has attracted others, even a prestigious adult. All involved enjoy a hearty laugh.

Five-year-old Sybil is playing with a pack of picture/word cards. "Car, star," she says aloud to herself. "Car, star, far, *Harr*," says the smiling adult who is passing by, participating a little bit in what each cluster of children or individual is doing, as she makes her supervisory rounds. Sybil is overjoyed — her last name is Harr. She laughs and cavorts. The adult laughs and continues the sport, saying other rhyming pairs of words and word families, "bell, tell, sell, smell," "sit, fit, hit." Sybil's activity has been extended and expanded. She feels endorsed. Her thinking stretches. Her teacher likes her, approves of her. She feels good about herself, she likes her teacher; *she respects her teacher.*

Because becoming *competent* is an important theme in early childhood development, children think it's very funny when an adult pretends to be *in*competent. The child, in comparison, feels "big" and capable. Therefore, any time a teacher or parent pretends *in*competence in an activity children

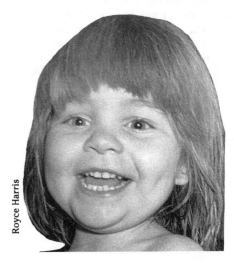
Royce Harris

Many potential "me-against-you" situations in which a heavy hand is needed can be avoided by using the light touch — distraction to something interesting and fun, directions in the form of a jingle or song, or a joke, *not* at the child's expense, of course.

Because adults of differing social classes may have different goals in childrearing, they might intentionally use humor toward *their* goals.

Dena Bawinkel

have just mastered, the children will think it very funny. "Oops!" says Sybil's teacher, "Now I've forgotten how to do it. Run, sun, sat, is that right?" "No!" shouts Sybil, beaming broadly. "Run, sun, *fun!*" "Why not sat?" asks the teacher, feigning ignorance, ". . . sun, sat." "No," Sybil admonishes, "they have to *end* the same: sun, fun." "Oh, I remember," says the teacher, smiling conspiratorially to remind Sybil that she's merely playing. "How about fat, sat?" "Right," says Sybil, her voice authoritative.

Caution: Incompetent adults, or adults who simulate incompetence in any area more important than a small physical or cognitive skill, *do not amuse children, but instead cause unnerving anxiety.* For example, a father we know, who jokes that he can't cook,

and at dinner time says to the two-year-old, "What will we do?" *scares* the child Dad thinks he's joshing. Children want to be able to trust the ability of adults to know how to take care of them, and to know in general.

Another caution: As is the case with us adults, feeling confused and stupid is not funny to children. Therefore, using sarcasm, sophisticated puns, and other "humor" that's beyond the child's bio-psychological developmental ability to fully comprehend — regardless of how smart she is — is unwise. Our purpose in fooling around with children is to bond with them, not to undermine their confidence.

A third caution: Being frightened is not fun. It's not fun for a child too young to be able to distinguish fact from fantasy (younger than five) to be teasingly told, for example, that you are crunching the bones of a skeleton, when you are crunching ice. Humor should relax and warm a child, not tense and chill him.

Discipline is essential, but shouldn't be painful

Humor, playfulness, an attitude of "we're a team, we're all on the same side, we're all trying to help our day go well," *averts* many a potential discipline problem, even when one is on the verge of arising. Adults with a "me-against-you" attitude have many more power struggles with children than do adults who view themselves as guides, whose job it is to intelligently steer children clear of doing wrong, whose job it is to gently steer children toward cooperative interactions with other children and with adults.

Directions can be given smilingly, and in the language of the play children are involved in:

"Tell the spacepeople to race *around* the spacegarden; we don't want to squoosh our tomatoes," rather than, "Stop your running! Get out of that vegetable garden! What do you think you're doing?"

"It's time for the mothers and fathers to put away their things, wash up well, and come to lunch," rather than, "I want everything in that housekeeping area cleaned up by the time I count to 10."

"Red light! Stop! Quick!", rather than, "I told you not to play cars, you'll run into someone."

"Here we go, Henry, hop, skip, jump, hop, skip, jump, let's see the frog go *this* way," rather than, "Henry, *will* you come with the class! You never come when I call people. Quit playing frog and let's go."

Speaking to a child in the language of her play works so well because she feels "seen," "heard," and therefore *respected.* She also feels that her "frogness" or whatever — her *imaginativeness and creativity*—have come through and have been respected.

Ginger Howard

If the goal is to teach children "to stay in their place" in childhood and later on as adults in our society, embarrassing and subduing work best.

Little children do and say so many amusing things that can make a caregiver's day! Sharing delightful tidbits with other adults (privately so as not to embarrass the child) is one of the joys of the job.

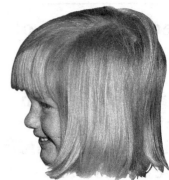

Marietta Lynch

And, of course, naptime instructions can be spontaneously improvised using favorite lullaby tunes. Playful or pleasing directions like these, given with a sparkling face and voice, add the spice of humor to the humdrum occasions that dot our days.

Instructions can be made into a chant, a jingle, or song. Children get a kick out of grown-up creativity—which they are aware these improvisations are.

Staff Photo

"One, two, walking to the bathroom, one, two, walking to the bathroom, one, two, walking to the bathroom," might not delight you, but little children like rhythmic repetition.

(To the tune of "Happy Birthday")
"Pickup time has come now,
Pickup time has come now,
Now it is pickup time,
Pickup time has come now."

Two - and - three - quarter - year - old Matija doesn't come when called; the group is going outside. She's deeply involved in practicing hopping. This is

an advanced skill for such a young child. We want to reward the effort Matija is investing in this difficult endeavor. We also need her to come.

"Matija, can you hop all the way over here?" She arrives almost instantly, on one foot.

The teacher tells two-and-a-half-year-old Ahmet it's time to go pee-pee, we're going to the playground. Ahmet pouts and refuses.

"Are you joking?" the teacher laughs.

"Sure, I'm just joking!" Ahmet shouts gaily, and races to the bathroom. As a strong stream arcs into the toilet, he says, quite pleased with himself, "My penis was just joking you."

How bossy does the boss have to be?

It's hard for children to take orders from dawn to dusk—one reason why they refuse to obey. Jokes, jingles, playful directions, all ease the tension. Grown-ups are in charge. They make the rules, the schedules, the decisions. But they needn't rub children's noses in this fact by being bluntly bossy. A little tact, a little humor, and life among the young is easier all around.

Gail Perry

If the goal is to develop free people with high self-esteem and aspiration levels, gentle guidance is most effective. Which is your goal?

CHAPTER 10

11

Avoiding "Me Against You" Discipline

QUESTION: I see why they are termed the terrible twos. I have constant discipline problems with most of the children in my group. There are several children who give me trouble, one incident on top of another. Last year I had four-year-olds. They were not so bad, but what do you do when children *are* bad? Some of my coworkers do not seem to believe in discipline.

Some adults see each individual child as being at this moment "good" and at that moment "bad." It all adds up to a view of a child as, overall, either a "good child" or a "bad child": She's a good girl; he's a hateful child, a really naughty boy.

Other adults, and certainly those of us well educated in child development, think differently about children. We consider all infants, toddlers, and young children *potentially* good people, naive little people with a very small amount of experience on Earth, who have much to learn, and **a great deal of motivation to please, to be accepted, to be approved, to be loved, to be cared for.** We see young children as generally receptive to guidance and usually eager to "do it right." (There are exceptional instances, and they sure keep us from falling asleep on the job!)

A child's concept of herself, her *self-concept,* is a powerful determiner of her behavior. If she believes she's a "bad

Renee Stockdale

One reason not to resort to frequent "no-no's," arguments, put-downs, and punishments when relating to young children is that a pattern of this treatment is permanently damaging to the child's long-term self-esteem.

Our profession believes in discipline, but rather than thinking of good versus bad children, it thinks of good versus bad approaches to discipline. Bad approaches to discipline diminish a child's self-esteem.

girl," she will *act* like a bad girl—she will behave badly. **To help develop "good character" in a child, we must help develop positive self-concept.** A child who believes she's a "good girl" will *try* to be a good girl, although, being merely mortal, and merely two-years-old, she may frequently fail.

We all believe in firm discipline

It's hard to imagine a sensible adult who does not "believe in discipline." You don't find mainstream adults trained in child development, child psychology, early childhood education, or parenting who don't believe in discipline. How would a young child learn self-control, daily self-help and family/school life procedures, how to get along with other children, values, parents' and teachers' standards, and "right from wrong" without explanations and expectations (discipline)? How would a child develop "good character"? *Our profession believes in discipline, but rather than thinking of good versus bad children thinks of good versus bad approaches to discipline.*

● *Bad approaches to discipline (if mental health is a goal)* diminish a child's self-esteem, make her feel worthless, make her feel victimized, make it impossible for her to begin to feel in control of—and to take responsibility for—some aspects of her own "destiny," make her blame "them," make her apathetic and disengaged, make her leave it all up to "fate," and make her not even try to "be good."

● *Good approaches to discipline (if a moderately high level of aspiration is a goal)* increase a child's self-esteem, allow her to feel valued, encourage her

to feel cooperative, enable her to learn gradually the many skills involved in taking responsibility for some aspects of what happens to her, motivate her to change her strategy rather than to blame others, help her take initiative, help her relate successfully, and help her problem solve.

Getting into a pattern of "me against you" confrontations with a crawler, toddler, or young child of any age can only lead to failure for the adult and bad news for the child's healthy emotional development.

Nothing is more consistently and intimately linked to a wide variety of emotional and behavioral disturbances than is a low opinion of oneself.

If the adult is doling out harsh orders, humiliating insults, or sharp smacks intended to make the child *stop* doing something (touch it, climb up it), she may superficially succeed: The giant adult is three or four times as big and strong as a young child, and the adult can terrorize the vulnerable little child, through the child's fear of loss of love and care, into compliance. But the adult will have *only* superficial success because each such incident in which the child's shaky, emerging

sense of individuality and independence is crushed leaves him angry (he will get revenge) and leaves him with lowered self-confidence.

If the adult is attempting to make the child *start* doing something (eat, sleep, be friendly, learn), she will undoubtedly fail and feel frustrated. (You can lead a horse to water but. . . .)

So one reason not to sink to the level of fighting with a two-year-old is that it is not likely to work even in the short term. A second reason not to resort to frequent "no-no's," arguments, put-downs, and punishments when relating to young children is that a pattern of this treatment is permanently damaging to the child's long-term self-esteem.

Methods of discipline must seldom interfere with the lifelong need for self-esteem

The search for a sense of personal worth steers much of what well-adjusted adults do (adults who have made an *unfortunate* adjustment may have *given up* the search and settled for *low* self-esteem). The search for a sense of personal worth is of pivotal importance to teenagers in their tumultuous identity struggles and is critical in the lives of small children.

Beyond providing physical care, perhaps the main child caring job of parents and other primary caregivers is providing a feeling of self-esteem to children, from earliest infancy onward. Not only in adults and adolescents, but in young children and even infants, the search for a sense of personal worth motivates much of each individual's ceaseless striving to develop and maintain meaningful attachments and meaningful work. The beginnings of a sense of being a valued individual come from loving interactions between mother and infant, and from loving interactions with other primary caregivers; *and* from encouragement of initiative and independence: Mother wants me to become myself, to make choices, to do it my way, to learn to do it acceptably with out having my spirit broken. Nothing is more consistently and intimately linked to a wide variety of emotional and behavioral distur-

Every day, discipline diminishes or enhances a child's feeling of worthlessness or self-worth.

Subjects & Predicates

Situations calling for limits to be set, standards to be established, and desired behaviors to be encouraged will arise with mobile infants, into-everything toddlers, and increasingly independent preschoolers. Therefore, we are continually faced with the questions: Am I disciplining in a way that hurts or helps this child's self-esteem? Am I disciplining in a way that attempts to control (to disempower) the child or in a way that attempts to develop in the child self-control (personal empowerment)? However, in spite of the complexity disciplining young children entails, they need to be disciplined.

bances than is a low opinion of oneself. Low self-esteem is always found in children/teens/adults who regularly do poorly in family life, friendships, school, jobs, and their lives in general.

Positive or negative self-image starts in infancy

Very early in an infant's/toddler's development, before he or she has effective language, an embryonic ability to self-evaluate has begun to evolve. This is the capacity (to some people the curse) to assess the aggregate of one's feelings, behaviors, competencies, and relationships — to judge oneself. Even toddlers, in an intuitional way if not in a way they could explain, pervasively feel they are perceived as precious, a pest, clever, stupid, wonderful, naughty, capable, helpless, or whatever. Astonishingly early, babies develop a *sense* of self as good or as unable and unworthy. We know people who seem not to know who they are, where they're going, what they want, or even what they have already accomplished. They do not appear to understand the coherence of their core *self*. Worse yet, we know people who have a strong sense of *negative* self: They feel

that at the center of themselves they are less than equal to others, a loser, deficient, dumb, unkind, unconscientious, incapable of successes — the ultimate success being that of feeling like a lovable person.

One's self-image, at all ages, but all the more so in infancy and early

---

A person's intuitive feeling of self-worth (or worthlessness) is formed at a very young age from a collection of perceptions about her body, race, intelligence, similarity to others in the peer group, socioeconomic status, and other "self-images." Probably the most major among them is the child's perception of parents' and significant others' continuing evaluation of her.

Do you help children problem solve, predict, plan, share, cooperate, empathize, and learn to understand how to get along in the world?

childhood, is dependent upon and interconnected with the judgments of higher authorities.

Adults, in many cases, will work hard without promotions or salary increases if they get encouragement, a degree of praise, and recognition from their supervisors.

Adolescents, confused as to whether they are going to be popular and make it in life, if fortunate enough to have loving and effective parents, get a significant amount of calming, stabilizing, and focus from parental conviction that *of course* they are going to find friends and mates, *of course* they are going to make it in life. In short, teenagers' positive self-image is reinforced by their parents' positive image of them.

Children will work hard in school for their teacher's approval; under normal, nonremedial circumstances, grades and stickers are not required. At the same time that parents and teachers strive to help each child develop independence, autonomy, individuality, and satisfaction in a job well done (intrinsic reward), we know that

our opinion of the child, and how we convey it to her, is a critical variable in her feeling of self-worth.

The human self is not solitary, self-contained, and completely autonomous. Human beings are social animals. We live in groups, we need each other to survive, and so we care what people think of us. Largely based on what the most significant people in our early lives think of us, we develop high, adequate, or low self-esteem.

Helping infants and toddlers develop self-esteem *and* self-discipline

We can structure our spaces at home and in the center, the schedule, diet, outings, frequency of visitors, and so on, to bring out the best in easily overwrought, easily exhausted babies and young children whose emotional and social systems quickly "short circuit" under stress. We can also structure our *own* lives to provide enough sleep, healthy food, time off, rewarding projects beyond the child, and other friends so that we can act with maximum maturity—can muster maximum patience and understanding. (Because they are egocentric, young children experience grown-ups' grumpiness as disapproval of *them;* feeling constantly disapproved of leads to low self-esteem.) All this is *preventive discipline.* Nonetheless, situations calling for limits to be set, standards to be established, and desired behaviors to be encouraged will arise with mobile infants, into-everything toddlers, sometimes virtually impossible boundary-testing two-year-olds, and increasingly independent preschoolers. Therefore, we are continually faced with the questions: Am I disciplining in a way that

hurts or helps this child's self-esteem? Am I disciplining in a way that attempts to control (to disempower) the child or in a way that attempts to develop *self*-control in the child (personal empowerment)?

Methods of discipline that promote self-worth

1. **Show that you recognize and accept the reason the child is doing what, in your judgment, is the wrong thing:**

"You want to play with the truck but . . ."
"You like to climb but . . ."
"You want me to stay with you but . . ."

This validates the legitimacy of the child's desires and illustrates to the child that you are an understanding person. It also is honest from the outset: The adult is wiser, in charge, and not afraid to be the leader, and occasionally has priorities other than the child's wishes.

2. **State the "but":**

"You want to play with the truck *but Jerisa is using it right now.*"
"You like to climb *but this will fall and hurt you; it's my job to keep you safe.*"
"You want me to stay with you *but now I need to (go out, help Jill, serve lunch, etc.).*"

This lets the child know that others have needs too. It teaches "perspective taking" and will lead later to the child's ability to put himself in other people's shoes. It will also gain you the child's respect; you are fair. And it will make the child feel safe; you are able to keep *him* safe.

As has previously been stated, this book addresses in-depth two concerns (1) How best to help children develop mental health to enable them to live happily in this particular very complex culture (the U.S.A. today), and (2) How best to help children "succeed" as members of America's middle class, while maintaining mental health and happiness.

---

3. Offer a solution:

"Soon you can play with the truck."

One-year-olds can begin to understand "just a minute" and will wait patiently if we always follow through 60 seconds later. Two- and three-year-olds can learn to understand "I'll tell you when it's your turn" if we always follow through within two or three minutes.

This assists children in learning how to delay gratification but is not thwarting in view of their short-term understanding of time, and teaches them to trust because you are fair.

4. Often, it's helpful to say something indicating your confidence in the child's ability and willingness to learn:

"When you get older I know you will (whatever it is you expect)."

"Next time you can (restate what is expected in a positive manner)."

This affirms your faith in the child, lets her know that you assume she has the capacity to grow and mature, transmits your belief in her good intentions, and establishes your expectation that "next time" she will do better.

5. In some situations, after firmly stating what is not to be done, you can demonstrate "how we do it," or "a better way":

"We don't hit. That *hurts* me. *Pat* my face *gently*" (gently stroke).

"Puzzle pieces are not for throwing. Let's put them in their places together" (offer help).

This sets firm limits yet helps the child feel that you two are a team, not enemies.

6. Toddlers are not easy to distract, but frequently they can be redirected to something similar but OK. Carry or lead the child by the hand, saying,

"That's the gerbil's paper. Here's Lindsay's paper."

"We don't jump in the scrub bucket. Lindsay can jump on the rug."

"Peter needs that toy. Here's a toy for Lindsay."

This endorses the child's right to choose what she will do, yet begins to

---

Creating a Positive Climate Promotes Self-Discipline (Required for Life in the Middle Class)

The stronger a child's motivation "to be good," the more effort he will exert in this direction. Therefore, there will be fewer "me against you" situations. If the child believes *you* believe he *is* good and is *capable* of learning new aspects of being good, and if he feels that you like him, he will be easier to live with.

Creating a positive climate for the very young includes

- spending lots of leisurely time with an infant or young child;
- sharing important activities and meaningful play;
- listening and answering as an equal (not as an instructor; for example, using labeling words when a toddler points inquiringly toward something, or discussing whatever topic the two-year-old is trying to tell you about);
- complimenting the child's efforts: "William is feeding himself!" "Juana is putting on her shoe!" (even if what you are seeing is only clumsy stabs in the right direction); and
- smiling, touching, caressing, kissing, cuddling, holding, rocking, hugging.

The young child should not have to "be good" to "earn" these indicators of caregivers' enjoyment. Children should freely be given affection and approval solely because they *exist.*

Even to babies and toddlers, it's important that we say every day

"Good morning!"

"Hi." (from time to time)

"Will you play with me?" or "Let's play _____ together."

"Come with me. We will . . ."

"I love you," or "You're my friend."

"Let's (sit, ride, rest, etc.) together."

"I'm glad you're in *my* (class, group, family)."

"I like to hug you."

Harmful, Negative Disciplinary Methods (If Successful Middle Class Living Is a Goal)

1. Frequently saying, "Stop that!" "Don't do it *that* way!" "That's not so bad considering that *you* did it." "If it weren't for you, . . ."
2. Criticizing
3. Discouraging
4. Creating constant obstacles and barriers
5. Blaming, shaming
6. Saying "You always . . . ," "You never . . ."
7. Using sarcastic, caustic, and cruel "humor"
8. Physical punishment
9. Using removal from the group or isolation (the time-out chair, the corner, the child's room) frequently during the day, or for more than two or three minutes at a time.

Any adult might *occasionally* do any of these things. Doing any or all of them more than once in a while means that a bad approach to discipline has become a habit and urgently needs to be addressed, analyzed, and altered before the child experiences low self-esteem as a permanent part of her personality.

Different socioeconomic and cultural groups discipline toddlers and two-year-olds in dramatically different ways. As we have seen in chapters 3, 5, and 9, this is one of several first steps in culture and class differentiation.

teach that other people have rights too. Blizzards of words further aggravate the situation. Make simple statements. Say simple things. There are times when just wordlessly carrying the child off to another scene is the most appropriate step to take.

7. Avoid accusing. Even with babies, communicate in respectful tones and words. This prevents lowering the child's self-image and promotes his tendency to cooperate.

8. For every "no," offer two *acceptable* choices:

"No! Rosie cannot bite Esther. That *hurts* Esther. I don't let children hurt children. Rosie can bite the rubber duck or the cracker."

"No, Jackie. That book is for teachers. Jackie can have *this* book or *this* book."

This encourages the child's independence and emerging decision-making skills, but sets boundaries. Children should *never* be allowed to hurt each other. It's bad for the hurter's self-image as well as for the self-esteem of the hurt.

9. If children have enough language, assist them in expressing their feelings, including anger, and their wishes. Assist them in thinking about alternatives and in thinking of a solution to the problem. Adults should never fear children's anger.

"You hate me because you're so very tired. It's hard to feel loving when you need to sleep. When you wake up, I think you'll feel more friendly."

"You feel terribly angry because I won't let you have candy. I *will* let you choose a banana or an apple. Which do you want?"

"You're angry because I said you can't grab all the books off the shelf in the library. Libraries and grown-ups don't let children grab all the books.

Which book would you like me to read you, this one or that one?"

This encourages characteristics we want to see emerge in children if we are preparing them for life in contemporary America's middle class, such as awareness of feelings and reasonable assertiveness, and gives children tools for solving problems without unpleasant scenes. It shows them that we are strong, so they are safe: We will not fall apart or cave in or harm them even if their rage scares *them*.

The fact that a parent or other caregiver "does everything right" does *not* mean that a child will never behave hideously or become furious. All children, especially two-year-olds, disintegrate into prolonged, hopelessly unstoppable howling occasionally. The least harmful thing to do, after a) everything preventive, and b) several patient, problem-solving things have been tried is to ignore the child. Engaging with an enraged toddler or two is a no-win thing to do. If at all possible, don't give in, and don't get involved (ha-ha! as if this were possible!).

10. Until a child is a year and a half or almost two years old, adults are completely responsible for his safety and comfort, and for creating the conditions that encourage "good behavior." After this age, while we are still responsible for his safety, adults increasingly, though extremely gradually, begin to transfer responsibility

Normal two-year-olds (24–36 months) have much more sense of self, interpersonal skill, large- and small-muscle control, language, and self-discipline than normal toddlers (12–24 months). Developmental miracles occur between 24 and 36 months because of physical maturation (studied by Gesellians) and mental maturation (studied by Piagetians). When all this is enhanced by insightful guidance rooted in understanding of psychological development (studied by Eriksonians), many two-year-olds often speak, play, and interact as maturely as less optimally nurtured three-year-olds.

for behaving acceptably to the child. Adults establish firm limits and standards as needed. They start expecting the child to become aware of other people's feelings. They begin to expect the child to think simple cause/effect (consequences) thoughts, if guided quietly through the thinking process. This is teaching the rudiments of "self-discipline."

11. When talking to children one year old and older, give clear, simple directions in a firm, friendly voice. While verbalizing, also use facial expressions, postures, and gestures to make your point even more clear. This avoids confusion, miscommunication, overwhelming a person new to the art of comprehension with a blizzard of words, and resulting refusal to comply.

12. Be aware that the job of a toddler, and to an extent the job of *all* young children, is to taste, touch, smell, squeeze, tote, poke, pour, sort, explore, and *test*. At times, toddlers are greedy, at times grandiose. They do not share well; they need time to experience ownership before they're expected to share. They need to assert themselves ("No," "I can't," "I won't," and "Do it myself"). They need to separate to a degree from their parents (individuate). One way to do this is to say *no* and not to do what is asked, or to *do* what is not wanted.

At times, two-year-olds are needy, at times bellicose. They do not understand where the limits to their grand new head-swelling competencies are, so they sometimes go way too far. They need to win (refuse to dress, refuse to cease and desist doing the forbidden). This has nothing to do with not understanding the rules. It's a developmentally appropriate (and maddening) aspect of developing **realistic self.** First children learn to feel competent. This leads those who are successful to feel *overconfident*—omnipotent. Especially during the year they're two, children need to learn how to meet the requirements of daily living and ordinary relationships: **They need to learn self-discipline.**

Two-and-a-half-year-olds are rather special people. Not a few have become great at dramatic play. Their dolls and teddies don't expect them to say please and thank you with perfect diction, or to talk seriously, as if they cared, about the marvels of toilets, or the pleasure of being straitjacketed in the car seat, or of waiting 300 tearful years for Mama to reappear and the sitter to leave. When listened to by their dolls and stuffed animals, twos perk up their ears and regard them with less wariness than they reserve for parents and other caregivers, who, they know, will get that condescending smile on the face and syrup in the voice as they say, meaning the opposite, "Good job!"

Twos can be self-possessed, cocky, articulate, house-trained, competent, and monstrous. They can be taught tricks and to come when called and to know what they shouldn't do. And in the tradition of a rabbit named Peter —a book that two-year-olds love— they can be bad on purpose. Then when they're caught (after an insufficiently supervised fraction of a sec-

Michael Tony-Topix

Nine times out of ten, families that find they have two-year-olds who generally won't obey and are usually "negative" inadvertently made them that way. In some cases, parents unnecessarily interrupt, irritatingly stifle, threaten, and arbitrarily boss around toddlers and twos. This would bring out the worst in any of us, and it does in toddlers. These parents don't have children with the degree of emerging self-discipline we expect because they dole out too much discipline but don't develop enough self. In other cases, parents go the opposite extreme: They provide no predictable, required routine and rules (behavior standards); they don't step in when children need help in sharing, turn-taking, and so on; they are absurdly permissive; and they don't firmly enforce "consequences." These parents don't have children with the degree of emerging self-discipline we expect because they allow far too much self and don't provide friendly but firm discipline.

As educarers, it's our job to confer with parents about these concepts, offer helpful reading materials to them, provide sensible speakers, and work collaboratively with them to assist the child in developing self-discipline.

ond) smearing the lipstick on the hall mirror or pouring the small blocks into the full potty, they'll stop and gaze at you balefully, without remorse. Few of them have a mean or deceitful bone in their bodies, but they don't have strong consciences or inner controls yet, either. If they're angry at you, they simply throw a shrieking tantrum for an hour and a half in the supermarket and are done with it. Occasionally, they're overcome with exhaustion or a feeling of to-hell-with-it-all. Then it's likely that they will leap into the garbage, overturn the nicely set table, or sweep all the glitter for the art project onto the floor.

Two-year-olds are wily creatures, and if they don't feel like getting dressed, they can't be bribed. A typical two spends some hours each day ricocheting gleefully off the furniture. Two-year-olds growl when you try to dress them, and guard their bodies with clamped arms and kicking legs. Though fierce when annoyed, they are usually pleasant people to be with in their own exuberant, opinionated way.

Are you a model and a gentle guide? This is the best kind of discipline because it fosters self-esteem and self-discipline.

They are, by turns, lovable, goofy, horrible, and cuddly. In a word, they're not easy to "discipline." Adults who live and work with two-year-olds need a good sense of self themselves, and a good sense of humor.

If adults understand children in this age range, they will create circumstances and develop attitudes that permit and promote development. **Development includes learning self-discipline.** It's better learned through guidance than through punishment.

It's better learned through a "We are a team, I am the leader, it's my job to help you grow up" approach than through a "me against you," self-esteem reducing, hostility-generating approach.

* * * * *

None of us control our own destiny. Our moment in history and our geographic place, the socioeconomic circumstances of the family we happen to be born into, disabilities or extra blessings we may find ours, our genetic inheritance and birth order, whether we have dreadful, sensational, or adequate parents, educational and other opportunities available or unavailable to us, and much, much more are matters, from an individual's point of view, of good or bad luck. But the goal of a good approach to discipline is to give each child ever-increasing control of his life, and a life in which adult love and commitment have been prominent and integral to his experiences from day one.

CHAPTER 12

What Kind of "Character" Are We Trying To Develop?
Eight Dozen Reasons To Feel Proud of Your Accomplishments With Infants, Toddlers, and Twos

QUESTION: My director doesn't want us to teach the infants and toddlers in our program anything. Aren't there any educational goals for this age group? Am I just a babysitter?

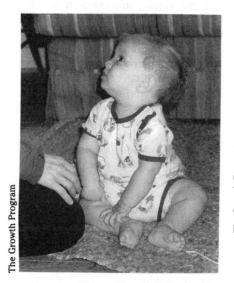

You are not just a babysitter. If you're doing a good job, you are helping to develop good human beings with a strong sense of independent self, high self-esteem, and emerging self-discipline **because these are the characteristics that help people succeed in this particular culture.**

It's important to note that the attributes valued by most mainstream middle-class Americans are not shared by all parents, particularly those from other countries, or from minority groups in *this* country. The desirability of certain behaviors varies through the centuries and across diverse cultures. What's right to some people is wrong to others. To a 17th Century Puritan parent, the development of piety and the suppression of sexuality were two primary objectives. In Chinese families, teaching sons filial loyalty to the father is a top priority. To elite parents in India, developing a detached attitude

Babies learn to respect (care for) the people who care for (respect) them.

from material possessions (and from the desperately poor people dying in the streets because they have neither possessions nor food) is an urgent virtue. Many Native American parents carefully foster cooperative behaviors; their children would rather fail than stand out above others. A large number of low-income American parents care more that their sons learn what's necessary to stay out of jail and get jobs than that they learn "cooperative behaviors." Japanese parents promote the social graces that hide hostility; hurting people's feelings and causing friction are strongly frowned upon. To the parents who supported the original Israeli kibbutzim, a far less intense than is customary relationship between child and mother and a much stronger *group* experience was the ideal.

Sensitive teachers and caregivers work collegially with parents in determining which behaviors all concur are to be encouraged. To do this, it's essential to challenge children physically, intellectually, socially, and emotionally, but almost always just at the frontier of the child's level of development so he or she can, with small but real effort, succeed. Admittedly, this can be tricky in a classroom where there are children of several cultures. Perhaps harder is the problem of reaching consensus about how to care for and educate children when there are *staff members* who don't "buy" mainstream middle class American assumptions; the assumptions promoted by the child development field.

If you ask American parents what they want for their children—what is their goal when they invest all these millions of childrearing minutes—many will come up with a list like this, not in any particular order. They want the child to:

- be in good health
- be happy
- be affectionate
- be kind and help others
- be friendly
- be self-confident
- be honest
- be cooperative/obedient

- be flexible, cope well
- be responsible
- be hard working
- do well, be motivated (in school, in sports, in life)
- have good morals and values
- have a good sense of humor
- get good jobs, achieve

Each of these characteristics promotes self-esteem, although some families and teachers value certain of the traits/goals more than others, which usually influences how esteem-enhancing *the child* will perceive the characteristic to *be*.

For example, if a child's parent(s) don't think being kind to others, being friendly, and being flexible are important, the child, even at a very young age, may not base much of his estimation of himself on these behaviors, whereas if parents *do* consider a moderate amount of kindness, friendliness, and flexibility in their two-year-olds important, the children will include this set of behaviors in their self-assessments.

To *all* children, physical competence is an important aspect of self. Yet children whose parents consider "winning" in sports of utmost importance will "weight" their judgment of this aspect of self very heavily—if they are not "winners," their self-esteem will be low—they may feel *overall* like losers. On the other hand, to a child whose parents are musicians, and who don't give two hoots about athletics, not being so hot in sports would be unlikely to affect more than a small, contained component of the child's self-esteem.

If a child's self-esteem is low in *general*, it usually negatively influences the characteristic.

The characteristics in the bulleted list above *are* the characteristics we're encouraging when we parent or give care such as that described and discussed in *Character Development: Encouraging Self-Esteem & Self-Discipline in Infants, Toddlers, & Two-Year-Olds*.

These are not necessarily the exact characteristics that parents from all ethnic, racial, and socioeconomic groups most desire to see developed in their children. All involved in raising,

caring for, and educating any specific young child need to engage in frank discussions of objectives, try to evolve some common goals, and learn to be a little flexible in order to meet the needs of those with whom they don't agree. If all of this isn't possible, this particular program may not be the most appropriate one for this child (or for this staff person to work in).

Moreover, we all need to be aware that families whose life experiences have unequivocally convinced them that it's their fate to remain on the bottom rung of society's success ladder usually do not *dare* rear their children for success. To do so would be, they fear, to head the children toward a heartbreaking, spirit-breaking fall—when the children realize what living their life ensnared in the cruel cycle of poverty really will be like. Therefore, the childrearing goals and concomitant methods adhered to by people who themselves are without hope of American-style success are not those described in this chapter, or indeed in this entire book. Most of the attributes on the above list of desired childrearing outcomes seem to such families peripheral, trivial, or contraindicated. The same is true of staff members whose personal lives have taught them to lack hope for the children in their charge.

Here are some eight dozen educational (developmental) accomplishments you and each child in this age group *you* work with will probably have achieved together, assuming that the child is not burdened by unusual hardships. **The child accomplishes these things, some of them through maturation, some with your help—through behavioral guidance and help you offer in understanding and handling feelings, and some through your assistance in interpreting puzzling or distressing aspects of the environment. This list of accomplishments and achievements has been derived from what expert practitioners (including parents) *do,* and from dialogue with them about what they *believe* they're striving to achieve with very young children. As** you care for each child, you may want to consider the ways in which you are

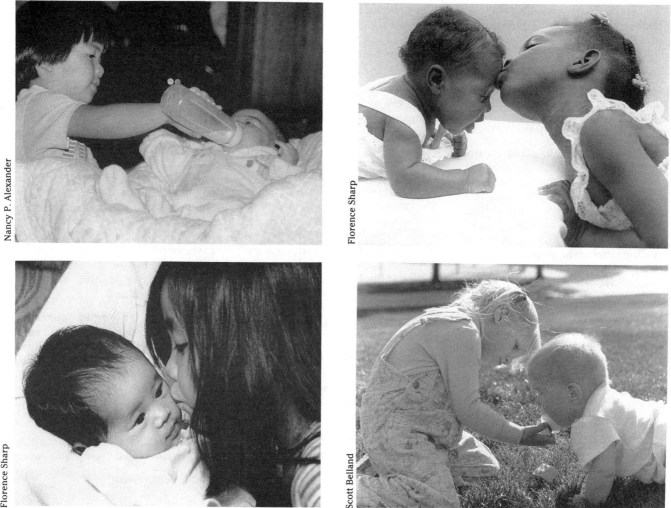

Florence Sharp

Florence Sharp

Scott Belland

If a cluster of characteristics you want children to develop includes empathy, insight, motivation, and skill in nurturing, perspective-taking, and respect for the needs of others, be sure to build into your daily program many opportunities for toddlers and two-year-olds to care for and help each other. Take time to notice and compliment each child when she or he shows these kindly behaviors.

continually but unintrusively promoting these abilities. We don't instruct, lecture, assign, assess, preach, or punish. **We guide, observing and fitting into natural situations as they arise, using these situations as our "learning materials."**

This is not an assessment "instrument." The child study movement has been in progress for the better part of the 20th century. Therefore, many expert practitioners, including this author and many readers of this book,

have read a large number of informal and formal, unpublished and published behavioral rating checklists and child study observational checklists. Most of them have much in common. Most of them present the physical, emotional, social, and intellectual ingredients of mental health, maturity, the characteristics, morality, and values that work for people living and doing well in a democracy. It is not a "tool" compiled by one pediatrician or

one distinguished developmental psychologist and his disciples. Pediatricians and research psychologists have much to offer us childrearers, but it is not up to them to decide what kind of people we are working so hard to raise. This is a set of behaviors and characteristics that many **expert parents and practitioners** agree are appropriate. It's a set of goals for parents and caregivers to work toward every day in every way.

What Kind of "Character" Are We Trying To Develop?

1. Seems generally satisfied with self (three months on; is a prerequisite of **self-esteem**).

2. Seems to feel secure with parents and/or other primary caregivers (indicates the presence of trust, an essential ingredient of positive **self-esteem,** and willingness to cooperate with adults, e.g., **self-discipline**).

3. Shows affection to primary caregivers (parents and others) and strongly prefers them to "insignificant others" (after approximately seven months, if not much earlier; drapes self against caregiver's body, molds into it, relaxes; indicates healthy attachment, emotional and social development, is essential for eventual positive **self-esteem**).

4. Seems purposefully involved in **self-selected** activities (from three months on; lays the foundation for motivation, initiative, perseverance, and **self-discipline** regarding work and play; contributes significantly to **self-esteem**).

5. Shows curiosity; investigates, explores, experiments, takes modest risks (increasingly as becomes mobile; reveals motivation to learn, the risk-taking needed to learn, intellectual eagerness, and initiative, all of which are related to self-confidence, also called positive **self-esteem**).

6. Separates **without acute distress** (though sometimes may cling and resist or cry for a short while) from one familiar caregiving person to another — parent to caregiver, caregiver to parent (indicates healthy attachment and growing mastery of abandonment anxiety, an important part of feeling good about oneself; children who have a deeply trusting relationship with one or more people, who have experienced happy caregiving by others, and whose grown-ups stay with them until they feel comfortable in new situations, usually have very little trouble separating **from one well-known person to another,** although some "normal" children seem to take separating very hard).

7. Asserts wants, needs, ideas appropriately; does not exhibit a pattern of passivity and "victim" behavior (nine months on; shows healthy **self-esteem**).

8. Imitates adults and other children (infants do this at an appropriately simple level; older toddlers do it through pretend play as well as in many, many other ways; two-year-olds do it through dramatic play with a story line and logical sequences of events — indicates attachment and identification, social responsiveness, motivation to learn and develop).

9. Shows concern for others: Older babies look dismayed when others cry; toddlers try to comfort unhappy or hurt companions or caregivers, perhaps by getting a tissue, "lovie," etc. for the person needing comfort; two-year-olds help others who seem to be in trouble (indicates developing perspective-taking, empathy, altruism; shows positive social development, which adds to **positive self-image** and **self-discipline**).

10. Carries on lengthy nonverbal communications with parents, caregivers, and possibly other children (nine months on; shows emerging sense of self as someone with something to say (e.g., positive self-esteem), social development, and suitable language development).

11. Is learning when to keep at a difficult, **self-selected** task, and when

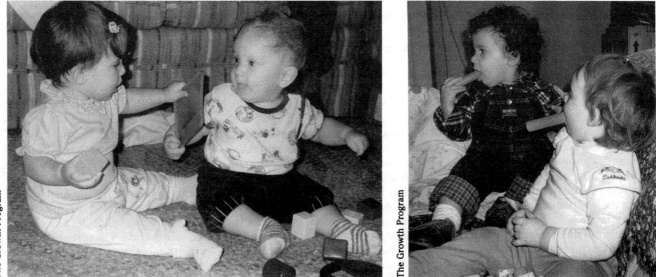

If you value friendship, allow babies and little children to play together. If necessary, help them work things out. At a very young age, many children prefer particular playmates. They seek each other out, greatly enjoy copying each other, and have fun being silly together. They seem unsettled when their special friend is absent.

to seek adult or older child assistance (12 months on; achieving a difficult self-chosen task contributes to **self-esteem,** reduces frustration, contributes to **self-discipline**).

12. Enjoys rhymes, songs, finger plays, and looking at books (12 months on; toddlers and two-year-olds who have had a great many happy times talking about *suitable* books will be advanced in this aspect of development; proves pre-literacy skills are developing well).

13. Feeds self with spoon (older babies, toddlers and twos; shows increasing autonomy; contributes to **self-esteem** and **self-discipline**).

14. Walks without assistance— toddles, lurches wide-leggedly from side to side, topples if an obstacle prevents staggering forward in a straight line (starting before 15 months, perhaps as early as 10 months; another step—literally—in the direction of autonomy, separate self, and positive **self-esteem**).

15. Climbs (soon after starts to walk; feeling physically competent is a big part of positive **self-esteem** for young children).

16. Enjoys push and pull toys (generates a sense of personal power, part of positive **self-esteem**).

17. Knows names of major body parts (12 to 18 months; shows that body image is beginning; indicates that language learning is well under way —good language is a literacy prerequisite; feeling intelligent is part of positive **self-esteem**).

18. Has beginning of a sense of humor (young toddlers; children whose parents and caregivers are very playful with them of course excel in this area; suggests that a vitally important social skill and creative coping skill is starting to form).

19. Shows pride in achievement of self-initiated tasks, social or language skills (12 months on; indicates self-appreciation, positive **self-esteem**).

20. Adjusts well to new experiences if they are appropriate, and if with a trusted adult (12 months on; **adds to image of self as a "can-do" person**).

21. Dares to express contrary behavior and hostile feelings to primary caregivers occasionally; toddlers and two-year-olds may say "no" and balk at cooperating quite often, and *more* so with their parents than with other adults (shows the development of healthy, separate **self,** self-confidence, and desirable assertiveness; children fight their best beloveds *hardest* because it's hardest to break away from them to gain independence).

22. Recognizes names of most familiar objects and points to them when they are named (12 to 24 months; indicates language learning is proceeding well; and again, feeling intelligent is part of a person's **self-esteem**).

23. Seeks to re-establish warm connections with loved ones and other primary caregivers after *brief* episodes of stubborn, oppositional, temperamental, or difficult behavior (after 12 months; shows the child highly values the relationship, is not too angry to reach out again, and has some **self-control:** a sign of good attachment, a social skill).

24. Expresses needs, and both positive and negative feelings, nonverbally, which is important—often in ways other than crying, whining, disrupting, or hurting (after 15 months, uses words more and more frequently when trying to communicate needs and feelings, including negative feelings; indicates growing **self-respect** and **self-discipline**).

25. Is becoming aware of and cares about own belongings, often says "Mine!", generally has trouble sharing and taking turns (younger than 18 months; protecting turf is a biological imperative—something all animals and nations do—this is not uniquely a toddler "problem"; contributes to **sense of self;** sense of possessing is the foundation of responsibility and **self-discipline**).

26. Enjoys parallel play with other children, sometimes with interaction —may, to some extent, treat them as fascinating objects (12 to 21 months; will lead to positive **self-image** as a person who has friends and successful interpersonal relations if adults encourage these clumsy beginnings).

27. Shares and takes turns often, but by no means always (12 to 18 months on; with steady guidance, occasionally shares or takes turns before 21 months; becomes quite good at these cooperative behaviors by 36 months; from 24 months on, many socially mature children—and of course there *are* mature and immature children from birth on, as there are mature and immature eight-, eighteen-, and eighty-year-olds —share and take turns very well with friends they regularly play with).

28. Runs (soon after learns to walk until approximately a year later; staggers, lurches, almost tumbles forward; physical accomplishments bring positive **self-esteem**).

29. Uses objects to represent others that are not really similar, for example, pretends to comb hair with stick or toothbrush (older babies, young toddlers; shows the beginning of creativity and evidence of ideas and thinking skills). Plays pretend with a grown-up—isolated play events without a "story line" (young toddlers; is the beginning of a sense of reality vs. fantasy, which takes two or three more years to fully develop; shows imagination).

30. Is interested in cause and effect —of spills and resulting puddles, of tripping and resulting tumbles, of behaviors and resulting reactions from others (15 months on; this intellectual progress will make it possible for the child, in a few years, to take responsibility for some "effects" by controlling the "causes." Taking responsibility for causing or not causing certain happenings in one's life, and taking responsibility for the effect one has on others, is part of feeling empowered—**positive self-esteem**—and of **self-discipline**— the solution to a problem will in part be solved by oneself).

31. Knows names of all family members, almost all people in group if in child care, a play group, etc. (18 to 24 months; indicates social awareness, memory, and mental retrieval skills; intellectual competence breeds **self-esteem**).

32. Engages in many kinds of activities and becomes quite absorbed in them for a considerable length of time (older babies, toddlers, two-year-olds;

children who are used to being interrupted, instructed, entertained, or denied opportunities to conduct their own play their own way will flit from activity to activity and will fuss a great deal; they protest because *their* ideas are not respected; this is harmful to the emergence of **self-esteem;** young children may have difficulty settling into an activity for other reasons as well.

33. Knows own drawers, shelves at home and cubby at child care and keeps personal things in these personal keeping places (twos; shows increasing sense of self, responsibility, competence; adds to **self-esteem, self-discipline).**

34. Says names of familiar objects and points to them, says names of action words, familiar events, and so on (after 15 months; language skills add to gestural, postural, and other communication skills, thus facilitate emotional, social, and cognitive capabilities, foster independence, **promote self-esteem,** and **make greater self-discipline possible).**

35. Usually (not always!) complies with adult requests if they are routine requests and tactfully made (15 to 36 months; indicates continuing social development in a cooperative, **self-disciplined** direction; though we expect a certain amount of balking and belligerency, which is an important aspect of autonomy, and this is part of **self-discipline** too; by 18 months, the child is beginning to respect limits set verbally or with a gesture, such as a "shh" finger across the lips, or a "get down" signal with the pointer finger; studies done in widely differing cultures show that, by 36 months, all children who have been taught to do so can understand the significance of an adult prohibition).

36. Often joins others when invited (indicates social development; being sought after socially and knowing how to fit in socially are important parts of positive **self-esteem** and of being accepted in our society—we Americans highly value social skills).

37. Is getting better and better at sharing, taking turns, and trading (toddlers and twos; contributes to sense of being a person who successfully functions with others and recognizes the rights of others, hence to **self-esteem;** this is a major part of social development and **self-discipline).**

38. Occasionally, approximately six to 20 times during the two years between 12 and 36 months, the child's fragile self-control will "short circuit" and the child will throw an all-out, howling, kicking tantrum (indicates "par for the course" immature ability to handle stress; more frequently, perhaps once every few weeks, toddlers and two-year-olds may make a stink about something seemingly silly, or have a very *mild* or *brief* crying fit, almost always when frustrated; *frequent* tantrums are evidence of much too much stress or of adult inability to set standards and insist upon suitable behaviors; two-year-olds know how they're supposed to behave, so when their grown-ups permit an aspect of their lives to be excessively stressful, or routinely allow ridiculously bad behavior, thus not expecting any **self-discipline, the child's self-esteem is lowered).**

39. Self-calms or accepts adult help in calming down after an upsetting experience such as a routine bump or scrape, being prevented from doing something, being required to do something, having to wait a few minutes (12 months on; after 24 months, we expect to see children exhibit the **self-discipline** revealed in the ability to terminate disintegrated or out-of-control behavior after a brief collapse and outburst, especially if an adult helps by putting the child's anger, frustration, or whatever into words and then attempting to interest the child in something else).

40. Knows, can explain (by shaking head negatively and saying, "No-no!" or in more complex language), and can usually cooperate with the basic no-no's of the program; often goes along with the general routines and procedures if all this is handled in a developmentally appropriate way (transition time, using car seats and belts in vehicles, naptime, etc.) (older toddlers, twos; is an important aspect of growing **self-discipline).**

41. Understands spatial relations as suggested by prepositions (12 months on; begins to grasp the most common of spatial concepts—above, after, around, behind, down, in, inside, off, on, out, outside, over, under, up; demonstrates understanding of more and more of these concepts as moves towards 36 months; these are language skills and also promote ability to follow directions, **self-discipline).**

42. Is developing a sense of spatial relations (18 to 24 months: can do three- to six-piece puzzle; 24 to 36 months: can do six- to 12-piece puzzle; tries to do age-appropriate puzzles, put together train tracks, popbeads, etc; competence, including these small muscle competencies, is a big part of **self-esteem** and, in large part, is the result of practice).

43. Notices changes in positions of furniture or toys in room, and significant changes in major routines (18 months on; shows awareness of environment and healthy interest in relevant matters beyond the self, pays attention—which is part of **self-discipline).**

44. Knows sequence of program routine (outside follows inside, snacks and stories follow outside, potty time and washing hands follow stories) (18 months on; is essential for the development of **self-discipline).**

45. Describes everyday objects and activities in pictures (toddlers and twos; indicates capability of understanding pictorial symbols, i.e., objects shown in pictures are symbolic of the real object—they are *not* the real object—a pre-literacy skill).

46. Says phrases, attempts sentences, expresses *ideas voluntarily* without an adult goading speech (18 to 36 months; although we don't expect it, many 24-month-olds speak fluently; children without well-developed language by ages five, six, and seven have trouble learning to read; language is an important part of readiness to read single words, phrases, or sentences; having good language, writing, and reading skills in elementary school is part of positive **self-esteem** and **self-discipline. Children with serious academic problems are often discipline problems).**

47. Can sustain substantial *verbal* communications with parents, caregivers, and other children (24 to 36 months on; shows social development, thinking skills, and appropriate language development; makes **self-discipline** more feasible because a child can often "talk it over" instead of struggling with feelings, desires, or ideas *physically*).

48. Often asks, "What's dis?" (15 to 24 months; indicates growing interest and facility in acquiring language).

49. Climbs without help (after 18 months; gross motor skills are critical to all physical fitness at all stages of life; shows growing initiative, independence, and risk-taking skills—all are needed for academic, interpersonal, and job success; a large part of a child's positive or negative **self-esteem** comes from being physically adept, even if in later years physical prowess becomes unimportant to a particular individual).

50. Tells adult when fresh diaper is needed (toddlers and twos; increasing self-awareness, communication skills, and initiative build **self-esteem** and lead to **self-discipline**).

51. Seems pleased with family members, family life (strong family and good relationship to family, contributes to positive **self-esteem** and security).

52. Knows names of more detailed body parts, including penis and vagina, or substitute words *easily understood by nonfamily members* (from 18 to 24 months; is part of language and pre-literacy development, as well as developing physical **self-image** and favorable feelings about one's body—another part of positive **self-esteem**).

53. Responds sensibly to questions (being able to do this makes a young child feel competent, thus this ability, like all other abilities, enhances positive **self-esteem**).

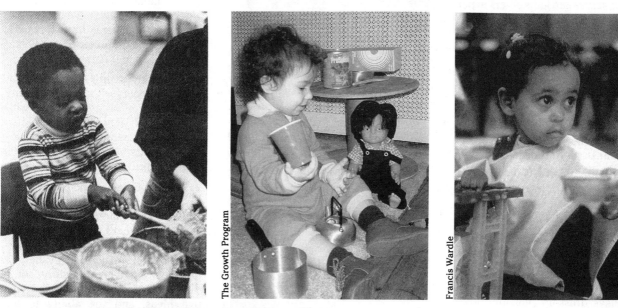

Barbara Rios

The Growth Program

Francis Wardle

Tom McGuire

The Growth Program

If you value perseverance, attention span, and stick-to-itiveness, be sure not to interrupt a busily absorbed toddler or two-year-old unless you absolutely have to.

What Kind of "Character" Are We Trying To Develop?

54. Speaks clearly enough so people who aren't regular caregivers can understand much of what is said (older toddlers and twos; again, being able to do this makes a young child feel competent, thus this ability, like all other abilities, enhances positive **self-esteem**).

55. Walks (coordinated, looks like a preschooler's walk; older toddlers and twos; because the child no longer *toddles*, we no longer term her a *toddler*).

56. Invites children or adults to join in the fun (toddlers and twos; indicates social development; social success is a big part of **self-esteem**).

57. Observes and joins others in pursuing activities started by them (nine months on; is a foundation of cooperative abilities, though it may be a bother to the other children, who may need "protection" from the baby's disruption).

58. Attempts to help clean up (senior babies, toddlers, and twos; contributes to competence, thus **self-esteem**; contributes to responsibility, thus **self-discipline**).

59. Throws ball toward someone (gross motor control brings with it positive **self-esteem**).

60. Catches a ball if carefully thrown from a very small distance (gross motor control brings with it positive **self-esteem**).

61. Plays dress-up (imitating loved ones and other admired people is a major way in which young children become socialized, e.g., learn **self-discipline** as well as **self-esteem** — it feels good to be like Mom or Dad; toddlers usually enjoy just putting on and taking off dress-up clothes and accessories, seeing themselves in the mirror, and having others admire them; many two-year-olds also *play* grown-up, acting out *both* a) what their grown-ups do with them, *and* b) their reactions to it).

62. Feeds self with fork (24 to 36 months; increasing autonomy contributes to **self-confidence** and **self-discipline**).

63. Knows the names of those in own group and notices when a special adult

It isn't easy to become a positive, well-integrated, mentally healthy "self," and to like who you are. Young children need us to encourage their self-esteem and self-discipline, and to gently guide them toward becoming people of good character.

or a child friend is absent (older toddlers and twos; social awareness contributes to social competence, and social competence contributes to positive **self-esteem** and **self-discipline**).

64. Helps group (older toddlers and twos; feeling altruistic and socially competent are big parts of positive **self-esteem** and **self-discipline**).

65. Uses potty occasionally, increasing to regularly (21 to 36 months; indicates cooperation, competence, achievement; contributes to **self-esteem** and **self-discipline** if it's the *child's* project, not if it's pushed by adults or a battle with them; even toddlers and two-year-olds know subtle coercion when they sense it!).

66. Washes hands, gets own paper towel, throws it in the trash (toddler and twos; shows growing competence, independence, and responsibility; contributes to **self-esteem** and **self-discipline**).

67. Serves snacks to self (older toddlers and twos; increasing initiative and independence contributes to **self-esteem** and **self-discipline**).

68. Says fragments of songs, stories and fingerplays frequently sung, read, or done together (older toddlers and twos; excellent language development, a prerequisite for later learning to read).

69. Enjoys interactive play with other children, with some parallel play— knows how to get others to pick up on his or her ideas (older toddlers and two-year-olds; having friends and successful social relations boosts **self-esteem**).

70. Demonstrates intentionality; can generate an idea about what she wants to do, get whatever is necessary to do it, and carry out the plan without being distracted from it (21 months on).

71. Can increasingly negotiate conflicts with peers without injuring anyone or anyone's project, and without adult assistance (older toddlers and twos; promotes **self-esteem** as a socially capable person, promotes **self-discipline**).

72. Engages in pretend play with one or more other children (21 to 36 months; at 24 months, pretend play with dolls, blocks, and so on usually consists of separate one- or two-minute episodes, but increasingly the child plays out a self-created story; shows the emergence of complex and creative ideas, and the ability to link ideas together).

73. Can describe and express feelings of self and others in words and through play—this includes dependent, angry, shy, and sad feelings (24 to 30 months; indicates growing self-awareness; is an ingredient of empathy for others; self-awareness and empathy are essentials of **self-discipline**).

74. Demonstrates creative use of objects and toys, comes up with solutions to solve problems, contributes good ideas to play (24 months on; creativity, problem-solving, thinking skills, and helpful contributions to the group all lead to positive **self-image**).

75. Uses crayons, markers, paint brushes (18 months on; promotes expression of feelings and ideas, thus promotes positive **self-esteem** if adults show approval).

76. Uses toy versions of real objects appropriately (21 months; telephone, blanket, etc.).

77. Uses many common prepositions fairly correctly, fairly frequently in speech (24 to 36 months; indicates spatial relations, language, and pre-literacy development).

78. Uses past and future tenses fairly correctly, fairly frequently, in speech (24 to 36 months; indicates that understanding of time and language are developing).

79. Participates in the social amenities and conventions—usually says, "hi," "bye-bye," "please," and "thank you," unless feeling shy with strangers (24 months on; because our mainstream, middle-class culture highly values friendliness and the social graces, children who are not socially adroit are seriously disadvantaged).

80. Has special same-age friends (older babies and young toddlers who are twins, who are almost same-age siblings, or who frequently play together often form best friendships; if children have the *opportunity* to develop friendships, we expect to see them from 24 months on, although many children have them much sooner).

81. Recognizes many colors and knows their names **without direct teaching;** spontaneously notices if two objects are the same color (two-year-olds; proves mental development, self-initiative, and mental competence are progressing; child is constructing knowledge, which contributes to positive **self-esteem**).

82. Recognizes major shapes and knows their names (circle, square, triangle, rectangle) **without direct teaching;** spontaneously notices if two objects are the same shape (two-year-olds; child is constructing knowledge, which contributes to positive **self-esteem**).

83. Recognizes several letters, most often those prominent in his or her own name **without instruction,** but simply **because adults have been say-** ing the letter name each time they write it for a year or so (after 30 months; it always adds to a child's positive **self-esteem** to know things society values if learning them is not stressful).

84. Jumps on two feet (24 to 36 months; physical agility promotes positive **self-esteem**).

85. Pulls off shoes and socks (after 24 months; fine-motor skill; competence creates **self-esteem**).

86. Puts on shoes and socks (36 months; fine-motor skill; competence produces positive **self-esteem**).

87. Beginning to undress/dress self (24 months; growing independence contributes to positive **self-esteem** and **self-discipline**).

88. Runs (36 months; coordinated, looks like a preschooler's run; physical agility is much more important to children than to many adults; being a fast runner promotes positive **self-esteem**).

89. Follows two-step directions if appropriate (24 months on; part of **self-discipline**).

90. Comprehends plans explained carefully and repeatedly (24 months on; significantly helps a child be self-disciplined to know what to expect and what's happening).

91. Can operate doorknobs (24 to 36 months; indicates small muscle skill progress; adds greatly to a child's sense of achievement—positive **self-esteem**).

92. Regresses temporarily to an earlier stage of maturity at stressful times (any young child; when masters something new and panics about too much scary independence, *or* during a move, divorce, when starting a new day care program, and so on; but with extra nurturing and support for a few days, weeks, or months, depending upon the seriousness of the stress-generating situation, soon resumes normal behavior and level of **self-discipline**).

93. Enjoys own body and being a boy or a girl, knows that boys have penises and girls have vaginas and that this anatomical fact is perhaps the chief difference between them; usually uses *he* and *she, him* and *her, his* and *hers* cor- rectly (30 to 36 months; being comfortable with one's body and gender is part of positive **self-esteem**).

94. Enjoys both traditionally boy and traditionally girl activities, shows no stereotypic biases (24 to 36 months; part of respecting others; which, in turn, is part of **self-discipline** and positive **self-esteem**).

95. Notices and accepts diversity—children and adults with leg braces, wheelchairs, a missing limb, neurological problems that make them flop or jerk; people with various skin colors and ethnic backgrounds—perhaps mixed-culture backgrounds; different family constellations, such as single-father or -mother families, two-father or -mother families, grandmother as childrearer, only child, adopted child, many children, and so on (24- to 36-month-old children may very well begin observing and reacting to *"differentness"*—because they have had enough experience to know what is *usual;* an important part of **self-esteem** in a pluralistic society and world is to view oneself as **equal** to others, no worse and **no better; as two-year-olds begin to notice these differences, adults directly discuss them in words and through play,** trying to make the unfamiliar feel OK; **all biased comments or behaviors are immediately confronted;** seeing oneself as a just person is part of positive **self-esteem;** behaving in a self-disciplined way with regard to the rights of others is part of being a good citizen in a democratic society).

96. Almost never hurts other children (babies and beginning toddlers—children younger than 18 months—will *occasionally* pinch, bop, scratch, even bite each other, either because they're curious and don't realize that it hurts, or because they have few social skills with which to "work things out"; indicates the need for firm guidance from grown-ups—a **disapproving,** slightly sharp, certainly not sweet and loving **tone,** combined with a **frowning face** and **physical removal** from the other child, with distraction into another activity; teaching from 18 to 36 months to solve interpersonal problems **verbally,** and **to feel powerful without inflicting pain on others,** is

The Growth Program

Providing high-quality child care is a great deal of work. But isn't helping to create great people worth it?

part of parents' and caregivers' core curriculum; by 24 months we expect to see **very** little hurting; by 36 months, intentionally hurting another child should be a rare happening indeed).

Two-year-olds (without exceptional handicaps) whose (gifted) parent(s) and (gifted) caregiver(s) succeed in regularly aiming at these eight dozen achievements are usually observably more advanced in all dimensions mentioned than are other two-year-olds, especially in self-esteem, self-discipline, and "character" development — solid mental health

If two-year-olds have excellent parents (according to the definition spelled out in this list) and/or have been in an excellent early childhood program (i.e., one with sensitive and skilled educarers who "believe in" the particular objectives listed above),

they will be very much more mature than toddlers and than the *average* two-year-old. Not everyone will agree with this entire list of objectives. Some people may disagree with a *number* of these specific items. Nonetheless, many expert parents and expert educarers have found throughout much of the 20th Century that trying to steer infants, toddlers, and two-year-olds toward these behaviors pays off: The children have greater ego strength **(self-esteem)**, greater inner control **(self-discipline)**, and stronger **character,** thus good chances for good lives. Recently, researchers from fields other than psychoanalytic psychology have joined expert practitioners (the psychoanalytic field gave us insights all along) in gathering evidence to support this approach to people-making. Research findings are currently bolstering experts' experiential findings.

If two-year-olds spend the whole day every day in infant/toddler rooms, or even in a group entirely made up of toddlers (12- or 18- to 24-month-olds), which is often the case in infant/toddler child care programs, ***they will probably not get adequate challenges***

- *to promote continuing development,*
- *to provide continuing fuel to feed positive self-esteem, and*
- *to avoid the discipline problems that result from boredom.*

All two-year-olds, regardless of how advanced they are in language, ability to play, interpersonal relations, mental organization, and emotional development are still only two years old. They need lots of time with their families, assuming that there is some sort of minimally adequate family for them. If in full-time, center-based care, they need to be in the toddler room (unless there is a room solely for two-year-olds). They should not be there exclusively, however; each child needs challenges. Advanced two-year-olds benefit from daily opportunities to spend 45 minutes or so mixing and free-playing with three-year-olds, four-year-olds, etc., because their conversation is usually much more complex and interesting than that of toddlers, and whose pretend play is far more involved and sophisticated. Based on knowledge of individual children, staff should determine which of the two-year-olds *who have been in the program for a while and feel secure* should regularly go to the three-, four-, or five-year-old teacher for a daily play time. Two-year-olds can also benefit from simple art, science, music and movement, and from a developmentally appropriate off-site "field trip" each week. To feel really good about ourselves, each of us needs to feel we are successfully meeting challenges. A few mature almost-three-year-olds might be better placed in a group of three's.

Two-year-olds in mixed-age family child care homes do get the language enrichment provided by the older children in the group.

If *you* successfully meet the challenges entailed in **enabling** infants and toddlers in all of these dimensions, you're teaching plenty, you *are* helping children achieve many educational goals, and *you* are much more than "just a babysitter." In fact, you're an expert child developer.

CHAPTER 12

INDEX

judgment, lack of: 128, 144
masturbation: 126
messy eating: 123
oppositional: 88, 89, 177–178
  dawdling: 87, 126
  refusing to cease: 130, 177, 178
  refusing to dress: 177
  refusing to pay attention: 137, 184
  sleep problems: 151, 153
  stubbornness: 155–156
  tantrums: 130, 184
  tempestuousness: 141
  testing limits: 177
  throwing food, things: 123, 154
  problems, related to family life: 31
rigid: 151, 152
routines, acceptance of: 184
sucking thumbs/fingers/pacifiers: 126
upset due to a move: 151, 155
wiggling & squirming: 137
wild: 42
Bias/biased:
  gender, middle-class, people who are "different," racial: 15–16, 115
  people's conclusions are biased by their values & experiences: 33, 50
Bio-psychological/psychobiological: 2, 87, 161, 163, 166, 169
"Bio-underclass": 22
Body & soul nourishing activities (cuddling, carrying, lap play, etc.): 5, 8, 23, 39, 46, 75–76, 175
Bottles/nursing mothers: 119, 154

C

Caregivers/educarers (parents & professionals):
  and children's language development (See also Language development):
    chat with children: 4, 5, 45, 70–73, 98, 101, 103, 104, 107, 109, 120, 129, 142, 143, 152, 154, 155, 156, 157, 161–166, 167–170, 175, 177, 182
    communicate with children in many ways: 4, 5, 39, 71–73
    communicate with children through play: 45, 68, 70–73, 131
    communication difficulties: 117
    foster language competence while providing routine care: 71, 73, 162
    give reasons: 4
    help children verbalize feelings, needs, & wants: 67, 70, 73, 184
    listen to/accept what children communicate, including feelings: 68, 83, 85
    model language: 71, 161–166
    name/explain/comment on: 71, 163
    neglecting children's language development: 166
    negotiate each communication: 164–165
    repeat rhyming words frequently: 71
  and parents:
    detailed daily record sheet (for social/

emotional as well as other), keep: 46, 68
  disagreements with: 128–129
  disapproval of: 43, 95
  disempowering: 42–44
  employed mothers, appreciation of/disapproval of: 28, 46
  help parents connect with one another: 46
  lack training in working with: 50
  parent/child relationships, strengthen: 41–43, 119
  parent/child time in program during the day, promote & provide for: 46, 119
  work tactfully/respectfully with parents as partners: 5, 28, 35, 36, 41, 46, 52, 88–89, 98, 102, 106, 114, 116–120, 125, 127, 130, 132, 133, 138, 153, 155, 157, 165, 180
anger, fear of children's: 152, 154, 155, 172, 176, 184
angry: 4, 93, 107, 125, 126
as behavioral detectives: 151
as child guidance specialists (See also Child guidance approach to character development/childrearing discipline): 5, 67–68, 70, 73
as "unbossy bosses": 170
authoritarian, overcontrolling, take over children's business (disempower children): 4, 36, 89, 127, 153, 155, 156, 173–174, 176
beliefs/feelings/values of: 95, 98, 103
  attitude toward child's body, body products, etc.: 73, 76
blame, accuse, criticize children: 172, 175, 176
challenge children (gently) on all frontiers (See also Activities; Learning): 165, 166, 180
character developers/character development specialists: 25, 30, 42, 67–74, 75, 78, 79, 81, 98, 121, 144
character of: 3, 4, 5, 8, 14, 25
child development, knowledge of, helps: 5, 125, 171
childishness of: 125, 126
co-caregivers (give caregivers a lift): 130
cold personality of: 4
comfort, reassure: 68, 153, 155, 156, 183
common sense of: 5, 67–74
competitiveness of: 19
conformity, force destructive: 36
"connect" well with children/develop trusting relationships (See also Friendship, between adult & child): 8, 20, 67–68, 72, 127, 163
cooperate with children, foster cooperative attitude: 167–170, 175, 182
correct behavior, give cues & clues about: 153
create conditions that cause or promote desired behaviors: 181
dependence/independence issues in our

own lives, have resolved: 126
developmental delays & abnormalities, recognize: 107
disagreements among: 128–129, 146
disempowered: 28
emotionally responsive, empathetic, caring: 8, 25, 118, 155
empower children: 173
encourage . . . :
  age-appropriate independence (See also Self-discipline): 68, 69, 139
  child/child conversation (See also Language development): 69, 137
  creative coping behavior in children: 36, 73
  curiosity in children: 36, 69
  desired characteristics. See Characteristics
  emotional organization & mental competence: 151–160
  family diversity, interest in: 44
  "good" behavior, as culturally defined: 167–170, 171–178
  intellectual curiosity & development. See Language; Learning
  physical development & competence: 68–70, 139
  social skills & competence, as culturally defined: 131, 137, 144, 146
  what an infant, toddler, or two-year-old is striving to master: 67–68
encourage, demonstrate kindly attitude/approach (show approval, thus motivate children): 5, 68, 172, 174, 181, 183, 186
enjoy children at this age: 67, 121, 125, 126
enthusiastic/lacking enthusiasm: 125, 128, 182
establish behavioral expectations, be firm (See also Discipline): 106, 107, 108, 121, 122–124, 174, 177, 184
even if perfect . . . : 176
example, set good: 108, 121
exhausted/distracted much of the time: 129
expert: 53, 129
familiar people, continuous (important to very young children): 8, 67, 103, 182
flexible personality (relating to children in a flexible way): 4, 68, 154, 158, 180
"good with children," being: 28, 125, 126
greet each child & adult daily: 135
harsh, insulting: 172
healthy/mentally healthy: 125, 126
help children . . . :
  calm themselves: 184
  help themselves: 5
  solve social problems & facilitate social development: 73, 136, 139
  understand their own & each other's behavior: 139, 180
high turnover of: 50
hit/smack/spank children: 68, 108, 155
inform children of next event (but not too far ahead): 155

indecisive: 83
insightful: 82, 85, 95, 181
intellectual competence, confidence about: 162
intelligence: 46
language competence. *See* Language
loner: 138
mental health: 31, 67
morality (embryonic sense of justice, wish to be good): 75, 86, 90, 180
motivation: 46, 69
    foundations of: 182
    to become competent: 143
    to do well: 180
    to please/win approval/"be good": 90, 167, 168, 171
obedience: 83, 111, 180
opposition: 183, 184
patience: 175
perseverance (attention span): 68, 138, 140, 143, 182–183, 185
personal power: 70, 92–93, 117, 138, 143, 148–149
perspective-taking: 174, 181
physical/motor competence. *See* Physical/motor accomplishments/competencies/skills
pleasant: 89
predicting, planning: 131, 158, 174
problem-solving/can help settle disputes: 73, 143, 146–147, 174, 176, 186
questioning/resisting authority: 87
rejected by peers: 84
resourceful/self-reliant: 68, 129, 143
respect:
    of adults: 125, 134, 143, 144
    of other children: 174, 179, 181
    of self: 183
responsibility: 180, 183, 184
risk-taking: 81, 85, 182, 185
seek intimacy: 81
self-confidence, suitable pride: 180
self-sabotage: 80
sense of humor: 167–170, 180
shyness: 69, 87, 186
social competence. *See* Social skills, competence
timid: 83
trust: 3, 68, 81, 118
values (beginning to form): 180
warmth: 46
withdrawn: 73, 80, 138
wonder: 68, 85
worry: 152, 155, 156
Child abuse/neglect:
    by families: 3, 12, 20, 38, 78, 84, 86, 88
    by governments: 7–22, 38
    remedial funds cut: 13
    tolerated/accepted/approved by society: 2, 19
Child care policies/regulations: 40, 48, 49, 52–53, 54–55, 56–57, 62–63, 65
    employer policies: 49
    for child care program settings: 129
    national, about families: 48

Child care settings & programs (center-based & family day care): 98
child guidance philosophy: 127
close friendships may develop within a group: 33
cost of care: 29, 30, 45, 125, 132
day care centers (specifically): 25, 26, 32, 125–150
emotionally negligent: 3
environment: 130, 134
    chaotic: 73
    temperature of rooms: 8, 10, 30
family day care (specifically): 25, 26, 28, 29, 67, 70, 75, 116, 130, 132, 133, 138, 154, 157
family day care homes, satellite: 29
family day care systems: 29
fifty hours a week?: 39, 46
for . . . :
    children from low-income families (*See also* Parents, without choice): 13
    infants: Where should babies be—at home or in non-kin substitute care? different parental shifts/part-time/flex-time/full-time or fifty-hour week?: 1, 23–66, 124
    special needs children: 113–114
full-time: 45
health, hygiene, & safety in: 25, 45, 71, 73, 130, 131, 141
homelike: 5, 50, 67, 70, 101–102, 124, 129, 132, 135, 136
nurturing: 46
outings: 50, 69, 101
policies/regulations. *See* Child care policies/regulations
quality of:
    high-quality: 2, 3, 32, 37, 39, 45, 46, 49, 51–53, 121, 138, 162
    low-quality: 4, 39, 50, 51–53
    optimal (*See also* Child development, *optimal*): 5, 51–53
    When will we have adequate child care nationwide?: 3–6, 51–53
    researchers' values about: 33
    socializing children into social classes: 35
    subsidized by government?: 15, 125
Child-caring community as activists/advocates for *all* children: 7, 9, 10, 18, 19, 20, 21, 22, 48, 134
    question the way it is, question authority: 15
Child development (*See also* Developmental accomplishments; Infants; Toddlers; Two-year-olds):
    keep track of each individual's general progress in all "domains": 68, 179–188
    optimal: 3, 4, 5, 23–25, 33, 36, 37, 39, 40, 44–47, 50, 51, 52–53, 57, 65, 73, 162
Child guidance approach to character development/childrearing/discipline: 5, 68, 73, 75–100, 167–170, 171–180, 181, 183, 184, 187
Childhood, history of: 1–2

Child labor: 2
Childproofing. *See* Discipline, preventive
Childrearing goals: 179–188
    parents/teachers discuss: 128–129
Childrearing, optimal. *See* Child development, *optimal*
Children with special needs (*See also* Child abuse/neglect; Child care settings & programs [center-based & family day care], special needs children in): 7–22, 76–77, 78, 106
    chronically ill (asthma, heart disease, etc.): 107
    "crack" cocaine babies: 22
    diagnosis, early: 107, 109
    giftedness: 152
    good character, developing, in: 129
    hearing impairments: 77, 103, 106, 163
    independence: 113
    language problems: 103
    limits, need firm: 121
    love & encouragement: 113, 114
    mental retardation: 77, 107
    orthopedic/motor/neurological difficulties: 77, 103, 106–107
    parents of. *See* Parents, of special needs children
    psychiatric illness: 78, 103
    seizures: 21
    vision impairments: 21, 77, 103
Children's allowance (from government): 11, 17
Children's Defense Fund: 10, 14, 20, 22
Child study. *See* Child development, keep track of each individual's progress; Staff development/supervision, studying child development
Child study movement: 3, 8, 136, 181
Church, religion (*See also* Diversity): 19, 21, 75
Class/classism/socioeconomic aspects (*See also* Child abuse/neglect, by governments; Social reproduction theory & practice; Poverty): 23–66, 168, 169, 184
    affluence/privilege: 2, 6
    children as a social class: 9
    class inequity: 7–22
    different approaches to discipline among: 176
Cognitive development. *See* Intellectual development; Mental development
Competence, competencies. *See* Caregivers/educarers (parents & professionals); Characteristics
Conscience. *See* Personality, **superego** (conscience)
Core curriculum (*See also* Activities for zero-to-three-year-olds; Characteristics): 67, 74
    building good character, individuals, relationships (adult/child, child/child): 53, 67, 74, 101, 127
    enabling children to master developmental milestones & become age-appro-

between adult & child: 32, 50, 68, 71, 131, 167–170, 175

between children: 69, 143, 162, 182

inviting friends to play: 186

G

Gender:

androgynous: 5

attitudes & behaviors, development of: 76

decision making, imbalance in: 14–16

perspectives: 1, 5, 9, 14, 16

stereotyping: 4

Government(s) (*See also* Child care policies/regulations, national, about families): 7, 8, 22

Group/grouping:

avoiding most large group activities: 136–137, 139

becoming an individual before becoming part of a nonfamily group: 134, 136

becoming part of family/culture: 162

human beings live in: 163

mixed-age: 33, 101–102, 138

relationships within, very important: 180

same-age: 102

size: 3, 33, 70

small, spontaneous clusters: 129, 144

Guide/guidance (*See also* Caregivers/educarers [parents & professionals]; Child guidance approach to character development/childrearing/discipline; Discipline; Self-discipline): 68, 143, 146, 148, 163, 178, 179–188

H

Habits: 152

Head Start: 13

Health care/health care systems: 8, 9, 10, 11, 13, 17, 20, 22, 48, 49

health insurance: 11, 12, 29

Medicaid: 13, 20

prenatal: 8, 9, 10, 11, 20

safe births: 8, 9

Homelessness. *See* Shelter

Home life (*See also* Family): 23–24, 25, 26–28, 31, 38–48, 51

Humor (*See also* Characteristics): 158, 167–170

developing a sense of: 183

having fun with children: 153, 167–170

laughing at children, mean teasing: 68, 154, 156

puns, sarcasm, not funny to young children: 169

Hunger/starvation: 7, 10, 17, 19, 21

I

Independence, initiative (*See also* Caregivers/educarers [parents & professionals], encouraging; Characteristics, autonomy/independence/individuality/initiative): 8

foundations of: 182, 183, 186

through physical prowess & self-sufficiency: 185

through self-help competencies: 186

Individual/individuality (*See also* Caregivers/educarers [parents & professionals], encouraging; Characteristics, autonomy/independence/individuality/initiative): 5, 73, 94, 95, 172

adult approval of: 174

asserting: 177

becoming: 136

development in each dimension at own pace: 140, 148, 182–188

differences in separation behavior: 182

interests: 138

of adults: 23–31

of babies: 25, 26, 30, 58–60, 62–63

of children: 37, 39, 69

of men: 9

one-on-one relationship, playtime, chatting with adult: 5, 128

personalities: 138

Infants (0–12 months) (*See also* Child care settings & programs): 101–124, 173, 182–183

adults listen to, communicate with: 68

anger: 107

are individuals: 46, 120, 122

behavior, difficult, cause of: 107

development (emotional, physical, social, intellectual): 67–74, 101–124

employed mothers of: 3

fear: 107

in care part-time: 49

language: 3, 67, 71, 162, 163, 165–166

learn by observing older children: 102

memory: 116

motivation: 102

need affection, appreciation, approval, lots of leisurely time (especially from parents): 49–50, 68, 124

overstimulation: 70, 72, 73, 102, 105, 120

perseverance (attention span): 107

preventive "discipline": 174

self-awareness: 121

"senior babies": 76, 90

stress/distress: 20, 40, 107, 120

survival needs should be met first: 7, 19, 22

urge to learn: 68, 69, 102

Where should babies be to develop optimally?: 23–66

Infant/toddler competence (*See also* Characteristics): 5, 8, 182–188

Information overload: 7

Instruction: 4, 70

director does not want direct: 179

not the way infants, toddlers, & two-year-olds learn best: 5, 102–103, 127, 181

Intellectual development (*See also* Characteristics; Learning; Literacy; Mental development): 10, 180

J

Jobs, job training (*See also* Parents, Staff development/supervision): 8, 11, 15, 127

funds cut: 13

K

Knowledge:

about . . . :

adjacent fields, lacking in early childhood educators: 33–34

child development, different from child developing/character developing skills: 181

child development, not the same as being a child developer: 32–33

children:

arbitrarily (& unfortunately for child developers) splintered: 7, 166

helpful to child developers: 5, 125, 171

infant child care: 37, 40

children need experiential knowledge before they can develop language: 164

increase in, children's: 139

. . . is not everything that goes into decision making: 37

of what use if we ignore it?: 39

useless to child developer unless he/she has appropriate personality: 126, 127

L

Language (*See also* Caregivers/educarers [parents & professionals], communicating with children in many ways, chatting with children: 46, 70–73, 161–166

adult's: 152

answer children: 175

explain to children: 152–153

give children reasons: 4

greet children in a friendly manner at arrival time/give frequent affirmations when child is working hard at something: 175

include frequent chants, fingerplays, improvised & standard songs & rhymes, repetition, lullabies, etc.: 170, 183

instructions, phrase tactfully: 170

listen to children: 175

nonverbal gestures, postures, facial expressions: 177

. . . of play, playfulness: 167–170

puns/sarcasm, not understood by young children: 175

restricted: 5

speak to children respectfully: 150, 176

too much verbiage: 176

use, to set limits: 157

child's: 151, 155, 161–166

ability . . . :

to answer questions: 185

to converse, discuss: 67, 185

acquisition: 166

advanced in: 188

asking questions: 185

confidence that he/she will be understood: 158

delays: 165

development: 71–73
enjoyment of books encourages: 183
facilitating: 166
in infants:
  attempting words: 163–164
  listening skills: 163
  nonverbal: 163
in toddlers & twos: 182
knows . . . :
  body part names: 183
  body part names, more detailed: 185
  names of all people in his life: 186
  names of family members & friends: 183
  /says color, shape, letter names: 187
language competence entwined with personal competence: 163, 166
language interactions, pleasant, has plenty of: 162
language-rich environments: 165
learning . . . :
  grammar: 164
  pronunciation: 164
  through experience: 164
  through imitation: 164
  through maturation: 164
learning to express needs, feelings:
  nonverbally: 183
  verbally: 155, 156, 176, 184, 186
limits, verbally set, beginning to comply with: 184
motivation to learn: 163
past/future tenses, often uses correctly: 187
pre-literacy skills: 183, 184, 186
pride in using: 183
prior to words/nonverbal language: 71, 162, 173
psycholinguistic: 165
says . . . :
  "Mine!": 183
  some words/phrases of familiar songs, books: 186
  words for familiar objects, actions, events, & people: 184
sings: 69, 71
(often) solves interpersonal problems verbally: 187
speaks clearly enough that child-attuned, nonregular caregivers can understand: 186
speaks in phrases or sentences: 184
talks to other children: 69
tells when needs . . . :
  diaper change: 185
  to go potty. See Toilet learning
understands . . . :
  pictures: 184
  spatial relations words: 184
  two-step instructions: 187
  well-explained plans: 187
  words for familiar objects, actions, events, & people: 183
  words for routines, routine instructions, prohibitions: 184

uses . . . :
  gestures to signify words: 184
  many prepositions: 187
  words to describe feelings of others: 186
  words to express creative thinking: 186
  words with peers to play & negotiate: 186
Learning (See also Instruction):
  classifying: 97
  development of: 182–188
  expands from what child already understands: 156
  language, motivation for: 163
  later, foundations of: 182
  love of (motivation): 102, 106, 182
  situations: 181
  social skills, successful interactions: 5, 20, 172
  through . . . :
    exploration, examination: 78, 108, 109
    imitation: 138, 143, 161–166, 182, 186
    reinforcement: 161–162
    self-selected activities/self-regulation: 78, 106, 135, 148
    senses & bodies (sensorimotor stage): 5, 141, 143, 182–188
  to manage their environment: 139
  to trust: 121, 144
Literacy, age zero to three (See also Language):
  excellent language basic to high literacy: 162
  looking at books together, discussing, reading/telling stories: 5, 71, 110, 136, 153–154, 176, 183
  motivation to read: 110
  scribbling: 70, 142
Loneliness (See also Abandoned/abandonment/desertion; Separation): 129
Low birth weight, premature birth: 22
Lying:
  adults to children: 153

M

Masculinist perspective: 1, 15
Materialism/consumerism: 40, 42
Maturation (biologically caused): 8, 37, 148, 158, 159, 161, 162, 165, 166, 169, 180–188
Maturity (encouraged by parents & other caregivers): 77–78, 84–91, 94, 158, 175, 181, 182–188
Memory, development of. See Mental development, memory
Men. See Caregivers/educarers (parents & professionals), male; Fathers; Parents
Mental development (how minds & thinking develop, cognitive skills, mental competence, higher level thinking skills, planning): 2, 5, 20, 87, 151–160, 163, 169
can plan: 186
knows routines: 184

memory: 90, 157, 158, 183
  spatial comprehension: 184
Mental health: 1, 2, 3, 6, 15, 23, 45, 47, 67, 98, 107, 124, 127, 158, 162, 172
  developing: 182–188
  foundations of: 8
  invest in: 48, 49
  (emotional) unwellness: 6, 38–45
Mental health professionals: 41
Mental ill health/unwellness/emotional problems/destructive, unhappy people: 6, 38–45
Mental (psychiatric) illness: 79, 85
Minimum guaranteed income: 15
Mothers (See also Democratic/egalitarian practice; Parents; Women): 5, 25, 39, 41, 70, 80
  expert: 25, 129, 130
  feelings: 42
  mother/child relationship: 42–46
  work/working: 24–65
    ambivalence about being away from baby/feel guilty/guilt-free: 26, 52
    conditions: 68–70, 87
    employed part-time/flex-time/full-time/job-sharing/job security/benefits/plus commute equals fifty-hour week: 46, 48–50
    history of: 1, 2
    How much should they do relative to fathers?: 30, 50
    hurried: 50
    need good child care: 3, 5, 6

N

Naptime/bedtime: 122, 151, 153, 154, 170
National budgets/national values (See also Child care policies/regulations): 8, 10, 12, 13, 15
  military spending: 13, 19
Natural learning situations: 181
Nutrition/food: 8, 9, 13, 15, 20, 22
  Food Stamps program: 13, 21
  school lunch program: 21
  WIC (Women & Infant Care program): 20

O

Observing children/observation (See also Child study): 181
Optimal development/true quality care (See also Child development, optimal): 4, 5, 23, 27
  for these children?: 10

P

Parents/parenting: 23–66
  and decision making: 5
  and staff: 5, 77, 93
  are busy: 82
  behavioral expectations, have reasonable: 45
  childrearing goals/values: 23–31, 33–37, 39–42, 62–64, 95, 129, 180
  competitive with paid caregiver: 42–44
  conferences/collaboration with: 5